SHYLOCK

Major Literary Characters

THE ANCIENT WORLD THROUGH THE SEVENTEENTH CENTURY

ACHILLES
Homer, *Iliad*

CALIBAN
William Shakespeare, *The Tempest*
Robert Browning, *Caliban upon Setebos*

CLEOPATRA
William Shakespeare, *Antony and Cleopatra*
John Dryden, *All for Love*
George Bernard Shaw, *Caesar and Cleopatra*

DON QUIXOTE
Miguel de Cervantes, *Don Quixote*
Franz Kafka, *Parables*

FALSTAFF
William Shakespeare, *Henry IV, Part I, Henry IV, Part II, The Merry Wives of Windsor*

FAUST
Christopher Marlowe, *Doctor Faustus*
Johann Wolfgang von Goethe, *Faust*
Thomas Mann, *Doctor Faustus*

HAMLET
William Shakespeare, *Hamlet*

IAGO
William Shakespeare, *Othello*

JULIUS CAESAR
William Shakespeare, *Julius Caesar*
George Bernard Shaw, *Caesar and Cleopatra*

KING LEAR
William Shakespeare, *King Lear*

MACBETH
William Shakespeare, *Macbeth*

ODYSSEUS/ULYSSES
Homer, *Odyssey*
James Joyce, *Ulysses*

OEDIPUS
Sophocles, *Oedipus Rex, Oedipus at Colonus*

OTHELLO
William Shakespeare, *Othello*

ROSALIND
William Shakespeare, *As You Like It*

SANCHO PANZA
Miguel de Cervantes, *Don Quixote*
Franz Kafka, *Parables*

SATAN
The Book of Job
John Milton, *Paradise Lost*

SHYLOCK
William Shakespeare, *The Merchant of Venice*

THE WIFE OF BATH
Geoffrey Chaucer, *The Canterbury Tales*

THE EIGHTEENTH AND NINETEENTH CENTURIES

AHAB
Herman Melville, *Moby-Dick*

ISABEL ARCHER
Henry James, *Portrait of a Lady*

EMMA BOVARY
Gustave Flaubert, *Madame Bovary*

DOROTHEA BROOKE
George Eliot, *Middlemarch*

CHELSEA HOUSE PUBLISHERS

Major Literary Characters

DAVID COPPERFIELD
Charles Dickens, *David Copperfield*

ROBINSON CRUSOE
Daniel Defoe, *Robinson Crusoe*

DON JUAN
Molière, *Don Juan*
Lord Byron, *Don Juan*

HUCK FINN
Mark Twain, *The Adventures of
Tom Sawyer, Adventures of
Huckleberry Finn*

CLARISSA HARLOWE
Samuel Richardson, *Clarissa*

HEATHCLIFF
Emily Brontë, *Wuthering Heights*

ANNA KARENINA
Leo Tolstoy, *Anna Karenina*

MR. PICKWICK
Charles Dickens, *The Pickwick Papers*

HESTER PRYNNE
Nathaniel Hawthorne, *The Scarlet Letter*

BECKY SHARP
William Makepeace Thackeray, *Vanity Fair*

LAMBERT STRETHER
Henry James, *The Ambassadors*

EUSTACIA VYE
Thomas Hardy, *The Return of the Native*

TWENTIETH CENTURY

ÁNTONIA
Willa Cather, *My Ántonia*

BRETT ASHLEY
Ernest Hemingway, *The Sun Also Rises*

HANS CASTORP
Thomas Mann, *The Magic Mountain*

HOLDEN CAULFIELD
J. D. Salinger, *The Catcher in the Rye*

CADDY COMPSON
William Faulkner, *The Sound and the Fury*

JANIE CRAWFORD
Zora Neale Hurston, *Their Eyes Were
Watching God*

CLARISSA DALLOWAY
Virginia Woolf, *Mrs. Dalloway*

DILSEY
William Faulkner, *The Sound and the Fury*

GATSBY
F. Scott Fitzgerald, *The Great Gatsby*

HERZOG
Saul Bellow, *Herzog*

JOAN OF ARC
William Shakespeare, *Henry VI*
George Bernard Shaw, *Saint Joan*

LOLITA
Vladimir Nabokov, *Lolita*

WILLY LOMAN
Arthur Miller, *Death of a Salesman*

MARLOW
Joseph Conrad, *Lord Jim, Heart of
Darkness, Youth, Chance*

PORTNOY
Philip Roth, *Portnoy's Complaint*

BIGGER THOMAS
Richard Wright, *Native Son*

CHELSEA HOUSE PUBLISHERS

Major Literary Characters

S H Y L O C K

Edited and with an introduction by
HAROLD BLOOM

CHELSEA HOUSE PUBLISHERS
New York ◊ Philadelphia

16 75

Jacket illustration: Sir Henry Irving as Shylock (The Folger
Shakespeare Library). *Inset:* Title page from the first quarto edition
of *The Merchant of Venice* (London: Printed by I. R. for Thomas Heyes, 1600)
(The Folger Shakespeare Library).

Chelsea House Publishers

Editor-in-Chief   Remmel T. Nunn
Managing Editor   Karyn Gullen Browne
Picture Editor   Adrian G. Allen
Art Director   Maria Epes
Manufacturing Manager   Gerald Levine

Major Literary Characters

Senior Editor   S. T. Joshi
Associate Editor   Richard Fumosa
Designer   Maria Epes

Staff for SHYLOCK

Picture Researcher   Patricia Burns
Assistant Art Director   Noreen Romano
Production Manager   Joseph Romano
Production Coordinator   Marie Claire Cebrián

Printed and bound in the United States of America

First Printing

1   3   5   7   9   8   6   4   2

Library of Congress Cataloging-in-Publication Data

Shylock / edited and with an introduction by Harold Bloom.
        p.   cm.—(Major literary characters)
        Includes bibliographical references and index.
        ISBN 0-7910-0930-0.—ISBN 0-7910-0985-8 (pbk.)
1. Shakespeare, William, 1564–1616. Merchant of Venice.   2. Shakespeare,
William, 1564–1616—Characters—Shylock.   3. Shylock (Fictitious character)
        4. Jews in literature.   I. Series.
                PR2825.S46   1991
                822.3'3—dc20
                90-49708
                CIP

CONTENTS

CONTENTS

THE ANALYSIS OF CHARACTER

Harold Bloom

"Character," according to our dictionaries, still has as a primary meaning a graphic symbol, such as a letter of the alphabet. This meaning reflects the word's apparent origin in the ancient Greek *charactēr,* a sharp stylus. *Charactēr* also meant the mark of the stylus' incisions. Recent fashions in literary criticism have reduced "character" in literature to a matter of marks upon a page. But our word "character" also has a very different meaning, matching that of the ancient Greek *ēthos,* "habitual way of life." Shall we say then that literary character is an imitation of human character, or is it just a grouping of marks? The issue is between a critic like Dr. Samuel Johnson, for whom words were as much like people as like things, and a critic like the late Roland Barthes, who told us that "the fact can only exist linguistically, as a term of discourse." Who is closer to our experience of reading literature, Johnson or Barthes? What difference does it make, if we side with one critic rather than the other?

Barthes is famous, like Foucault and other recent French theorists, for having added to Nietzsche's proclamation of the death of God a subsidiary demise, that of the literary author. If there are no authors, then there are no fictional personages, presumably because literature does not refer to a world outside language. Words indeed necessarily refer to other words in the first place, but the impact of words ultimately is drawn from a universe of fact. Stories, poems, and plays are recognizable as such because they are human utterances within traditions of utterances, and traditions, by achieving authority, become a kind of fact, or at least the sense of a fact. Our sense that literary characters, within the context of a fictive cosmos, indeed are fictional personages is also a kind of fact. The meaning and value of every character in a successful work of literary representation depend upon our ideas of persons in the factual reality of our lives.

Literary character is always an invention, and inventions generally are indebted to prior inventions. Shakespeare is the inventor of literary character as we know it; he reformed the universal human expectations for the verbal imitation of personality, and the reformation appears now to be permanent and uncannily inevitable. Remarkable as the Bible and Homer are at representing personages, their characters are relatively unchanging. They age within their stories, but their habitual modes of being do not develop. Jacob and Achilles unfold before us, but without metamorphoses. Lear and Macbeth, Hamlet and Othello severely modify themselves not only by their actions, but by their utterances, and most of all through *overhearing themselves,* whether they speak to themselves or to others. Pondering what they themselves have said, they will to change, and actually do change, sometimes extravagantly yet always persuasively. Or else they suffer change, without willing it, but in reaction not so much to their language as to their relation to that language.

I do not think it useful to say that Shakespeare successfully imitated elements in our characters. Rather, it could be argued that he compelled aspects of character to appear that previously were concealed, or not available to representation. This is not to say that Shakespeare is God, but to remind us that language is not God either. The mimesis of character in Shakespeare's dramas now seems to us normative, and indeed became the accepted mode almost immediately, as Ben Jonson shrewdly and somewhat grudgingly implied. And yet, Shakespearean representation has surprisingly little in common with the imitation of reality in Jonson or in Christopher Marlowe. The origins of Shakespeare's originality in the portrayal of men and women are to be found in the *Canterbury Tales* of Geoffrey Chaucer, insofar as they can be located anywhere before Shakespeare himself. Chaucer's savage and superb Pardoner overhears his own tale-telling, as well as his mocking rehearsal of his own spiel, and through this overhearing he is emboldened to forget himself, and enthusiastically urges all his fellow-pilgrims to come forward to be fleeced by him. His self-awareness, and apocalyptically rancid sense of spiritual fall, are preludes to the even grander abysses of the perverted will in Iago and in Edmund. What might be called the character trait of a negative charisma may be Chaucer's invention, but came to its perfection in Shakespearean mimesis.

The analysis of character is as much Shakespeare's invention as the representation of character is, since Iago and Edmund are adepts at analyzing both themselves and their victims. Hamlet, whose overwhelming charisma has many negative components, is certainly the most comprehensive of all literary characters, and so necessarily prophesies the labyrinthine complexities of the will in Iago and Edmund. Charisma, according to Max Weber, its first codifier, is primarily a natural endowment, and implies a primordial and idiosyncratic power over nature, and so finally over death. Hamlet's uncanniness is at its most suggestive in the scene of his long dying, where the audience, through the mediation of Horatio, itself is compelled to meditate upon suicide, if only because outliving the prince of Denmark scarcely seems an option.

Shakespearean representation has usurped not only our sense of literary character, but our sense of ourselves as characters, with Hamlet playing the part of the largest of these usurpations. Insofar as we have an idea of human disinterestedness, we tend to derive it from the Hamlet of Act V, whose quietism has about it a ghostly authority. Oscar Wilde, in his profound and profoundly witty dialogue, "The Decay of Lying," expressed a permanent insight when he insisted that art shaped every era, far more than any age formed art. Life imitates art, we imitate Shakespeare, because without Shakespeare we would perish for lack of images. Wilde's grandest audacity demystifies Shakespearean mimesis with a Shakespearean vivaciousness: "This unfortunate aphorism about art holding the mirror up to Nature is deliberately said by Hamlet in order to convince the bystanders of his absolute insanity in all art-matters." Of *Hamlet*'s influence upon the ages Wilde remarked that: "The world has grown sad because a puppet was once melancholy." "Puppet" is Wilde's own deconstruction, a brilliant reminder that Shakespeare's artistry of illusion has so mastered reality as to have changed reality, evidently forever.

The analysis of character, as a critical pursuit, seems to me as much a Shakespearean invention as literary character was, since much of what we know about how to analyze character necessarily follows Shakespearean procedures. His hero-villains, from Richard III through Iago, Edmund, and Macbeth, are shrewd and endless questers into their own self-motivations. If we could bear to see Hamlet, in his unwearied negations, as another hero-villain, then we would judge him the supreme analyst of the darker recalcitrances in the selfhood. Freud followed the pre-Socratic Empedocles, in arguing that character is fate, a frightening doctrine that maintains the fear that there are no accidents, that overdetermination rules us all of our lives. Hamlet assumes the same, yet adds to this argument the terrible passivity he manifests in Act V. Throughout Shakespeare's tragedies, the most interesting personages seem doom-eager, reminding us again that a Shakespearean reading of Freud would be more illuminating than a Freudian exegesis of Shakespeare. We learn more when we discover Hamlet in the Freudian Death Drive, than when we read *Beyond the Pleasure Principle* into *Hamlet*.

In Shakespearean comedy, character achieves its true literary apotheosis, which is the representation of the inner freedom that can be created by great wit alone. Rosalind and Falstaff, perhaps alone among Shakespeare's personages, match Hamlet in wit, though hardly in the metaphysics of consciousness. Whether in the comic or the modern mode, Shakespeare has set the standard of measurement in the balance between character and passion.

In Shakespeare the self is more dramatized than theatricalized, which is why a Shakespearean reading of Freud works out so well. Character-formation after the passing of the Oedipal stage takes the place of fetishistic fragmentings of the self. Critics who now call literary character into question, and who proclaim also the death of the author, invariably also regard all notions, literary and human, of a stable character as being mere reductions of deeper pre-Oedipal desires. It becomes

clear that the fortunes of literary character rise and fall with the prestige of normative conceptions of the ego. Shakespeare's Iago, who wars against being, may be
the first deconstructionist of the self, with his proclamation of "I am not what I am."
This constitutes the necessary prologue to any view that would regard a fixed ego
as a virtual abnormality. But deconstructions of the self are no more modern than
Modernism is. Like literary modernism, the decentered ego came out of the
Hellenistic culture of ancient Alexandria. The Gnostic heretics believed that the
psyche, like the body, was a fallen entity, mechanically fashioned by the Demiurge
or false creator. They held however that each of us possessed also a spark or
pneuma, which was a fragment of the original Abyss or true, alien God. The soul
or psyche within every one of us was thus at war with the self or pneuma, and only
that sparklike self could be saved.

Shakespeare, following after Chaucer in this respect, was the first and remains
still the greatest master of representing character both as a stable soul and a
wavering self. There is a substance that endures in Shakespeare's figures, and there
is also a quicksilver rendition of the unsettling sparks. Racine and Tolstoy, Balzac and
Dickens, follow in Shakespeare's wake by giving us some sense of pre-Oedipal
sparks or drives, and considerably more sense of post-Oedipal character and
personality, stabilizations or sublimations of the fetish-seeking drives. Critics like Leo
Bersani and René Girard argue eloquently against our taking this mimesis as the only
proper work of literature. I would suggest that strong fictions of the self, from the
Bible through Samuel Beckett, necessarily participate in both modes, the sublima-
tion of desire, and the persistence of a primordial desire. The mystery of Hamlet
or of Lear is intimately invested in the tangled mixture of the two modes of
representation.

Psychic mobility is proposed by Bersani as the ideal to which deconstructions
of the literary self may yet guide us. The ideal has its pathos, but the realities of
literary representation seem to me very different, perhaps destructively so. When
a novelist like D. H. Lawrence sought to reduce his characters to Eros and the
Death Drive, he still had to persuade us of his authority at mimesis by lavishing upon
the figures of *The Rainbow* and *Women in Love* all of the vivid stigmata of
normative personality. Birkin and Ursula may represent antithetical and uncanny
drives, but they develop and change as characters pondering their own pronounce-
ments and reactions to self and others. The cost of a non-Shakespearean representation is enormous. Pynchon, in *The Crying of Lot 49* and *Gravity's Rainbow*,
evades the burden of the normative by resorting to something like Christopher
Marlowe's art of caricature in *The Jew of Malta*. Marlowe's Barabas is a marvelous
rhetorician, yet he is a cartoon alongside the troublingly equivocal Shylock. Pynchon's personages are deliberate cartoons also, as flat as comic strips. Marlowe's
achievement, and Pynchon's, are beyond dispute, yet they are like the prelude and
the postlude to Shakespearean reality. They do not wish to engage with our hunger
for the empirical world and so they enter the problematic cosmos of literary
fantasy.

No writer, not even Shakespeare or Proust, alters the available stock that we agree to call reality, but Shakespeare, more than any other, does show us how much of reality we could encounter if only we retained adequate desire. The strong literary representation of character is already an analysis of character, and is part of the healing work of a literary culture, which implicitly seeks to cure violence through a normative mimesis of ego, *as if it were stable,* whether in actuality it is or is not. I do not believe that this is a social quest taken on by literary culture, but rather that we confront here the aesthetic essence of what makes a culture *literary,* rather than metaphysical or ethical or religious. A culture becomes literary when its conceptual modes have failed it, which means when religion, philosophy, and science have begun to lose their authority. If they cannot heal violence, then literature attempts to do so, which may be only a turning inside out of the critical arguments of Girard and Bersani.

I conclude by offering a particular instance or special case as a paradigm for the healing enterprise that is at once the representation and the analysis of literary character. Let us call it the aesthetics of being outraged, or rather of successfully representing the state of being outraged. W. C. Fields was one modern master of such representation, and Nathanael West was another, as was Faulkner before him. Here also the greatest master remains Shakespeare, whose Macbeth, himself a bloody outrage, yet retains our imaginative sympathy precisely because he grows increasingly outraged as he experiences the equivocation of the fiend that lies like truth. The double-natured promises and the prophecies of the weird sisters finally induce in Macbeth an apocalyptic version of the stage actor's anxiety at missing cues, the horror of a phantasmagoric stage fright of missing one's time, of always reacting too late. Macbeth, a veritable monster of solipsistic inwardness but no intellectual, counters his dilemma by fresh murders, that prolong him in time yet provoke him only to a perpetually freshened sense of being outraged, as all his expectations become still worse confounded. We are moved by Macbeth, however estrangedly, because his terrible inwardness is a paradigm for our own solipsism, but also because none of us can resist a strong and successful representation of the human in a state of being outraged.

The ultimate outrage is the necessity of dying, an outrage concealed in a multitude of masks, including the tyrannical ambitions of Macbeth. I suspect that our outrage at being outraged is the most difficult of all our affects for us to represent to ourselves, which is why we are so inclined to imaginative sympathy for a character who strongly conveys that affect to us. The Shrike of West's *Miss Lonely-hearts* or Faulkner's Joe Christmas of *Light in August* are crucial modern instances, but such figures can be located in many other works, since the ability to represent this extreme emotion is one of the tests that strong writers are driven to set for themselves.

However a reader seeks to reduce literary character to a question of marks on a page, she will come at last to the impasse constituted by the thought of death, her death, and before that to all the stations of being outraged that memorialize her own drive towards death. In reading, she quests for evidences that are strong representations, whether of her desire or her despair. Such questings constitute the necessary basis for the analysis of literary character, an enterprise that always will survive every vagary of critical fashion.

EDITOR'S NOTE

This book brings together a representative selection of the best criticism that has been devoted to Shylock, of Shakespeare's *The Merchant of Venice*, considered as a major literary character. I am indebted to Richard Fumosa for his skill and dedication in helping me to edit this volume.

My introduction centers upon what I find most problematical in Shakespeare's representation of Shylock: the Jew's forced conversion, and his muted reaction to that outrage. The critical extracts, arranged like the critical essays in the chronological order of their original publication, begin with August Wilhelm von Schlegel's and William Hazlitt's portraits of Shylock, and go on through such major figures as Victor Hugo and Georg Brandes, and then culminate in our century with a number of eminent interpreters, including Northrop Frye, Leslie Fiedler, W. H. Auden, and C. L. Barber.

The critical essays commence with E. E. Stoll's crucial corrective to the Romantic tradition in which Shylock becomes the play's instance of heroic pathos, rather than its comic villain. John Middleton Murry chooses to emphasize the drama's fairy-tale elements, so as to exclude Shylock's pathos, while Harold C. Goddard fiercely finds Portia liable for not living up to her own exaltation of Christian mercy.

In the view of Graham Midgley, Shylock and Antonio parallel each other, each retiring at last into his own loneliness. John Russell Brown, in a purely theatrical analysis, sees the fifth act providing a final perspective upon the absent Shylock, while Bernard Grebanier ironically highlights Shylock's prophetic intimation of the triumph of "the philosophy of banks," beyond compassion.

Barbara K. Lewalski illuminates the Biblical aspects of Shylock, in which the New Testament vision of mercy is set against what Christians judge to be the Old Testament's insistence upon the Law. In John Palmer's historicizing exegesis, Shylock's story "lingers in the memory as an old, unhappy tale," standing up against the play's "pretty confusion of rings and posies."

For Alan C. Dessen, Shylock is another instance of the stage Jew, and so should be regarded more as a theatrical device than as an anti-Semitic stereotype. Lawrence Danson judges the play to be a progressive weakening of Shylock, so that his acceptance of forced conversion is the result of profound exhaustion.

In a remarkable account of the image of the scapegoat, René Girard tries to emancipate us from the ceaseless interplay of interpretations emphasizing the contraries of Shylock's pathos and Shylock's dreadful villainy. Derek Cohen concludes this volume by taking us back full circle to the stance of E. E. Stoll and of my introduction, since Cohen also sees Shylock as the central figure in "a profoundly and crudely anti-Semitic play."

INTRODUCTION

Of Shakespeare's displaced spirits, those enigmatic figures who sometimes seem to have wandered into the wrong play, Shylock clearly remains the most problematical. We need always to keep reminding ourselves that he is a *comic* villain, partly derived from the grandest of Marlovian scoundrels, Barabas, Jew of Malta. In some sense, that should place Shylock in the Machiavellian company of two villains of tragedy, Edmund and Iago, yet none of us wishes to see Shylock there. Edmund and Iago are apocalyptic humorists; self-purged of pathos, they frighten us because continually they invent themselves while manipulating others. Shylock's pathos is weirdly heroic; he was meant to frighten us, to be seen as a nightmare made into flesh and blood, while seeking the audience's flesh and blood. It seems clear to me that if Shakespeare himself were to be resurrected, in order to direct a production of *The Merchant of Venice* on a contemporary stage in New York City, there would be a riot, quite without the assistance of the Jewish Defense League. The play is both a superb romantic comedy, and a marvelously adequate version of a perfectly Christian, altogether murderous anti-Semitism, of a kind fused into Christianity by the Gospel of John in particular.

In that latter assertion, or parts of it, I follow after the formidable E. E. Stoll, who observed that Shylock's penalty was the heaviest to be discovered in all the pound-of-flesh stories. As Stoll said, in none of them "does the money-lender suffer like Shylock—impoverishment, sentence of death, and an outrage done to his faith from which Jews were guarded even by decrees of German Emperors and Roman pontiffs." Of all the enigmas presented by *The Merchant of Venice*, to me the most baffling is Shylock's broken acceptance of forced conversion. Is it persuasive? Surely not, since Shakespeare's Shylock, proud and fierce Jew, scarcely would have preferred Christianity to death. Consistency of character in Shylock admittedly might have cost Shakespeare the comedy of his comedy; a Shylock put to death might have shadowed the ecstasy of Belmont in Act V. But so does the forced conversion, for us, though clearly not for Shakespeare and his contemporary audience. The difficult but crucial question becomes: why did Shakespeare inflict the cruelty of the

I

false conversion, knowing he could not allow Shylock the tragic dignity of dying for his people's faith?

I find it astonishing that this question never has been asked anywhere in the published criticism of *The Merchant of Venice.* No other Shakespearean character who has anything like Shylock's representational force is handled so strangely by Shakespeare, and ultimately so inadequately. That Shylock should agree to become a Christian is more absurd than would be the conversion of Coriolanus to the popular party, or Cleopatra's consent to become a vestal virgin at Rome. We sooner could see Falstaff as a monk, than we can contemplate Shylock as a Christian. Shakespeare notoriously possessed the powers both of preternatural irony, and of imbuing a character with more vitality than a play's context could sustain. I cannot better the judgment upon Christian conversion that Launcelot Gobbo makes in his dialogue with the charmingly insufferable Jessica, that Jewish Venetian princess:

> JESSICA: I shall be sav'd by my husband, he hath made me a Christian!
> LAUNCELOT: Truly, the more to blame he; we were Christians enow before, e'en as many as could well live one by another. This making of Christians will raise the price of hogs. If we grow all to be pork-eaters, we shall not shortly have a rasher on the coals for money.

But Shakespeare takes care to distance this irony from the play's comic catastrophe, when the Jew is undone by Christian mercy. It is Antonio, the pious Jew-baiter, who adds to the Duke's pardon the requirement that Shylock immediately become a Christian, after which Shakespeare seems a touch anxious to get Shylock offstage as quietly and quickly as possible:

> DUKE: He shall do this, or else I do recant
> The pardon that I late pronounced here.
> PORTIA: Art thou contented, Jew? what dost thou say?
> SHYLOCK: I am content.
> PORTIA: Clerk, draw a deed of gift.
> SHYLOCK: I pray you give me leave to go from hence.
> I am not well. Send the deed after me,
> And I will sign it.

And in a moment, Shylock walks out of the play, to the discord of what must seem to us Gratiano's Nazi-like jeers and threats. In our post-Holocaust universe, how can we accommodate Shylock's "I am content," too broken for irony, too strong for any play whatsoever? That question, I think, is unanswerable, and does not belong to literary criticism anyway. What is essential for criticism is to ask and answer the double question: why did Shakespeare so represent his stage Jew as to make possible the Romantic interpretation that has proceeded from Hazlitt and Henry Irving right through to Harold C. Goddard and innumerable actors in our century, and having done so, why did the playwright then shatter the character's consistency by imposing upon him the acceptance of the humiliating forced conversion to that religion of mercy, the Christianity of Venice?

In his lively essay on the play, W. H. Auden remarks on a different kind of implausibility that Shakespeare confers upon Shylock:

> After Portia has trapped Shylock through his own insistence upon the letter of the law of Contract, she produces another law by which any alien who conspires against the life of a Venetian citizen forfeits his goods and places his life at the Doge's mercy. Even in the rush of a stage performance, the audience cannot help reflecting that a man as interested in legal subtleties as Shylock, would, surely, have been aware of the existence of this law and that, if by any chance he had overlooked it, the Doge surely would very soon have drawn his attention to it. Shakespeare, it seems to me, was willing to introduce what is an absurd implausibility for the sake of an effect which he could not secure without it.

Auden is very shrewd here, but I cite him primarily to help suggest that Shylock's acceptance of enforced Christianity is a far more severe implausibility, and one that distracts from dramatic or even theatrical effect. Indeed, as drama Shylock's "I am content" is necessarily a puzzle, not akin say to Iago's "From this time forth I never will speak word." Iago will die, under torture, in absolute silence: a dramatic death. We anticipate that Shylock the broken new Christian will live in silence: not a dramatic life. Is it that Shakespeare wished to repeal Shylock, as it were, and so cut away the enormous pathos of the character? We have seen no weaknesses in Shylock's will, no signs indeed that he can serve the function of a comic villain, a new Barabas. No red wig and giant nose will transform the speaker of Shylock's three hundred and sixty dark lines into a two-dimensional character. Shylock, however monstrous his contemplated revenge, is all spirit, malign and concentrated, indifferent to the world and the flesh, unless Antonio be taken to represent both for him. Displaced spirit and so villain as he is, Shylock confronts in the heroically Christian merchant of Venice his tormentor and his double, the play's best Christian, who demonstrates the authenticity of his religious and moral zeal by his prowess in spitting at and cursing Shylock. I intend no irony there, and I fear that I read Shakespeare as he meant to *be* read. And yet every time I teach *The Merchant of Venice,* my students rebel at my insistence that Shylock is not there to be sympathized with, whereas Antonio is to be admired, if we are to read the play that Shakespeare wrote. One had best state this matter very plainly: to recover the comic splendor of *The Merchant of Venice* now, you need to be either a scholar or an anti-Semite, or best of all an anti-Semitic scholar.

E. E. Stoll sensibly said that if you sympathize with Shylock, then you must turn against Portia, a lesson that modern directors refuse to learn, preferring to have it both ways: a Shylock of sublime pathos, and a Portia triumphant and wholly delightful. What is a serious reader to do with the more severe difference that is confronted when Goddard and C. L. Barber, two of the handful of great critics of

Shakespeare in our time, are juxtaposed on the question of Shylock? Barber deftly improves upon Stoll, first by noting that we never encounter Shylock alone, which denies the villain his inwardness, and makes him subject to a group perspective. Second, Barber goes on:

> This perspective on him does not exclude a potential pathos. There is always potential pathos, behind, when drama makes fun of isolating, anti-social qualities. Indeed, the process of *making fun of* a person often works by exhibiting pretensions to humanity so as to show that they are inhuman, mechanical, not validly appropriate for sympathy.

Barber's persuasive view cannot be reconciled with Goddard's grand sentence: "Shylock's conviction that Christianity and revenge are synonyms is confirmed." For Goddard, Portia becomes one with the golden casket, and fails her own inner self. On that reading, we return to a Shylock of tragic pathos, and hardly to Barber's comic butt. René Girard, our contemporary authority on scapegoating, attempts to solve contradictory readings by ironizing Shakespeare:

> Ultimately we do not have to choose between a favorable and an unfavorable image of Shylock. The old critics have concentrated on Shylock as a separate entity, an individual substance that would be merely juxtaposed to other individual substances and remain unaffected by them. The ironic depth in *The Merchant of Venice* results from a tension not between two static images of Shylock, but between those textual features that strengthen and those features that undermine the popular idea of an insurmountable difference between Christian and Jew.

I am myself a survivor of those "old critics" whom Girard scorns, and like them I do not speak of entities, substances, textual features, and ironic differences. One learns from Shakespeare to speak of characters, and the issue remains: why did Shakespeare ultimately refuse consistency to his Jew, whether viewed as comic or as a figure of profound pathos? I cannot find more than a few aesthetic flaws in Shakespeare, and Shylock's acceptance of conversion seems to me much the most egregious, surpassing the peculiar final scene of *Measure for Measure* and even the brutal treatment of Malvolio at the end of *Twelfth Night.* Since Act V of *The Merchant of Venice* is a triumphal ecstasy, the collapse of Shylock's pride in his Jewishness perhaps becomes an artistic blemish only when I brood on it in my study, but then I have never seen, will never see, and could not bear seeing a production of the play that is consonant with the play's own values.

Shylock is one of Shakespeare's displaced spirits, together with Barnardine, Lear's Fool, Malvolio, in some sense even Caliban, perhaps even an aspect of Sir John Falstaff, perhaps even the outcast Edgar, who is so slow to abandon his mask as poor Tom o'Bedlam. We do not know who wrote the great lyric, "Tom o'Bedlam," found in a manuscript commonplace that scholars date about 1620, but being very unscholarly I always cheerfully assume that it was Shakespeare, because it is too good to be by anyone else. I cite its final stanza here because it sums up, for me, the ethos of the ultimately displaced spirit, the Shakespearean outsider who needs a context less alien than Shakespeare will provide for him:

With an host of furious fancies
Whereof I am commander,
With a burning spear and a horse of air,
To the wilderness I wander.
By a knight of ghosts and shadows
I summoned am to a tourney
Ten leagues beyond the wide world's end:
Methinks it is no journey.
Yet will I sing, Any food, any feeding,
Feeding, drink, or clothing;
Come dame or maid, be not afraid,
Poor Tom will injure nothing.

One can hardly say that poor Shylock, incessantly demanding that he will have his bond, will injure nothing, and even I would hesitate at speaking of "poor Shylock" had not Shakespeare invented the monstrosity of the forced conversion. But the great Tom o'Bedlam song, whoever wrote it, manifests the same mixture of unbearable pathos and visionary intensity that I find in all of Shakespeare's displaced spirits: Shylock, Barnardine, Lear's Fool, Malvolio, and in a weird mode, Caliban. Ambivalence emanates from all of these, as it does from the alienated Edgar, and ambivalence is part of our response to them also. Oddly the least original of these, Shylock is too much the Belial figure of Christian tradition, and one wonders why Shakespeare could accept so much crudity of stock representation, even as he allowed the apparent pathos in Shylock that continues to divide critics. I suspect that the enigmas concerning Shylock can be resolved only if we return Shakespeare's Jew to his agonistic context, the Shakespearean need to compete with and overgo Marlowe's superb villain, Barabas, the Jew of Malta. Barabas is a farcical hero-villain, while Shylock is a comic villain, yet the contrast between them tends to abolish such distinctions. Could we conceive of Barabas accepting an imposed conversion? The question's absurdity turns upon Marlowe's dramatic art, which works here as the purest caricature, excluding any possibilities of pathos. Barabas could no more say "If you prick us, do we not bleed? If you tickle us, do we not laugh?" than Shylock could roar out the parodic outrageousness and exuberance of Marlowe's Jew:

As for myself, I walk abroad a-nights,
And kill sick people groaning under walls;
Sometimes I go about and poison wells.

Marlowe, subverting every established order and tradition, loathes Christians, Muslims, and Jews with admirable impartiality, and so he is happy to have Barabas satirize the Christian myth of the Jewish sport of poisoning wells. Shakespeare hardly could have missed the jest, but for him Marlowe always represented, in art as in life, the way down and out, the way not to go. The savage gusto of Barabas is deliberately lacking in the rugged Shylock, whose only exuberance is his will to revenge himself, and his people, upon that sincere Christian, the noble Antonio. Antonio's superior goodness is shown to us by his righteous contempt for Shylock. Splendid as this must have been for Shakespeare's audience, it is now our largest burden, I sometimes think, in reading *The Merchant of Venice*. Antonio is a Jew-baiter, plain and simple. Marlowe gives us no such figure in *The Jew of Malta*, yet I suspect that Marlowe provoked Shakespeare into the ambivalence of our having to accept Antonio and Portia as angels, and Shylock as the Devil, albeit a Devil with strong feelings, akin to Marlowe's Mephistopheles in *Doctor Faustus*.

Though Barabas seems to me Shakespeare's prime model for Richard III and even for Aaron the Moor in *Titus Andronicus*, Barabas has nothing Shakespearean about him. There is a mad zest in Barabas, a kind of antic ferocity, that Shakespeare rejected as too raw, a rejection of great consequence, since it spurred Shakespeare into the creation of Edmund and Iago. That Marlovian parody, Ancient Pistol, is Shakespeare's sardonic commentary upon Marlowe's exaltation of self-celebratory and exuberant ferocity. "I'll show you a Jew!" Shakespeare says to us by Shylock, thus implying that Barabas is no Jew, but simply is: Kit Marlowe. Barabas of course is a superbly outrageous representation of a Jew; he is no more Jewish than Marlowe's Christians are Christians or his Muslims are Muslims. Is there a more vivid, a more memorable representation of a Jew in post-Biblical literature than Shakespeare's Shylock? Well, there is the Fagin of Charles Dickens, clearly more memorable than George Eliot's Daniel Deronda, but about as acceptable to a post-Holocaust sensibility as Shylock. Jewish novelists from Disraeli to the present hardly have given us a being as intense as Shylock, or as eloquent, though Shylock's eloquence is somber, even so rancid:

> You'll ask me why I rather choose to have
> A weight of carrion flesh than to receive
> Three thousand ducats. I'll not answer that,
> But say it is my humor. Is it answered?
> What if my house be troubled with a rat,
> And I be pleased to give ten thousand ducats
> To have it baned? What, are you answered yet?
> Some men there are love not a gaping pig,
> Some that are mad if they behold a cat,
> And others, when the bagpipe sings i' th' nose,
> Cannot contain their wine; for affection,
> Master of passion, sways it to the mood
> Of what it likes or loathes.

Extraordinary psychologist as Shakespeare has made him (akin in this to Edmund and Iago), Shylock is totally unable to achieve self-understanding. If "affection" (innate antipathy) totally dominates "passion" (any authentic emotion) in him, that is because he wills such domination. But thus he plays the Christian's game, and unlike Barabas he can only lose. Barabas goes down in pained but clamorous triumph, cursing Christians and Muslims with his final burst of spirit. Shylock, as Shakespeare deftly creates him, defeats himself, as Iago will, and ends in the terrible humiliation of being "content" to become a Christian, when in some sense (the Venetian one) he has been Christianized already, by accepting their exaltation of antipathy governing emotion, as in the good Antonio. Is this Shakespeare's irony, or does it not belong instead to a commonplace older than Shakespeare, as old as the Talmud? If, as Blake grimly insisted, we become what we behold, it is an ancient lesson, far older even than Hebraic morality. Shakespeare's comic villain undoes himself as Barabas does not, in a critique of Marlowe that nevertheless was expensive for the play, *The Merchant of Venice,* since it ultimately destroys Shylock's heretofore strong plausibility as a character.

A displaced spirit, in Shakespeare, never ceases to be spirit, and though it is warped by displacement, such a spirit contaminates the drama through which it passes, and of necessity contaminates the audience as well. To stage the play of Antonio, Portia, and Shylock now is to attempt what is virtually impossible, since only an audience at ease with its own anti-Semitism could tolerate a responsible and authentic presentation of what Shakespeare actually wrote. In this one play alone, Shakespeare was very much of his age, and not for all time.

—H. B.

CRITICAL EXTRACTS

AUGUST WILHELM VON SCHLEGEL

The *Merchant of Venice* is one of Shakspeare's most perfect works: popular to an extraordinary degree, and calculated to produce the most powerful effect on the stage, and at the same time a wonder of ingenuity and art for the reflecting critic. Shylock, the Jew, is one of the inimitable masterpieces of characterization which are to be found only in Shakspeare. It is easy for both poet and player to exhibit a caricature of national sentiments, modes of speaking, and gestures. Shylock, however, is everything but a common Jew: he possesses a strongly-marked and original individuality, and yet we perceive a light touch of Judaism in everything he says or does. We almost fancy we can hear a light whisper of the Jewish accent even in the written words, such as we sometimes still find in the higher classes, notwithstanding their social refinement. In tranquil moments, all that is foreign to the European blood and Christian sentiments is less perceptible, but in passion the national stamp comes out more strongly marked. All these inimitable niceties the finished art of a great actor can alone properly express. Shylock is a man of information, in his own way, even a thinker, only he has not divorced the region where human feelings dwell; his morality is founded on the disbelief in goodness and magnanimity. The desire to avenge the wrongs and indignities heaped upon his nation is, after avarice, his strongest spring of action. His hate is naturally directed chiefly against those Christians who are actuated by truly Christian sentiments: a disinterested love of our neighbour seems to him the most unrelenting persecution of the Jews. The letter of the law is his idol; he refuses to lend an ear to the voice of mercy, which, from the mouth of Portia, speaks to him with heavenly eloquence: he insists on rigid and inflexible justice, and at last it recoils on his own head. Thus he becomes a symbol of the general history of his unfortunate nation. The melancholy and self-sacrificing magnanimity of Antonio is affectingly sublime. Like a princely merchant, he is surrounded with a whole train of noble friends. The contrast which this forms to the selfish cruelty of the usurer Shylock was necessary to redeem the honour of human nature. The danger which almost to the close of the fourth act, hangs over Antonio, and which the imagination is almost afraid to approach, would fill the mind with too painful anxiety, if the poet did not also provide for its recreation and diversion. This is effected in an especial manner by the scenes at Portia's country-seat, which transport the spectator into quite another world. And yet they are closely connected with the main business by the chain of cause and effect: Bassanio's preparations for his courtship are the cause of Antonio's subscribing the dangerous bond; and Portia again, by the counsel and advice of her uncle, a famous lawyer, effects the safety of her lover's friend. But the relations of the dramatic composition are the while admirably observed in yet another respect. The trial between Shylock and Antonio is indeed recorded as being a real event, still, for all that, it must ever remain an unheard-of and singular case.

—AUGUST WILHELM VON SCHLEGEL, *Lectures on Dramatic Art and Literature*
[1809], tr. John Black [1816], rev. A. S. W. Morrison (London:
Henry G. Bohn, 1846), pp. 388–90

WILLIAM HAZLITT

This is a play that in spite of the change of manners and prejudices still holds undisputed possession of the stage. Shakespear's malignant has outlived Mr. Cumberland's benevolent Jew. In proportion as Shylock has ceased to be a popular bugbear, "baited with the rabble's curse," he becomes a half-favourite with the philosophical part of the audience, who are disposed to think that Jewish revenge is at least as good as Christian injuries. Shylock is a *a good hater;* "a man no less sinned against than sinning." If he carries his revenge too far, yet he has strong grounds for "the lodged hate he bears Anthonio," which he explains with equal force of eloquence and reason. He seems the depositary of the vengeance of his race; and though the long habit of brooding over daily insults and injuries has crusted over his temper with inveterate misanthropy, and hardened him against the contempt of mankind, this adds but little to the triumphant pretensions of his enemies. There is a strong, quick, and deep sense of justice mixed up with the gall and bitterness of his resentment. The constant apprehension of being burnt alive, plundered, banished, reviled, and trampled on, might be supposed to sour the most forbearing nature, and to take something from that "milk of human kindness," with which his persecutors contemplated his indignities. The desire of revenge is almost inseparable from the sense of wrong; and we can hardly help sympathising with the proud spirit, hid beneath his "Jewish gaberdine," stung to madness by repeated and undeserved provocations, and labouring to throw off the load of obloquy and oppression heaped upon him and all his tribe by one desperate act of "lawful" revenge, till the ferociousness of the means by which he is to execute his purpose, and the pertinacity with which he adheres to it, turn us against him; but even at last, when disappointed of the sanguinary revenge with which he had glutted his hopes, and exposed to beggary and contempt by the letter of the law on which he had insisted with so little remorse, we pity him, and think him hardly dealt with by his judges. In all his answers and retorts upon his adversaries, he has the best not only of the argument but of the question, reasoning on their own principles and practice. They are so far from allowing of any measure of equal dealing, of common justice or humanity between themselves and the Jew, that even when they come to ask a favour of him, and Shylock reminds them that "on such a day they spit upon him, another spurned him, another called him dog, and for these curtesies request he'll lend them so much monies"—Anthonio, his old enemy, instead of any acknowledgment of the shrewdness and justice of his remonstrance, which would have been preposterous in a respectable Catholic merchant in those times, threatens him with a repetition of the same treatment—

I am as like to call thee so again,
To spit on thee again, to spurn thee too.

After this the appeal to the Jew's mercy, as if there were any common principle of right and wrong between them, is the rankest hypocrisy, or the blindest prejudice; and the Jew's answer to one of Anthonio friends, who asks him what his pound of forfeit flesh is good for, is irresistible—

To bait fish withal; if it will feed nothing else, it will feed my revenge. He hath disgrac'd me, and hinder'd me of half a million, laughed at my losses, mock'd at my gains, scorn'd my nation, thwarted my bargains, cool'd my friends, heated mine enemies; and what's his reason? I am a Jew. Hath not a Jew eyes; hath not a Jew hands, organs, dimensions, senses, affections, passions; fed with the same food, hurt with the same weapons, subject to the same diseases, healed by the same means, warmed and cooled by the same winter and summer that a Christian is? If you prick us, do we not bleed? If you tickle us, do we not laugh? If you poison us, do we not die? And if you wrong us, shall we not revenge? If we are like you in the rest, we will resemble you in that. If a Jew wrong a Christian, what is his humility? revenge. If a Christian wrong a Jew, what should his sufferance be by Christian example? why revenge. The villainy you teach me I will execute, and it shall go hard but I will better the instruction.

The whole of the trial-scene, both before and after the entrance of Portia, is a master-piece of dramatic skill. The legal acuteness, the passionate declamations, the sound maxims of jurisprudence, the wit and irony interspersed in it, the fluctuations of hope and fear in the different persons, and the completeness and suddenness of the catastrophe, cannot be surpassed. Shylock, who is his own counsel, defends himself well, and is triumphant on all the general topics that are urged against him, and only fails through a legal flaw. Take the following as an instance:—

SHYLOCK: What judgment shall I dread, doing no wrong?
You have among you many a purchas'd slave,
Which like your asses, and your dogs, and mules,
You use in abject and in slavish part.
Because you bought them:—shall I say to you,
Let them be free, marry them to your heirs?
Why sweat they under burdens? let their beds
Be made as soft as yours, and let their palates
Be season'd with such viands? you will answer,
The slaves are ours:—so do I answer you:
The pound of flesh, which I demand of him,
Is dearly bought, is mine, and I will have it:
If you deny me, fie upon your law!
There is no force in the decrees of Venice:
I stand for judgment: answer; shall I have it?

The keenness of his revenge awakes all his faculties; and he beats back all opposition to his purpose, whether grave or gay, whether of wit or argument, with an equal degree of earnestness and self-possession. His character is displayed as distinctly in other less prominent parts of the play, and we may collect from a few sentences the history of his life—his descent and origin, his thrift and domestic economy, his affection for his daughter, whom he loves next to his wealth, his courtship and his first present to Leah, his wife! "I would not have parted with it" (the ring which he first gave her) "for a wilderness of monkies!" What a fine Hebraism is implied in this expression! ⟨...⟩

When we first went to see Mr. Kean in Shylock, we expected to see, what we had been used to see, a decrepid old man, bent with age and ugly with mental deformity, grinning with deadly malice, with the venom of his heart congealed in the expression of his countenance, sullen, morose, gloomy, inflexible, brooding over one idea, that of his hatred, and fixed on one unalterable purpose, that of his revenge. We were disappointed, because we had taken our idea from other actors, not from the play. There is no proof there that Shylock is old, but a single line, "Bassanio and *old* Shylock, both stand forth,"—which does not imply that he is infirm with age—and the circumstance that he has a daughter marriageable, which does not imply that he is old at all. It would be too much to say that his body should be made crooked and deformed to answer to his mind, which is bowed down and warped with prejudices and passion. That he has but one idea, is not true; he has more ideas than any other person in the piece; and if he is intense and inveterate in the pursuit of his purpose, he shews the utmost elasticity, vigour, and presence of mind, in the means of attaining it. But so rooted was our habitual impression of the part from seeing it caricatured in the representation, that it was only from a careful perusal of the play itself that we saw our error. The stage is not in general the best place to study our author's characters in. It is too often filled with traditional common-place conceptions of the part, handed down from sire to son, and suited to the taste of *the great vulgar and the small.*—" 'Tis an unweeded garden: things rank and gross do merely gender in it!" If a man of genius comes once in an age to clear away the rubbish, to make it fruitful and wholesome, they cry, " 'Tis a bad school: it may be like nature, it may be like Shakespear, but it is not like us." Admirable critics!

—WILLIAM HAZLITT, *Characters of Shakespear's Plays*
(London: C. H. Reynell, 1817)

CHARLES KNIGHT

The generosity of Antonio's nature unfitted him for a contest with the circumstances amid which his lot was cast. The Jew says—

> In low simplicity,
> He lends out money gratis.

He himself says—

> I oft deliver'd from his forfeitures
> Many that have at times made moan to me.

Bassanio describes him as—

> The kindest man,
> The best condition'd and unwearied spirit
> In doing courtesies.

To such a spirit, whose "means are in supposition"—whose ventures are "squander'd abroad"—the curse of the Jew must have sometimes presented itself to his own prophetic mind:—

> This is the fool that lends out money gratis.

Antonio and his position are not in harmony. But there is something else discordant in Antonio's mind. This kind friend, this generous benefactor, this gentle spirit, this man "unwearied in doing courtesies," can outrage and insult a fellow-creature, because he is of another creed:—

> SHY.: Fair sir, you spet on me on Wednesday last;
> You spurn'd me such a day; another time
> You call'd me dog; and for these courtesies
> I'll lend you thus much monies.
> ANT.: I am as like to call thee so again,
> To spet on thee again, to spurn thee too.

Was it without an object that Shakspere made this man, so entitled to command
our affections and our sympathy, act so unworthy a part, and not be ashamed of
the act? Most assuredly the poet did not intend to justify the indignities which were
heaped upon Shylock; for in the very strongest way he has made the Jew remember the insult in the progress of his wild revenge:—

> Thou call'dst me dog, before thou hadst a cause:
> But, since I am a dog, beware my fangs.

Here, to our minds, is the first of the lessons of charity which this play teaches.
Antonio is as much to be pitied for his prejudices as the Jew for his. They had both
been nurtured in evil opinions. They had both been surrounded by influences
which more or less held in subjection their better natures. The honoured Christian
is as intolerant as the despised Jew. The one habitually pursues with injustice the
subjected man that he has been taught to loathe; the other, in the depths of his
subtle obstinacy, seizes upon the occasion to destroy the powerful man that he has
been compelled to fear. The companions of Antonio exhibit, more or less, the
same reflection of the prejudices which have become to them a second nature.
They are not so gross in their prejudices as Launcelot, to whom "the Jew is the very
devil incarnation." But to Lorenzo, who is about to marry his daughter, Shylock is
a "faithless Jew." When the unhappy father is bereft of all that constituted the solace
of his home, and before he has manifested that spirit of revenge which might well
call for indignation and contempt, he is to the gentlemanly Solanio "the villain Jew,"
and "the dog Jew." When the unhappy man speaks of his daughter's flight, he is met
with a brutal jest on the part of Salarino, who, within his own circle, is the pleasantest of men;—"I, for my part, knew the tailor that made the wings she flew
withal." We can understand the reproaches that are heaped upon Shylock in the
trial scene as something that might come out of the depths of any passion-stirred
nature: but the habitual contempt with which he is treated by men who in every
other respect are gentle and good-humoured and benevolent is a proof to us that
Shakspere meant to represent the struggle that must inevitably ensue, in a condition
of society where the innate sense of justice is deadened in the powerful by those
hereditary prejudices which make cruelty virtue; and where the powerless, invested by accident with the means of revenge, say with Shylock, "The villainy you
teach me I will execute; and it shall go hard but I will better the instruction." The
climax of this subjection of our higher and better natures to conventional circumstances is to be found in the character of the Jew's daughter. Young, agreeable,
intelligent, formed for happiness, she is shut up by her father in a dreary solitude.
One opposed to her in creed gains her affections; and the ties which bind the father
and the child are broken for ever. But they are not broken without compunction:—

> Alack! what heinous sin is it in me
> To be ashamed to be my father's child!

This is nature. But when she has fled from him, robbed him, spent fourscore ducats in one night, given his turquoise for a monkey, and, finally, revealed his secrets, with an evasion of the ties that bound them which makes one's flesh creep,—

When I was *with him*,—

we see the poor girl plunged into the most wretched contest between her duties and her pleasures by the force of external circumstances. We grant, then, to all these our compassion; for they commit injustice ignorantly, and through a force which they cannot withstand. Is the Jew himself not to be measured by the same rule? We believe that it was Shakspere's intention so to measure him.

When Pope exclaimed of Macklin's performance of Shylock,—

This is the Jew
That Shakspere drew!

the higher philosophy of Shakspere was little appreciated. Macklin was, no doubt, from all traditionary report of him, perfectly capable of representing the subtlety of the Jew's malice and the energy of his revenge. But it is a question with us whether he perceived, or indeed if any actor ever efficiently represented, the more delicate traits of character that lie beneath these two great passions of the Jew's heart. Look, for example, at the extraordinary mixture of the personal and the national in his dislike of Antonio. He hates him for his gentle manners:—

How like a fawning publican he looks!

He hates him, "for he is a Christian;"—he hates him, for that "he lends out money gratis;"—but he hates him more than all, because

He hates our sacred nation.

It is this national feeling which, when carried in a right direction, makes a patriot and a hero, that assumes in Shylock the aspect of a grovelling and fierce personal revenge. He has borne insult and injury "with a patient shrug;" but ever in small matters he has been seeking retribution:—

I am not bid for love; they flatter me:
But yet I'll go in hate, to feed upon
The prodigal Christian.

The mask is at length thrown off—he has the Christian in his power; and his desire of revenge, mean and ferocious as it is, rises into sublimity, through the unconquerable energy of the oppressed man's wilfulness. "I am a Jew: Hath not a Jew eyes? hath not a Jew hands, organs, dimensions, senses, affections, passions? fed with the same food, hurt with the same weapons, subject to the same diseases, healed by the same means, warmed and cooled by the same winter and summer, as a Christian is? If you prick us, do we not bleed? if you tickle us, do we not laugh? if you poison us, do we not die? and, if you wrong us, shall we not revenge? If we are like you in the rest, we will resemble you in that." It is impossible, after this exposition of his feelings, that we should not feel that he has properly cast the greater portion of the odium which belongs to his actions upon the social circumstances by which he has been hunted into madness. He has been made the thing he is by society. In the extreme wildness of his anger, when he utters the harrowing imprecation,—"I would my daughter were dead at my foot, and the jewels in her ear! 'would she were hearsed at my foot, and the ducats in her coffin," the tenderness that belongs to our common humanity, even in its most passionate forgetfulness of the dearest ties, comes across him in the remembrance of the mother of that execrated child:—"Out upon her! Thou torturest me, Tubal: it was my turquoise; I had it of Leah when I was a bachelor."

It is in the conduct of the trial scene, that, as it appears to us, is to be sought the concentration of Shakspere's leading idea in the composition of this drama. The merchant stands before the Jew a better and a wiser man than when he called him "dog:"—

> I do oppose
> My patience to his fury; and am arm'd
> To suffer, with a quietness of spirit,
> The very tyranny and rage of his.

Misfortune has corrected the influences which, in happier moments, allowed him to forget the gentleness of his nature, and to heap unmerited abuse upon him whose badge was sufferance. The Jew is unchanged. But, if Shakspere in the early scenes made us entertain some compassion for his wrongs, he has now left him to bear all the indignation which we ought to feel against one "uncapable of pity." But we cannot despise the Jew. His intellectual vigour rises supreme over the mere reasonings by which he is opposed. He defends his own injustice of every-day occurrence—and no one ventures to answer him:—

> You have among you many a purchas'd slave,
> Which, like your asses, and your dogs, and mules,
> You use in abject and in slavish parts,
> Because you bought them:—Shall I say to you,
> Let them be free, marry them to your heirs?
> Why sweat they under burthens? let their beds
> Be made as soft as yours, and let their palates
> Be season'd with such viands? You will answer,
> The slaves are ours:—So do I answer you.
> The pound of flesh, which I demand of him,
> Is dearly bought; 't is mine, and I will have it:
> If you deny me, fie upon your law!

It would have been exceedingly difficult for the Merchant to have escaped from the power of the obdurate man, so strong in the letter of the law, and so resolute to carry it out by the example of his judges in other matters, had not the law been found here, as in most other cases, capable of being bent to the will of its administrators. Had it been the inflexible thing which Shylock required it to be, a greater injustice would have been committed than the Jew had finally himself to suffer. Mrs. Jameson has very justly and ingeniously described the struggle which Portia had to sustain in abandoning the high ground which she took in her great address to the Jew;—"She maintains at first a calm self-command, as one sure of carrying her point in the end: yet the painful heart-thrilling uncertainty in which she keeps the whole court, until suspense verges upon agony, is not contrived for effect merely; it is necessary and inevitable. She has two objects in view: to deliver her husband's friend, and to maintain her husband's honour by the discharge of his just debt, though paid out of her own wealth ten times over. It is evident that she would rather owe the safety of Antonio to anything rather than the legal quibble with which her cousin Bellario has armed her, and which she reserves as a last resource. Thus all the speeches addressed to Shylock, in the first instance, are either direct or indirect experiments on his temper and feelings. She must be understood, from the beginning to the end, as examining with intense anxiety the effect of her own words on his mind and countenance; as watching for that relenting spirit which she hopes to awaken either by reason or persuasion."

Had Shylock relented after that most beautiful appeal to his mercy, which Shakspere has here placed as the exponent of the higher principle upon which all law and right are essentially dependent, the real moral of the drama would have been destroyed. The weight of injuries transmitted to Shylock from his forefathers, and still heaped upon him even by the best of those by whom he was surrounded, was not so easily to become light, and to cease to exasperate his nature. Nor would it have been a true picture of society in the sixteenth century had the poet shown the judges of the Jew wholly magnanimous in granting him the mercy which he denied to the Christian. We certainly do not agree with the Duke, in his address to Shylock, that the conditions upon which his life is spared are imposed—

That thou shalt see the difference of our spirit.

Nor do we think that Shakspere meant to hold up these conditions as anything better than examples of the mode in which the strong are accustomed to deal with the weak. There is still something discordant in this, the real catastrophe of the drama. It could not be otherwise, and yet be true to nature.

—CHARLES KNIGHT, *Studies of Shakspere* (London: Charles Knight, 1849),
pp. 236–39

CHARLES COWDEN CLARKE

If I were required to adduce a signal proof of the question that Shakespeare lived beyond his age as a moral and social philosopher, I should not hesitate to ground my proof upon the way in which he has worked out the story of the *Merchant of*

Venice, as regards the character, behaviour, and treatment of the most important person in the drama—the Jew.

Shakespeare lived in an age when the general feeling towards the sect in which Shylock was born and educated could scarcely be called a prejudice—'tis too mild a term—it was a rancour, a horror, venting itself in injustice and violence, pillage, expulsion, and, if possible, extermination of the race. I cannot suppose that he was wholly untainted with the antipathy that had been fostered for centuries before him, for he was familiar with the legends of revenge and cruelty that had, at various periods, been perpetrated by Jews, when individual opportunities of gratifying their own natural lust of retaliation had presented themselves. He was familiar with the story of Hugh of Lincoln, and with the murder of the Christian babe in Chaucer's story of the Nun's Tale; and he felt that here was atrocity for atrocity committed,—a course that never yet produced, and never will produce, the redress of an original wrong. He belonged to that faith, and throughout his writings he has urged its grand tenet, which inculcates the wickedness as well as the folly of revenge. But Shakespeare, in becoming the social and moral reformer of his species, possessed that point of wisdom in knowing, as it were by instinct, that he who desires to change a master-section in an age's code, whether it be civil or social, will not accomplish his end half so readily and effectually by un unconditional and wholesale opposition, as by a partial and rational extenuation. They who aim at reforming the masses,—who desire to lead, must at all events make a show of following. Nothing does the common mind resent more vehemently than the presumption of a single individual professing to be wiser than, and to dictate to, his whole race—the experience of all ages and of every day proves this. It was not for Shakespeare, whose profession it was to provide for the intellectual entertainment of his nation, to perk in their faces his individual opinions: it was much that he did not foster their prejudices, that he did not pander to their vices and inflate their self-love,—and he has not done this. He himself has laid down the principle upon which the drama should be constructed and sustained, and upon no other will it survive.

Upon this, his grand principle, therefore, it appears that the poet, in delineating the character and conduct of Shylock, as well as of his Christian opponents, has, with his large wisdom, preached a homily upon injustice to each sect and denomination of religionists, with a force and perspicuity of argument, as well as knowledge of human nature in its melancholy prejudices, that, to me, as I reflect upon his impartiality, his honest dispensation of justice, as displayed in this drama, place him centuries in advance of his age, and the production itself among the greatest efforts of human genius. If any reader have a doubt of the poet's sense of justice towards that most ill-used tribe, let him read the works of other writers of the period where the character of the Jew has been introduced. It is true, Shylock has been punished for his motive of revenge,—and justly; for it was an atrocious refinement of the passion, claimed and substantiated upon the worst of all unjust grounds—the right of legal justice;—no tyranny being equal to the wrenching of law for penal purposes. It is also true that the injuring party, in the first instance—the Christian—is brought off triumphantly; but in that age, or indeed in any age, the multitude could never have sympathised in a rigid fulfilment of such a compact, or of any compact that should sacrifice the one party for the benefit of the other.

But, after all, who does not sympathise with Shylock? Who, with the most ordinary notions of right and wrong, derives any gratification from the merchant Antonio's being brought off by a quirk of law, and that law an unjust one, which decreed the demolition of the Jew's whole wealth and estate? Shakespeare has made out a strong case for Shylock,—startling, indeed, it must have been to the commonalty in his time. Shylock says the finest things in the play, and he has the advantage in the argument throughout. If the motion of revenge *be* justifiable, (and his own moral code, "An eye for an eye, and a tooth for a tooth," bear him out,) he has all the odds against his adversaries:—

> Hath not a Jew eyes? hath not a Jew hands, organs, dimensions, senses, affections, passions? fed with the same food, hurt with the same weapons, subject to the same diseases, healed by the same means, warmed and cooled by the same winter and summer as a Christian is? If you prick us, do we not bleed? if you tickle us, do we not laugh? if you poison us, do we not die? and if you wrong us, shall we not revenge? If we are like you in the rest, we will resemble you in that. If a Jew wrong a Christian, what is his humility? revenge: if a Christian wrong a Jew, what should his sufferance be *by Christian example?* why, revenge. The villainy you teach me I will execute; and it shall go hard but I will better the instruction.

This is strong "lex talionis," or tooth-for tooth argument; and strong extenuation for that age; ay, and even for our own very Christian age.

But who shall say that this very play has not been instrumental in breaking down the barriers and mounds of intolerance and persecution for faith's sake? This noble production has, I believe, among other philosophical appeals, tended to assuage the fury of class and party prejudice, and persecution. Its course through those deep and savage ravines, wherein the stream of class-opinion was confined, and amid which it brawled and raved, tearing and wasting all before it, is gradually becoming diverted; and if it still exist, (which, alas! we all can sadly answer,) it has, nevertheless, mainly expended its force, and is slowly spreading in an inert ooze over the social champaign. The age of Diabolism is passing away; and a spirit of bearing and forbearing—the "doing unto others as we would be done by"—is becoming recognised and largely debated; and only let a question be brought to the debating point, its settlement is at no very remote distance. It is now the few only who hold fast by the integrity of the "right of might;" and the "might" is changing with the many into a calm principle of equitable adjustment.

So much is the leading principle of Christianity doing for us; gradually, but as surely as the progress of matter: and so much, in the pure spirit of its principle, did our Shakespeare anticipate and provide nearly three centuries ago.

It gives me pleasure to find that my feeling of the ethical working of this play is confirmed in a pamphlet lately brought out by Victor Hugo. The eloquent French writer has a beautiful passage in illustration; he says:—"Shylock has gained what is better than his cause—he has gained the cause of an entire people. He has caused the unknown rights of his race to be recognised, and enabled them to prevail by the exemplary condemnation of that exterminatory code which hitherto had kept them in abeyance. * * * Shakespeare has been the judge of peace in this great litigation; he has reconciled the parties by a compromise, which imposes on them reciprocal concessions. In exacting that Shylock should be converted to Christianity, he did not intend to violate the principle, unknown in his day, of liberty of conscience, he has solely desired that Jew and Christian should alike practise that ideal religion which preaches forgiveness of injuries." ⟨. . .⟩

Shylock's "morality" appears to me founded on the great law of wild nature, *ratified by his own national code;* and all his arguments and all his actions are the offspring of the horrible injustice burnt into his own feelings and those of all his tribe: hence his scorpion-like hatred of the Christians; and not merely because one man lent out money without interest, bating the rate of usance in the money-market,—that is an apology; and a natural one for such a man to urge to himself. No; Shakespeare, with his consistent love of justice, has punished him for his cruelty; but, in the persecution exercised towards him by the professors of a sect who are enjoined to "do justice and love mercy," he has read a lesson which ought, if it do not, to last through all time.

And now, for a pleasant wind-up, "talk we of Master Launcelot; or, Master Launcelot Gobbo; or, good Gobbo; or, good Master Launcelot Gobbo;" who is a foster-brother, if not of the same family with Master Launce, in *The Two Gentlemen of Verona.* In the old editions, Gobbo is called a clown, and in character he is a sort of mongrel between the thoroughbred jester-clown and the cur errand-boy. The vein of humour that distinguishes this class of persons must have been popular in Shakespeare's time, since he has repeated the character on various occasions; and although it has passed away from us, yet it still possesses more than an obsolete interest by reason of its quaint idiosyncrasy. Launcelot is a sort of "arabesque" character in the order of humanity; exhibiting the prevalent feature of likeness, with a portentous flourish of half-meaning, and which passes for embellishment. He is a fellow who will scramble through the world with a "light heart and a thin pair of inexpressibles." His spare diet at the Jew's does not waste his humour, and conscience will scarcely sit heavily on him in the night-watches, since the gravest misdemeanour that can be laid to his charge is that he runs away from a master in whose service he swears he is "famished:"—his master's character of him being—

The patch is kind enough, but a *huge feeder.*

Nevertheless he says—"You may tell every finger I have with my ribs." And yet, with all this inducement, he sedately balances the question between his conscience to remain, and the temptation of Old Scratch to run away; and Old Scratch being right—for once—carries the debate;—

> Certainly, my conscience will serve me to run from this Jew, my master. The fiend is at my elbow, and tempts me, saying to me, "Gobbo, Launcelot Gobbo, good Launcelot, or good Gobbo, or good Launcelot Gobbo, use your legs, take the start, run away." My conscience says, "No; take heed, honest Launcelot; take heed, honest Gobbo;" or, as aforesaid, "honest Launcelot Gobbo; do not run; scorn running with thy heels." Well, the most courageous fiend bids me pack:—"Via!" says the fiend; "Away!" says the fiend; "for the heavens, rouse up a brave mind," says the fiend, "and run." Well, my conscience, hanging about the neck of my heart, says very wisely to me, "My honest friend, Launcelot, being an honest man's son,"—or rather an honest woman's son; for, indeed, my father did something smack, something grow to, he had a kind of taste;—well, my conscience says, "Launcelot, budge not." "Budge," says the fiend. "Budge not," says my conscience. Conscience, say I, you counsel well; fiend, say I, you counsel well:—to be ruled by my conscience, I should stay with the Jew, my master, who (Heaven bless the mark!) is a kind of devil; and to run away from the Jew, I should be ruled by the fiend who, saving your reverence, is the devil himself. Certainly the Jew is the very devil incarnation; and, in my conscience, my conscience is but a kind of hard conscience to offer to counsel me to stay with the Jew. The fiend gives the more friendly counsel:—I will run, fiend; my heels are at your commandment. I will run.

—CHARLES COWDEN CLARKE, *"Merchant of Venice," Shakespeare-Characters; Chiefly Those Subordinate* (London: Smith, Elder, 1863), pp. 389–93, 410–12

VICTOR HUGO

A type does not reproduce any man in particular; it cannot be exactly superposed upon any individual; it sums up and concentrates under one human form a whole family of characters and minds. A type is no abridgment: it is a condensation. It is not one, it is all. Alcibiades is but Alcibiades, Petronius is but Petronius, Bassompierre is but Bassompierre, Buckingham is but Buckingham, Fronsac is but Fronsac, Lauzun is but Lauzun; but take Lauzun, Fronsac, Buckingham, Bassompierre, Petronius, and Alcibiades, and bray them in the mortar of the dream, and there issues from it a phantom more real than them all,—Don Juan. Take usurers individually, and no one of them is that fierce merchant of Venice, crying: "Go, Tubal, fee me an officer, bespeak him a fortnight before; I will have the heart of him if he forfeit." Take all the usurers together, from the crowd of them is evolved a total,—Shylock. Sum up usury, you have Shylock. The metaphor of the people, who are never mistaken, confirms unawares the invention of the poet; and while Shakespeare makes Shylock, the popular tongue creates the bloodsucker. Shylock is the embodiment of Jewishness; he is also Judaism,—that is to say, his whole nation, the high as well as the low, faith as well as fraud; and it is because he sums up a whole race, such as oppression has made it, that Shylock is great. The Jews are, however, right in saying that none of them—not even the mediæval Jew—is Shylock. Men of pleasure may with reason say that no one of them is Don Juan. No leaf of the orange-tree when chewed gives the flavor of the orange; yet there is a deep affinity, an identity of roots, a sap rising from the same source, a sharing of the same subterranean shadow before life. The fruit contains the mystery of the tree, and the type contains the mystery of the man. Hence the strange vitality of the type.

—VICTOR HUGO, *William Shakespeare* [1864], tr. Melville B. Anderson
(Chicago: A. C. McClurg, 1887), pp. 224–25

H. N. HUDSON

If Portia is the beauty of this play, Shylock is its strength. He is a standing marvel of power and scope in the dramatic art; at the same time appearing so much a man of Nature's making, that we can hardly think of him as a creation of art. In the delineation Shakespeare had no less a task than to fill with individual life and peculiarity the broad, strong outlines of national character in its most revolting form. Accordingly Shylock is a true representative of his nation; wherein we have a pride which for ages never ceased to provoke hostility, but which no hostility could ever subdue; a thrift which still invited rapacity, but which no rapacity could ever exhaust; and a weakness which, while it exposed the subjects to wrong, only deepened their hate, because it kept them without the means or the hope of redress. Thus Shylock is a type of national sufferings, national sympathies, national antipathies. Himself an object of bitter insult and scorn to those about him; surrounded by enemies whom he is at once too proud to conciliate and too weak to oppose; he can have no life among them but money; no hold on them but interest; no feeling towards them but hate; no indemnity out of them but revenge. Such being the case, what wonder that the elements of national greatness became congealed and petrified into malignity? As avarice was the passion in which he mainly lived, the Christian virtues that thwarted this naturally seemed to him the greatest of wrongs.

With these strong national traits are interwoven personal traits equally strong. Thoroughly and intensely Jewish, he is not more a Jew than he is Shylock. In his hard, icy intellectuality, and his dry, mummy-like tenacity of purpose, with a dash now and then of biting sarcastic humour, we see the remains of a great and noble nature, out of which all the genial sap of humanity has been pressed by accumulated injuries. With as much elasticity of mind as stiffness of neck, every step he takes but the last is as firm as the earth he treads upon. Nothing can daunt, nothing disconcert him; remonstrance cannot move, ridicule cannot touch, obloquy cannot exasperate him: when he has not provoked them, he has been forced to bear them; and now that he does provoke them, he is hardened against them. In word, he may be broken; he cannot be bent.

Shylock is great in every scene where he appears, yet each later scene exhibits him in a new element or aspect of greatness. For as soon as the Poet has set forth one side or phase of his character, he forthwith dismisses that, and proceeds to another. For example, the Jew's cold and penetrating sagacity, as also his malignant and remorseless guile, are finely delivered in the scene with Antonio and Bassanio, where he first solicited for the loan. And the strength and vehemence of passion, which underlies these qualities, is still better displayed, if possible, in the scene with Antonio's two friends, Solanio and Salarino, where he first avows his purpose of exacting the forfeiture. One passage of this scene has always seemed to me a peculiarly idiomatic strain of eloquence, steeped in a mixture of gall and pathos; and I the rather notice it, because of the wholesome lesson which Christian may gather from it. Of course the Jew is referring to Antonio:

"He hath disgraced me, and hindered me half a million; laughed at my losses, mocked at my gains, scorned my nation, thwarted my bargains, cooled my friends, heated mine enemies; and what's his reason? I am a Jew. Hath not a Jew eyes? hath not a Jew hands, organs, dimensions, senses, affections, passions? fed with the same food, hurt with the same weapons, subject to the same diseases, healed by the same means, warmed and cooled by the same Winter and Summer, as a Christian is? If you prick us, do we not bleed? if you tickle us, do we not laugh? if you poison us, do we not die? and if you wrong us, shall we not revenge? if we are like you in the rest, we will resemble you in that. If a Jew wrong a Christian, what is his humility? revenge: if a Christian wrong a Jew, what should his sufferance be by Christian example? why, revenge. The villainy you teach me, I will execute; and it shall go hard but I will better the instruction."

I have spoken of the mixture of national and individual traits in Shylock. It should be observed further, that these several elements of character are so at-tempered and fused together, that we cannot distinguish their respective influence. Even his avarice has a smack of patriotism. Money is the only defence of his brethren as well as of himself, and he craves it for their sake as well as his own; feels indeed that wrongs are offered to them in him, and to him in them. Antonio has scorned his religion, balked him of usurious gains, insulted his person: therefore he hates him as a Christian, himself a Jew; hates him as a lender of money gratis, himself a griping usurer; hates him as Antonio, himself Shylock. Moreover, who but a Christian, one of Antonio's faith and fellowship, has stolen away his daughter's heart, and drawn her into revolt, loaded with his ducats and his precious, precious jewels? Thus his religion, his patriotism, his avarice, his affection, all concur to stimulate his enmity; and his personal hate thus reinforced overcomes for once his greed, and he grows generous in the prosecution of his aim. The only reason he will vouchsafe for taking the pound of flesh is, "if it will feed nothing else, it will feed my revenge"; a reason all the more satisfactory to him, forasmuch as those to whom he gives it can neither allow it nor refute it: and until they can rail the seal from off his bond, all their railings are but a foretaste of the revenge he seeks. In his eagerness to taste that morsel sweeter to him than all the luxuries of Italy, his recent afflictions, the loss of his daughter, his ducats, his jewels, and even the precious ring given him by his departed wife, all fade from his mind. In his inexorable and imperturbable hardness at the trial there is something that makes the blood to tingle. It is the sublimity of malice. We feel that the yearnings of revenge have silenced all other cares and all other thoughts. In his rapture of hate the man has grown superhuman, and his eyes seem all aglow with preternatural malignity. Fearful, however, as is his passion, he comes not off without moving our pity. In the very act whereby he thinks to avenge his own and his brethren's wrongs, the national curse overtakes him. In standing up for the letter of the law against all the pleadings of mercy, he has strengthened his enemies' hands, and sharpened their weapons, against himself; and the terrible Jew sinks at last into the poor, pitiable, heart-broken Shylock.

The inward strain and wrenching of his nature, caused by the revulsion which comes so suddenly upon him, is all told in one brief sentence, which may well be quoted as an apt instance how Shakespeare reaches the heart by a few plain words, when another writer would most likely pummel the ears with a high-strung oration. When it turns out that the Jew's only chance of life stands in the very mercy which he has but a moment before abjured; and when, as the condition of that mercy, he is required to become a Christian, and also to sign a deed conveying to his daughter and her husband all his remaining wealth; we have the following from him:

I pray you, give me leave to go from hence;
I am not well: send the deed after me,
And I will sign it.

Early in the play, when Shylock is bid forth to Bassanio's supper, and Launcelot urges him to go, because "my young master doth expect your reproach," Shylock replies, "So do I his." Of course he expects that reproach through the bankruptcy of Antonio. This would seem to infer that Shylock has some hand in getting up the reports of Antonio's "losses at sea"; which reports, at least some of them, turn out false in the end. Further than this, the Poet leaves us in the dark as to how those reports grew into being and gained belief. Did he mean to have it understood that the Jew exercised his cunning and malice in plotting and preparing them? It appears, at all events, that Shylock knew they were coming, before they came. Yet I suppose the natural impression from the play is, that he lent the ducats and took the bond, on a mere chance of coming at his wish. But he would hardly grasp so eagerly at a bare possibility of revenge, without using means to turn it into something more. This would mark him with much deeper lines of guilt. Why, then, did not Shake-speare bring the matter forward more prominently? Perhaps it was because the doing so would have made Shylock appear too steep a criminal for the degree of interest which his part was meant to carry in the play. In other words, the health of the drama as a work of *comic* art required his criminality to be kept in the background. He comes very near overshadowing the other characters too much, as it is. And Shylock's character is *essentially tragic;* there is none of the proper timber of comedy in him.

—H. N. HUDSON, *Shakespeare: His Life, Art and Characters*
(Boston: Ginn & Co., 1872; 4th rev. ed. 1882), Vol. I, pp. 291–95

G. H. RADFORD

It is proposed here to treat the character of Shylock as if Shakspeare was *not* an inspired writer. It is only courteous to make this announcement at the outset, so that those who do not care to read anything based on a hypothesis so gratifying to the profane may skip the remarks that follow. To such readers as remain to us we have to suggest that the people who say, or repeat the saying, that Shylock is a great creation do not for the most part know how great a creation it is. We are so familiar with the Jews as an element not to be ignored in our national life that we are apt to forget that for centuries the wisdom of our ancestors rigidly excluded them from this realm. For two centuries after the Conquest, Jews had indifferent entertainment in this country, and it was during this period that

> by way of mild reminders
> That he needed coin, the Knight
> Day by day extracted grinders
> From the howling Israelite.

But in the year 1290 Edward I expelled them all, and it was not till the Commonwealth that the decree of banishment was rescinded. The late Mr. J. R. Green goes a little too far when he says that from the time of Edward to that of Cromwell no Jew touched English ground. Now and then during these centuries a stray Jew, protected by royal favour or stimulated by hopes of gain, found his way hither; but in Shakspeare's time the business of London (incredible as this may appear) was transacted without any help from the Jews, and it is quite likely that Shakspeare never saw a Jew in his life. It is, of course, possible that he may have met Roderigo Lopez, "a Portingale," who was chief physician to Queen Elizabeth, and was hanged in 1594 on unsatisfactory evidence for attempting to poison her. Sir Edward Coke says, with the venal scurrility of the lawyers of that day, that he was "a perjured and murdering villain and Jewish doctor worse than Judas himself;" but Gabriel Harvey, a contemporary without a professional bias, says that, though descended of Jews, he was himself a Christian. Nearly twenty years earlier Lopez was physician to Leicester, who was patron to Burbage, who was Shakspeare's "fellow," so there are links for those who want to make a chain to prove that the doctor and the dramatist may have come together.

However this may be, in presenting a Jew as one of the chief characters of the *Merchant of Venice,* Shakspeare was introducing a specimen of a species practically unknown both to the author and his audience. The Philistines among the latter no doubt held that the play was designed to inculcate by example the wisdom of our legislators in excluding the Jews from the country and the folly of the Venetians in admitting them. Frenchmen, Welshmen, and other "mountain foreigners" Shakspeare knew, and in depicting Fluellen and Dr. Caius he had numerous models on which to work; but in drawing Shylock he had to exercise his imagination, probably unassisted by any living model. Shylock is therefore a creation in the same sense that Caliban is.

But if there was no living model there was ample material to feed and stimulate imagination. Shakspeare knew the sacred writings of the Hebrews, and the traditional stories of the Jews descended from the Middle Ages. More specially suggestive material was also ready to his hand in Marlowe's *Jew of Malta,* then newly written, and the *Pecorone* of Ser Giovanni Fiorentino. The former contains a powerful delineation of a Jew turning with the fury of revenge on his Christian oppressors, and the latter has the very story which is followed in most of its details in Shakspeare's play. It is not known that there was any Elizabethan English translation of the *Pecorone,* and we are driven to the conclusion that Shakspeare had (notwithstanding his small Latin and less Greek) a facility for reading Italian, or that he had the help of a friend who had this facility. This presents an alternative that has no doubt been discussed by the New Shakspere Society, and this Society can probably inform any inquiring Hebrew whether Shakspeare read Italian; and why, among Shakspeare relics, an edition of the *Pecorone* (Milano, 1558) with Shakspeare's autograph thriftily inscribed on the title page is not yet forthcoming, and when it may be expected; and who among the poet's friends read the *Pecorone,* and which of them translated at sight for his dramatisation.

At any rate, Shakspeare had all this material out of which to construct his Shylock, and he, of course, used his material in his own masterly way. The marauding mind which possesses the English dramatist who has got hold of a likely foreign original was fully developed in Shakspeare, and no useful detail in Giovanni's story was left unappropriated. The old Jew, however, is not a portrait, but a kind of grim conjecture. If Shakspeare had had the advantage of intercourse with the Jews now possessed by every playwright and journalist he would have turned out something more lifelike and (possibly) more amiable.

But it seems that Shakspeare's aim in the *Merchant of Venice* was not by any means solely to hold the mirror up to nature. This is one way of delighting an audience, but not the only one. To blend the agreeable with the surprising is an ancient prescription for producing the same result, and this is done in the character of Antonio, the Christian merchant who had scruples about usury and lent out his money gratis. Now, though Shakspeare did not know the Jews, he well knew the City, and that he had the City largely represented in his audience. *They* knew the Christian merchant, but the Christian merchant with these scruples was entirely new to them, and no doubt delighted them hugely. The statute-book shows us clearly what was the practice of merchants at this time. *An Acte against Usurie,* 13

Eliz. c. 8, declares that "all usurie being forbidden by the laws of God, is sinne and detestable," but it does not make it illegal. It only declares all contracts void upon which "there shall be reserved or taken above the rate of X. pounds for the hundred for one yere." Recognising the hardness of heart of the Christian merchant, the legislature, while licensing the sin, merely sought to limit the evils of it by fixing ten per cent. as the maximum rate of interest. A house half-filled with usurers and borrowers was highly amused by the wildly improbable character of Antonio.

But the *rôle* of Portia is still more improbable, and consequently more diverting. Allowing everything that can be demanded and granted for the indulgence of dramatic illusion, the appearance of this young lady in a Court of Justice, which (to use an Americanism) she proceeds to "run" herself, is an incident which the audience felt to be impossible, and enjoyed none the less on that account. The incident was at least as impossible in Shakspeare's time (or Giovanni's, for that matter) as it is now.

Imagine Mary Anderson, primed with lines written for her (alas, it is difficult to imagine who could write them!), having borrowed Mr. Lockwood's wig and gown, sweeping into the Lord Chief Justice's Court, gently taking the case of the injured defendant out of the hands of the benign Chief who looks on amazed but quiescent while the extortionate plaintiff is not only non-suited but committed for trial at the Old Bailey—imagine all this, and you have a modern counterpart of the glorious day's work of the breezy Portia. Here is not realism but something much rarer and more delightful. This is not a digression, as the learned (and courteous) reader may suppose. On the contrary it is intended to lead him by the pleasantest route to the conclusion that Shylock himself is not realistic, is not, as has been foolishly said, a libel on the Jews, but a personage whose character is determined by the requirements of the plot. Shakspeare wanted a villain vindictive enough to endanger the life and peace of the virtuous members of the cast, but not sufficiently heroic to interfere with a happy *dénoûement*, and he devised just such a villain in Shylock.

Let us consider the character in broad outlines. He is a great and prosperous merchant, and he has many and excellent reasons for the hatred of Antonio, which has become his ruling passion. The two are alien in race. This is something. The saying of the old Meynell that foreigners are fools is quoted with approval by the Christian philosopher Johnson. But it is a second-rate patriotism which dubs a foreigner only a fool. Philologists tell us that *hostis* originally meant a foreigner; but we only knew it at school as an enemy. It is all the same. This alone was reason enough for hatred, but there were other reasons. Antonio was a Christian, and the follower of one religion is ready to believe evil of the follower of another. "Some Jews are wicked, as *all* Christians are," says Marlowe's Jew of Malta. Moreover, the Jews were but tolerated in Venice for commercial reasons, and subject to persecution and indignity which only stopped short at the point where such treatment would have deprived the Republic of the commercial advantages obtained through the Jews. Difference of race, difference of religion, persecution—this is enough to make Shylock hate *any* Christian at sight. But there were special reasons for hating Antonio. It seems he had been accustomed to spit on Shylock. This is a practice which may violently stimulate even a slight antipathy. Antonio, too, was a rival in business, and while we do not forget the possibility of a Jewish reader, it is no breach of confidence to confess that fellow-Christians have quarrelled under such circumstances. The most galling incident of the rivalry appears to be that Antonio had cut down Shylock's profits as a usurer by lending money without interest, and so "brought down the rate of usance." We presume this is sound political economy: and there seems to be a suppressed proposition that the larger the number of borrowers at interest the higher the rate the lenders can exact. It does not matter, for an antipathy founded on an economic heresy is likely to be quite as strong as if based on a perfectly orthodox doctrine. The conclusion does not seem as obvious as that drawn by Launcelot Gobbo, who found that if Lorenzo converted his Jewish bride to Christianity, he would be damned for raising the price of pork.

This *is* a digression. To return to Shylock's antipathy. Besides the general grounds above hinted at and those arising from personal reasons, Shylock was at the moment irritated by events for which Antonio was not to blame. His daughter Jessica had not only eloped in a tailor-made suit with a detrimental Christian, but had carried with her quite a cargo of jewels and ready-money, and the young couple were living in Genoa on Shylock's money at the gorgeous rate of 80 ducats a night. With this respectable, old-established, and one may almost say reasonable hatred intensified by Jessica's conduct, Shylock suddenly finds himself in a position to take revenge. Antonio has made default in payment on the day, and Shylock is entitled to exact the forfeiture, "a pound of flesh to be by him cut off nearest the merchant's heart." He can kill his enemy, as he understands the laws of Venice, without incurring any risk of injury to himself. The temptation was great. There are several Christian merchants of blameless character (we mean they have never been in prison) at whose mercy we should be very sorry to be under similar circumstances. Shylock was ready to strike the blow. It was not murder, as he was advised, but justice. He could have Antonio's life without as much as standing an action for assault and battery. It was true that by so doing he would not recover the 3000 ducats secured by the bond, but he was ready to submit to this loss and even to forego the handsome profit held out by Antonio's friends who offered thrice the principal for his release. Shylock was avaricious, but his revenge rises superior to his avarice: he will not be balked of his revenge for money. This is the noblest point in his not very noble character. He refuses the cash and stands for the law. But it is always risky to rely on a strict view of the law when the court is dead against you on the merits. The judge, or even the jury, will lay hold of some quibble to justify a finding adverse to a suitor of whose conduct they disapprove. Such a quibble was raised by Portia on the language of the bond. It had not been drawn by an Equity draughtsman of the old school, in which case it would no doubt have stipulated that the creditor was entitled not only to the pound of flesh, but also to the epidermis, cartilages, arteries, veins, capillaries, blood or sanguinary fluid, and all other appurtenances thereunto belonging or therewith usually held and enjoyed. This careless draughtsmanship enabled the Court, in accordance with its inclinations, to hold that Shylock was entitled to no drop of blood. The plaintiff was baffled by this quibble. By shedding a drop of blood he would break the law and commit a capital offence. He was not prepared to run this risk. His desire for revenge is strong enough to make him unusually indifferent to money, but not strong enough to make him regardless of his life. This is not the revenge of tragedy, and Shylock is not a hero, though the vanity of certain modern actors has exalted the character to such a pitch that they cannot "climb down" in the fourth act without being ridiculous. But Shakspeare's Shylock climbs down without absurdity and with reasonable alacrity. He is the serviceable villain, serviceable, that is, for the action of the play, who has frightened the ladies by whetting his knife, and now gratifies them by dropping (reluctantly) all thoughts of bloodshed. Antonio must be saved. The pains and penalties with which Shylock is threatened by the Bench effectually secure this end. Then comes retribution. Both the life and fortune of Shylock, according to the laws of Venice, are held to be forfeited. But it would be distressing to kill him, and his life is spared on condition that he becomes a Christian and gives up the bulk of his fortune. Shylock accepts the terms imposed on him. He appears only to retain a life interest in half his property, and the whole of it is to go on his death to the gentleman who lately stole his daughter. Shylock leaves the stage promising to execute the necessary documents, and we hear of him no more. What became of him subsequently is merely matter of conjecture, but his conduct in court justifies us in inferring that he accepted the inevitable and made the best of it. Had he lived in our day we might conjecturally sketch his subsequent career thus: His baptism was performed with pomp in a historic temple by a distinguished ecclesiastic who knows that there is Eternal Hope for Jews if not for publishers. His marriage later on with a Dowager Countess who largely endowed the Society for Propagation of the Gospel among the Jews made his social position impregnable, and the money he subsequently made by publishing a financial newspaper far exceeded anything ever acquired by him in his old profession of usury.

—G. H. RADFORD, "Shylock," *Shylock and Others: Eight Studies*
(New York: Dodd, Mead, 1894), pp. 9–26

GEORG BRANDES

We learn from Ben Jonson's *Volpone* (iv. 1) that the traveller who arrived in Venice first rented apartments, and then applied to a Jew dealer for furniture. If the traveller happened to be a poet, he would thus have an opportunity, which he lacked in England, of studying the Jewish character and manner of expression. Shakespeare seems to have availed himself of it. The names of the Jews and Jewesses who appear in *The Merchant of Venice* he has taken from the Old Testament. We find in Genesis (x. 24) the name Salah (Hebrew Schelach; at that time appearing as the name of a Maronite from Lebanon: Scialac) out of which Shakespeare has made Shylock; and in Genesis (xi. 29) there occurs the name Iscah (she who looks out, who spies), spelt "Jeska" in the English translations of 1549 and 1551, out of which he made his Jessica, the girl whom Shylock accuses of a fondness for "clambering up to casements" and "thrusting her head into the public street" to see the masquers pass.

Shakespeare's audiences were familiar with several versions of the story of the Jew who relentlessly demanded the pound of flesh pledged to him by his Christian debtor, and was at last sent empty and baffled away, and even forced to become a Christian. The story has been found in Buddhist legends (along with the adventure of the Three Caskets, here interwoven with it), and many believe that it came to Europe from India. It may, however, have migrated in just the opposite direction. Certain it is, as one of Shakespeare's authorities points out, that the right to take payment in the flesh of the insolvent debtor was admitted in the Twelve Tables of ancient Rome. As a matter of fact, this antique trait was quite international, and Shakespeare has only transferred it from old and semi-barbarous times to the Venice of his own day.

The story illustrates the transition from the unconditional enforcement of strict law to the more modern principle of equity. Thus it afforded an opening for Portia's eloquent contrast between justice and mercy, which the public understood as an assertion of the superiority of Christian ethics to the Jewish insistence on the letter of the law.

One of the sources on which Shakespeare drew for the figure of Shylock, and especially for his speeches in the trial scene, is *The Orator* of Alexander Silvayn. The 95th Declamation of this work bears the title: "Of a Jew who would for his debt have a pound of the flesh of a Christian." Since an English translation of Silvayn's book by Anthony Munday appeared in 1596, and *The Merchant of Venice* is mentioned by Meres in 1598 as one of Shakespeare's works, there can scarcely be any doubt that the play was produced between these dates.

In *The Orator* both the Merchant and the Jew make speeches, and the invective against the Jew is interesting in so far as it gives a lively impression of the current accusations of the period against the Israelitish race:—

> But it is no marvaile if this race be so obstinat and cruell against us, for they doe it of set purpose to offend our God whom they have crucified: and wherefore? Because he was holie, as he is yet so reputed of this worthy Turkish nation: but what shall I say? Their own bible is full of their rebellion against God, against their Priests, Judges, and leaders. What did not the verie Patriarks themselves, from whom they have their beginning? They sold their brother ... &c.

Shakespeare's chief authority, however, for the whole play was obviously the story of Gianetto, which occurs in the collection entitled *Il Pecorone,* by Ser Giovanni Fiorentino, published in Milan in 1558.

A young merchant named Gianetto comes with a richly laden ship to a harbour near the castle of Belmonte, where dwells a lovely young widow. She has many suitors, and is, indeed, prepared to surrender her hand and her fortune, but only on one condition, which no one has hitherto succeeded in fulfilling, and which is stated with mediæval simplicity and directness. She challenges the aspirant, at nightfall, to share her bed and make her his own; but at the same time she gives him a sleeping-draught which plunges him in profound unconsciousness from the moment his head touches the pillow, so that at daybreak he has forfeited his ship and its cargo to the fair lady, and is sent on his way, despoiled and put to shame.

This misfortune happens to Gianetto; but he is so deeply in love that he returns to Venice and induces his kind foster-father, Ansaldo, to fit out another ship for him. But his second visit to Belmonte ends no less disastrously, and in order to enable him to make a third attempt his foster-father is forced to borrow 10,000 ducats from a Jew, upon the conditions which we know. By following the advice of a kindly-disposed waiting-woman, the young man this time escapes danger, becomes a happy bridegroom, and in his rapture forgets Ansaldo's obligation to the Jew. He is not reminded of it until the very day when it falls due, and then his wife insists that he shall instantly start for Venice, taking with him a sum of 100,000 ducats. She herself presently follows, dressed as an advocate, and appears in Venice as a young lawyer of great reputation, from Bologna. The Jew rejects every proposition for the deliverance of Ansaldo, even the 100,000 ducats. Then the trial-scene proceeds, just as in Shakespeare; Gianetto's young wife delivers judgment, like Portia; the Jew receives not a stiver, and dares not shed a drop of Ansaldo's blood. When Gianetto, in his gratitude, offers the young advocate the whole 100,000 ducats, she, as in the play, demands nothing but the ring which Gianetto has received from his wife; and the tale ends with the say gay unravelling of the sportive complication, which gives Shakespeare the matter for his fifth act. ⟨. . .⟩

The great value of *The Merchant of Venice* lies in the depth and seriousness which Shakespeare has imparted to the vague outlines of character presented by the old stories, and in the ravishing moonlight melodies which bring the drama to a close.

In Antonio, the royal merchant, who, amid all his fortune and splendour, is a victim to melancholy and spleen induced by forebodings of coming disaster, Shakespeare has certainly expressed something of his own nature. Antonio's melancholy is closely related to that which, in the years immediately following, we shall find in Jaques in *As You Like It,* in the Duke in *Twelfth Night,* and in Hamlet. It forms a sort of mournful undercurrent to the joy of life which at this period is still dominant in Shakespeare's soul. It leads, after a certain time, to the substitution of dreaming and brooding heroes for those men of action and resolution who, in the poet's brighter youth, had played the leading parts in his dramas. For the rest, despite the princely elevation of his nature, Antonio is by no means faultless. He has insulted and baited Shylock in the most brutal fashion on account of his faith and his blood. We realise the ferocity and violence of the mediæval prejudice against the Jews when we find a man of Antonio's magnanimity so entirely a slave to it. And when, with a little more show of justice, he parades his loathing and contempt for Shylock's money-dealings, he strangely (as it seems to us) overlooks the fact that the Jews have been carefully excluded from all other means of livelihood, and have been systematically allowed to scrape together gold in order that their hoards may always be at hand when circumstances render it convenient to plunder them. Antonio's attitude towards Shylock cannot possibly be Shakespeare's own. Shylock cannot understand Antonio, and characterises him (iii. 3) in the words—

This is the fool that lent out money gratis.

But Shakespeare himself did not belong to this class of fools. He has endowed Antonio with an ideality which he had neither the resolution nor the desire to emulate. Such a man's conduct towards Shylock explains the outcast's hatred and thirst for revenge. ⟨. . .⟩

The central figure of the play, however, in the eyes of modern readers and spectators, is of course Shylock, though there can be no doubt that he appeared to Shakespeare's contemporaries a comic personage, and, since he makes his final exit before the last act, by no means the protagonist. In the humaner view of a later age, Shylock appears as a half-pathetic creation, a scapegoat, a victim; to the Elizabethan public, with his rapacity and his miserliness, his usury and his eagerness to dig for another the pit into which he himself falls, he seemed, not terrible, but ludicrous. They did not even take him seriously enough to feel any real uneasiness as to Antonio's fate, since they all knew beforehand the issue of the adventure. They laughed when he went to Bassanio's feast "in hate, to feed upon the prodigal Christian;" they laughed when, in the scene with Tubal, he suffered himself to be bandied about between exultation over Antonio's misfortunes and rage over the prodigality of his runaway daughter; and they found him odious when he exclaimed, "I would my daughter were dead at my foot and the jewels in her ear!" He was, simply as a Jew, a despised creature; he belonged to the race which had crucified God himself; and he was doubly despised as an extortionate usurer. For the rest, the English public—like the Norwegian public so lately as the first half of this century—had no acquaintance with Jews except in books and on the stage. From 1290 until the middle of the seventeenth century the Jews were entirely excluded from England. Every prejudice against them was free to flourish unchecked.

Did Shakespeare in a certain measure share these religious prejudices, as he seems to have shared the patriotic prejudices against the Maid of Orleans, if, indeed, he is responsible for the part she plays in *Henry VI.?* We may be sure that he was very slightly affected by them, if at all. Had he made a more undisguised effort to place himself at Shylock's standpoint, the censorship, on the one hand, would have intervened, while, on the other hand, the public would have been bewildered and alienated. It is quite in the spirit of the age that Shylock should suffer the punishment which befalls him. To pay him out for his stiff-necked vengefulness, he is mulcted not of the sum he lent Antonio, but half his fortune, and is finally, like

Marlowe's *Jew of Malta,* compelled to change his religion. The latter detail gives something of a shock to the modern reader. But the respect for personal conviction, when it conflicted with orthodoxy, did not exist in Shakespeare's time. It was not very long since the Jews had been forced to choose between kissing the crucifix and mounting the faggots; and in Strasburg, in 1349, nine hundred of them had in one day chosen the latter alternative. It is strange to reflect, too, that just at the time when, on the English stage, one Mediterranean Jew was poisoning his daughter, and another whetting his knife to cut his debtor's flesh, thousands of heroic and enthusiastic Hebrews in Spain and Portugal, who, after the expulsion of the 300,000 at the beginning of the century, had secretly remained faithful to Judaism, were suffering themselves to be tortured, flayed, and burnt alive by the Inquisition, rather than forswear the religion of their race.

It is the high-minded Antonio himself who proposes that Shylock shall be forced to become a Christian. This is done for his good; for baptism opens to him the possibility of salvation after death; and his Christian antagonists, who, by dint of the most childish sophisms, have despoiled him of his goods and forced him to forswear his God, can still pose as representing the Christian principle of mercy, in opposition to one who has taken his stand upon the Jewish basis of formal law.

That Shakespeare himself, however, in nowise shared the fanatical belief that a Jew was of necessity damned, or could be saved by compulsory conversion, is rendered clear enough for the modern reader in the scene between Launcelot and Jessica (iii. 5), where Launcelot jestingly avers that Jessica is damned. There is only hope for her, and that is, that her father may not be her father:—

> JESSICA: That were a kind of bastard hope, indeed: so the sins of my mother should be visited upon me.
> LAUNCELOT: Truly then I fear you are damned both by father and mother: thus when I shun Scylla, your father, I fall into Charybdis, your mother. Well, you are gone both ways.
> JES.: I shall be saved by my husband; he hath made me a Christian.
> LAUN.: Truly, the more to blame he: we were Christians enow before; e'en as many as could well live one by another. This making of Christians will raise the price of hogs: if we grow all to be pork-eaters, we shall not shortly have a rasher on the coals for money.

And Jessica repeats Launcelot's saying to Lorenzo:—

> He tells me flatly, there is no mercy for me in heaven, because I am a Jew's daughter: and he says, you are no good member of the commonwealth, for, in converting Jews to Christians, you rise the price of pork.

No believer would ever speak in this jesting tone of matters that must seem to him so momentous.

It is none the less astounding how much right in wrong, how much humanity in inhumanity, Shakespeare has succeeded in imparting to Shylock. The spectator sees clearly that, with the treatment he has suffered, he could not but become what he is. Shakespeare has rejected the notion of the atheistically-minded Marlowe, that the Jew hates Christianity and despises Christians as fiercer money-grubbers than himself. With his calm humanity, Shakespeare makes Shylock's hardness and cruelty result at once from his passionate nature and his abnormal position; so that, in spite of everything, he has come to appear in the eyes of later times as a sort of tragic symbol of the degradation and vengefulness of an oppressed race.

There is not in all Shakespeare a greater example of trenchant and incontro-vertible eloquence than Shylock's famous speech (iii. I):—

> I am a Jew. Hath not a Jew eyes? hath not a Jew hands, organs, dimensions, senses, affections, passions? fed with the same food, hurt with the same weapons, subject to the same diseases, healed by the same means, warmed and cooled by the same winter and summer, as a Christian is? If you prick us, do not we bleed? if you tickle us, do we not laugh? if you poison us, do we not die? and if you wrong us, shall we not revenge? If we are like you in the rest, we will resemble you in that. If a Jew wrong a Christian, what is his humility? revenge. If a Christian wrong a Jew, what should his sufferance be by Christian example? why, revenge. The villany you teach me, I will execute; and it shall go hard but I will better the instruction.

But what is most surprising, doubtless, is the instinct of genius with which Shakespeare has seized upon and reproduced racial characteristics, and emphasised what is peculiarly Jewish in Shylock's culture. While Marlowe, according to his custom, made his Barabas revel in mythological similes, Shakespeare indicates that Shylock's culture is founded entirely upon the Old Testament, and makes com-merce his only point of contact with the civilisation of later times. All his parallels are drawn from the Patriarchs and the Prophets. With what unction he speaks when he justifies himself by the example of Jacob! His own race is always "our sacred nation," and he feels that "the curse has never fallen upon it" until his daughter fled with his treasures. Jewish, too, is Shylock's respect for, and obstinate insistence on, the letter of the law, his reliance upon statutory rights, which are, indeed, the only rights society allows him, and the partly instinctive, partly defiant restriction of his moral ideas to the principle of retribution. He is no wild animal; he is no heathen who simply gives the rein to his natural instincts; his hatred is not ungoverned; he restrains it with its legal rights, like a tiger in its cage. He is entirely lacking, indeed, in the freedom and serenity, the easy-going, light-hearted carelessness which char-acterises a ruling caste in its virtues and its vices, in its charities as in its prodigalities; but he has not a single twinge of conscience about anything that he does; his actions are in perfect harmony with his ideals.

Sundered from the regions, the social forms, the language, in which his spirit is at home, he has yet retained his Oriental character. Passion is the kernel of his nature. It is his passion that has enriched him; he is passionate in action, in calcu-lation, in sensation, in hatred, in revenge, in everything. His vengefulness is many times greater than his rapacity. Avaricious though he be, money is nothing to him in comparison with revenge. It is not until he is exasperated by his daughter's robbery and flight that he takes such hard measures against Antonio, and refuses to accept three times the amount of the loan. His conception of honour may be unchivalrous enough, but, such as it is, his honour is not to be bought for money. His hatred of Antonio is far more intense than his love for his jewels; and it is this passionate hatred, not avarice, that makes him the monster he becomes.

From this Hebrew passionateness, which can be traced even in details of diction, arises, among other things, his loathing of sloth and idleness. To realise how essentially Jewish is this trait we need only refer to the so-called Proverbs of Solomon. Shylock dismisses Launcelot with the words, "Drones hive not with me." Oriental, rather than specially Jewish, are the images in which he gives his passion utterance, approaching, as they so often do, the parable form. (See, for example, his appeal Jacob's cunning, or the speech in vindication of his claim, which begins, "You have among you many a purchased slave.") Specially Jewish, on the other hand, is the way in which this ardent passion throughout employs its images and parables in the service of a curiously sober rationalism, so that a sharp and biting logic, which retorts every accusation with interest, is always the controlling force. This sober logic, moreover, never lacks dramatic impetus. Shylock's course of thought perpetually takes the form of question and answer, a subordinate but characteristic trait which appears in the style of the Old Testament, and reappears to this day in representations of primitive Jews. One can feel through his words that there is a chanting quality in his voice; his movements are rapid, his gestures large. Externally and internally, to the inmost fibre of his being, he is a type of his race in its degradation.

Shylock disappears with the end of the fourth act in order that no discord may mar the harmony of the concluding scenes. By means of his fifth act, Shakespeare dissipates any preponderance of pain and gloom in the general impression of the play.

—GEORG BRANDES, *William Shakespeare: A Critical Study,* tr. William Archer
(London: William Heinemann, 1898), Vol. I, pp. 186–90, 194–98

LEVIN L. SCHÜCKING

In no department of Shakespeare's art do we find such irregularity as in his dealing with the motives for action. It has therefore become the happy hunting-ground of the most daring and extravagant critics, the starting-point of the most fundamentally diverse interpretations of his characters. But as has been shown in the preceding chapters, it will not be impossible to base our conclusions on the firm ground of facts if we try to form a picture of his method of working that is not contradictory to the results we have so far obtained.

The first peculiarity that strikes us is one that cannot surprise us, knowing, as

we do, how he strove after a plain and popular form of expression. Information
that in a modern drama must be deduced from the action itself, or gathered
indirectly from the dialogue of the principal or secondary personages, the monologues of the heroes serving at most to supplement it, is here imparted, in all
essentials, by just these monologues, which especially in the great tragedies give us,
ready made, all the knowledge necessary for our judgment of the speaker's character. Brutus, for instance, unreservedly opens his soul to the penetrating gaze of
the spectator, and exposes the motives of his actions in his monologue, and Macbeth, with that self-knowledge of which, against all probability, even the villains of
Shakespeare are capable, carefully enlightens the audience:

> I have no spur
> To prick the sides of my intent, but only
> Vaulting ambition, which o'erleaps itself
> And falls on the other.   (I, vii)

What clearly distinguished reasons, too, does Shylock give when he discloses
the threefold root of his hatred against Antonio in the following speech:

> I hate him for he is a Christian,
> But more for that in low simplicity
> He lends out money gratis and brings down
> The rate of usance here with us in Venice.
> If I can catch him once upon the hip,
> I will feed fat the ancient grudge I bear him.
> He hates our sacred nation, and he rails,
> Even there where merchants most do congregate,
> On me, my bargains and my well-won thrift,
> Which he calls interest.   (I, iii)

This absolutely plain and unmistakable exposition of the Jew's point of view
has been seized upon and subjectively interpreted, according to their own personal
point of view, by critics who are accustomed to read more *between* the lines than
in them. They have endeavoured to upset the ethical balance which Shakespeare
intended to establish between the parties, being induced to take this line by the fact
that the standards of morality have changed in many respects since his time. We
now regard Shylock's enemies, the gay cavaliers and dowry-hunters, the royal
merchant suffering from an aristocratic weariness of the world, largely as drones
from whom we have but little sympathy. On the other hand, we sympathize with
the Jew, who voices the bitter feeling of his race, due to incessant insults, in such
powerful and touching language. The contention of these critics would be acceptable only if the Jew's behaviour were not in agreement with the reasons expressed
in his words. Now the fact is that there is a perfect agreement. As most characteristic, we need point out only the cunning manner in which he utilizes the chance
of laying a snare for the merchant by getting him to sign the bond. When Antonio's

friend, grown suspicious, warns him against signing the gruesome document Shylock pretends, with masterly hypocrisy, that the whole affair is nothing more than a joke; he even goes the length of simulating offence because the arrangement is taken seriously at all:

> O father Abram, what these Christians are,
> Whose own hard dealings teaches them suspect
> The thoughts of others! Pray you, tell me this;
> If he should break his day, what should I gain
> By the exaction of the forfeiture? (I, iii)

We see clearly that a conception which regards Shylock as the avenger who by chance obtains an opportunity of exacting retribution for his downtrodden race, and who cannot be expected to show mercy to his enemies who, on their part, treat him without pity, strays far from the poet's intention. This passage alone suffices to show how, on the contrary, he tries to entrap his unsuspecting enemy by cunning and perfidy. Nor can we overlook the fact that the fury of the Jew, due to sordid avarice against the merchant who lends money without interest, and the hatred against the Christian, which springs from racial pride, are meant to be important motives, in conjunction with the vindictiveness of one who has been oppressed and ill-treated.

Scientific Shakespearean criticism, however, has never taken the so-called Shylock question very seriously; the text of the drama was too clear an argument against it. Still, the case is useful as affording instruction of the degree of arbitrariness and neglect of the text to which Shakespearean exegesis can sink in a comparatively simple instance. Similar mistakes, of almost the same gravity, are committed on other occasions by many of the most exact interpreters who in the case of Shylock rightly admit the poet's own words to be the only canon of judgment.

—LEVIN L. SCHÜCKING, Character Problems in Shakespeare's Plays
(London: George G. Harrap & Co., 1922), pp. 203–5

J. L. CARDOZO

We have all pondered the question at issue between Anthonio and Shylocke, or rather between the Church and the world. Strange to say, though Shylocke is made to quote the Old Testament, the question is not debated on Biblical principles; both Anthonio and Bassanio deprecate the adduction of Holy Writ: 'The Devil can cite Scripture for his purpose' says Anthonio. 'In religion any damned error can be blessed and approved with a text' says Bassanio. However, texts of obvious relevancy are not wanting in the Testaments:

"If thou lend money to any of my people that is poor by thee, thou shalt not be to him as an usurer, neither shalt thou lay upon him usury (Ex. 22). If thy brother be waxen poor and fallen in decay with thee thou shalt relieve him, yea though he be a stranger or a sojourner; that he may live with thee. Thou shalt not give him thy money upon usury, nor lend him thy victuals for increase (Lev. 25)." Shylocke's defence would have been that the prohibition was against taking usury from *poor* people and particularly poor Israelites: "Thou shalt not lend upon usury to thy brother, usury of money, usury of victuals, usury of anything that is lent upon usury; Unto a stranger thou mayest lend upon usury, but unto thy brother thou shalt not lend upon usury (Deut. 23)." Shylocke I suppose observed that distinction; we may take for granted that those who at times made moan to Anthonio to be delivered from Shylocke's forfeitures, were not Jews. Thomas of Aquino condemned the discrimination against 'a stranger', ruling that 'God did not approve, but would not punish that *sin*'. Likewise Anthonio could have appealed to Nu. 15: "One ordinance shall be both for you of the congregation and also for the stranger that sojourneth with you." Shylocke would counter with the criticism that *he* was a stranger in *their* gate, not they in his; that he would welcome the general application of legal equality, but that a *conjonction fraternelle* could not be partial. The time to reproach him for taking usury would not come till Christians, especially the court of Rome, had given up the practise. Anthonio: "Lord, who shall abide in thy Tabernacle? . . . he that putteth not out his money to usury (Ps. 14–15); he that hath not given forth upon usury, nor hath taken any increase. (Ez. 18); he that by usury and unjust gain increaseth his substance, he shall gather it for him that will pity the poor. (Prov. 28. Will this justify the despoiling of usurers by the charitable?)." Anthonio could have ended his exhortation with: "Lend, hoping for nothing again." Shylocke: "What, not barely my principal?" Anthonio: "If ye lend to them of whom ye hope to receive, what thank have ye? for sinners also lend to sinners to receive as much again." (Luke VI) Shylocke: "As much again as they have lent out? Do you mean centum per cento? Where can a man get that? We are only allowed a legal rate of twelve per cent a year." No doubt Anthonio need not have stinted there for lack of matter.

—J. L. CARDOZO, *The Contemporary Jew in Elizabethan Drama*
(Amsterdam: J. H. Paris, 1925), pp. 310–11

HARLEY GRANVILLE-BARKER

There remains Shylock. He steps into the play, actual and individual from his first word on, and well might in his strength (we come to feel) have broken the pinchbeck of his origin to bits, had a later Shakespeare had the handling of him. As it is, his actuality is not weakened by the fantasy of the bond, as is Portia's by her caskets. For one thing, our credulity is not strained till the time comes for its maturing, and by then—if ever—the play and its acting will have captured us. For another, the law and its ways are normally so uncanny to a layman that the strict court of an exotic Venice might give even stranger judgments than this and only confirm us in our belief that once litigation begins almost anything may happen. Despite the borrowed story, this Shylock is essentially Shakespeare's own. But if he is not a puppet, neither is he a stalking horse; he is no more a mere means to exemplifying the Semitic problem than is Othello for the raising of the colour question. 'I am a Jew.' 'Haply, for I am black. . . .' Here we have—and in Shylock's case far more acutely and completely—the *circumstances* of the dramatic conflict; but at the heart of it are men; and we may surmise, indeed, that from a maturer Shakespeare we should have had, as with Othello, much more of the man, and so rather less of the alien and his griefs. However that may be, he steps now into the play, individual and imaginatively full-grown, and the scene of his talk with Bassanio and Antonio is masterly exposition.

The dry taciturnity of his

Three thousand ducats, well?

(the lure of that thrice-echoed 'Well'!) and the cold dissecting of the business in hand are made colder, drier yet by contrast with the happy sound of Portia's laughter dying in our ears as he begins to speak. And for what a helpless innocent Bassanio shows beside him; over-anxious, touchy, over-civil! Shylock takes his time; and suddenly we can see him peering, myopic, beneath his brows. Who can the new comer be? And the quick brain answers beneath the question's cover: They must need the money badly if Antonio himself comes seeking me. Off goes Bassanio to greet his friend; and Shylock in a long aside can discharge his obligations to the plot. (This is one of the ever-recurring small strokes of stagecraft that are hardly appreciable apart from an Elizabethan stage. Shylock and Bassanio are to the front of the platform. Antonio, near the door, is by convention any convenient distance off; by impression too, with no realistic scenery to destroy the impression. Shylock is left isolated, so isolated that the long aside has all the importance and the force of a soliloquy.) These eleven lines are worth comment. In them is all the motive power for drama that the story, as Shakespeare found it, provides; and he throws this, with careless opulence, into a single aside. Then he returns to the upbuilding of *his* Shylock.

Note the next turn the scene takes. From the snuffling depreciation of his present store, from his own wonted fawning of these Christian clients, Shylock unexpectedly rises to the dignities of

When Jacob grazed his uncle Laban's sheep. . . .

And with this the larger issue opens out between Gentile and Jew, united and divided by the scripture they revere, and held from their business by this tale from it—of flocks and herds and the ancient East. Here is another Shylock; and Antonio may well stare, and answer back with some respect—though he recovers contempt for the alien creature quickly enough. But with what added force the accusation comes:

> Signior Antonio, many a time and oft
> In the Rialto you have rated me. . . .
> You called me misbeliever, cut-throat dog
> And spet upon my Jewish gaberdine. . . .

The two Venetians see the Ghetto denizen again, and only hear the bondman's whine. But to us there is now all Jewry crouched and threatening there, an ageless force behind it. They may make light of the money bond, but we shall not.

Shakespeare keeps character within the bounds of story with great tact; but such a character as this that has surged in his imagination asks more than such a story to feed on. Hence, partly at least, the new theme of Jessica and her flight, which will give Shylock another and more instant grudge to satisfy. It is developed with strict economy. Twenty-one lines are allowed to Jessica and Launcelot, another twenty or so to her lover and their plans; then, in a scene not sixty long, Shylock and his household are enshrined. As an example of dramatic thrift alone this is worth study. The parting with Launcelot: he has a niggard liking for the fellow, is even hurt a little by his leaving, touched in pride too, and shows it childishly.

> Thou shalt not gormandize
> As thou has done with me. . . .

But he can at least pretend that he parts with him willingly and makes some profit by it. The parting with Jessica, which we of the audience know to be a parting indeed; that constant calling her by name, which tells us of the lonely man! He has looked to her for everything, has tasked her hard, no doubt; he is her gaoler, yet he trusts her, and loves her in his extortionate way. Uneasy stranger that he is within these Venetian gates; the puritan, who, in a wastrel world, will abide by law and prophets! So full a picture of the man does the short scene give that it seems hardly possible we see no more of him than this between the making of the bond and the climacteric outbreak of passion upon Jessica's loss and the news of Antonio's ruin.

References to him abound; Shylock can never be long out of our minds. But how deliberate is the thrift of opportunity we may judge by our being shown the first effect of the loss on him only through the ever-useful eyes of Salarino and Solanio. This is politic, however, from other points of view. Look where the scene in question falls, between Morocco's choice of his casket and Aragon's. Here or hereabouts some such scene must come, for the progress of the Antonio and Shylock story cannot be neglected. But conceive the effect of such a tragic outcry as Shylock's own,

> So strange, outrageous and so variable. . . .

—of such strong dramatic meat sandwiched between pleasant conventional rhetoric. How much of the credibility of the casket story would survive the association, with how much patience should we return to it? But Salarino and Solanio tone down tragedy to a good piece of gossip, as it becomes young men of the world to do. We avoid an emotional danger zone; and, for the moment at least, that other danger of an inconvenient sympathy with 'the dog Jew.' When Shylock's outbreak of anguish does come, the play is nearer to its climax, Bassanio's choice is about to free Portia's story from its unreality, and his savage certainty of revenge upon Antonio will now depress the sympathetic balance against him.

But, considering the story's bounds, what a full-statured figure we already have! Compare the conventional aside, the statement of the theme, in the earlier scene, the bald

I hate him for he is a Christian. . . .

with the deluge of molten passion which descends upon the devoted Solanio and Salarino, obliterating their tart humour; compare the theme, that is to say, with its development, mere story with character, and measure in the comparison Shakespeare's growing dramatic power.

In tone and temper and method as well this scene breaks away from all that has gone before. The very start in prose, the brisk

Now, what news on the Rialto?

even, perhaps, Solanio's apology for former

. . . slips of prolixity or crossing the plain highway of talk:

seem to tell us that Shakespeare is now asserting the rights of his own imagination, means, at any rate, to let this chief creature of it, his Shylock, off the leash. For verily he does.

The scene's method repays study. No whirling storm of fury is asked for; this is not the play's climax, but preparation for it still. Shylock is wrapped in resentful sorrow, telling over his wrong for the thousandth time. Note the repetition of thought and praise. And how much more sinister this sight of him with the wound festering than if we had seen the blow's instant fall! His mind turns to Antonio, and the thrice told

. . . let him look to his bond.

is a rope of salvation for him; it knots up the speech in a dreadful strength. Then, on a sudden, upon the good young Salarino's reasonable supposition that what a money-lender wants is his money back; who on earth would take flesh instead?—

What's that good for?

—there flashes out the savagery stripped naked of

To bait fish withal: if it will feed nothing else, it will feed my revenge.

Now we have it; and one salutes such purity of hatred. There follows the famous speech—no need to quote it—mounting in passionate logic, from its

He hath disgraced me . . . and what's his reason? I am a Jew.

to the height of

If a Jew wrong a Christian, what is his humility? Revenge. If a Christian wrong a Jew, what should his sufferance be by Christian example? Why, revenge. The villainy you teach me I will execute, and it shall go hard but I will better the instruction.

This is a Shylock born of the old story, but transformed, and here a theme of high tragedy, of the one seemingly never-ending tragedy of the world. It is the theme for a greater play than Shakespeare was yet to write. But if this one cannot be sustained on such a height, he has at least for the moment raised it there.

Solanio and Salarino are quite oblivious to the great moral issue opened out to them; though they depart a little sobered—this Jew seems a dangerous fellow. There follows the remarkable passage with Tubal; of gruesome comedy, the apocalyptic Shylock shrunk already to the man telling his ill-luck against his enemy's, weighing each in scales (love for his daughter, a memory of his dead wife thrown in!) as he is used to weigh the coin which is all these Christians have left him for his pride. It is technically a notable passage, in that it is without conflict or contrast, things generally necessary to dramatic dialogue; but the breaking of a rule will be an improvement, now and then, upon obedience to it. So Shakespeare, for a finish, lowers the scene from its climax, from that confronting of Christian and Jew, of hate with hate, to this raucous assonance of these two of a kind and mind, standing cheek to cheek in common cause, the excellent Tubal fueling up revenge.

Such a finish, ousting all nobility, both shows us another facet of Shylock himself (solid man enough now to be turned any way his maker will) and is, as we saw, a shadow against which the high romance of Bassanio's wooing will in a moment shine the more brightly. Sharp upon the heels of this, he comes again; but once more apocalyptic, law incarnate now.

SHYLOCK: Gaoler, look to him; tell me not of mercy;
This is the fool that lent out money gratis:
Gaoler, look to him.
ANTONIO: Hear me yet, good Shylock.
SHYLOCK: I'll have my bond; speak not against my bond:
I have sworn an oath that I will have my bond.

Verse and its dignity are needed for this scene; and note the recurring knell of the phrases:

I'll have my bond; I will not hear thee speak:
I'll have my bond, and therefore speak no more.
I'll not be made a soft and dull-eyed fool,
To shake the head, relent, and sigh, and yield
To Christian intercessors. Follow not;
I'll have no speaking: I will have my bond.

Here is a Shylock primed for the play's great scene; and Shakespeare's Shylock wrought ready for a catastrophe, which is a deeper one by far than that the story yields. For not in the missing of his vengeance on Antonio will be this Shylock's tragedy, but in the betrayal of the faith on which he builds.

I've sworn an oath that I will have my bond...

How many times has the synagogue not heard it sworn?

An oath, an oath. I have an oath in Heaven...

He has made his covenant with an unshakable God:

What judgment shall I dread, doing no wrong?

—and he is to find himself betrayed.

It is the apocalyptic Shylock that comes slowly into Court, solitary and silent, to face and to outface the Duke and all the moral power of Venice. When he does speak he answers the Duke as an equal, setting a sterner sanction against easy magnanimity—at other people's expense! One could complain that this first appeal for mercy discounts Portia's. To some extent it does; but the more famous speech escapes comparison by coming when the spell of the young doctor is freshly cast on us, and by its finer content and larger scope. Structurally, the Duke's speech is the more important, for it sets the lists, defines the issue and provokes that

> I have possessed your grace of what I purpose;
> And by our holy Sabbath have I sworn
> To have the due and forfeit of my bond...

So confident is he that he is tempted to shift ground a little and let yet another Shylock peep—the least likable of all. He goes on

> You'll ask me, why I rather choose to have
> A weight of carrion flesh, than to receive
> Three thousand ducats: I'll not answer that,
> But say it is my humour...

Legality gives license to the hard heart. Mark the progression. While the sufferer cried

> The villainy you teach me I will execute; and it shall go hard but I will better the instruction.

with the law on his side it is

> What judgment shall I dread, doing no wrong?...

from which he passes, by an easy turn, to the mere moral anarchy of

> The pound of flesh, which I demand of him,
> Is dearly bought; 'tis mine, and I will have it...

and in satanic heroism stands defiant:

If you deny me, fie upon your law!
There is no force in the decrees of Venice.
I stand for judgment. Answer: shall I have it?

There is a dreadful silence. For who, dwelling unquestioningly under covenant of law, shall gainsay him?

It says much for the mental hypnosis which the make-believe of the theatre can induce that this scene of the trial holds us so spellbound. Its poetry adds to the enchantment—let anyone try re-writing it in prose—and the exotic atmosphere helps. But how much more is due to the embroidering of character upon story so richly that the quality of the fabric comes to matter little! Shakespeare, at any rate, has us now upon the elemental heights of drama. He cannot keep us there. Portia must perform her conjuring trick; perhaps this is why he gives Shylock full scope before she arrives. But he brings us down with great skill manœuvring character to the needs of the story, and turning story to character's account.

The coming of the young judge's clerk does not impress Shylock. How should it? Little Nerissa! He has won, what doubt of it? He can indulge then—why not?—the lodged hate and loathing he bears Antonio. The Duke is busy with Bellario's letter and the eyes of the Court are off him. From avenger he degenerates to butcher; to be caught, lickerish-lipped, by Bassanio, and Gratiano's rough tongue serves him as but another whetstone for savagery. He turns surly at first sight of the wise young judge—what need of such a fine fellow and more fine talk?—and surlier still when it is talk of mercy. He stands there, he tells them yet again, asking no favours, giving none.

My deeds upon my head! I crave the law,
The penalty and forfeit of my bond.

Why does Shakespeare now delay the catastrophe by a hundred lines, and let Portia play cat and mouse with her victim? From the story's standpoint, of course, to keep up the excitement a while longer. We guess there is a way out. We wonder what it can be; and yet, with that knife shining, Antonio's doom seems to come nearer and nearer. This is dramatic child's play, and excellent of its sort. But into it much finer stuff is woven. We are to have more than a trick brought off; there must be a better victory; this faith in which Shylock abides must be broken. So first she leads him on. Infatuate, finding her all on his side, he finally and informally refuses the money—walks into the trap. Next she plays upon his fanatical trust in his bond, sets him searching in mean mockery for a charitable comma in it—had one escaped his cold eye—even as the Pharisees searched their code to convict Christ. Fold by fold, the prophetic dignity falls from him. While Antonio takes his selfless farewell of his friend, Shylock must stand clutching his bond and his knife, only contemptible in his triumph. She leads him on to a last slaveringly exultant cry: then the blow falls.

Note that the tables are very precisely turned on him.

> . . . if thou tak'st more,
> Or less, than a just pound, be it so much
> As makes it light or heavy in the substance,
> Or the division of the twentieth part
> Of one poor scruple, nay, if the scale do turn
> But in the estimation of a hair. . . .

is exact retaliation for Shylock's insistence upon the letter of his bond. Gratiano is there to mock him with his own words, and to sound, besides, a harsher note of retribution than Portia can; for the pendulum of sympathy now swings back a little—more than a little, we are apt to feel. But the true catastrophe is clear. Shylock stood for law and the letter of the law; and it seemed, in its kind, a noble thing to stand for, ennobling him. It betrays him, and in the man himself there is no virtue left.

> Is *that* the law?

he gasps helplessly. It is his only thought. The pride and power in which legality had wrapped him, by which he had outfaced them all, and held Venice herself to ransom, are gone. He stands stripped, once more the sordid Jew that they may spit upon, greedy for money, hurriedly keen to profit by his shame.

> I take this offer then; pay the bond thrice,
> And let the Christian go.

Here is Shakespeare's Shylock's fall, and not in the trick the law plays him.

He is given just a chance—would the story let him take it!—to regain tragic dignity. What is passing in his mind that prompts Portia's

> Why doth the Jew pause? Take thy forfeiture.

No, nothing, it would seem, but the thought that he will be well out of the mess with his three thousand ducats safe.

Shakespeare has still to bring his theme full circle. He does it with doubled regard to character and story.

> Why, then the devil give him good of it!
> I'll stay no longer question.

If he were not made to, by every canon of theatrical justice Shylock would be let off too lightly; wherefore we find that the law has another hold on him. It is but a logical extending of retribution, which Gratiano is quick to reduce to its brutal absurdity. Here is Shylock with no more right to a cord with which to hang himself than had Antonio to a bandage for his wound. These quibbling ironies are for the layman among the few delights of law. Something of the villainy the Jew taught them the Christians will now execute; and Shylock, as helpless as Antonio was, takes on a victim's dignity in turn. He stays silent while his fate, and the varieties of official and unofficial mercy to be shown him, are canvassed. He is allowed no comment upon his impoverishing for the benefit of 'his son Lorenzo' or upon his forced apostasy. But could eloquence serve better than such a silence?

> PORTIA: Art thou contented, Jew? What dost thou say?
> SHYLOCK: I am content.

With the three words of submission the swung pendulum of the drama comes to rest. And for the last of him we have only

> I pray you give me leave to go from hence;
> I am not well. Send the deed after me,
> And I will sign it.

Here is the unapproachable Shakespeare. 'I am not well.' It nears banality and achieves perfection in its simplicity. And what a completing of the picture of Shylock! His deep offence has been to human kindness; he had scorned compassion and prayed God himself in aid of his vengeance. So Shakespeare dismisses him upon an all but ridiculous appeal to our pity, such as an ailing child might make that had been naughty; and we should put the naughtiness aside. He passes out silently, leaving the gibing Gratiano the last word, and the play's action sweeps on without pause. There can be no greater error than to gerrymander Shylock a strenuously 'effective exit'—and most Shylocks commit it. From the character's point of view the significant simplicity of that

> I am not well.

is spoilt; and from the point of view of the play the technical skill with which Shakespeare abstracts from his comedy this tragic and dominating figure and avoids anti-climax after is nullified.

> —HARLEY GRANVILLE-BARKER, "Shylock," *Prefaces to Shakespeare: Second Series* (London: Sidgwick & Jackson, 1930), pp. 92–106

LEAH WOODS WILKINS

It has been generally accepted that the reason for Shylock's discourse on Jacob and the flocks of Laban was merely to justify his practice of usury through the example of his blessed forbear, Jacob. Some critics have seen this speech as rambling and irrelevant to the discussion of the projected loan to Bassanio; some see him as rising to heights of dignity and racial pride as he expounds reverently upon the Biblical tale. On the other hand, a surprising number of critics have completely ignored this speech in their comments on *The Merchant of Venice,* even when they write at length on Shylock's character and motives and this particular scene. The writer believes that the story of Jacob and Laban indicates Shylock's preoccupation with the problem of how he may feed his grudge against Antonio, how he may match the cunning of his ancestor, how he may collect interest without taking interest. He is groping for an idea as to what kind of bond he can take from Antonio which will answer these requirements.

Shylock's mind is not wandering from the issue between him and Antonio on usury, or from the fact that Antonio "neither lends nor borrows upon advantage," when he remarks thoughtfully:

> When Jacob graz'd his uncle Laban's sheep—
> This Jacob from our holy Abraham was
> (As his wise mother wrought in his behalf)
> The third possessor; ay, he was the third—   (I, iii, 72–75)

Shylock pauses significantly, as if he were reviewing in his own mind the story of how Rebekah connived and Jacob lied to receive the blessing given by God to Abraham, which should have passed on to Isaac's first-born son. We can imagine Shylock's sly half-smile as he replies to Antonio's impatient question about Jacob:

> ANT.: And what of him? Did he take interest?
> SHY: No, not take interest; not as you would say,
> Directly interest.   (I, iii, 76–78)

Note that Shylock must accent the word "you"; Antonio would not say that Jacob took interest in the same sense that he was expecting Shylock to demand interest. Antonio is here concerned with money, and it was not in money that Jacob was paid. But Shylock would say that Jacob took interest! He continues firmly:

> Mark what Jacob did.
> When Laban and himself were compromis'd
> That all the eanlings which were streak'd and pied
> Should fall as Jacob's hire. . . .   (I, iii, 78–81)

He uses the word *hire;* it is used in the Bible passage—but Shylock has another connotation in mind. It is to Antonio that he will hire his money, so it will earn its wages for him.

Shakespeare summarized in eleven lines the story of how Jacob trickily obtained for himself the better portion of his uncle Laban's cattle, sheep and goats. The Elizabethans knew this Biblical story well; they were accustomed to thinking of animals in connection with usury; they were used to thinking of animals as payment for services. Shylock herein finds the answer to his ruminations. Since Jacob took his wages in the form of flesh, Shylock would also take his in terms of flesh. Evilly he decides to practice trickery with human flesh as his ancestor did with animal flesh.

Antonio, though he might perhaps have been warned by this tale to suspect trickery, only inquires with impatience at the story, "Was this inserted to make interest good?" The Elizabethan conviction that "interest" was not "good" supplied the answer "No!" "Or is your gold and silver ewes and rams?" Antonio adds. Traditionally livestock was recognized as a valid medium for payment; if flocks, or flesh, were hire, or money to Jacob, then to Shylock, also, money could be equivalent to flesh. Yes! his gold and silver equals ewes and rams, but to Antonio he gives an evasive answer: "I cannot tell; I make it breed as fast." Indirectly he admits that it is.

That this story inspired Shylock with the idea of asking for Antonio's flesh as bond is proved, the writer believes, by his subsequent return to the idea of Laban's flocks, some seventy lines later. When final arrangements are about to be made for the signing of the bond, he craftily argues:

> If he should break his day, what should I gain
> By the exaction of the forfeiture?
> A pound of man's flesh taken from a man
> Is not so estimable, profitable neither,
> As flesh of muttons, beefs or goats. (I, iii, 64–68)

The audience knows that his "exaction of the forfeiture" would be a great, if most unlikely, victory for him; that for his devilish purpose this "pound of man's flesh taken from a man" would mean the death of the one whom he has sworn to undo. To put such a scheme into effect would call for machinations even cleverer than Jacob's. If he should win the forfeiture, he would avenge the insults to his "tribe," while gaining greater glory for his "sacred nation" by adding to their history of ingenious cozenage. And finally, there is the paraphrasing of Laban's cattle, sheep and goats in the "flesh of muttons, beefs and goats." In this one sentence Shylock links the idea of a pound of man's flesh with the flesh of Laban's flocks. Surely they originally became linked in his mind when he first brought forth this ancient story.

—LEAH WOODS WILKINS, "Shylock's Pound of Flesh and Laban's Sheep," *Modern Language Notes* 62, No. 1 (January 1947): 28–30

C. L. BARBER

When Shylock comes on in the third scene, the easy, confident flow of colorful talk and people is checked by a solitary figure and an unyielding speech:

SHYLOCK: Three thousand ducats—well.
BASSANIO: Ay, sir, for three months.
SHYLOCK: For three months—well.
BASSANIO: For the which, as I told you, Antonio shall be bound.
SHYLOCK: Antonio shall become bound—well.
BASSANIO: May you stead me? Will you pleasure me? Shall I know your answer?
SHYLOCK: Three thousand ducats for three months, and Antonio bound.
(I.iii.1–10)

We can construe Shylock's hesitation as playing for time while he forms his plan. But more fundamentally, his deliberation expresses the impersonal logic, the mechanism, involved in the control of money. Those *well's* are wonderful in the way they bring bland Bassanio up short. Bassanio assumes that social gestures can brush aside such consideration:

SHYLOCK: Antonio is a good man.
BASSANIO: Have you heard any imputation to the contrary?
SHYLOCK: Ho, no, no, no, no! My meaning in saying he is a good man, is to have you understand me that he is sufficient. (I.iii.12–17)

The laugh is on Bassanio as Shylock drives his hard financial meaning of "good man" right through the center of Bassanio's softer social meaning. The Jew goes on to calculate and count. He connects the hard facts of money with the rocky sea hazards of which we have so far been only picturesquely aware: "ships are but boards"; and he betrays his own unwillingness to take the risks proper to commerce: "and other ventures he hath, squand'red abroad."

    . . . I think I may take his bond.
BASSANIO: Be assur'd you may.
SHYLOCK: I will be assur'd I may; and, that I may be assured, I will bethink me. (I.iii.28–31)

The Jew in this encounter expresses just the things about money which are likely to be forgotten by those who have it, or presume they have it, as part of a social station. He stands for what we mean when we say that "money is money." So Shylock makes an ironic comment—and *is* a comment, by virtue of his whole tone and bearing—on the folly in Bassanio which leads him to confuse those two meanings of "good man," to ask Shylock to dine, to use in this business context such social phrases as "Will you *pleasure* me?" When Antonio joins them, Shylock (after a soliloquy in which his plain hatred has glittered) becomes a pretender to fellowship, with an equivocating mask:

SHYLOCK: This is kind I offer.
BASSANIO: This were kindness.
SHYLOCK: This kindness I will show. (I.iii.143–144)

We are of course in no doubt as to how to take the word "kindness" when Shylock proposes "in a merry sport" that the penalty be a pound of Antonio's flesh.

In the next two acts, Shylock and the accounting mechanism which he embodies are crudely baffled in Venice and rhapsodically transcended in Belmont. The solidarity of the Venetians includes the clown, in whose part Shakespeare can use conventional blacks and whites about Jews and misers without asking us to take them too seriously:

To be ruled by my conscience, I should stay with the Jew my master, who (God bless the mark) is a kind of devil. . . . My master's a very Jew. (II.ii.24–25, III)

Even the street urchins can mock Shylock after the passion which "the dog Jew did utter in the streets":

> Why, all the boys in Venice follow him,
> Crying his stones, his daughter, and his ducats.   (II.viii.23–24)

Historical changes in stock attitudes have made difficulties about Shylock's role as a butt, not so much in the theater, where it works perfectly if producers only let it, but in criticism, where winds of doctrine blow sentiments and abstractions about. The Elizabethans almost never saw Jews except on the stage, where Marlowe's Barabas was familiar. They did see *one*, on the scaffold, when Elizabeth's unfortunate physician suffered for trumped-up charges of a poisoning plot. The popular attitude was that to take interest for money was to be a loan shark—though limited interest was in fact allowed by law. An aristocrat who like Lord Bassanio ran out of money commanded sympathy no longer felt in a middle-class world. Most important of all, suffering was not an absolute evil in an era when men sometimes embraced it deliberately, accepted it as inevitable, and could watch it with equanimity. Humanitarianism has made it necessary for us to be much more thoroughly insulated from the human reality of people if we are to laugh at their discomfiture or relish their suffering. During the romantic period, and sometimes more recently, the play was presented as a tragi-comedy, and actors vied with one another in making Shylock a figure of pathos. I remember a very moving scene, a stock feature of romantic productions, in which George Arliss came home after Bassanio's party, lonely and tired and old, to knock in vain at the door of the house left empty by Jessica. How completely unhistorical the romantic treatment was, E. E. Stoll demonstrated overwhelmingly in his essay on Shylock in 1911, both by wide-ranging comparisons of Shylock's role with others in Renaissance drama and by analysis of the *optique du théâtre*.

To insert a humanitarian scene about Shylock's pathetic homecoming prevents the development of the scornful amusement with which Shakespeare's text presents the miser's reaction in Solanio's narrative:

> I never heard a passion so confus'd,
> So strange, outrageous, and so variable,
> As the dog Jew did utter in the streets.
> "My daughter! O my ducats! O my daughter!
> Fled with a Christian! O my Christian ducats! ..."   (II.viii.12–16)

Marlowe had done such a moment already with Barabas hugging in turn his money bags and his daughter—whom later the Jew of Malta poisons with a pot of porridge, as the Jew of Venice later wishes that Jessica "were hears'd at my foot, and the ducats in her coffin" (III.i.93–94). But the humanitarian way of playing the part develops suggestions that are *also* in Shakespeare's text:

> I am bid forth to supper, Jessica.
> There are my keys. But wherefore should I go?

I am not bid for love; they flatter me.
But yet I'll go in hate, to feed upon
The prodigal Christian.   (II.v.11–15)

Shakespeare's marvelous creative sympathy takes the stock role of Jewish usurer and villain and conveys how it would feel to be a man living inside it. But this does not mean that he shrinks from confronting the evil and the absurdity that go with the role; for the Elizabethan age, to understand did not necessarily mean to forgive. Shylock can be a thorough villain and yet be allowed to express what sort of treatment has made him what he is:

You called me misbeliever, cutthroat dog,
And spet upon my Jewish gaberdine,
And all for use of that which is mine own.   (I.iii.112–114)

We can understand his degradation and even blame the Antonios of Venice for it; yet it remains degradation:

Thou call'dst me dog before thou hadst a cause;
But, since I am a dog, beware my fangs.   (III.iii.6–7)

Shylock repeatedly states, as he does here, that he is only finishing what the Venetians started. He can be a drastic ironist, because he carries to extremes what is present, whether acknowledged or not, in their silken world. He insists that money is money—and they cannot do without money either. So too with the rights of property. The power to give freely, which absolute property confers and Antonio and Portia so splendidly exhibit, is also a power to refuse, as Shylock so logically refuses:

You have among you many a purchas'd slave,
Which, like your asses and your dogs and mules,
You use in abject and in slavish parts,
Because you bought them. Shall I say to you,
"Let them be free, marry them to your heirs!..."
                            You will answer,
"The slaves are ours." So do I answer you.
The pound of flesh which I demand of him
Is dearly bought, 'tis mine, and I will have it.   (IV.i.90–100)

At this point in the trial scene, Shylock seems a juggernaut that nothing can stop, armed as he is against a pillar of society by the principles of society itself: "If you deny me, fie upon your law!... I stand for judgement. Answer. Shall I have it." Nobody does answer him here, directly; instead there is an interruption for Portia's entrance. To answer him is the function of the whole dramatic action, which is making a distinction that could not be made in direct, logical argument.

Let us follow this dramatic action from its comic side. Shylock is comic, so far as he is so, because he exhibits what should be human, degraded into mechanism.

The reduction of life to mechanism goes with the miser's wary calculation, with the locking up, with the preoccupation with "that which is mine own." Antonio tells Bassanio that

> My purse, my person, my extremest means
> Lie all unlock'd to your occasions.   (I.i.138–139)

How open! Antonio has to live inside some sort of rich man's melancholy, but at least he communicates with the world through outgoing Bassanio (and, one can add, through the commerce which takes his fortunes out to sea). Shylock, by contrast, who breeds barren metal, wants to keep "the vile squeeling of the wry-neck'd fife" out of his house, and speaks later, in a curiously revealing, seemingly random illustration, of men who "when the bagpipe sings i'th'nose, / Cannot contain their urine" (IV.i.49–50). Not only is he closed up tight inside himself, but after the first two scenes, we are scarcely allowed by his lines to feel with him. And we never encounter him alone; he regularly comes on to join a group whose talk has established an outside point of view towards him. This perspective on him does not exclude a potential pathos. There is always potential pathos, behind, when drama makes fun of isolating, anti-social qualities. Indeed, the process of *making fun of* a person often works by exhibiting pretensions to humanity so as to show that they are inhuman, mechanical, not validly appropriate for sympathy. With a comic villain such as Shylock, the effect is mixed in various degrees between our responding to the mechanism as menacing and laughing at it as ridiculous.

So in the great scene in which Solanio and Salerio taunt Shylock, the potentiality of pathos produces effects which vary between comedy and menace:

> SHYLOCK: You knew, none so well as you, of my daughter's flight.
> SALERIO: That's certain. I, for my part, knew the tailor that made the wings she
>   flew withal.   (III.i.27–30)

Shylock's characteristic repetitions, and the way he has of moving ahead through similar, short phrases, as though even with language he was going to use only what was his own, can give an effect of concentration and power, or again, an impression of a comically limited, isolated figure. In the great speech of self-justification to which he is goaded by the two bland little gentlemen, the iteration conveys the energy of anguish:

> —and what's his reason? I am a Jew. Hath not a Jew eyes? Hath not a Jew
> hands, organs, dimensions, senses, affections, passions? fed with the same food,
> hurt with the same weapons, subject to the same diseases, healed by the same
> means, warmed and cooled by the same winter and summer as a Christian is?
> If you prick us, do we not bleed? If you tickle us, do we not laugh? If you poison
> us, do we not die? And if you wrong us, shall we not revenge? If we are like
> you in the rest, we will resemble you in that.   (III.i.60–71)

Certainly no actor would deliver this speech without an effort at pathos; but it is a pathos which, as the speech moves, converts to menace. And the pathos is quali fied, limited, in a way which is badly falsified by humanitarian renderings that open all the stops at "Hath not a Jew hands, etc. . . ." For Shylock thinks to claim only a *part* of humanness, the lower part, physical and passional. The similar self-pitying enumeration which Richard II makes differs significantly in going from "live with bread like you" to social responses and needs, "Taste grief, / Need friends" (*Richard II* III.ii.175–176). The passions in Shylock's speech are conceived as reflexes; the parallel clauses draw them all towards the level of "tickle . . . laugh." The same assumption, that the passions and social responses are mechanisms on a par with a nervous tic, appears in the court scene when Shylock defends his right to follow his "humor" in taking Antonio's flesh:

> As there is no firm reason to be render'd
> Why he cannot abide a gaping pig,
> Why he a harmless necessary cat,
> Why he a woollen bagpipe—but of force
> Must yield to such inevitable shame
> As to offend himself, being offended;
> So I can give no reason, nor I will not,
> More than a lodg'd hate and a certain loathing
> I bear unto Antonio . . .   (IV.i.52–61)

The most succinct expression of this assumption about man is Shylock's response to Bassanio's incredulous question:

> BASSANIO: Do all men kill the things they do not love?
> SHYLOCK: Hates any man the thing he would not kill?   (IV.I.66–67)

There is no room in this view for mercy to come in between "wrong us" and "shall we not revenge?" As Shylock insists, there is Christian example for him: the irony is strong. But the mechanism of stimulus and response is only a part of the truth. The reductive tendency of Shylock's metaphors, savagely humorous in Iago's fash- ion, goes with this speaking only the lower part of the truth. He is not cynical in Iago's aggressive way, because as an alien he simply doesn't participate in many of the social ideals which Iago is concerned to discredit in self-justification. But the two villains have the same frightening, ironical power from moral simplification.

Shylock becomes a clear-cut butt at the moments when he is himself caught in compulsive, reflexive responses, when instead of controlling mechanism he is controlled by it: "O my daughter! O my ducats!" At the end of the scene of taunting, his menace and his pathos become ridiculous when he dances like a jumping jack in alternate joy and sorrow as Tubal pulls the strings:

> TUBAL: Yes, other men have ill luck too. Antonio, as I heard in Genoa—
> SHYLOCK: What, what, what? Ill luck, ill luck?

TUBAL: Hath an argosy cast away coming from Tripolis.
SHYLOCK: I thank God, I thank God!—Is it true? is it true?
TUBAL: I spoke with some of the sailors that escaped the wrack.
SHYLOCK: I thank thee, good Tubal. Good news, good news! Ha, ha! Where? in Genoa?
TUBAL: Your daughter spent in Genoa, as I heard, one night fourscore ducats.
SHYLOCK: Thou stick'st a dagger in me. I shall never see my gold again. Fourscore ducats at a sitting! Fourscore ducats!
TUBAL: There came divers of Antonio's creditors in my company to Venice that swear he cannot choose but break.
SHYLOCK: I am very glad of it. I'll plague him; I'll torture him. I am glad of it.
TUBAL: One of them show'd me a ring that he had of your daughter for a monkey.
SHYLOCK: Out upon her! Thou torturest me, Tubal. It was my turquoise; I had it of Leah when I was a bachelor. I would not have given it for a wilderness of monkeys.
TUBAL: But Antonio is certainly undone.
SHYLOCK: Nay, that's true, that's very true. (III.i.102–130)

This is a scene in the dry manner of Marlowe, Jonson, or Molière, a type of comedy not very common in Shakespeare: its abrupt alternations in response convey the effect. Bergson describes so well in Le Rire, where the comic butt is a puppet in whom motives have become mechanisms that usurp life's self-determining prerogative. Some critics have left the rhythm of the scene behind to dwell on the pathos of the ring he had from Leah when he was a bachelor. It is like Shakespeare once to show Shylock putting a gentle sentimental value on something, to match the savage sentimental value he puts on revenge. There is pathos; but it is being fed into the comic mill and makes the laughter all the more hilarious.

In the trial scene, the turning point is appropriately the moment when Shylock gets caught in the mechanism he relies on so ruthlessly. He narrows everything down to his roll of parchment and his knife: "Till thou canst rail the seal from off my bond ..." (IV.i.139). But two can play at this game:

as thou urgest justice, be assur'd
Thou shalt have justice more than thou desir'st. (IV.i.315–316)

Shylock's bafflement is comic, as well as dramatic, in the degree that we now see through the threat he has presented, recognizing it to have been, in a degree, unreal. For it is unreal to depend so heavily on legal form, on fixed verbal definition, on the mere machinery by which human relations are controlled. Once Portia's legalism has broken through his legalism, he can only go on the way he started, weakly asking "Is that the law?" while Gratiano's jeers underscore the comic symmetry:

A Daniel still say I, a second Daniel!
I thank thee, Jew, for teaching me that word.   (IV.i.340–341)

The turning of the tables is not, of course, simply comic, except for the bold, wild and "skipping spirit" of Gratiano. The trial scene is a species of drama that uses comic movement in slow motion, with an investment of feeling such that the resolution is in elation and relief colored by amusement, rather than in the evacuation of laughter. Malvolio, a less threatening kill-joy intruder, is simply laughed out of court, but Shylock must be ruled out, with jeering only on the side lines. The threat Shylock offers is, after all, drastic, for legal instruments, contract, property are fundamental. Comic dramatists often choose to set them hilariously at naught; but Shakespeare is, as usual, scrupulously responsible to the principles of social order (however factitious his "law" may be literally). So he produced a scene which exhibits the limitations of legalism. It works by a dialectic that carries to a more general level what might be comic reduction to absurdity. To be tolerant, because we are all fools; to forgive, because we are all guilty—the two gestures of the spirit are allied, as Erasmus noted in praising the sublime folly of following Christ. Shylock says before the trial "I'll not be made a soft and dull-ey'd fool" by "Christian intercessors" (III.iii.14–15). Now when he is asked how he can hope for mercy if he renders none, he answers: "What judgement shall I dread, doing no wrong?" As the man who will not acknowledge his own share of folly ends by being more foolish than anyone else, so Shylock, who will not acknowledge a share of guilt, ends by being more guilty—and more foolish, to judge by results. An argument between Old Testament legalism and New Testament reliance on grace develops as the scene goes forward. (Shylock's references to Daniel in this scene, and his constant use of Old Testament names and allusions, contribute to the contrast.) Portia does not deny the bond—nor the law behind it; instead she makes such a plea as St. Paul made to his compatriots:

                    Therefore, Jew,
Though justice be thy plea, consider this—
That, in the course of justice, none of us
Should see salvation. We do pray for mercy,
And that same prayer doth teach us all to render
The deeds of mercy.   (IV.i.97–102)

Mercy becomes the word that gathers up everything we have seen the Venetians enjoying in their reliance on community. What is on one side an issue of principles is on the other a matter of social solidarity: Shylock is not one of the "we" Portia refers to, the Christians who say in the Lord's Prayer "Forgive us our debts as we forgive our debtors." All through the play the word Christian has been repeated, primarily in statements that enforce the fact that the Jew is outside the easy bonds of community. Portia's plea for mercy is a sublime version of what in

less intense circumstances, among friends of a single communion, can be conveyed
with a shrug or a wink:

> Dost thou hear, Hal? Thou knowest in the state of innocency Adam fell; and
> what should poor Jack Falstaff do in the days of villany?
>
> (*1 Henry IV* III.iii.185–188)

Falstaff, asking for an amnesty to get started again, relies on his festive solidarity with
Hal. Comedy, in one way or another, is always asking for amnesty, after showing
the moral machinery of life getting in the way of life. The machinery as such need
not be dismissed—Portia is very emphatic about not doing that. But social solidarity,
resting on the buoyant force of a collective life that transcends particular mistakes,
can set the machinery aside. Shylock, closed off as he is, clutching his bond and his
knife, cannot trust this force, and so acts only on compulsion:

> PORTIA: Do you confess the bond?
> ANTONIO: I do.
> PORTIA: Then must the Jew be merciful.
> SHYLOCK: On what compulsion must I? Tell me that.
> PORTIA: The quality of mercy is not strain'd;
> It droppeth as the gentle rain from heaven
> Upon the place beneath. It is twice blest—
> It blesseth him that gives, and him that takes.   (IV.i.181–187)

It has been in giving and taking, beyond the compulsion of accounts, that Portia,
Bassanio, Antonio have enjoyed the something-for-nothing that Portia here summarizes in speaking of the gentle rain from heaven. ⟨. . .⟩

I must add, after all this praise for the way the play makes its distinction about
the use of wealth, that *on reflection*, not when viewing or reading the play, but
when thinking about it, I find the distinction, as others have, somewhat too easy.
While I read or watch, all is well, for the attitudes of Shylock are appallingly
inhuman, and Shakespeare makes me feel constantly how the Shylock attitude rests
on a lack of faith in community and grace. But when one thinks about the Portia-
Bassanio group, not in opposition to Shylock but alone (as Shakespeare does not
show them), one can be troubled by their being so very very far above money:

> What, no more?
> Pay him six thousand, and deface the bond.
> Double six thousand and then treble that . . .   (III.ii.298–300)

⟨. . .⟩

About Shylock ⟨. . .⟩ there is a difficulty which grows on reflection, a difficulty
which may be felt too in reading or performance. His part fits perfectly into the
design of the play, and yet he is so alive that he raises an interest beyond its design.
I do not think his humanity spoils the design, as Walter Raleigh and others argued,
and as was almost inevitable for audiences who assumed that to be human was to
be ipso-facto good. But it is true that in the small compass of Shylock's three

hundred and sixty-odd lines, Shakespeare provided material that asks for a whole additional play to work itself out. Granville-Barker perceptively summarizes how much there is in the scene, not sixty lines long, in which Shylock is seen at home:

> The parting with Launcelot: he has a niggard liking for the fellow, is even hurt a little by his leaving, touched in pride, too, and shows it childishly.
>
>   Thou shalt not gormandize
> As though hast done with me . . .
>
> . . . The parting with Jessica, which we of the audience know to be a parting indeed; that constant calling her by name, which tells us of the lonely man! He has looked to her for everything, has tasked her hard, no doubt; he is her jailer, yet he trusts her, and loves her in his extortionate way. Uneasy stranger that he is within these Venetian gates; the puritan, who, in a wastrel world, will abide by law and prophets!

To have dramatized "he has looked to her for everything, has tasked her hard, no doubt," would have taken Shakespeare far afield indeed from the prodigal story he was concerned with—as far afield as *King Lear*. Yet the suggestion is there. The figure of Shylock is like some secondary figure in a Rembrandt painting, so charged with implied life that one can forget his surroundings. To look sometimes with absorption at the suffering, raging Jew alone is irresistible. But the more one is aware of what the play's whole design is expressing through Shylock, of the comedy's high seriousness in its concern for the grace of community, the less one wants to lose the play Shakespeare wrote for the sake of one he merely suggested.

—C. L. BARBER, "The Merchant and the Jew of Venice: Wealth's Communion and an Intruder," *Shakespeare's Festive Comedy: A Study of Dramatic Form and Its Relation to Social Custom* (Princeton: Princeton University Press, 1959), pp. 172–73, 178–86, 189–91

W. H. AUDEN

Shylock is a Jew living in a predominantly Christian society, just as Othello is a Negro living in a predominantly white society. But, unlike Othello, Shylock rejects the Christian community as firmly as it rejects him. Shylock and Antonio are at one in refusing to acknowledge a common brotherhood.

> I will buy with you, sell with you, talk with you, walk with you, and so following, but I will not eat with you, drink with you, nor pray with you.   (Shylock.)

> I am as like
> To spit on thee again, to spurn thee, too.
> If thou wilt lend this money, lend it not
> As to thy friends . . .

But lend it rather to thine enemy,
Who if he break, thou mayst with better face
Exact the penalty.   (Antonio.)

In addition, unlike Othello, whose profession of arms is socially honorable, Shylock is a professional usurer who, like a prostitute, has a social function but is an outcast from the community. But, in the play, he acts unprofessionally; he refuses to charge Antonio interest and insists upon making their legal relation that of debtor and creditor, a relation acknowledged as legal by all societies. Several critics have pointed to analogies between the trial scene and the medieval *Processus Belial* in which Our Lady defends man against the prosecuting Devil who claims the legal right to man's soul. The Roman doctrine of the Atonement presupposes that the debtor deserves no mercy—Christ may substitute Himself for man, but the debt has to be paid by death on the cross. The Devil is defeated, not because he has no right to demand a penalty, but because he does not know that the penalty has been already suffered. But the differences between Shylock and Belial are as important as their similarities. The comic Devil of the mystery play can appeal to logic, to the letter of the law, but he cannot appeal to the heart or to the imagination, and Shakespeare allows Shylock to do both. In his "Hath not a Jew eyes . . ." speech in Act III, Scene I, he is permitted to appeal to the sense of human brotherhood, and in the trial scene, he is allowed to argue, with a sly appeal to the fear a merchant class has of radical social revolution:

You have among you many a purchased slave
Which, like your asses and your dogs and mules,
You use in abject and in slavish parts,

which points out that those who preach mercy and brotherhood as universal obligations limit them in practice and are prepared to treat certain classes of human beings as things.

Furthermore, while Belial is malevolent without any cause except love of malevolence for its own sake, Shylock is presented as a particular individual living in a particular kind of society at a particular time in history. Usury, like prostitution, may corrupt the character, but those who borrow upon usury, like those who visit brothels, have their share of responsibility for this corruption and aggravate their guilt by showing contempt for those whose services they make use of.

It is, surely, in order to emphasize this point that, in the trial scene, Shake-speare introduces an element which is not found in *Pecorone* or other versions of the pound-of-flesh-story. After Portia has trapped Shylock through his own insis-tence upon the letter of the law of Contract, she produces another law by which any alien who conspires against the life of a Venetian citizen forfeits his goods and places his life at the Doge's mercy. Even in the rush of a stage performance, the audience cannot help reflecting that a man as interested in legal subtleties as Shylock, would, surely, have been aware of the existence of this law and that, if by any chance he had overlooked it, the Doge surely would very soon have drawn his attention to it. Shakespeare, it seems to me, was willing to introduce what is an absurd implausibility for the sake of an effect which he could not secure without it: at the last moment when, through his conduct, Shylock has destroyed any sympathy we may have felt for him earlier, we are reminded that, irrespective of his personal character, his status is one of inferiority. A Jew is not regarded, even in law, as a brother.

If the wicked Shylock cannot enter the fairy story world of Belmont, neither can the noble Antonio, though his friend, Bassanio, can. In the fairy story world, the symbol of final peace and concord is marriage, so that, if the story is concerned with the adventures of two friends of the same sex, male or female, it must end with a double wedding. Had he wished, Shakespeare could have followed the *Pecorone* story in which it is Ansaldo, not Gratiano, who marries the equivalent of Nerissa. Instead, he portrays Antonio as a melancholic who is incapable of loving a woman. He deliberately avoids the classical formula of the Perfect Friends by making the relationship unequal. When Salanio says of Antonio's feelings for Bassanio

I think he only loves the world for him

we believe it, but no one would say that Bassanio's affections are equally exclusive. Bassanio, high-spirited, elegant, pleasure loving, belongs to the same world as Gratiano and Lorenzo; Antonio does not. When he says:

I hold the world but as the world, Gratiano,
A stage, where everyman must play a part,
And mine a sad one

Gratiano may accuse him of putting on an act, but we believe him, just as it does not seem merely the expression of a noble spirit of self-sacrifice when he tells Bassanio:

I am a tainted wether of the flock,
Meetest for death; the weakest kind of fruit
Drops earliest to the ground, and so let me.

It is well known that love and understanding breed love and understanding.

The more people on high who comprehend each other,
the more there are to love well, and the more
love is there, and like a mirror, one giveth
back to the other.   (*Purgatorio*, XV.)

So, with the rise of a mercantile economy in which money breeds money, it became an amusing paradox for poets to use the ignoble activity of usury as a metaphor for love, the most noble of human activities. Thus, in his *Sonnets*, Shakespeare uses usury as an image for the married love which begets children.

Profitless usurer, why does thou use
So great a sum of sums, yet canst not live?
For having traffic with thyself alone
Thou of thyself thy sweet self dost deceive.   (*Sonnet* IV.)

That use is not forbidden usury
Which happies those that pay the willing loan,
That's for myself, to breed another thee,
Or ten times happier, be it ten for one.   (VI.)

And, even more relevant, perhaps, to Antonio are the lines

But since she pricked thee out for women's pleasure
Mine be thy love, and thy love's use their treasure.   (XXXIII.)

There is no reason to suppose that Shakespeare had read Dante, but he must have
been familiar with the association of usury with sodomy of which Dante speaks in
the Ninth Canto of the *Inferno.*

It behoves man to gain his bread and to prosper. And because the usurer
takes another way, he contemns Nature in herself and her followers, placing
elsewhere his hope.... And hence the smallest round seals with its mark
Sodom and the Cahors....

It can, therefore, hardly be an accident that Shylock the usurer has as his antagonist
a man whose emotional life, though his conduct may be chaste, is concentrated
upon a member of his own sex.

In any case, the fact that Bassanio's feelings are so much less intense makes
Antonio's seem an example of that inordinate affection which theologians have
always condemned as a form of idolatry, a putting of the creature before the
creator. In the sixteenth century, suretyship, like usury, was a controversial issue.
The worldly-wise condemned the standing surety for another on worldly grounds.

Beware of standing suretyship for thy best friends; he that payeth another
man's debts seeketh his own decay: neither borrow money of a neighbour or
a friend, but of a stranger.   (Lord Burghley.)

Suffer not thyself to be wounded for other men's faults, or scourged for other
men's offences, which is the surety for another: for thereby, millions of men
have been beggared and destroyed. . . . from suretyship as from a manslayer
or enchanter, bless thyself.   (Sir Walter Raleigh.)

And clerics like Luther condemned it on theological grounds.

Of his life and property a man is not certain for a single moment, any more
than he is certain of the man for whom he becomes surety. Therefore the
man who becomes surety acts unchristian like and deserves what he gets,
because he pledges and promises what is not his and not in his power, but in

the hands of God alone. . . . These sureties act as though their life and property
were their own and were in their power as long as they wished to have it; and
this is nothing but the fruit of unbelief. . . . If there were no more of this
becoming surety, a man would have to keep down and be satisfied with a
moderate living, who now aspires night and day after high places, relying on
borrowing and standing surety.

The last sentence of this passage applies very well to Bassanio. In *Pecorone*, the
Lady of Belmonte is a kind of witch and Gianetto gets into financial difficulties
because he is the victim of magic, a fate which is never regarded as the victim's fault.
But Bassanio had often borrowed money from Antonio before he ever considered
wooing Portia and was in debt, not through magic or unforeseeable misfortune, but
through his own extravagances,

> 'Tis not unknown to you, Antonio,
> How much I have disabled my estate
> By something showing a more swelling port
> Than my faint means would grant continuance

and we feel that Antonio's continual generosity has encouraged Bassanio in his spendthrift habits. Bassanio seems to be one of those people whose attitude towards
money is that of a child; it will somehow always appear by magic when really needed.
Though Bassanio is aware of Shylock's malevolence, he makes no serious effort to
dissuade Antonio from signing the bond because, thanks to the ever-open purse of
his friend, he cannot believe that bankruptcy is a real possibility in life.

Shylock is a miser and Antonio is openhanded with his money; nevertheless,
as a merchant, Antonio is equally a member of an acquisitive society. He is trading
with Tripoli, the Indies, Mexico, England, and when Salanio imagines himself in
Antonio's place, he describes a possible shipwreck thus:

> . . . the rocks
> Scatter all her spices on the stream,
> Enrobe the roaring waters with my silks.

The commodities, that is to say, in which the Venetian merchant deals are not
necessities but luxury goods, the consumption of which is governed not by physical
need but by psychological values like social prestige, so that there can be no
question of a Just Price. Then, as regards his own expenditure, Antonio is, like
Shylock, a sober merchant who practices economic abstinence. Both of them avoid
the carnal music of this world. Shylock's attitude towards the Masquers

> Lock up my doors and when you hear the drum
> And the vile squeaking of the wry-necked fife
> Clamber not you up the casement then,
> Let not the sound of shallow foppery enter
> My sober house

finds an echo in Antonio's words a scene later:

> Fie, fie Gratiano. Where are all the rest?
> Tis nine o'clock: our friends all stay for you.
> No masque to-night—the wind is come about.

Neither of them is capable of enjoying the carefree happiness for which Belmont stands. In a production of the play, a stage director is faced with the awkward problem of what to do with Antonio in the last act. Shylock, the villain, has been vanquished and will trouble Arcadia no more, but, now that Bassanio is getting married, Antonio, the real hero of the play, has no further dramatic function. According to the Arden edition, when Alan McKinnon produced the play at the Garrick theatre in 1905, he had Antonio and Bassanio hold the stage at the final curtain, but I cannot picture Portia, who is certainly no Victorian doormat of a wife, allowing her bridegroom to let her enter the house by herself. If Antonio is not to fade away into a nonentity, then the married couples must enter the lighted house and leave Antonio standing alone on the darkened stage, outside the Eden from which, not by the choice of others, but by his own nature, he is excluded.

Without the Venice scenes, Belmont would be an Arcadia without any relation to actual times and places, and where, therefore, money and sexual love have no reality of their own, but are symbolic signs for a community in a state of grace. But Belmont is related to Venice though their existences are not really compatible with each other. This incompatibility is brought out in a fascinating way by the difference between Belmont time and Venice time. Though we are not told exactly how long the period is before Shylock's loan must be repaid, we know that it is more than a month. Yet Bassanio goes off to Belmont immediately, submits immediately on arrival to the test of the caskets, and has just triumphantly passed it when Antonio's letter arrives to inform him that Shylock is about to take him to court and claim his pound of flesh. Belmont, in fact, is like one of those enchanted palaces where time stands still. But because we are made aware of Venice, the real city, where time is real, Belmont becomes a real society to be judged by the same standards we apply to any other kind of society. Because of Shylock and Antonio, Portia's inherited fortune becomes real money which must have been made in this world, as all fortunes are made, by toil, anxiety, the enduring and inflicting of suffering. Portia we can admire because, having seen her leave her Earthly Paradise to do a good deed in this world (one notices, incidentally, that in this world she appears in disguise), we know that she is aware of her wealth as a moral responsibility, but the other inhabitants of Belmont, Bassanio, Gratiano, Lorenzo and Jessica, for all their beauty and charm, appear as frivolous members of a leisure class, whose carefree life is parasitic upon the labors of others, including usurers. When we learn that Jessica has spent fourscore ducats of her father's money in an evening and bought a monkey with her mother's ring, we cannot take this as a comic punishment for Shylock's sin of avarice; her behavior seems rather an example of the opposite sin of conspicuous waste. Then, with the example in our minds of self-sacrificing love as displayed by Antonio, while we can enjoy the verbal felicity of the love duet between Lorenzo and Jessica, we cannot help noticing that the pairs of lovers they recall, Troilus and Cressida, Aeneas and Dido, Jason and Medea, are none of them examples of self-sacrifice or fidelity. Recalling that the inscription on the leaden casket ran, "Who chooseth me, must give and hazard all he hath," it occurs to us that we have seen two characters do this. Shylock, however unintentionally, did, in fact, hazard all for the sake of destroying the enemy he hated, and Antonio, however unthinkingly he signed the bond, hazarded all to secure the happiness of the friend he loved. Yet it is precisely these two who cannot enter Belmont. Belmont would like to believe that men and women are either good or bad by nature, but Shylock and Antonio remind us that this is an illusion: in the real world, no hatred is totally without justification, no love totally innocent.

—W. H. AUDEN, "Brothers & Others," *The Dyer's Hand and Other Essays* (New York: Random House, 1962), pp. 227–35

NORTHROP FRYE

Comedy, like tragedy, has its catharsis, sympathy and ridicule being what correspond to pity and terror in tragedy. The action of *The Merchant of Venice* moves from justice to mercy, and mercy is not opposed to justice, but is an authority which contains or internalizes justice. The justice of Shylock's bond is external, and the fall of Shylock is part of the process of internalizing justice ⟨...⟩. To regard Shylock ultimately either with sympathy or with contempt is a response of mood only: either attitude would keep him externalized. Shylock is the focus of the comic catharsis of the play because both moods are relevant to him. We feel the possibility of both, but neither is the comic point of Shylock's role.

We approach nearer to this comic point when we recognize the strength of the dramatic tension between Shylock and the rest of the play. The sense of festivity, which corresponds to pity in tragedy, is always present at the end of a romantic comedy. This takes the form of a party, usually a wedding, in which we feel, to some degree, participants. We are invited to the festivity and we put the best face we can on whatever feelings we may still have about the recent behavior of some of the characters, often including the bridegroom. In Shakespeare the new society is remarkably catholic in tolerance; but there is always a part of us that remains a spectator, detached and observant, aware of other nuances and values. This sense of alienation, which in tragedy is terror, is almost bound to be represented by somebody or something in the play, and even if, like Shylock, he disappears in the fourth act, we never quite forget him. We seldom consciously feel identified with him, for he himself wants no such identification: we may even hate or despise him, but he is there, the eternal questioning Satan who is still not quite silenced by the vindication of Job. Part of us is at the wedding feast applauding the loud bassoon; part of us is still out in the street hypnotized by some graybeard loon and listening to a wild tale of guilt and loneliness and injustice and mysterious revenge. There seems no way of reconciling these two things. Participation and detachment, sympathy and ridicule, sociability and isolation, are inseparable in the complex we call comedy, a complex that is begotten by the paradox of life itself, in which merely to exist is both to be a part of something else and yet never to be a part of it, and in which all freedom and joy are inseparably a belonging and an escape. ⟨. . .⟩

The action of a Shakespearean comedy ⟨. . .⟩ is not simply cyclical but dialectical as well: the renewing power of the final action lifts us into a higher world, and separates that world from the world of the comic action itself. This dialectical element in Shakespeare's comic structure we have now to examine. The first feature of it is the parallel between the structure of a romantic comedy and the central myth of Christianity: the parallel that made Dante call his poem a *commedia*. The framework of the Christian myth is the comic framework of the Bible, where man loses a peaceable kingdom, staggers through the long nightmare of tyranny and injustice which is human history, and eventually regains his original vision. Within this myth is the corresponding comedy of the Christian life. We first encounter the law in its harsh tyrannical form of an external barrier to action, a series of negative commands, and we are eventually set free of this law, not by breaking it, but by internalizing it: it becomes an inner condition of behavior, not an external antagonist as it is to the criminal.

Two of Shakespeare's comedies present the action within this familiar Christian setting. In *The Merchant of Venice* the supporter of the irrational is a Jew, or at least what Shakespeare's audience assumed to be a Jew. Shylock is frequently called a devil, because his role at the trial is the diabolical one of an accuser who demands death. When he says: "My deeds upon my head!" and prefers the seed of Barabbas to Christians, he is echoing the Jews at the trial of Christ. The redeeming power which baffles him is the blood that he cannot have. His insistence on his bond and on justice is countered by Portia's explicitly Christian appeal to mercy, and his claim to his bond is not denied until he has renounced mercy. In the background of the imagery are allusions to the story of the prodigal son, the parable which sums up, in epitome, the whole Christian story of the exile and return of man to his home.

> —NORTHROP FRYE, *A Natural Perspective: The Development of Shakespearean Comedy and Romance* (New York: Columbia University Press, 1965), pp. 102–4, 133–34

E. M. W. TILLYARD

In some ways there is little need to speak of Shylock, for present opinion, represented for instance by the editors of the new Arden and Players' editions of the *Merchant*, has settled into a satisfactory position between the tough and the tender interpreters. But something I must say, for I conjecture that the blackening of Antonio's friends depends ultimately on a false conception of Shylock

Shakespeare's Shylock has been the victim of the great actor. No other male character in the *Merchant* offered sufficient scope for him. All you can do with Bassanio is to make him, the male charmer, as manly and as charming as possible; there are no lateral possibilities. And mere male charm does not suffice the great actor. Antonio lacks emphasis and is too passive and withdrawn to meet the requirements. It would indeed be possible to specialize him into the tortured homosexual and extract a bit of sensationalism in that way; but that would not have suited the taste of the last two centuries, when the big actor's Shylock was being created. These exhaust the list of the other potentially major male parts, and Shylock remained the one possible victim of fruitful distortion. By exaggerating certain lines where we are invited to see Shylock's point of view and playing down or forgetting others that balance the impression made by these it was possible to fabricate a Shylock who was more sinned against than sinning, an intruder from the realm of tragedy, and thus a man of a dimension nobler than that of any other male character: in sum, a character worth the attention of the great actor.

This weighting of Shylock was bound to have consequences beyond itself. In the measure in which you increase your sympathy with him in the same measure you turn against those who rejoice or gloat over his downfall. Antonio's companions cease to be decent young men and become callous wasters. Then, any upsetting of the balance causes an unduly violent reaction. Thus, those who have seen that Shakespeare's text simply will not admit of the great actor's Shylock, for instance E . E. Stoll and René Pruvost, have, in reaction, made just a little too much of Shylock's undoubted affinity to the conventional types of usurer, Puritan, and Pantaloon familiar to an Elizabethan audience, as if Shakespeare was not capable of having it both ways: that is of satisfying conventional expectations up to a point and yet preserving his freedom to extend his sympathies beyond anything his audience could have glimpsed and to make the conventional issue into the unique. They thus do an injustice to Shakespeare as surely as do those who hold that Shylock ran away with him during composition and forced his maker to enlarge the stature for which he was first designed.

It cannot be too strongly asserted that Shylock, uninflated and unsentimentalized, remains one of Shakespeare's most wonderful creations and that he perfectly suits and promotes the romantic comedy in which he occurs. The 'tough' critics are correct in holding that Shylock was malevolent from the beginning and is never anything else; but in the scene where he first appears, and which should dictate our feelings about him, the strongest impression he gives, one that Shakespeare creates immediately with an incredible economy of words, is of strangeness. Shylock is utterly and irretrievably the alien. His slowness of speech, with its repetitions of what Bassanio has already said—'Three thousand ducats, for three months, and Antonio bound', etc.—betokens not only a man temperamentally repugnant to the lively Venetians but a whole alien code of manners. The Venetians can be formal enough on occasions, but Bassanio is far too contemptuous of the processes of finance to be willing to bestow the gift of his formality on *them*. On the other hand they are a big portion of Shylock's restricted existence, and he loves to draw them out and to savour them. That love, alien to the Venetians, is yet a conceivable human feeling; and Shakespeare, who was interested in all such human feelings, puts himself in Shylock's place and puts words in Shylock's mouth expressive of that love. In so doing he may be said to sympathize with Shylock, but only in a restricted sense of the word. In no sense does he take sides with him. When, in actual life, we encounter abruptly alien habits of mind we experience revulsion in the first place, but on it curiosity may quickly follow. The Venetians in encountering Shylock never got beyond revulsion; and Shakespeare was being true enough to life in thus restricting them. But he was free also to express his own curiosity and larger vision by causing Shylock to present here and elsewhere his own strange world. He does not expect us to like the picture. Shylock's house was a hell of gloom, puritanical and museless; and his Jessica is justified in leaving it in favour of light and the prospects of a Christian heaven. But in the background there is the synagogue and the antique world of the Old Testament; and I think we are justified in thinking that Shylock's reference to his wife and her ring is meant to denote a kind of ordered domestic life in past days. And as to his daughter, at least he was vulnerably dependent on her and perhaps loved her in his harsh way. Again, there is 'sympathy', but of the restricted kind.

What may not have been noted about Shylock is his spiritual stupidity. If the Venetians take no stock of Shylock's world, neither does he of theirs; and with less excuse. It is an unpleasant fact of life that a dominant class is less apt to study the dispositions of its subordinates than the other way round. It is also common sense, if you are a subordinate, to recognize the fact and to fall in with your fellows. Hence my assertion that Shylock had less excuse. He is quite self-absorbed and incapable of watching others. Shakespeare brings this out wonderfully in his great speeches (III,i) to Salario and Solanio about Antonio's scorn and *all* of his hostile acts to racial prejudice. It never begins to enter his head that Antonio may have genuine scruples about usury and that his acts in redeeming the debts of imprisoned Christians may have been motivated by disinterested kindness. And Shylock's stupidity becomes all the more convincing dramatically, when, in his lashings out, he strikes in the Christians the very sin he has been in the act of exemplifying. 'If a Jew wrong a Christian, what is his humility? Revenge.' I say the same sin as Shylock's, for the Venetians, in excluding the Jew from the scope of their Christian code of conduct, were indeed being stupid, were denying to a portion of the human race something which of its very essence applied, if to any, to all. Again, it is a mistake to think that Shakespeare was here so carried away by his Shylock that he took sides with him against his enemies. If it is necessary to define Shakespeare's position, it is this: the Venetians are better than the Jew, but they do not always act on that betterness; the Jew is worse, but not without excuse for being so. But, of course, Shakespeare does not take sides: he presents things as he sees them, to the enlargement of our sympathies if we are content to follow him. One more example of Shylock's stupidity is his mentioning his daughter and his ducats in the same breath. He has not the sense to see that others may find here an incongruity. Shakespeare is not any the less understanding of Shylock for having made him stupid. He created him as he created another character, stupid in her own way, Mrs Quickly; and no one would dream of saying that he failed in sympathy here. He also had a good reason for making his Shylock stupid. Experience has shown that in the trial scene producers and readers have sought to enlarge Shylock into a figure of tragic dimensions, to the detriment of the whole shape of the play. Tragic is precisely what Shylock should not be; and Shakespeare made his Shylock stupid, as Conrad in the *Secret Agent* made Winnie Verlock stupid, in order to preserve the comic predominance of his composition. Stupid people can be pathetic, but tragic never. Shylock's culminating stupidity occurs in the trial scene; and I have written at length about it in my *Essays Literary and Educational* (1962). There I maintain that Portia, in her role as Mercy, knowing she has her infallible charm for saving Antonio's life, spends her eloquence in trying to make Shylock save his own soul, an attempt which he cannot even begin to recognize.

I can now revert to the first point I made in talking of Shylock: the strangeness of his Jewish world. It is because of that strangeness that we can move to the other strange world of Belmont and the romantic improbabilities of the casket theme, without inconvenience. Many elements went to the composition of Shylock, as they did to that of Falstaff; but, situated at Belmont, we can, on account of that strangeness, see him not as the pantaloon of comedy, or as the joyless Puritan, but as the hero's enemy in the fairy-tale, the simple embodiment of the powers of evil.

> —E. M. W. TILLYARD, "Shylock," *Shakespeare's Early Comedies*
> (New York: Barnes & Noble, 1965), pp. 189–94

LESLIE A. FIEDLER

The Merchant of Venice is surely one of the most popular of Shakespeare's works, but by the same token, perhaps, one of the least well understood. The common error which takes the "Merchant" of the title to be Shylock is symptomatic of a whole syndrome of misconceptions about a play which few of us have ever really confronted, so badly is it customarily annotated, taught, and interpreted on the stage and so totally does the Jew now dominate its action. The play has captured our imagination, but Shylock has captured the play, turning, in the course of that conquest, from grotesque to pathetic, from utter alien to one of us

And why not, since the Jew is, to begin with, an archetype of great antiquity and power, a nightmare of the whole Christian community, given a local habitation and a name by Shakespeare, so apt it is hard to believe that he has not always been called "Shylock," has not always walked the Rialto. The contest between him and the play's other characters—Antonio, for instance, that projection of the author's private distress, or Portia, that not-far-from-standard heroine in male garb—is as unequal as that between mythic Joan and historic Talbot in *Henry VI, Part I*. Even the sort of transformation he has undergone is not unprecedented in the annals of theater. Molière's "Misanthrope," for example, was converted much more quickly, in less than a generation, rather than over nearly two centuries, from absurd buffoon to sympathetic dissident. But Molière's margin of ambivalence toward Alceste was greater by far than Shakespeare's toward Shylock, and a major revolution in taste and sensibility had begun before he was long dead.

Shakespeare, on the other hand, though not without some prophetic reservations about the wickedness of Jews, had to wait two centuries or more before such reservations had moved from the periphery to the center of the play. To be sure, the original entry in the Stationer's Register for 1598 refers to the play as "a booke of the Marchaunt of Venyce, or otherwise called the Jewe of Venyce"; and by 1701, Lord Lansdowne had quite rewritten it as *The Jew of Venice*. But even at that point, the appeal of Shylock was not so much pathetic as horrific and grotesque. It took three generations of nineteenth-century romantic actors to make the Jew seem sympathetic as well as central, so that the poet Heine, sitting in the audience, could feel free to weep at his discomfiture. The final and irrevocable redemption of Shylock, however, was the inadvertent achievement of the greatest anti-Semite of all time, who did not appear until the twentieth century was almost three decades old. Since Hitler's "final solution" to the terror which cues the uneasy laughter of *The Merchant of Venice*, it has seemed immoral to question the process by which Shylock has been converted from a false-nosed, red-wigged monster (his hair the color of Judas's), half spook and half clown, into a sympathetic victim.

By the same token, it proved possible recently to mount a heterodox production of *The Merchant* as an anti-Semitic play within the larger play of anti-Semitic world history—by enclosing it in a dramatic frame which made clear to the audience that the anti-Semitic travesty they watched was a command performance put on by doomed Jewish prisoners in a Nazi concentration camp. The play within a play turned out in this case to lack a fifth act, since the actor-Shylock "really" stabbed a guard with the knife he whetted on his boot; and that same actor spoke all his speeches in a comic Yiddish accent, except for those scant few lines in which Shakespeare permits the Jew to plead his own humanity. But none of this seems as important finally as its renewed insistence on what everyone once knew: that the play in some sense celebrates, certainly releases ritually, the full horror of anti-Semitism. A Jewish child, even now, reading the play in a class of Gentiles, feels this in shame and fear, though the experts, Gentile and Jewish alike, will hasten to assure him that his responses are irrelevant, even pathological, since "Shakespeare rarely 'takes sides' and it is certainly rash to assume that he here takes an unambiguous stand 'for' Antonio and 'against' Shylock. . . ."

It is bad conscience which speaks behind the camouflage of scholarship, bad conscience which urges us to read Edmund Keane's or Heinrich Heine's Shylock into Shakespeare's lovely but perverse text, as it had almost persuaded us to drop

Henry VI, Part I (which means, of course, the Pucelle) quite out of the canon. And which finally is worse: to have for so long forgotten Joan, or to persist in misremembering Shylock? In either case, we have, as it were, expurgated Shakespeare by canceling out or amending the meanings of the strangers at the heart of his plays.

The problem is that both of these particular strangers, the woman and the Jew, embody stereotypes and myths, impulses and attitudes, images and metaphors grown unfashionable in our world. Not that we have been emancipated from those impulses and attitudes, whatever superficial changes have been made in the stereotypes and myths, the images and metaphors which embody them; but we have learned to be ashamed, *officially* ashamed of them at least. And it irks us that they still persist in the dark corners of our hearts, the dim periphery of our dreams. What is demanded of us, therefore, if we would find the real meaning of these plays again, is not so much that we go back into the historical past in order to reconstruct what men once thought of Jews and witches, but rather that we descend to the level of what is most archaic in our living selves and there confront the living Shylock and Joan.

Obviously, it is easier to come to terms with such characters on the "enlightened" margin of Shakespeare's ambivalence. We are pleased to discover how much he is like what we prefer to think ourselves, when, for instance, he allows Shylock a sympathetic apology for himself: "Hath not a Jew eyes? Hath not a Jew hands, organs, dimensions, senses, affections, passions? Fed with the same food, hurt with the same weapons, subject to the same diseases, healed by the same means, warmed and cooled by the same winter and summer as a Christian is? If you prick us, do we not bleed? If you tickle us, do we not laugh? If you poison us, do we not die?"

And we are similarly delighted when Shakespeare lets him for an instant speak out of deep conjugal love: "It was my turquoise, I had it of Leah when I was a bachelor. I would not have given it for a wilderness of monkeys," or when Shakespeare permits him to rehearse the list of indignities he has suffered at Antonio's hands:

> Signior Antonio, many times and oft
> In the Rialto you have rated me
> About my moneys and my usances.
> Still I have borne it with a patient shrug,
> For sufferance is the badge of all our tribe.
> You call me misbeliever, cutthroat dog,
> And spit upon my Jewish gaberdine. . . .

But we must not forget that immediately following that first speech, Shylock is crying "revenge" and vowing that he will practice "villainy," and that scarcely has he spoken the second, when he is dreaming that he will "have the heart of" the Christian merchant. True, he bows and fawns and flatters throughout the third, but in a tone so obviously false, it could fool no one but gullible Antonio. And we would do better, therefore, to face that in ourselves which responds to the negative, which is to say, the stronger, pole of Shakespeare's double view: the uneasiness we feel before those terrible others whom we would but cannot quite believe no longer alien to us and all that we prize.

—LESLIE A. FIEDLER, "The Jew as Stranger; or, 'These Be the Christian Husbands,' " *The Stranger in Shakespeare* (New York: Stein & Day, 1972), pp. 97–100

HANS MAYER

Shakespeare's Shylock ⟨. . .⟩ has been fleshed out with many real characteristics of Jewish historical life. It is a historical fact that an act of Parliament in 1522 forbade Christians in England the taking of usurious interest, while some few Jews expelled from Spain and let into the country were admitted to that occupation. It is historical fact as well that one of them, Dr. Lopez, once again Jew and physician in the infamous "Faustian" concatenation, was charged at the time Shakespeare was staying in London, an imaginary charge to be sure, of having planned to assassinate Queen Elizabeth with poison. He was subsequently racked and hanged.

The stage figure of Shylock underscores this connection of rumor and scarcely understood reality. Nonetheless the wealth of individual and national traits in the rich Jew and usurer of Venice is surprising. He is proud of his religion and despises the Christians and their faith. He hates Antonio, who as Christian and Venetian merchant "lends out money gratis." He entertains relations with the other Jews of Venice and does not wish to be unworthy of them. His famous lament before the do-nothing parasite Salarino on the mocked and persecuted Jewish nation (III, 1) is neither Machiavellian nor egocentric: it is a universal Jewish lamentation. His hatred for Antonio is proxy for his whole race. "He hates our sacred nation," or "Cursed be my tribe if I forgive him." He, the widower, loves his deceased Leah and sentimentally holds in high honor the turquoise ring she once gave him, now stolen by their daughter and traded for a monkey. That he loves his daughter Jessica, who finds her vexed and avaricious father's house a hell, is patent. Her flight and betrayal first conjure up the real possibility of the strange contract with Antonio and its perfidious content: now to have revenge once for all! The outsider, spat upon, buffeted, and cheated by society in a monstrous manner, now transforms himself into a monster in his own right. And in this fashion the fateful transformation takes place: heretofore the Jew and usurer of the Rialto had been more or less a Jewish Everyman. Now he becomes a singular monster. He becomes Shylock.

In so doing, however, he becomes the mortal adversary of another man who for his own part cannot pretend to be a Venetian, Christian Everyman. Antonio is a Venetian merchant who has grown wealthy in the sea trade but who, as good Christian and law-abiding citizen, lends money out at no interest. A burgher, apparently, who consorts with young and extravagant noblemen. The man who he loves is for him always "Lord Bassanio."

The merchant of Venice is a monster as well, in the disguise of the decent burgher, who lives in solitude and spreads it about himself, a burgher and provider of money among profligate aristocrats. As Bassanio's loving friend he is supposed to help the young dandies attain their ladies. The question of mime—how Shakespeare could conceive this figure who speaks so few lines and scarcely has a "great scene" as the eponymous hero of his comedy—is wrongly put. It is the confrontation between the two outsiders, Antonio and Shylock, who have no other course, who are irreversible, to use Sartre's terminology—that is to say, robbed of all possibility of freedom of decision, since the one cannot stop being a Jew and the other cannot "switch over" his feelings and love—that makes possible the structure and dimensions of the play.

—HANS MAYER, "Shylock," *Outsiders: A Study in Life and Letters* [1975], tr. Denis M. Sweet (Cambridge, MA: MIT Press, 1982), pp. 278–80

R. CHRIS HASSEL, JR.

Though they are vastly different characters, Shylock and Antonio are spiritual communicants in their common Hebraic and Puritanical self-righteousness and in their related dependence upon fulfilling the Law. Their similarity is enhanced when each becomes the other's scapegoat. Since Antonio exemplifies both the best and the worst of the Christian community in the eyes of his adversary, he is most meet for Shylock's sacrificial knife. Assured of his own righteousness, Antonio seems ethically as much a stage Jew as a Christian throughout the play, but especially when he spits out uncharitably upon Shylock in the Rialto. Shylock is just as obviously Antonio's scapegoat and ours, embodying as he does both the vices of the Venetian business community and those of the comic *alazon*. When he is expelled after the fourth act, poetic justice and the form of New Comedy are admirably fulfilled and we are glad to see him thwarted. But the Christian idealism that has been coexisting with the comic structure suffers something of a setback. For again, the Christian community should need no other scapegoat than Christ, once only offered for the remission of the sins of all men. Punishing and expelling Shylock in the guise of baptising him is thus a failure without parallel in Shakespeare's comedies. At worst it is blasphemous. But it is at least an act devoid of Shrovetide humility, forgiveness, and the communal Christian acknowledgment of universal human imperfection. To St. Paul shared human error should unite, not separate, Jew and Gentile. Here, because the Christians cannot perceive their communion in imperfection with the Jew, he is baptized literally but never spiritually. His absence in Act V makes that failure clear to all of us.

Shylock shares the literal-mindedness and the self-righteousness of his Christian enemies, even though he cannot share their sacraments. As Antonio tries literally to fulfill the law and stand for sacrifice, so Shylock pursues the bloody, literal sacrifice of the old covenant. As he himself interprets his actions:

> The villainy you teach me I will execute, and it shall go hard but I will better
> the instruction.   (III.i.62–64)

Additional exegesis of Romans 12:I, the passage Portia alludes to when she remarks on the breach between Christian precept and Christian practice, indicates how well-equipped Shylock might have been as a Jew to better their instruction. According to Colet, St. Paul, in urging the Romans to present their bodies as living sacrifices, "is covertly reproving the sacrifices of . . . the Jews, who . . . were accustomed to make oblations of victims on festival days by slaughtering thousands of sheep, and to glut the whole temple with blood; thinking that by this act they gave great pleasure to God."

But if such bloody sacrifice could be associated with Colet with the Jews, and therefore by Shakespeare's audience with Shylock's literal attempt upon the body and blood of a Christian, it could also be cited by William Tyndale to attack the Catholic doctrine of transubstantiation. According to Tyndale, the Jews abhorred the eating of Christ because they "could not see that Christ's flesh, broken and crucified, and not bodily eaten, should be our salvation and this spiritual meat." But the Catholics, continues Tyndale, who believe in "sacrifice" and transubstantiation, have even less faith than the Jews: "Our fleshy Papists (being of the Jews' carnal opinion) yet abhor it not, neither cease they daily to crucify and offer him up again, which was once for ever and all offered, as Paul testifieth." Embarrassing as such polemics might seem today, they were the stock-in-trade of Reformation sectarian exchanges. They were readily available to Shakespeare's contemporaries, in texts like Tyndale's, in sermons, and in the catechism. *Certaine Sermons or Homilies,* for example, calls this Catholic belief in sacrifice and transubstantiation "a grosse carnall feeding, basely objecting and binding ourselves to the elements and creatures"; "we must then take heed," the homily says elsewhere, "lest of the memory, it be made a sacrifice, lest of a communion, it be made a private eating." Nowell's *Catechism* says transubstantiation would "fill them with abhorring that receive the sacrament, if we should imagine his body . . . to be enclosed in so narrow a room, . . . or his flesh to be chawed in our mouth with our teeth, and to be bitten small, and eaten as other meat." The literal and repeated sacrifice of flesh and blood relates both to the frequent sectarian debates about the nature of the sacrament and to the relationships of Jews, Catholics, and Anglicans. That the key term, *sacrifice,* is alluded to and key issues enacted in *The Merchant of Venice* suggests again that Shakespeare was using this well-known controversy to investigate the complicated ironies of an imperfect but self-satisfied Christian community and a Jew whose lust for Antonio's body and blood could finally be satisfied neither literally nor symbolically.

Reinforcing such undercurrents of the controversy are the play's repeated references to eating and starving. To suggest like Coriat that Shylock's problem is anal-erotic makes little sense in the context of the dramatic actions or the understandings of Shakespeare's contemporaries. But to suggest that because he is persistently spurned by the Christian community he is driven in revenge to enact a bloody sacrifice reminiscent of Christian Communion is directly within the spirit of the play. Denied all spiritual communion by the Christians (who stole Jessica) as well as by his own villainy, he pursues in his hunger a literal anti-Communion instead, one encouraged further by Antonio's own misunderstandings of "sacrifice" and righteousness. As a Jew Shylock might well commit a bloody, literal, vengeful sacrifice, a "grosse carnall feeding," a "private eating." For as Shylock finally tells Jessica, he would "feed upon" this "prodigal Christian" in hate if he cannot dine with Christians in love. Such references to the "meals" of Jew and Christian fill out the symbolic dimensions of Shylock's obsessive appetite for Antonio's body and blood. They also suggest that Shylock's final revenge upon the Christians is his exposure of their own imperfect treatment of a bitter enemy, and their unawareness of that imperfection.

At Shylock's first appearance in the play his language unconsciously expresses a perverse hunger. Almost immediately he says about Antonio,

> If I can catch him once upon the hip,
> I will feed fat the ancient grudge I bear him.   (I.iii.42–43)

Antonio's appearance is then greeted by the most astonishing "Freudian slip" in Shakespeare:

> Rest you fair, good signior!
> Your worship was the last man in our mouths.   (I.iii.55–56)

When Shylock is invited to dinner with the Christians earlier in the scene, he categorically turns it down, showing his conscious disgust over eating with them. Simultaneously, however, his language indicates how closely Shylock associates Christian dining and Christian worship: "I will not eat with you, drink with you, nor pray with you" (I.iii.33–34). In these ways, feasting and flesh consistently relate to the human communion which Shylock desperately needs and will never experience, and the mystical Christian Communion he does not understand. They also suggest the universal communion with foolish, imperfect mankind that this Christian community never achieves.

Shylock is consistently uneasy when he tries to explain his desire for the strange terms of the bond. In many scenes he is dumbfounded and irritated by his own irrational and thriftless behavior (I.iii.161–63; III.i.44–47). As late as the trial Shylock responds to the question of his desire for Antonio's flesh with a defiant and evasive reply:

> You'll ask me why I rather choose to have
> A weight of carrion flesh than to receive
> Three thousand ducats. I'll not answer that,
> But say it is my humor.   (IV.i.40–43)

Incapable of understanding the impulse himself, incapable of explaining how a Jew would prefer worthless, carrion flesh to so much money, beset by a perplexing symbolic condition he can neither explain nor comprehend, Shylock evades the question, publicly and personally. All Shylock knows, and all he can communicate, is that he desires the body and the blood of a Christian.

Shylock's complex attitude toward the Christians' dinners furthers our sense that dinners have communal implications in the play. As in no other Shakespearean play, characters so frequently refer to dining together that such dining becomes our sense of the natural Christian condition. Dinners are consistently focal points for celebration and companionship. For example, Lorenzo promises to meet Gratiano after dinner (I.i.104), and Portia delays Morocco's hazard until the same time (II.i.44). Gratiano promises to meet Bassanio at suppertime (II.i.192). The Duke celebrates the trial's happy conclusion by inviting Portia to dinner (IV.i.399); his generosity is almost ritually followed by Gratiano's similar invitation of Portia to a celebratory meal (IV.ii.7–8). Lorenzo, Launcelot, and Jessica joke at length about dinners and festivity (III.v.39–83). Finally, Bassanio deems an elegant dinner the reward for love: "I do feast tonight / My best esteemed acquaintance" (II.ii.158–59). Like Communion these dinners celebrate and reward shared love.

Shylock, in contrast, is niggardly with his food. His skinny servant must laugh hollowly when his master upbraids him for eating too much: "Thou shalt not gormandize / As thou hast done with me" (II.v.3–4). Shylock seems to have starved his whole household in his material and spiritual thrift. Jessica, for example, mentions the "taste of tediousness" (II.iii.3) that pervades their house. But though Shylock instinctively refuses his one invitation to dine with the Christians (I.ii.31–34), he then compulsively and ambiguously reverses his decision and decides to attend:

> I am bid forth to supper, Jessica
> There are my keys. But wherefore should I go?
> I am not bid for love—they flatter me—
> But yet I'll go in hate to feed upon
> The prodigal Christian.   (II.v.11–15)

Here Shylock almost articulates for us the submerged irony of his compulsion to eat with—nay, "upon"—the Christian. His supper will not be one of love, that communal meal shared by Christians and traditionally called "love" in the homily and the catechism. Instead it will be a supper celebrating their hatred for him and his for them, a complete reversal of the sacrament of Communion and the image of Christian dining established elsewhere in the play. Even worse, while he dines with Antonio and Bassanio, their Christian friends steal away with Shylock's last remnant of human communion, his daughter Jessica. The meal is doubly prodigal: Shylock is hypocritical to attend thus in hatred, but his hosts share his hypocrisy and as Christians should perceive this common error much more readily than Shylock. They never do.

Of course, Shylock does not get the chance to carve out Antonio's body and blood, even in hatred. Portia mercifully tricks him, after first arousing him to a feverish expectation during the trial. The Duke recalls an old law against aliens, and strips him of his wealth. And then Shylock is given literally what he never knew he wanted. He is forced to join the Christian community after all. The Shrovetide and Communion ironies intensify again in this scene. Antonio wants only to stand for sacrifice and exhibit perfect, Christlike love. Consequently he has renounced the world and prepared himself to die. Instead he is given the life and later the goods he had willingly resigned. Simultaneously, his attempts to act Christlike have made him less so, more presumptuous, more contemptuous of imperfection. Shylock pursues a literal, bloody, ritualistic Communion of retribution upon the greatest Christian in his community. He is diverted from his literal bond only to be made through baptism a Christian communicant, a fellow of enemies who seem no more capable of forgiving him than he can forgive them. Ostensibly their forced conversion is merciful, directing a monstrous cannibalism to the Table of our Lord. But the aesthetic sense of the moment is one of defeat and exclusion, not Shylock's salvation. That is why so many readers, viewers, and actors have found the moment unsatisfactorily slick. When Portia denies Shylock the blood and offers him only the flesh (IV.i.304), Shakespeare may remind us of the Communion controversy once again: the Catholic communicant, unlike the Protestant, is given the wafer but not the wine. When the Christians have to resort to the letter of the law, it seems that they have joined the Jew rather than defeating him. In fact, Shylock's absence from the fellowship of Act V announces the negative thrust of their partial and ironic victory. Both Antonio and Shylock, two central and occasionally parallel characters, suffer the same imperfect mercy at the end of the play, and its festivity is the more ambiguous because their fates are so similar.

—R. CHRIS HASSEL, JR., "Shylock's Frustrated Communion,"
Faith and Folly in Shakespeare's Romantic Comedies
(Athens: University of Georgia Press, 1980), pp. 189–95

MARK TAYLOR

Various Shakespearean fathers object to suitors for their daughters' hands because of the inferior social or economic position of the suitors (Cymbeline, Page in *The Merry Wives*, the Duke of Milan in *The Two Gentlemen*, and others), but only in *Othello* and *The Merchant of Venice* is the alliance transcultural and transracial as well, between white and black or between gentile and Jew. If we could ask the majority of the characters in each play how successful the marriages are for the girls, they would surely hold that though Desdemona lowered herself by marrying beneath the station to which she was born, Jessica raised herself by marrying into a higher station. On pragmatic grounds, the first marriage seems a failure, the second a success, since in both cases it is the woman who joins the man, and not he her. There is, of course, no reason that Shylock, who is as proud of his racial heritage, and as bent on maintaining its purity, as the Christians are of their own, should share this view; but Jessica unquestionably earns perquisites, like entrance into the world of Belmont, that she had lacked. Or perhaps it is more accurate to say, not that she earns these perquisites, but that she purchases them with money stolen from her father.

Like Antonio and Portia when first we meet them, Jessica announces her unhappiness with her lot; but whereas the first two are made unhappy by something that has just happened, Bassanio's falling in love, or by a temporary situation, the need to wait and to see who chooses the lead casket, Jessica's unhappiness is evidently a long-term condition. She tells Launcelot,

> I am sorry thou wilt leave my father so;
> Our house is hell, and thou a merry devil
> Didst rob it of some taste of tediousness.   (2.3.1–3)

There is no reason for us to doubt the legitimacy of Jessica's indictment, and Launcelot, who sees service in a Christian household as preferable to service in Shylock's, offers a kind of confirmation of Jessica's view. On the other hand, it is natural to wish for more objective evidence of conditions—hellish? tedious?—in Shylock's home than the play offers. Unless we can accept Jessica's situation as truly intolerable, and perhaps even if we do, we must regard her leaving with his gold as a terrible betrayal for any daughter. Here, as so often in the play, we must make up our minds, for less than conclusive reasons exist about the sort of man Shylock is, and then let that judgment determine subsequent judgments about everything that happens to him. It is much easier to do this in the theater, where the director will foist his decisions on us, than in the study, where almost any unambiguous view is likely to seem extreme. As a partial justification for leaving Shylock, Launcelot tells old Gobbo,

> I am famished in his service; you may tell every finger I have with my ribs.
>   (2.2.98–99)

That sounds bad indeed, but Gobbo, who is "more than sand-blind, high-gravel-blind" (32–33) and cannot even recognize his son, is unable to substantiate the report. By contrast, Shylock tells Launcelot that, when he goes over to Bassanio,

> Thou shalt not gormandize
> As thou hast done with me.   (2.5.3–4)

It is tempting to laugh at this hypocrisy, but we cannot be sure it is hypocrisy; it may be, rather, that Launcelot, like Jessica, simply seeks social preferment for its own sake, not because the circumstances of his life are really very bad. Again, there is Solanio's report of Shylock's outcry in the streets:

> "My daughter! O my ducats! O my daughter!
> Fled with a Christian! O my Christian ducats!
> Justice! the law! my ducats and my daughter!

A sealèd bag, two sealèd bags of ducats,
Of double ducats, stol'n from me by my daughter!
And jewels—two stones, two rich and precious stones.
Stol'n by my daughter!"   (2.8.15–21)

which, if accurate (as it need not be), is not necessarily prejudicial to our sympathy for Shylock. Probably everyone laughs at these words and their implied equivalence of the two losses, a daughter and gold, but if the first loss should be regarded as infinitely more severe than the second, the two together still add up to everything the man owns. Furthermore, even if Solanio is providing a verbatim transcript of Shylock's words, it is unlikely that he is trying to duplicate Shylock's tone.

(Irrespective of Solanio's accuracy, however, one thing about this speech is highly significant: the pun on testicles implicit in "two sealèd bags" and "two stones, two rich and precious stones." Since these bags, or stones, were stolen by Jessica, as Shylock says, it follows by corollary that he has been disembowelled, castrated, unmanned by the departure of his daughter. The point is not that this wound is present in Shylock's mind, though it may well be, but that in his words, or those of Solanio, as in those of Antigonus, there lies the association of a daughter's coming to maturity and a father's loss of sexual potency.)

Having lost his daughter, Shylock calls on the state for restitution. Solanio says,

The villain Jew with outcries raised the Duke,
With him went to search Bassanio's ship.   (2.8.4–5)

Like Brabantio, Shylock believes that the power of the state will preserve a father's control over his daughter. The social insider and the social outsider are for a moment one in their appeals to external authority for buttressing of their personal authority when it is challenged within their families. The state's response to each man is ultimately the same. Though we may feel more sympathy for Desdemona than for Jessica, and though we cannot attribute the same or even similar motives to the Duke in *Othello* and the Duke in *The Merchant of Venice,* we may recognize that it is the proper business of both to allow girls to grow up, whether their fathers will or no.

—MARK TAYLOR, "The Lords of Duty," *Shakespeare's Darker Purpose: A Question of Incest* (New York: AMS Press, 1982), pp. 100–102

ABBA RUBIN

The most libelous early work by far was Lord Lansdowne's travesty of *The Merchant of Venice*. Shakespeare's play was not much read and not at all performed in the eighteenth century until 1741, when it made a dramatic comeback. Until then Lansdowne's play (first produced in 1701) was popular. The general outline of the story is the same as Shakespeare's. There is the unequal rivalry between Shylock and Antonio and the bond of the pound of flesh; the resolution of the problem is the same. Shylock's daughter robs him and runs off with a Christian, and Shylock is the only, and complete, loser. The comparative literary qualities of the two plays is beyond the scope of this argument; it is therefore necessary to deal directly with Lansdowne's treatment of Shylock the Jew; in *The Jew of Venice* he is reduced from a powerful figure to one petty in his viciousness. In speaking of the possible forfeiture in case of Antonio's default, Shylock now suggests: "What think you of your nose, or of an eye—or of—a pound of flesh." In a thoroughly original scene, Antonio, Bassanio, and others, together with Shylock, are found sitting "as at an entertainment." Shylock is apart, seated at a table lavishly spread with food. After the others have toasted their friends or mistresses, Shylock rises to a new toast:

> I have a Mistress, that outshines 'em all— Commanding yours—and yours tho' the whole sex: O may her charms encrease and multiply; My money is my Mistress! Here's to Interest upon Interest.

The character is small and ridiculous. In the place of dignity there is absurdity; in the place of vengeful hate there is conspicuous greed. The character shows the influence of tradition together with the rumored greed and wealth of the Jews on the stock exchange. It ceases to be a portrayal of a monstrous, yet insidiously believable, villain. The original Shylock was feared and hated for his character and as the embodiment of all that was thought to be evil in the Jews. Lansdowne's Shylock, however, is laughable as the embodiment of the greedy and ridiculous Jew. But Lord Lansdowne's work is primarily the work of fancy coupled to tradition instead of truth. In general, truths about the Jews only slowly and subtly began to make themselves felt in literature.

—ABBA RUBIN, *Images in Transition: The English Jew in English Literature 1660–1830* (Westport, CT: Greenwood Press, 1984), pp. 52–53

HARRIETT HAWKINS

⟨. . .⟩ it was out of fear that it ⟨*The Merchant of Venice*⟩ would encourage anti-Semitism that the New York School Board banned *The Merchant of Venice* from all schools under its jurisdiction. And the fact is that Shakespeare's play was exploited as a vehicle for anti-Semitic propaganda in productions mounted in Berlin and Vienna during the Third Reich, in one of which the star of the Nazi film *Jud Süss* (1940) played Shylock. I am indebted to Professor Werner Habicht for this information: there was a notorious Viennese production in 1943 with Werner Krauss as Shylock, and a Berlin production in 1942 where professional actors were distributed among the audience to boo at Shylock (played by Georg August Koch). In the earlier Nazi years, *Merchant* was put on quite often; there were about fifty German productions between 1933 and 1939, according to the known statistics.

—HARRIETT HAWKINS, *The Devil's Party: Critical Counter-interpretations of Shakespearean Drama* (Oxford: Clarendon Press, 1985), p. 53

KIERNAN RYAN

The crux of *The Merchant* is of course Shylock and the significance of his revenge. Conventional criticism has unflaggingly distorted or repressed the full implications of this problem, persisting for the most part in the romantic idealist conception of the play. According to this, *The Merchant* is a tragically tinged but, in the end, delightful romantic comedy, in which the ruling-class Christians triumph, by virtue of their selfless love and merciful generosity, over the threat posed to their happiness by the pitiable but essentially evil Jew. In John Russell Brown's representative view: 'We cannot doubt that Shylock must be condemned. However lively Shylock's dialogue may be, however plausibly and passionately he presents his case, however cruelly the lovers treat him, he must still be defeated, because he is an enemy to love's wealth and its free, joyful and continual giving.'

A telling endorsement of this position was provided several years ago by the eminent Shakespeare scholar, Samuel Schoenbaum. Reviewing a whole season of RSC productions, he singled out as the highpoint a production of *The Merchant* which had been 'rapturously received by an audience consisting almost entirely of Shakespeare scholars'. The virtue of the production, in Schoenbaum's eyes, was the director's 'refusal to be seduced by the opposing voice of the play', the voice, that is, of Shylock. The production is applauded for not being 'sentimental', despite 'the holocaust and the history of European Jewry in this century'. It is acclaimed for its 'courage to be faithful' to what Schoenbaum regards as the historically given 'main thrust of the play' against 'the Devil Jew'.

Conventional Marxist interpretations, moreover, are in complete agreement with this standard view of the play's 'main thrust'. The only real difference is their negative evaluation of the play as the blind tool of whatever they take to be the dominant Elizabethan ideology. Thus Elliot Krieger's *A Marxist Study of Shakespeare's Comedies* reads *The Merchant* as having forged by the end an elaborate ideological resolution designed to consolidate the sway of the aristocracy (Portia and Belmont) over the rising bourgeoisie (Venice and Shylock). While in Christian Enzensberger's long, ambitious study the play is no less reductively diagnosed as an ideological allegory of the triumph of merchant capitalism over Shylock's reactionary practice of usury, with Act V as the romantically refracted celebration of a merchant capitalist utopia. For Enzensberger the text cunningly dramatises and solves an in fact subordinate conflict of the period—mercantilism versus usury—as if it were the main conflict within society. It thus strives to conceal the really central contradiction between a racist capitalism and humanity.

But this contradiction, I would argue, is precisely what the play exposes to the gaze of a genuinely historical and dialectical approach. The cited critics are doomed, whether by their unhistorical impressionism or their one-dimensional historicism, to remain deaf from the start to the 'opposing voice' centred in Shylock, and therefore blind to the alternative and more valuable interpretive possibilities stored within the text. In responding to the play, we should not suppress the critical awareness we ought to have of 'the holocaust and the history of European Jewry in this century', nor should we resist the change in the angle of reception which such a modern consciousness creates. The extent to which the vision of *The Merchant of Venice* contradicts or coincides with the progressive viewpoint of the present must be proved first and foremost on the evidence of the text. But in the process we should not fail to take into account, at the historical pole of the interpretive dialectic, the fact that the conditions of literary production in Shakespeare's time made it possible for his plays to undermine rather than reproduce the normative ideological assumptions of his society. I will say more about this later in the chapter. Suffice it for the moment to suggest that, if one does bring these potentially converging past and present perspectives to bear upon the text together, *The Merchant of Venice* turns out to be dynamised by a profound struggle between conflicting impulses. Its true achievement consists in its relentless subversion of its own conventional commitments.

This process of self-subversion is organised through Shylock. It reaches its first explicit and devastating expression, of course, in his speech rebuking the Jew-baiting Christians on the grounds of their virtual common humanity:

> Hath not a Jew eyes? Hath not a Jew hands, organs, dimensions, senses, affections, passions; fed with the same food, hurt with the same weapons, subject to the same diseases, heal'd by the same means, warm'd and cool'd by the same winter and summer, as a Christian is? If you prick us, do we not bleed? If you tickle us, do we not laugh? If you poison us, do we not die? And if you wrong us, shall we not revenge? If we are like you in the rest, we will resemble you in that ... The villainy you teach me, I will execute, and it shall go hard but I will better the instruction.   (III.i.59–73)

With this speech there erupts into the play the full, protesting force of an irresistible egalitarian vision, whose basis in the shared faculties and needs of our common physical nature implicitly indicts all forms of inhuman discrimination. The speech provokes a radical shift of emotional allegiance, from which our perception of the comedy's Christian protagonists never recovers. Through Shylock, *The Merchant* proceeds to broach within itself a counter-perspective which cracks the received readings wide open and transfigures our understanding of the play.

The key line is that which defines the rationale of Shylock's revenge: '*The villainy you teach me, I will execute*'. The consequences of this line are worth thinking fully through. For what it makes plain is that Shylock's revenge signifies much more than the accustomed evil threat to the idyllic world of romance. It explains that Shylock's bloodthirsty cruelty is not simply the result of the Venetians' treatment of him, but the deliberate mirror-image of their concealed real nature. The revenge declares itself as a bitterly ironic parody of the Christians' own actual values, a calculated piercing of their unconsciously hypocritical facade. The whole point of Shylock's demanding payment of 'a *pound* of flesh', and of Antonio's heart in particular (III.i.127), lies in its grotesquely graphic attempt to translate the moral heartlessness of Venice into reality. For Venice is a world where the human heart is literally a quantifiable lump of meat, where indeed, as Shylock sardonically remarks,

> A pound of man's flesh, taken from a man,
> Is not so estimable, profitable neither,
> As flesh of muttons, beefs, or goats. (I.iii.165–7)

The revenge opens up the normally covert reality of a money-centred society, which has created Shylock in its own avaricious image only to victimise the Jew by projecting upon him its suppressed guilty hatred of itself.

This process of demystification climaxes in the trial scene. Once again it's a question of fully unpacking the implications of the text, of spelling out completely in this case the meaning of Shylock's insistence on his bond, on his acknowledged legal right to his pound of flesh. Castigated by the Christians for his merciless bloodlust, Shylock reminds them that by their own principles, in the eyes of their own law—as they themselves explicitly concede—he is 'doing no wrong'. On the contrary:

> You have among you many a purchas'd slave,
> Which like your asses, and your dogs and mules,
> You use in abject and in slavish parts,
> Because you bought them. Shall I say to you,
> 'Let them be free! Marry them to your heirs!
> Why sweat they under burthens?...'
> ... You will answer,
> 'The slaves are ours'. So do I answer you:
> The pound of flesh which I demand of him
> Is dearly bought as mine, and I will have it.
> If you deny me, fie upon your law! (IV.i.90–101)

What the established criticism has always repressed here is Shylock's irrefutable demonstration that his 'wolvish, bloody, starv'd, and ravenous' cruelty (IV.I.138) is the very foundation and institutionalised norm of this society, whose inhumanity is ratified as 'justice' by its laws. The play as romantic comedy has nothing to say in reply that can compensate for this annihilating realisation.

This is not to say, of course, that the play ends up justifying or excusing Shylock by turning its sympathy over to him. *The Merchant of Venice* operates at a level beyond the simplistic polarities of such sentimental moralism. To define the play in terms of which party deserves the blame and which the absolution, with readings and productions swinging now to Shylock and now to the Christians, is to miss the point. For what is at stake is the deeper recognition cutting across this that, through the revenge plot and the trial, through the ironies and contradictions they lay bare, *The Merchant* engineers a dramatic situation in which an apparently civilised form of society is unmasked as in fact premised on barbarity, on the ruthless priority of money-values over human values, of the rights of property over the most fundamental rights of men and women. The point lies not in the justification of the Jew at the expense of the Christians, or of the Christians at the expense of the Jew, but in the explanation and critique of the structural social forces which have made them both become what they are, for better and for worse.

What is fascinating, moreover, is the way the pressure exerted by this reinterpretation of the Shylock plot throws further latent dimensions of the text into unexpected relief, and thus brings them likewise within the scope of present appropriation.

It becomes evident, for example, that the casket-choosing plot at Belmont does more than test the moral competence of Portia's prospective husbands. It persistently underlines the contradiction between the apparent and the real nature of people and things, between conventionally supposed worth and actual value: 'All that glisters is not gold, / . . . Gilded tombs do worms enfold' (II.vii.65–9); 'So may the outward shows be least themselves' (III.ii.73). In so doing the casket-scenes serve to tune us to the frequency of the play's opposing voice. They educate our expectations in the seditious logic of inversion running through the play as a whole, reinforcing the central discovery of the Shylock plot that the social world of this comedy is the brutal reverse of what it seems and of how its heroes and heroines see it.

We might also reconsider, to take another instance, that intriguing first appearance of Launcelot Gobbo (II.ii.), where the clown presents himself in monologue as violently torn back and forth between his conscience's demand that he stay with his master the Jew and the devil's insistence that he abandon him. This ostensibly inconsequential scene can now be perceived to signify more than mere comic relief. As in other plays, especially *King Lear, As You Like It* and *Twelfth Night*, the fool acts here as a kind of personified index of the text's evolving overall viewpoint. Thus what Gobbo gives us in the passage in question is a condensed comic version of the crisis of moral allegiance provoked by Shylock at the heart of *The Merchant of Venice*. What has hitherto lain submerged as no more than a farcical interlude in the action proper surfaces as a key strategy of dramatic estrangement, as an internal objectification of the play's own tormented subconscious.

We can now begin to decipher as well the central enigma of Antonio, the merchant of Venice himself. The play's opening scene fastens at once upon the inexplicable mystery of Antonio's sadness, writhing itself into a knot of frustrated interrogation which is never subsequently unravelled. From then on the titular hero of the play remains a cryptically still and passive negative presence, the absence centre around which the action of the play revolves. But therein lies Antonio's true significance as the embodiment of the void at the heart of Venice. For it is in the text's rebellion against the expectations of its own title, in its conspicuously advertised refusal to project the merchant capitalist as hero, that the play's anguished rejection of the values increasingly prevailing over Shakespeare's world finds its distorted expression.

Furthermore, once we have allowed a consciously modern grasp of the Shylock problem to awaken us to the deep-seated prejudice and constitutional inhumanity of society in *The Merchant of Venice*, an equally undisguised present-day concern with sexual injustice enables us to recognise the play's disabused preoccupation with women's status as the alienated objects of masculine vision, choice and possession. As Portia exclaims:

> O me, the word choose! I may neither choose who I would, nor refuse who I dislike; so is the will of a living daughter curb'd by the will of a dead father.
> (I.ii.22–5)

For Bassanio she is first and foremost the means 'to get clear of all the debts I owe' (I.i.135)—'a lady richly left' (I.i.161) and imprisoned as her own image in a leaden casket: 'I am lock'd in one of them' (III.ii.40). The freedom of thought, speech, and behaviour she displays when alone with her maid Nerissa, or when disguised in male apparel as the lawyer Balthazar, only accentuates the rigid constrictions of her normal female identity as obedient daughter and, subsequently, submissive wife: 'Myself, and what is mine, to you and yours/Is now converted' (III.ii.166–7).

Re-examined from this angle of interest in the play, the fifth-act closure in supposed romantic harmony emerges as in fact fraught with malevolent insinuations. Even the first idyllic moonlit exchange cannot escape the shadow cast across the comedy by what Shylock's tale has taught us. Lorenzo and Jessica's hymning of their love is infected by a rash of sinister allusions to tragically doomed lovers: Troilus and Cressida, Pyramus and Thisbe, Dido and Aeneas, Jason and Medea (V.i.1–14). In the subsequent bantering encounter between the newly-wed couples (Portia and Bassanio, Gratiano and Nerissa) disquieting doubts are raised about the quality of the men's love by their failure of the love-test in giving away their rings: 'You swore to me,' protests Nerissa, 'when I did give it you, /That you would wear it till your hour of death' (V.i.152–3). The fact that the men unknowingly gave the rings to the disguised Portia and Nerissa themselves does not succeed in overriding the intractable reproaches in which the women persist for a third of the entire act (V.i.142–246). The sense of discord is amplified by Portia's and Nerissa's teasing threats of revenge through sexual infidelity: 'Lie not a night from home,' warns Portia, 'Watch me like Argus' (V.i.230). And it is on a note of equivocally contained male sexual anxiety that Gratiano ends the play; 'while I live I'll fear no other thing/ So sore, as keeping safe Nerissa's ring' (V.i.306–7).

Perhaps most unsettling of all, though, is the moment shortly before this, when Antonio offers to heal the rift between the lovers by pledging himself once again as surety for Bassanio:

> I once did lend my body for his wealth,
> . . . I dare be bound again,

My soul upon the forfeit, that your lord
Will never more break faith advisedly.   (V.i.249–53)

What is remarkable here is the ominous duplication on the sexual level of the triangular financial bond upon whose implications the would-be comedy has foundered, but with Portia now cast in the role previously assigned to Shylock. The conscious parallel conveys a subliminal oppression of the Jew and the sexual oppression of the female.

I have no space to do more than outline these embryonic insights into the changing meaning of *The Merchant of Venice,* all of which are confirmable, I would contend, through close textual analysis. The point I want to stress here is that the interpretive strategy responsible for these readings is neither arbitrary nor unhistorical. It postulates a historically produced semantic potential, a determinate range of verifiable, latent readings genetically secreted by the text. The context and angle of the work's reception will dictate which of these potential dimensions of meaning will subsequently be realised and which remain undiscerned or repressed. What *The Merchant of Venice* means today depends as much, in other words, on what we are prepared to make of it as it does on Shakespeare's text. The reading I have privileged represents a textually supported interpretive option inherent in the work, objectively encoded in the structure of words which constitutes the edition of the play being read. It is a demonstrably available interpretation, which could not be perceived and actualised within the successive horizons of the play's reception in the past, but which *can* be realised and elected to priority within the horizon of its politically progressive reception today.

For those who share the basic values which define that horizon, the perspective provided by a knowledge of the holocaust of the Jewish people, and a horror of that lethal juncture where capitalism and racism continue to intersect, should by no means be suppressed as anachronistic or extraneous, as Professor Schoenbaum suggests. On the contrary, that perspective ought to serve as the obligatory point of departure for any enlightened engagement with *The Merchant of Venice* at this point in history, so that it becomes increasingly inconceivable to evade or refuse the oppositional vision which the text invites us to appropriate today. The appropriation of this vision involves, moreover, the illuminating discovery that all along the play knew more about the world of its time and, indeed, our own than historicist criticism in particular deemed it capable of knowing; that it lay ready and waiting to reveal unexplored shores of imaginative perception in the fresh light of modern experience and understanding.

—KIERNAN RYAN, "Re-reading *The Merchant of Venice,*" *Shakespeare*
(Atlantic Highlands, NJ: Humanities Press, 1989), pp. 14–24

CRITICAL ESSAYS

Elmer Edgar Stoll

SHYLOCK

His beard was red; his face was made
Not much unlike a witches.
His habit was a Jewish gown,
That would defend all weather;
His chin turned up, his nose hung down,
And both ends met together.

So Shylock was made up, according to the report of the old actor Thomas Jordan in 1664, on a stage that was still swayed by the tradition of Alleyn and Burbage. Macklin kept all of this—nose and chin enough he had of his own—when, in the forties of the eighteenth century, he restored to the stage "the Jew that Shakespeare drew," and he ventured a red hat in early Venetian style for the old "orange-tawney",[1] into the bargain. "By Jove! Shylock in a black wig!" exclaimed a first-rater as Kean, seventy years after, appeared in the wings of Drury Lane for his first performance. And the part was played by Sir Henry Irving, in our day, in a grey beard and a black cap. Changes in costume (on the stage at least) are but the outward and visible tokens of change. Macklin's grotesque ferocity gave place to Kean's vast and varied passion, and it, in turn, to Macready's and Irving's Hebraic picturesqueness and pathos. Taste had changed, and racial antipathy, in art if not in life, had faded away. Macklin, in an age when a part must be either comic or tragic, and not both together, dropped the butt and kept the villain, and this he played with such effect that the audience shrank visibly from him, and, during the play and after it, King George II lost sleep. Kean made the Jew an injured human being, an outraged father. And Macready and Irving lifted him, in the words of Edmund Booth, "out of the darkness of his native element of revengeful selfishness into the light of the venerable Hebrew, the martyr, the avenger."

With this movement criticism has kept pace, or has gone before. Macklin's

From *Journal of English and Germanic Philology* 10 (1911): 236–37, 239–46, 249, 260–61, 266–79.

conception is in sympathy with Rowe's; Kean's with Hazlitt's and Skottowe's; and Macready and Irving take the great company of the later critics with them in their notions of racial pathos, and, despite the declarations of a Spedding, a Furnivall, and a Furness,[2] in their plea for toleration. Few critics have recognized the prejudices of the times, the manifest indications of the poet's purpose, and his thoroughly Elizabethan taste for comic villainy. The few are mostly foreigners—Brandes, Brandl, Creizenach, Morsbach, and Sarcey. Others take account of this point of view only to gainsay it. "We breathed a sigh of relief", says the New York *Nation* (as if the worst were over) in a review of Professor Baker's book on Shakespeare, "when we found him confessing his belief that Shakespeare did not intend Shylock to be a comic character;"[3] and the distinguished critics Bradley and Raleigh may be supposed to have done the same. As much as fifteen years ago Professor Wendell expressed the opinion that Shylock was rightly represented on the stage in Shakespeare's time as a comic character, and rightly in our time as sympathetically human; but the dramatist's intention he left in the dark. Undertaking, perhaps, to abolish this antinomy and to bridge the gap between Shakespeare's time and ours, Professor Schelling perceives in Shylock, quite subtly, a grotesqueness bordering on laughter and a pathos bordering on tears.[4] ⟨. . .⟩

To get at Shakespeare's intention is, after all, not hard. As with popular drama, great or small, he who runs may read—he who yawns and scuffles in the pit may understand. The time is past for speaking of Shakespeare as impartial or inscrutable; study of his work and that of his fellows as an expression of Elizabethan ideas and technique is teaching us better. The puzzle whether the *Merchant of Venice* is not meant for tragedy, for instance, clears up when, as Professor Baker suggests, we forget Sir Henry Irving's acting, and remember that the title,[5] and the hero, is not the *Jew of Venice* as he would lead us to suppose, that the play itself is, like such a comedy as *Measure for Measure* or *Much Ado,* not clear of the shadow of the fear of death, and that in closing with an act where Shylock and his knife are forgotten in the unraveling of the mystery between the lovers and the crowning of Antonio's happiness in theirs, it does not, from the Elizabethan point of view, perpetrate an anticlimax, but, like many another Elizabethan play, carries to completion what is a story for story's sake. "Shylock is, and has always been, the hero," says Professor Schelling. But when, then, does Shakespeare drop his hero out of the play for good before the fourth act is over? It is a trick which he never repeats—a trick, I am persuaded, of which he is not capable.

Hero or not, Shylock is given a villain's due. His is the heaviest penalty to be found in all the pound of flesh stories, including that in *Il Pecorone,* which served as a model for this. Not in the Servian, the Persian, the African version, or even that of the *Cursor Mundi* does the money-lender suffer like Shylock—impoverishment, sentence of death, and an outrage done to his faith from which Jews were guarded even by decrees of German Emperors and Roman pontiffs. It was in the old play, perhaps, but that Shakespeare retained it shows his indifference to the amenities, to say the least, as regards either Jews or Judaism. Shylock's griefs excite no commiseration; indeed, as they press upon him they are barbed with gibes and jeers. The lot of Coriolanus is not dissimilar, but we know that the poet is with him. We know that the poet is not with Shylock, for on that head, in this play as in every other, the impartial, inscrutable poet leaves little or nothing to suggestion or surmise. As is his custom elsewhere, by the comments of the good characters, by the method pursued in the disposition of scenes, and by the downright avowals of soliloquy, he constantly sets us right.

As for the first of these artifices, all the characters who come in contact with Shylock except Tubal, among them being those of his own house—his servant and his daughter—have a word or two to say on the subject of his character, and never a good one. And in the same breath they spend on Bassanio and Antonio, his enemies, nothing but words of praise. Praise or blame, moreover, is, after Shakespeare's fashion, usually in the nick of time to guide the hearer's judgment. Lest the Jew should make too favorable an impression by his Scripture quotations, Antonio observes that the devil can cite Scripture for his purpose; lest the Jew's motive in foregoing interest, for once in his life, should seem like the kindness Antonio takes it to be, Bassanio avows that he likes not fair terms and a villain's mind; and once the Jew has caught the Christian on the hip, every one, from Gaoler to Duke, has words of horror for him and of compassion for his victim. As for the second artifice, the ordering of the scenes is such as to enforce this contrast. First impressions are momentous, every playwright knows (and no one better than Shakespeare himself), particularly for the purpose of ridicule. Launcelot and Jessica, in separate scenes, are introduced before Shylock reaches home, that, hearing their story, we may side with them, and, when the old curmudgeon appears, may be moved to laughter as he complains of Launcelot's gormandizing, sleeping, and rending apparel out, and as he is made game of by the young conspirators to his face. Still more conspicuous is this care when Shylock laments over his daughter and his ducats. Lest then by any means the tender-hearted should grieve, Solanio reports his outcries—in part word for word—two scenes in advance, as matter of mirth to himself and all the boys in Venice. And as for the third artifice, that a sleepy audience may not make the mistake of the cautious critic and take the villain for the hero, Shakespeare is at pains to label the villain by an aside at the moment the hero appears on the boards:

> I hate him for he is a Christian,
> But more for that in low simplicity
> He lends out money gratis, and brings down
> The rate of usance here with us in Venice.

Those are his motives, confessed repeatedly,[6] and either one brands him as a villain more unmistakably in that day, as we shall see, than in ours. Of the indignities which he has endured he speaks, too, and of revenge; but of none of these has he anything to say at the trial. There he pleads his oath, perjury to his soul should he break it, his "lodged hate", or his "humor"; but here to himself and to Tubal—"were he out of Venice I can make what merchandise I will"—he tells, in the thick of the action, the unvarnished truth. As with Shakespeare's villains generally, Aaron, Iago, or Richard III, only what they say concerning their purposes aside or to their confidants can be relied upon; and Shylock's oath, or his horror of perjury, is belied, as Dr. Furness[7] observes, by his clutching at thrice the principal when the pound of flesh escapes him, just as is his money-lender's ruse of borrowing the cash from "a friend" (avowed as such by Moses in the *School for Scandal*) by his going home "to purse the ducats straight." His arguments, too, are given a specious, not to say grotesque, coloring. Hazlitt and other critics say that in argument Shylock has the best of it.

> What if my house be troubled with a rat
> And I be pleas'd to give *ten* thousand ducats
> To have it ban'd?

This rat is a human being, but the only thing to remark upon, in Shylock's opinion, is his willingness to squander ten thousand ducats on it. Even in Hazlitt's day, moreover, a choice of "carrion flesh" in preference to ducats could not be plausibly compared as a "humor" with an aversion to pigs or the bag-pipe, or defended as a right by the analogy of holding slaves;[8] nor could the practice of interest-taking find a warrant in Jacob's pastoral trickery while in the service of Laban; least of all in the day when Sir John Hawkins, who initiated the slave-trade with the Earls of Pembroke and Leicester and the Queen herself for partners, bore on the arms[9] which were granted him for his exploits a demi-Moor, proper, in chains, and in the day when the world at large still held interest-taking to be but theft. Very evidently, moreover, Shylock is discomfited by Antonio's question "Did he take interest?" for he falters and stumbles in his reply—

> No, not take interest, not, as you would say,
> Directly, interest,—

and is worsted, in the eyes of the audience if not in his own, by the use of the old Aristotelian argument of the essential barrenness of money, still gospel in Shakespeare's day, in the second question,

> Or is your gold and silver ewes and rams?

For his answer is meant for nothing better than a piece of complacent shameless-ness:

> I cannot tell: I make it breed as fast.

Only twice does Shakespeare seem to follow Shylock's pleadings and reason-ings with any sympathy—"Hath a dog money?" in the first scene in which he appears, and "Hath not a Jew eyes?" in the third act—but a bit too much has been made of this. Either plea ends in such fashion as to alienate the audience. To Shylock's reproaches the admirable Antonio, "one of the gentlest and humblest of all the men in Shakespeare's theatre",[10] praised and honored by every one but

Shylock, retorts, secure in his virtue, that he is just as like to spit on him and spurn him again. And Shylock's celebrated justification of his race runs headlong into a justification of his villainy:—"The villainy which you teach me I will execute, and it shall go hard but I will better the instruction." "Hath not a Jew eyes?" and he proceeds to show that your Jew is no less than a man, and as such has a right, not to respect or compassion as the critics of a century have had it, but to revenge. Neither large nor lofty are his claims. Quite as vigorously and, in that day, with as much reason, the detestable and abominable Aaron defends his race and color, and Edmund, the dignity of bastards. The worst of his villains Shakespeare allows to plead their cause: their confidences in soliloquy, if not, as here, slight touches in the plea itself, sufficiently counteract any too favorable impression. This, on the face of it, is a plea for indulging in revenge with all its rigors; not a word is put in for the nobler side of Jewish character; and in lending Shylock his eloquence Shakespeare is but giving the devil his due.[11]

By all the devices of Shakespeare's dramaturgy, then, Shylock is proclaimed, as by the triple repetition of a crier, to be the villain, a comic villain, though, or butt. Nor does the poet let pass any of the prejudices of that day which would heighten this impression. A miser, a money-lender, a Jew,—all three had from time immemorial been objects of popular detestation and ridicule, whether in life or on the stage. The union of them in one person is the rule in Shakespeare's day, both in plays and in "character"-writing: to the popular imagination a moneylender was a sordid miser with a hooked nose. So it is in the acknowledged prototype of Shylock, Marlowe's "bottle-nosed" monster, Barabas, the Jew of Malta. Though more of a villain, he has the same traits of craft and cruelty, the same unctuous friendliness hiding a thirst for a Christian's blood, the same thirst for blood outreaching his greed of gold, and the same spirit of unrelieved egoism which thrusts aside the claims of his family, his nation, or even his faith. If Barabas fawns like a spaniel when he pleases, grins when he bites, heaves up his shoulders when they call him dog, Shylock, for his part, "still bears it with a patient shrug", and "grows kind", seeking the Christian's "love" in the hypocritical fashion of Barabas with the suitors and the friars. If Barabas ignores the interests of his brother Jews, poisons his daughter, "counts religion but a childish toy", and, in various forms, avows the wish that "so I live perish may all the world", Shylock has no word for the generous soul but "fool" and "simpleton",[12] and cries, "fervid patriot" that he is, "martyr and avenger": "A diamond gone, cost me two thousand ducats in Frankfort! The curse never fell upon our nation until now. I never felt it till now." Such is his love of his race, which Professor Raleigh says is "deep as life".[13] And in the next breath he cries, "the affectionate father": "Two thousand ducats in that; and other precious, precious jewels. I would my daughter were dead at my foot, and the jewels in her ear ... and the ducats in her coffin." This alternation of daughter and ducats itself comes from Marlowe's play, as well as other ludicrous touches, such as your Jew's stinginess with food and horror of swine-eating, and the confounding of Jew and devil. This last is an old, wide-spread superstition: on the strength of holy writ the

Fathers, with the suffrage in late years of Luther, held that the Jews were devils and the synagogue the house of Satan.[14] In both plays it affords the standing joke, in the *Merchant of Venice* nine times repeated.[15] "Let me say Amen betimes", exclaims Salanio in the midst of his good wishes for Antonio, "lest the devil cross my prayer, for here he comes in the likeness of a Jew". And in keeping with these notions Shylock's synagogue is, as Luther devoutly calls it, *ein Teuffels Nest,* the nest for hatching his plot once he and Tubal and the others of his "tribe" can get together. "Go, go, Tubal", he cries in the unction of his guile, "and meet me at our synagogue; go, good Tubal, at our synagogue, Tubal!"[16] It is highly probable, moreover, that Shylock wore the red hair and beard, mentioned by Jordan, from the beginning, as well as the bottle-nose of Barabas. So Judas was made up from of old, and in their immemorial orange-tawny, highcrowned hats, and "Jewish gaberdines", the very looks of the two usurers welcomed horror and derision. In both plays the word Jew, itself a badge of opprobrium, is constantly in use instead of the proper name in question and as a byword for cruelty and cunning. ⟨...⟩

In the Elizabethan drama and character-writing, then, the Jew is both money-lender and miser, a villain who hankers after the Christians' blood, a gross egoist, even an atheist, though charged with dealings with the devil, and at the same time a butt, a hook-nosed niggard. A similar spirit of rude caricature and boisterous burlesque, with even less of characterization, prevails in the treatment of the Jews in early popular drama on the Continent. Such is the soil from which the figure of Shylock grew. For everything in Shakespeare is a growth, and strikes root deep in the present and the past, in stage tradition and in human life. ⟨...⟩

That the Jew was a devil, we remember, was a matter of common belief and pleasantry. Nor was the Jew, in medieval imagination at least, to be outdone, for according to Luther, who in his diatribe has all too much to say of spitting, meta-phorically or literally, a threefold expectoration accompanied the Jewish curse of Christ.[17]

Here we touch on one of the charges against the Jews which lie embedded in Shakespeare's other work, among the few casual references which he makes to them. "Liver of blaspheming Jew" is cast into the cauldron by the Witches in *Macbeth,* along with the other unholy odds and ends:—

> Nose of Turk and Tartar's lips,
> Finger of birth-strangled babe
> Ditch-deliver'd by a drab.

Blasphemy is a charge made from the time of the Fathers.[18] Three times daily the Jews were supposed to rail against Christ in their prayers. That they should be restrained from such blasphemy was a special recommendation of the committee appointed by the Council in 1655 to consider the re-settlement of the Jews in England.[19] In that day when a man had to look out for his God as well as for himself, Luther took this matter of blasphemy particularly hard. Again and again in his tractate he belabors the Jews for it; and he would have their synagogues and their houses, as the scenes of such impiety, burned down and removed forever from the sight of man. "Und solchs sol man thun unserm Herrn und der Christenheit zu Ehren, damit Gott sehe dass wir Christen seyn!" Hardness of heart is another implied accusation, several times repeated. "A Jew would have wept," sobs Launce, before his cruel-hearted cur, "to have seen our parting." Shylock himself is intended as a capital instance: the Duke, Antonio, Bassanio and Gratiano all recognize in him the "Jewish heart", "uncapable of pity"—"than which what's harder?"—and it is this that gave point, now lost, to Portia's praise of mercy. People generally—Protestants like Luther and Prynne, for instance—believed, as in some parts of Europe they believe still, that the Jews, especially about the time of the Passover, caught little Christians and crucified them, poisoned the wells or the air, and dealt death and destruction about them as freely as Barabas in the play.[20] After all this, one other charge, no more than vaguely hinted at in Shakespeare but made explicit, as we have seen, in Marlowe, that of atheism, need not surprise us. Absurd as it is, it comes down from ancient times, and it is no more absurd than Luther's charge of blasphemy and idolatry,[21] made a few years before Marlowe wrote.

Shylock, we do not forget, was also a usurer. Dr. Honigmann, who is of those who interpret the *Merchant of Venice* as a plea for toleration, says that in Shakespeare's day the word did not carry with it any stigma.[22] Never was opinion more mistaken. By laws civil and ecclesiastical, usury—that is, the exaction of interest of any sort—was a crime. With expanding trade and manufacture the practice was widening, but no one approved of it in principle. ⟨. . .⟩

Shylock was both money-lender and Jew. In him are embodied two of the deepest and most widely prevalent social antipathies of two thousand years, still sanctioned, in Shakespeare's day, by the teachings of religion. What was religious in them Shakespeare probably shared, like any other easy-going churchman, but all that was popular and of the people was part and parcel of his breath and blood.

It is impossible to undertake a minute and particular refutation. To show that Shakespeare is entering a plea, Shylock has on the one hand been conceived as a good man, much abused; and on the other hand as a bad man made bad. The misconception in the first case is so gross—as Professor Schelling has said, so preposterous—that we will not linger upon it. It is the result of reading Shakespeare as if he wrote but yesterday. Shakespeare, as we have seen, takes pains with first impressions and general effects, and is careless of detail: if the detail is important it is repeated or expatiated upon. Modern poets, as Browning, Ibsen and Maeterlinck, frame characters and plots that are problems and puzzles, in which detail is everything. We are likely at first to sympathize with Helmar instead of Nora, in the *Doll's House,* and with Guido instead of Prinzivalle or the heroine, in *Monna Vanna.* If we lose a word or a look, we lose the meaning of the whole. Turning straight from these to Shakespeare, we are likely to lose the meaning of the whole in our eagerness to catch every wandering word or look. Clues to the situation are found in matters such as the bits of satire in which Shylock, like Barabas, lets fling at the ways of Christians, which one might as wisely take for one's leading-strings as the

gibes of Mephistopheles in Faust;[23] or such as the Christians' willingness to feast with
the Jew, Launcelot's scruples against running away from him, or the Jew's opinion
of Launcelot as a lazy and gluttonous fellow. It is by this process of making the big
little and the little big, as in the reflection of a convex mirror, this process of reading
into Shakespeare a lot of considerations of which he knew nothing, and reading out
of him all his minor improbabilities and inconsistencies,[24] that Dr. Honigmann[25] and
Professor Jastrow[26] arrive at the conception of Shylock as advocate and avenger,—
injured by a daughter ill brought up, they say, by this Launcelot, actuated by a sense
of justice, swearing his oath in a paroxysm of moral self-coercion like another
William Tell, hating Antonio, not because he is a Christian, but because by lending
money gratis he deprives Hebrews of the means of livelihood, and inveigling him
into signing the bond that he may humble him and then by an act of generosity heap
coals of fire on his head! One wonders whether the language of Shakespeare is any
longer capable of conveying thought, or is become indeed a cryptogram. The
Christians feast the Jew not from respect for him, but to give Lorenzo a chance to
run away with Jessica; just as Lorenzo runs away with Jessica and the ducats, not,
as François Victor Hugo thinks, to satisfy his own or the dramatist's enlightened
convictions on the subject of intermarriage, but, so far as the purposes of the play
are concerned, to give point to Shylock's revenge. Both are matters of story, of
improbabilities not, in modern fashion, smoothed away, or, very likely, if Gosson's
play were known, a matter of sources. And as for Launcelot's scruples, they, like his
laziness and gluttony, are a joke, as in Shylock's sneer at[27] "these Christian husbands," Bassanio and Gratiano, who, in the presence of their newly wedded wives,
as only the audience is aware, vow, in the fervor of friendship, that to save their
friend they would sacrifice their wives and all. "Censure of profane swaggering
about the purest sentiments," observes Professor Jastrow, severely.

Those who will have it that Shylock, though bad, was made so, do violence to
Shakespeare in two different quarters. In the first place, they have recourse to an
all-pervading irony. Antonio, gentlest and humblest of Shakespeare's heroes, kicking
and spitting at Jews and thrusting salvation down their throats,—such, as they say,
is the spectacle of race-hatred to which Shakespeare points.[28] And those others
who will have it that Shylock is a noble spirit brought to shame, carry the irony still
farther, into the characterization of Antonio and his friends. He, not Shylock, is the
caricature![29] His virtues are but affectations and shams; his friends are debauchees,
parasites, and fribbles! That is, nothing is what it seems; a comedy ending in
moonlight blandishments and badinage is a tragedy, and the play written for the
customers of the Globe flies over their honest heads to the heights of nineteenth-
century transcendentalism! Irony is surely unthinkable unless the author intends it,
and here not the slightest trace of such an intention appears. Moreover, a play of
Shakespeare's is self-contained; the irony is within it, so to speak, not underneath
it. There is irony in the appearance of Banquo at the moment when Macbeth
presumes hypocritically to wish for his presence at the feast, or, more obviously
still, in the fulfillment of the Witches' riddling oracles, but there is no irony such as

Mr. Yeats discovers in the success of Henry V and the failure of Richard II.[30] Shakespeare does not dream that to fail and be a Richard is better than to succeed and be a Henry—or an Antonio. He knows not the ways of modern idealism, which sets the judgment of the world aside, nor the ways of modern artistic expression, which withholds the purport of the higher judgment from the world. No abysmal irony undermines his hard sense and straightforward meaning. Shylock is indeed condemned: Sir Henry Irving took no counsel of the poet when he made his exit from the ducal palace in pathetic triumph.

In the second place, they do violence to Shakespeare in representing Shylock as the product of his environment.[31] The thoughts of men had not begun to run in those channels; the ancient rigors of retribution held fast; men still believed in heaven and hell, in villains and heroes. Though in him there is little of George Eliot's moral rigor, as brought to bear on Tito Melema, for instance, Mr. Yeats errs, I think, in his opinion that Shakespeare's plays are, like all great literature, "written in the spirit of the Forgiveness of Sin." Macbeth is not forgiven, nor is Othello. Richard III and Iago were damned even in the making. And though the shortcomings of Falstaff, Bardolph, Pistol, and Nym serve a while as food for mirth, Shakespeare is in full accord with Henry V as he casts his fellows out of his company and out of his mind, to meet their end in the brothel or on the gallows. Except in comedy, he has not the spirit of forgiveness which, like Uncle Toby's for the Devil, comes of mere kindness of heart; and neither in comedy nor in tragedy has he the forgiveness of our psychological and social drama and novel, where villains and heroes are no more, which comes of fullness of knowledge. Thus he deals with poverty, the hard-handed, greasy, foul-smelling, ignorant, and ungrateful multitude for which he so often utters his aversion; and thus he deals with the kindred subject of heredity. If a scoundrel is a bastard, or is of mean birth, the fact is not viewed as an extenuating circumstance, but is turned to a reproach. It may in a sense explain his depravity, but never explain it away. It sets the seal upon it. It confirms the prejudice that there is a difference between noble blood and that of low degree. So, though our hearts are softened by Shylock's recital of the indignities he has suffered, the hearts of the Elizabethans, by a simpler way of thinking, are hardened. It confirms the prejudice that there is a difference between Christian and Jew. The Fathers, Protestant theologians like Luther, seventeenth-century lawyers like Coke and Prynne, review the pitiful story of the Jews in Europe grimly, with at best a momentary and furtive pathos.[32] It proves their notion of the curse. What else, in an age when it was the universal belief that Jew and Gentile alike took upon their heads the curse of Adam's sin on issuing from the mother's womb? Even today a man who is abused in the street is supposed, by bystanders, to deserve it; the world barks at rags and poverty like the dogs; and every one knows that there are certain scars—as of branding—which a wise man does not exhibit or complain of. And how much more in the days of literary and theological bludgeoning; when the reformers were to the common enemy, and to one another, dogs, hogs, and asses; when Shakespeare himself let one of his noblest characters cast it up to another that he possessed but one trunk of clothes; when Milton was reviled, in scholarly Latin, for his blindness and (in defiance of fact) for his guttering eyelids; and when Dryden never heard the last of the beating he got at the instigation of a fellow poet in a London street. For everything there is some one to blame, is the point of view, and who so much as he who has the worst of it?

> And every loss the men of Jebus bore,
> They still were thought God's enemies the more!

Such is the logic of Luther as he puts to the Jew the crushing question (naively exhorting Christians, if they must speak to Jews at all, to do likewise, and "not to quarrel with them"): "Hear'st thou, Jew, dost thou know that Jerusalem, your temple, and your priesthood have been destroyed now over fourteen hundred and sixty years?"[33] Even at the end of the seventeenth century Robert South, as he considers the universal detestation in which, through the ages, Jews have been held, must conclude that there is "some peculiar vileness essentially fixed in the genius of this people."[34] It does not occur to him that there is no one to blame, and that the cause of the detestation lies in race-hatred, the incompatibility of temperament and customs. "What's his reason?" cries Shylock. It is the reason which Antonio—that is, Shakespeare—is not analytical enough to recognize or cynical enough to avow. Steadily the Jewishness of Shylock is kept before us; like Barabas, he loses his name in his nationality—"the Jew," "the dog Jew," "the villain Jew," "his Jewish heart;"—and it is not merely according to the measure of his villainy that at the end and throughout the play he suffers. Shakespeare himself would have said, with Robert South, that the reason was his "essential Jewish vileness;" but we, who in the light of modern psychology and the history of society are aware that no man and no age can render adequately the reason why they themselves do anything, recognize that the famous reason given by Shylock himself, in the heat of his *ex parte* pleading with which Shakespeare so little sympathizes, curiously enough hits the mark.[35]

With this conventionality in mind we may approach the final question, whether villain and butt as Shylock is, he may not also be, as Professor Schelling thinks, a pathetic creation. Mr. Schelling speaks of Shylock as "semi-humorous",[36] a character in whom there is a grotesqueness bordering on laughter and a pathos bordering on tears.[37] The union of butt and villain is, as we have seen, common in Shakespeare's day, and it is as old as the stupid devils of the miracle-plays; and the union of villain and droll goes back to the cleverer devils, those of Dante, too, and medieval painting, and underlies the characterization of most of the villains—Aaron and Iago, for instance—in Shakespearean and Elizabethan drama. But villain, butt, and pathetic figure, all in one, is a thing hard to conceive. Drollery or ludicrousness and pathos coalesce, then as now, in Ibsen's Ulric Brendel or in Shakespeare's Mercutio and his clowns; but derision mingling with pathos would be like water poured into the fire. Round Shylock's words about Leah and the turquoise the question centers.

TUBAL: One of them showed me a ring that he had of your daughter for a monkey.

SHYLOCK: Out upon her. Thou torturest me, Tubal. It was my turquoise; I had it of Leah when I was a bachelor. I would not have given it for a wilderness of monkeys.

This, most critics assert, the great historian of the drama[38] almost alone dissenting, is pathos: it is not the ducats behind the turquoise (a diamond gone, cost me two thousand ducats in Frankfort!) but the thought of Leah that wrings his heart. "What a fine Hebraism is implied in this expression!" cries Hazlitt. "He has so deep a veneration for his dead wife," says Hawkins, with impenetrable gravity, "that a wilderness of monkeys would not compensate for the loss of the ring she had given him in youth."[39] More Elizabethan wit running to waste! We may not be used to laughing at a man as he mourns the flight of his daughter, the memory of his wife, or the theft of his ducats; but neither are we used, any more than Salanio or the boys of Venice, to the manner of his mourning.

I never heard a passion so confus'd,
So strange, outrageous, and so variable.

Shylock is a puppet, and Tubal pulls the string. Now he shrieks in grief for his ducats or his daughter, now in glee at Antonio's ruin. In his rage over the trading of a turquoise for a monkey, he blurts out, true to his instinct for a bargain, "not for a wilderness of monkeys," and the Elizabethan audience, as well as some few readers today, have the heart—or the want of it—to think the valuation funny. The rest may find it hard to laugh at that, as, in the opinion of Rousseau, Taine, Mantzius, and many another candid spirit, it is nowadays hard to laugh at the plight of Molière's Alceste, Georges Dandin, or Arnolphe, or, to come nearer home, as it is hard to laugh at the torments of Malvolio; but in all these instances the invitation to hilarity is plain and clear. It is too late in the day to modernize and transmogrify Molière; but in lands where Shylock's love for Leah moves men to tears, Mr. Sothern may presume, as Professor Baker has noted, to elicit sympathy for the "affection'd ass," pleading in his madman's chains to be set free. The mistake of the critics in the present case, however, is in part that of viewing the text piece by piece and not as a whole. Torn from the context, there are phrases, even sentences, that may, indeed, seem pathetic. But Shakespeare plays the familiar dramatic trick of taking the audience in for a moment—of clapping upon a seemingly pathetic sentiment a cynical, selfish, or simply incongruous one. Shylock cannot wish that his daughter were dead at his foot (if that be pathos) without, while he is at it, wishing that the jewels were in her ear, the ducats in her coffin;[40] he cannot think of Launcelot's kindness, as he parts with him, without also thinking of his appetite; and when he hears of his turquoise traded off for a monkey, thoughts of Leah, his bachelorhood, and a wilderness of monkeys clatter through his brain. Here is pathos side by side with laughter, but not according to Mr. Schelling's thought. The nuances, the harmony is lacking—in true Elizabethan style, there is glaring contrast instead. The pathos is a pretense, the laughter alone is real. The laughter is not restrained, either, but would be nothing less than a roar: the grotesqueness goes over the border of laughter—perhaps of tears.

The trial scene is another place where Shylock has seemed pathetic. Almost all critics make him so, in spite of the scales and the knife-whetting and the jeers at the Jew's discomfiture. Professor Baker holds that Shakespeare evinces a sense of dramatic values in presenting Shylock's disappointment as tragic through his eyes, amusing through Gratiano's. How is the tragic value presented? By the miser and usurer's prostrate prayer to the Duke to take his life if he will take his wealth, or by his plea that he is not well? The biter bit, is the gibe cast at him at the end of *Il Pecorone;*[41] and that, exactly, is the spirit of the scene. Nor is Gratiano the only one to crow. "Thou shalt have justice, more than thou desir'st.—Soft! The Jew shall have all justice—Why doth the Jew pause? Take thy forfeiture—Tarry, Jew; the law hath yet another hold on you—Art thou contented, Jew? What dost thou say?" Aimed at Shylock as he pleads and squirms, these words fall from lips which a moment before extolled the heavenly qualities of mercy! But here, as in Antonio's notion of conversion, or the Duke's notion of clemency to Jews, is the irony of history, not of art. Shakespeare's thought is as simple and sincere as is the old hagiographer's about the balancing of Jews' ledgers by royal edict. *Pacem operatur justicia.*

Professor Baker asks why "if Shakespeare wished to create laughter by Shylock, he kept him out of the fifth act, thus losing the many opportunities which his forlorn, defeated condition would have given to delight the Jew-baiters." But that would have been to make a point of the matter, and to raise the Jewish question in a play where the Jew's story is, and is meant to be, but an episode. That question, or the slavery question, which Professor Jastrow—not Shylock—raises,[42] or the sex question, or any other, had for Shakespeare, or his brother playwrights, no existence. To him things were solid and settled; he was a conservative in art, as well as in life; and in his plays he had no brief, followed no program. The Jews he made ridiculous not because he himself had a grudge against them, but, just as he made London citizens, Puritans, Frenchmen, and Welshmen ridiculous, because, as he might have said, they were so. He took the world as he found it, and in no respect more than in matters of mirth.

Nor by nature was Shakespeare a satirist. Shylock is the only full-length caricature, perhaps, he ever drew, and he is rather a burlesque,—a burlesque by virtue not only of the extravagance of the portrayal but of the inadvertent indulgence of it. Unlike Mr. Sidney Lee[43] (if he still holds to the view), I cannot find pathos in the remark

The patch is kind enough,

which Shylock makes as he looks after Launcelot dancing out the door, any more than I can in that about the turquoise. Our sympathies—even ours today—are engrossed and forestalled by Launcelot and Jessica, and we are not likely to concern ourselves, as Mr. Lee would have us do, about Launcelot's present deceptions and scant deservings. Any pathos, moreover, that the remark might have evoked would immediately have been swallowed up, as is the thought of Launcelot's kindliness in the miser's breast, by the words "but a huge feeder" which follow. The real significance of the remark, as of the other little touches in Shylock's character, his pride in his sober house, his memories of Leah, or the simplicity of his last words on the stage, lies in the casual quality of it—beyond the satiric scheme—a cozy individuality which Shakespeare adds almost unawares. Thus the logic of the characterization is disturbed, but the reality of it is heightened. It is thoroughly English, free-handed art, not French. Here, no doubt, lies one of the difficulties of the critics, imbued, as is all the modern world, with Gallic regularity and restraint. That at Harpagon, miser every inch of him, we are meant to laugh, there can be no question; but at Shylock, miser, usurer, and Jew we hesitate, at times, to laugh, because at those times he is something more.

So far and so far only is there any basis for the modern notion of Shylock as a sympathetic character. Yet most critics, I apprehend, will hold, as some hold already, that to us he must be a man more sinned against than sinning, a hero or martyr, despite the fact that to Shakespeare he was nothing of the sort. From of old the inroads of science and history have driven men to their refuge of the "two-fold truth." It is the weakness of our minds, perhaps their safeguard. The Romans enthroned the Greek and Egyptian gods by their own. A century and a half after Copernicus, Milton, the iconoclast, ventured to make room in his great poem for the Solar System only by the side of the Ptolemaic. But truth is not twofold, for all "the higher synthesis." The question is, is the earth—the twentieth century—the hub and centre of things? Is criticism to remain as naive and arrogant as the philosophy of many a primitive people, which has it that the navel of the earth is in Delphi, the Forum, or a certain spot in Greenland, and that the name "people" belongs to them alone?[44] If for us the real and permanent meaning of the *Merchant of Venice* was reserved, then Shakespeare must have reserved it knowingly or unknowingly. That the actor and gentleman-sharer, who never published a play, should have written for the globe a burlesque part which he meant, in some milder time, to be taken for nothing short of pathetic and tragic, is an hypothesis too colossal for my mind, at least, to compass. He, of all men, surely, was no alien and stranger to his age, no "pilgrim of eternity." And as for unconscious deviation from his purpose and inadvertent relenting toward the mark of his ridicule, traces of that I have pointed out above. But why not go farther? Why is Shylock, though meant to be butt and villain, not, in spite of the poet, a hero, like Milton's Satan? But Milton's Satan, like Dante's Farinata, is not a hero—we sentimentalize and wrest the text when we make him such—and is just such an instance of unconscious sympathy, artistic rather than moral, as we have already found. And neither Milton nor Dante swerves so far, consciously or unconsciously, as to turn burlesque comedy into tragedy, or villainy into vengeance and martyrdom? What poet could? For genius, though mysterious, is nothing mystical, and is not uplifted beyond reach of reason and common sense. It is no oracle, but the true and troubled voice of the age. It has no knowledge of the future—*sortes Homericae, Virgilianae, Biblicae,* forsooth! When will criticism have done with Apollo and his tripod, cast aside by poetry long ago? At present, the word "prescience" or "omniscience of genius" is little else than a critic's innocent method of begging the question. It lends color to the foisting into a sixteenth-century playhouse book of twentieth-century morals, ideas, and scientific facts. Why do they not find them in Beaumont or Webster, Jonson or Marlowe? Shakespeare's ways are their ways, and his thoughts their thoughts (and the ways and thoughts of many another, for that matter, before him); nor does his genius differ from theirs except in rank and degree. To hear the critics, you would think that on the twenty-third day of April, 1616, the earth yawned and the light of the sun and moon was darkened.[45]

As we have done with many another monster in history, literature, or holy writ, we have tanned and domesticated the "dog Jew", and drawn his "fangs." "He will speak soft words unto us," he no longer grins or bites. But Shakespeare and the Elizabethans, as we have seen, shuddered at him and laughed at him, and except at popular performances, where racial antipathy is rather to be allayed than fomented, so should we, as much as in us lies, today. Thus we shall come into sympathy with the manifest intention of the poet, with the acting of the part on the Elizabethan stage, with the conception of the money-lending Jew in the contemporary drama, character-writing, and ballad, and with the lively prejudices of the time. A villain and a butt, "une simple figure a gifles," as Francisque Sarcey shrewdly observes, "un monstrueux grotesque, sur le nez de qui tombent à l'envi d'effroyables nasardes",[46]—such, save for a few happily irrelevant touches, and for the splendor of poetry shed, like the rain and the light of heaven, on the just and the unjust, is the impression which Shylock makes after he has been duly restored to the sixteenth century, an impression in which pathos has no place, and with which our notions of justice and social responsibility, on the one hand, or of ironical art, on the other, have, so far as they are merely modern, nothing to do. So he is not lost to us. That Hebraic and picturesque figure will be remembered long after he has retreated from the warm circle of our sentiments, and be visited again and again, by an exhilarating sally of the imagination, in the midst of the harsh and sturdy life where he belongs.

NOTES

[1] Usurers should have orange-tawney Bonnets, because they doe Iudaize:—Bacon's Essay of Usury (Furness).
[2] See Furness's *Variorum Merchant of Venice*, pp. 433–5.
[3] August 15, 1907.
[4] Since this article was finished I have come upon the third volume of Mr. W. H. Hudson's *Elizabethan Shakespeare*, which contains the *Merchant of Venice*. In the introduction Mr. Hudson declares for historical criticism almost as unreservedly as heart could wish, and except for his silence concerning the comic aspects of Shylock, his interpretation of the character is in spirit almost identical with that presented in these pages.

[5] No great weight, of course, can, with justice, be given to this circumstance, but it is significant that modern critics and translators object to the title as it stands.

[6] *M. V.* I. 3, 13f; III. 1, 55f, 133, III. 3, 2—the fool that lends out money gratis; line 22t:
I oft delivered from his forfeitures
Many that have at times made moan to me:
Therefore he hates me.

[7] *Variorum M. V.* p. 233.

[8] *M. V.* IV. I, 35–100.

[9] See Hawkins in the *Dictionary of National Biography.*

[10] Cf. J. W. Hales, *English Historical Review* ix, p. 652f. Cf. p. 660 for an accumulation of the evidence for his goodness and amiableness. "A kinder gentleman treads not the earth."

[11] It is in these passages, no doubt, that, according to Mr. Hudson (*v. ante,* n. 4), the racial feeling rises superior to Shylock's greed and personal ferocity and Shylock becomes an impressive, tragic figure. I dislike to disagree with a critic with whom I have found myself, unawares, so often agreeing, but I think that at this point Mr. Hudson has not quite shaken off the spell of the *Zeitgeist,* of which, as he himself confesses, it is hard to rid the mind. As I show below, these appeals did not reach the hearts of the Elizabethans as they reach ours. Mr. Hudson explains them, like Professor Wendell, as moments where Shylock "got too much for Shakespeare", and said what he liked. But that dark saying I cannot comprehend—not in itself and still less on the lips of a critic who protests, so justly, against treating the characters of Shakespeare as if they were real people in a real world. What else are Mr. Hudson and Mr. Wendell doing when they let the poet be inspired by those whom he himself had inspired, and so say things in a spirit of racial sympathy beyond his ken? "Shylock spoke as Shylock would speak"—not Shakespeare—"spoke so simply because of the life which had been breathed into him." Granting that, Mr. Hudson surrenders all the ground he had gained for historical criticism. Shylock is thereupon free to say, regardless of his maker, whatever it enters into the head of the critic to have him say; and here is the entering in of the wedge for all those modernizing tendencies which Mr. Hudson, like a scholar, abhors.

[12] Cf. III. 3, where the word, as Cowden Clarke remarks, is significant. "This is the fool that lent out money gratis;"—"in low simplicity, he lends out money gratis."

[13] *Shakespeare,* p. 150.

[14] See *Jewish Encyclopaedia,* article *Church Fathers.* Pyrnne in his *Short Demurrer,* (1656, Pt. i, p. 35) quotes Matthew Paris, and (p. 7) Eadmerus, in passages where the Jew is identified with the devil. Other evidence I shall present shortly in a special article. In the cases cited here and below, *devil* is not used loosely as the equivalent of *villain.* Shylock is a devil because he is a Jew.

[15] Bartlett's Concordance, *Jew.*

[16] There is a medieval picture of such a meeting to be found in Lacroix, t. i., fol. viii, *Conspiration des Juifs,* a miniature in *Le Pélerinage de la vie humaine.* How they lay their heads together! For the unrealistic red hair and beard put upon the Jews in medieval literature and art there is a deal of evidence, some of which I hope soon to publish.

[17] *Von den Juden und ihren Lügen,* in *Werke* (Altenburg, 1662), Theil viii, p. 254.

[18] Justin, Origen, Epiphanius, Jerome. *V. Jewish Encyclopaedia,* article *Church Fathers.*

[19] Hyamson, *Jews in England,* p. 205.

[20] See Graetz passim; or any history of the Middle Ages.

[21] *Von den Juden und ihren Lügen.*

[22] *Jahrbuch,* xviii, p. 216.

[23] Shakespeare's intention is nowhere so evident as in the case of Shylock's outcry:
O Father Abraham, what these Christians are
Whose own hard dealings teaches them suspect
The thoughts of others!
The satire is not bad; but the critics forget (what Shakespeare had seen to it that the audience should not forget) that this is unctuous piety, to hide "a villain's mind." It is such satire as that of the atrocious Barabas and Zariph and the devils in the mysteries.

[24] See quantities of these in the appendix to Professor Bradley's *Shakespearean Tragedy.*

[25] *Shakespeare-Jahrbuch,* xvii, p. 200ff.

[26] *Penn Monthly,* 1880, p. 725f.

[27] *M. V.* IV. I, 205–7.

[28] C. A. Brown; Sir Theodore Martin; J. W. Hales, *English Historical Review* ix, p. 656; Frederick Hawkins, *Theatre,* Nov. 1879, p. 194 (quoted by Furness):—"In availing himself of the greatest popular

madness of the time, he sought to appease it." I sympathize with Mr. W. H. Hudson's impatience with the theory—"perilously near to talking downright nonsense." (Op. cit. p. xxxviii.)

[29] Jastrow, op. cit., p. 737.

[30] *Ideas of Good and Evil*, Essay entitled "At Stratford-on-Avon."

[31] Mr. Hudson also remarks upon this, op. cit., p. xxxvii.

[32] In his *Short Demurrer* Pyrnne tells at length the story of their sufferings, seldom with an epithet of commiseration, frequently in terms of reproach. Coke, in his comment on the Statute De Judaismo, tells the tale of the outrage committed in 1290 at the mouth of the Thames not without tokens of satisfaction at the "divine ultion."

[33] Op. cit., p. 208.

[34] *Sermons* (London, 1865) ii, p. 228.

[35] Yet it is no case of poetic divination or of writing for the comprehension of a later age. "I am a negro!" a victim of race-hatred will say today, with as little comprehension of the psychology of race-hatred or of Professor Summer's theory of the *mores*.

[36] *Elizabethan Drama*, i, p. 232.

[37] Ibid., *p. 373.*

[38] Creizenach, *Works*, iv, pp. 279–80.

[39] Quoted by Furness, p. 433. Cf. Jastrow, op. cit., p. 733, for a like interpretation.

[40] Professor Jastrow and Dr. Honigmann see no fun in these prompt afterthoughts, these anti-climaxes, which, if they had stood in the text of one of Robertson's plays, would have been printed each with a dash before it. "He would prefer *burying his child and his gold*," says the former, "to knowing them to be in the possession of the Christian fools."

[41] Talche chiunque v'era presente, di questo faceva grandissima allegrezza, e ciascuno si faceva beffe di questo Giudeo, dicendo, Tale si crede uccellare ch'e uccellato. Hazlitt's *Shakespeare's Library*, Pt. ii, vol. i, p. 348.

[42] P. 737: "The Jew reproaches the Christian with his sinful traffic in human flesh." Surely not; that would have spoiled Shylock's argument from analogy.

[43] *Academy*, Nov. 27, 1880.

[44] Cf. the etymology of the word Dutch or Deutsch, and similar instances of ethnocentrism in language given in Sumner, *Folkways*, p. 14.

[45] See a sensible scientific discussion of "inspiration" and the relation of the genius to his age in Joly, *Psychologie des grands hommes*, ch. v and vi. I hope to return to the subject so far as it concerns Shakespeare, before long.

[46] *Quarante ans de théâtre: Shylock.*

John Middleton Murry

SHAKESPEARE'S METHOD:
THE MERCHANT OF VENICE

The Merchant of Venice probably shares with *Hamlet* the distinction of being the most popular of all Shakespeare's plays. It was not always so. After the Restoration, *The Merchant of Venice* suffered eclipse. When it was at last revived (in a drastic adaptation) at the beginning of the eighteenth century, Shylock was played as a purely comic part. Not until 1741, when Macklin played Shylock at Drury Lane, did something near to Shakespeare's text come back to the stage. The return was triumphant. 'Macklin made Shylock malevolent,' says Mr. Harold Child, 'and of a forcible and terrifying ferocity.' Macklin's Shylock, which Pope accepted as Shakespeare's, dominated the stage for nearly fifty years; and it imposed the conception described by Hazlitt:

> When we first went to see Mr. Kean in Shylock, we expected to see, what we had been used to see, a decrepit old man, bent with age and ugly with mental deformity, grinning with deadly malice, with the venom of his heart congealed in the expression of his countenance, sullen, morose, gloomy, inflexible, brooding over one idea, that of his hatred, and fixed on one unalterable purpose, that of his revenge.

With this conception of Shylock *The Merchant of Venice* became truly popular. Garrick chose it for the opening performance of Drury Lane under his management in 1747, and in it Kean made his triumphant first appearance at the same theatre in 1814. It was Kean's Shylock, as Hazlitt makes plain, which caused a revolution in the attitude of criticism towards the character. 'In proportion as Shylock has ceased to be a popular bugbear, "baited with the rabble's curse,"' wrote Hazlitt, 'he becomes a half-favourite with the philosophical part of the audience, who are disposed to think that Jewish revenge is at least as good as Christian injuries.'

That is a singular and significant stage-history. For both these popular Shylocks

From *Shakespeare* (New York: Harcourt, Brace, 1936), pp. 153–66, 171–73.

are Shakespeare's: or rather both are to be found in Shakespeare. As the attitude to the Jew became more civilized, at the beginning of the nineteenth century, so it was discovered that the new attitude also was prophetically contained in Shakespeare's Jew.

But *The Merchant of Venice* is more than Shylock. It is, more even than *Hamlet,* more than any other of Shakespeare's plays, a matter-of-fact fairy tale: a true folk story, made drama; and it makes its secular appeal to that primitive substance of the human consciousness whence folk-tales took their origin. Or, without reaching back to these dark and dubious beginnings, we may say that it is, as nearly as possible, a pure melodrama or tragi-comedy, an almost perfect example of the art-form which being prior to art itself, most evidently and completely satisfies the primitive man in us all. If the English theatre be considered as a place of popular entertainment, strictly on a level with the football field, the prize-ring and the racecourse, then *The Merchant of Venice* is the type of entertainment the theatre should supply—villain discomfited, virtue rescued, happy marriages, clowning, thrills, and a modest satisfaction of the general appetite for naughtiness.

The Merchant of Venice happens to be Shakespeare's; but Shakespeare has not much to do with its popularity. True, *The Merchant of Venice* almost *is* Shakespeare in the popular mind. But this popular Shakespeare, who wrote *The Merchant of Venice* and *Richard III,* is scarcely a person. He is rather a name which gives to these satisfactions of our elementary appetites for melodrama the prestige of art. This impersonal 'Shakespeare' is a great stumbling-block to criticism, which is for ever engaged, consciously and unconsciously, in the effort to dissolve him out of existence. But he did most certainly exist: he is the Shakespeare who, in his own day as in ours, was veritably popular, who tickled the groundlings because his living lay that way (and surely it was a better way than being hand-fed by the aristocracy, gratification for dedication), who did what he could to season his caviare to the general appetite, and made not a virtue of his necessity—that was hardly his nature—but the best of it.

It is the more striking, therefore, that of all the plays of this period *The Merchant of Venice* is the most typical of Shakespeare—the most expressive of what Coleridge once called his 'omni-humanity.' It contains tragedy, comedy high and low, love lyricism; and, notably, it does not contain any 'Shakespearian' character. The Berowne-Mercutio-Benedick figure, witty, debonair, natural, is diffused into a group of young Venetian noblemen, all credible and substantial, but none possessing the inimitable individuality of their progenitor. Antonio, who stands apart from them, and was (if my judgment of the various verse-styles of the play is to be trusted) the last figure in it to have been elaborated, is a singular character. He supplies a background of sadness to the whole drama. He seems to be older than the friends who surround him, and detached from their thoughtless extravagance. Actually, in his final elaboration, by reason of the quality and colour given to him by Shakespeare's re-writing of Act I, Scene i, he becomes, as a character, slightly inconsistent with the contemptuous opponent of Shylock of later scenes; but it is not the function of Antonio to be primarily a dramatic 'character.' In that capacity, he is negative; he is a shadow beside Shakespeare and Portia, and unsubstantial even in comparison with his Venetian entourage. But as the vehicle of an atmosphere, he is one of the most important elements in the play. He provides, for the beginning of the play, what the lyrical antiphony of Lorenzo and Jessica supplies for the end of it—a kind of musical overtone which sets the spiritual proportions of the drama. He shades into the Duke of *Twelfth Night.*

The analogue between *The Merchant of Venice* and a musical composition is significant, I think, when taken in conjunction with the basic popularity of the play and the probability that its origin is to be sought in a play of many years before called 'The Jew,' which Stephen Gosson exempted from abuse in 1579 because it displayed 'the greediness of worldly chusers and the bloody mind of userers.' That is too apt a summary of the purely dramatic content of *The Merchant of Venice* to be accidental, and it fits too well with our impression of the play as the product of much re-writing to be ignored. Whether or not *The Merchant* is, as Malone suggested, the 'Venetian Comedy' mentioned by Henslowe in 1594—a date which would suit very well for Shakespeare's first drafting of *his* play—may be left undecided. The important fact is that in *The Merchant* we have, almost certainly, Shakespeare's treatment of a dramatic plot which came to him, substantially, as a datum.

Out of this substance Shakespeare wrought a miracle. He transformed it, and yet he left the popular substance essentially the same. What he did not, could not, and, so far as we can see or guess, would not do, was to attempt to make it an intellectually coherent whole. That seems to have been no part of his purpose; he did not entertain the idea because he knew it was impossible. The coherence of *The Merchant of Venice* is not intellectual or psychological; and there has been much beating of brains in the vain effort to discover in it a kind of coherence which it was never meant to possess.

As an example of what I believe to be a radical misunderstanding of the nature of *The Merchant of Venice*, we may take the edition of the play in the *New Cambridge Shakespeare*. It will serve as a typical example of a mistaken approach to Shakespeare, for *The Merchant* in its origins, its methods of composition, and its final splendour, is typical of Shakespeare's achievement. The very stubbornness of his material compelled, I believe, a more or less complete abeyance of Shakespeare's personality. In his work upon this play he was pre-eminently the 'artist,' but not in the modern and largely romantic sense of the word.

When the news of the disaster to Antonio's ventures comes to Belmont, in the very ecstasy of happiness there, Jessica adds her witness to Salerio's report of Shylock's implacability:

> When I was with him, I have heard him swear
> To Tubal and to Chus, his countrymen,
> That he would rather have Antonio's flesh

Than twenty times the value of the sum
That he did owe him: and I know, my lord,
If law, authority and power deny not,
It will go hard with poor Antonio.   (III. ii. 285–91)

On this passage, the New Cambridge editors have the following note:

> We are tempted to put this speech into square brackets as one from the old
> play which Shakespeare inadvertently left undeleted in the manuscript. Note
> (I) it jars upon a nerve which Shakespeare of all writers was generally most
> careful to avoid: that a daughter should thus volunteer evidence against her
> father is hideous . . .

This fits, precisely, with the description of Jessica given in the essay of general
introduction to the play:

> Jessica is bad and disloyal, unfilial, a thief; frivolous, greedy, without any more
> conscience than a cat, and without even a cat's redeeming love of home. Quite
> without heart, on worse than an animal instinct—pilfering to be carnal—she
> betrays her father to be a light-of-lucre carefully weighted with her father's
> ducats.

This is, indeed, to break a butterfly upon a wheel. But more alarming than the
severity of the sentence is its irrelevance. *The Merchant of Venice* is not a realistic
drama; and its characters simply cannot be judged by realistic moral standards.
Jessica, taken out of the play, and exposed to the cold light of moral analysis, may
be a wicked little thing; but in the play, wherein alone she has her being, she is
nothing of the kind—she is charming. She runs away from her father because she
is white and he is black; she is much rather a princess held captive by an ogre than
the unfilial daughter of a persecuted Jew. Whether or not it is true that Shakespeare
'of all writers' was most careful to avoid representing unfilial behaviour without
condemning it—and the proposition becomes doubtful when we think of *Romeo
and Juliet* and *Othello*—it is almost certainly true that he did not himself conceive,
or imagine that others would conceive, that Jessica's behaviour was unfilial. The
relations between the wicked father and the lovely daughter are governed by laws
nearly as old as the hills.

Yet even so, in rejecting Jessica's words as un-Shakespearian because morally
hideous, the *New Cambridge Shakespeare* is not consistent; for the introductory
essay discusses the problem how it is that Shylock is made 'sympathetic' to us, and
argues that it is because he is deserted by his bad and disloyal daughter: 'he is
intolerably wronged,' and we feel for him accordingly. We cannot have it both
ways; we cannot argue that Shakespeare deliberately made Jessica unfilial in order
to gain our sympathy for the Jew, and at the same time reject a passage as
un-Shakespearian because in it Jessica reveals herself unfilial. The dilemma is absolute, but it is of the modern critic's making, not Shakespeare's. It is the direct result

of applying to *The Merchant of Venice* a kind of criticism which it was never meant to satisfy.

Criticism of this kind seeks for psychological motives where none were intended or given. Shylock's hatred of Antonio is, in origin, a fairy-tale hatred, of the bad for the good. And perhaps this fairy-tale hatred is more significant than a hatred which can (if any hatred can) be justified to the consciousness. At any rate Shakespeare was at all times content to accept his antagonism of the evil and the good as self-explanatory. Not to speak of Iago, or Goneril, or Edmund, in the very next play in the Folio, *As You Like It,* which was probably written at about the same time as *The Merchant of Venice,* Oliver, in plotting Orlando's death, similarly confesses his elemental hatred of his brother: 'I hope I shall see an end of him; for my soul, yet I know not why, hates nothing more than he.' Some would explain these simple assertions of a primal antagonism as compelled by the conditions of the Elizabethan theatre, which required the characters clearly to label themselves as villains or heroes; but it is quite as likely that Shakespeare accepted the sheer opposition of good and evil as an ultimate fact of the moral universe. Assuredly, if it was a necessary convention of the Elizabethan theatre, it was a convention which Shakespeare found it easy to use for his own purposes. For the hatred of his villains always lies deeper than their consciousness.

Thus Shylock at one moment declares that he hates Antonio 'for he is a Christian'; at another, because he is a trade rival: 'I will have the heart of him if he forfeit, for were he out of Venice, I can make what merchandise I will.' If we take the psychological point of view, the contradiction should not trouble us. We may say that Shylock is trying, as later Iago will try, to rationalize his hatred of Antonio: that he contradicts himself in so doing, is in accord with everyday experience. Or, on a different level, we may say that Shakespeare himself is trying to rationalize his elemental story. Unlike Oliver, who appears only at the beginning and the end of *As You Like It,* unlike the unsubstantial Don John in *Much Ado,* Shylock is the main figure of the play. What is in reality the simple fact of his hatred has to be motivated. Oliver and Don John are not required to be credible; Shylock is.

But these two kinds of explanation are not contradictory, as some critics think they are. They are two modes, two levels, of the operation of the same necessity: the 'psychologization' of a story that is a datum. In the process, Antonio's character suffers some slight damage. He spits upon Shylock's Jewish gaberdine. If we reflect in cold blood on Antonio's reported behaviour to Shylock, we are in danger of thinking that Shylock's intended revenge was not excessive. But we are not meant or allowed to reflect upon it. We are not made to *see* this behaviour. It is a sudden shifting of the values in order to make Shylock sympathetic to us at the moment he is proposing the bond. This is a dramatic device of which Shakespeare was always a master. But because Shakespeare was Shakespeare it is something more than a dramatic device.

Shylock undoubtedly is, to a certain degree, made sympathetic to us; and it is important to discover how it is done. For this, almost certainly, was a radical change wrought by Shakespeare in the crude substance of the old play. But the effect was certainly not achieved by Shakespeare's representing Shylock as the victim of Jessica's ingratitude. On the contrary, Shakespeare is most careful to prevent any such impression from taking lodgment in our minds. At the moment when we might feel a little uneasy about Jessica's treatment of her father, any nascent misgiving is stifled by Salerio's description of Shylock's outcry at the discovery:

> My daughter! O my ducats! O my daughter!
> Fled with a Christian! O my Christian ducats!
> Justice! the law! my ducats, and my daughter!
> A sealed bag, two sealed bags of ducats,
> Of double ducats, stolen from me by my daughter!
> And jewels, two stones, two rich and precious stones,
> Stolen by my daughter! Justice! find the girl;
> She hath the stones upon her, and the ducats.   (II. viii. 14–22)

It is not the loss of his daughter that moves Shylock, but only the loss of his money. Shylock, at this moment, is presented as an ignoble being whom Jessica does well to escape and despoil.

Shylock is deliberately made unsympathetic when it is required to cover Jessica. He is made sympathetic when Shakespeare feels the need, or welcomes the opportunity of making a truly dramatic contrast between Shylock and Antonio. At critical moments he is given dignity and passion of speech and argument to plead his cause to us and to himself. His hatred then is represented as deep, irrational and implacable, but not as mean and mercenary. It is then a force of nature—something greater than himself:

> So can I give no reason, nor I will not,
> More than a lodged hate and a certain loathing
> I bear Antonio, that I follow thus
> A losing suit against him.   (IV. i. 59–62)

'A losing suit,' because he, who grieves more for his ducats than his daughter, refuses many times the value of his debt to have his bond of Antonio; and his implacability is supplied with excuses enough to more than half persuade us— Antonio's expressed contempt for him, and the magnificent speech, which may have been hardly less magnificent in the verse from which Shakespeare seems to have changed it.

> And if you wrong us, shall we not revenge?
> If we are like you in the rest, we will
> Resemble you in that. If a Jew wrong
> A Christian, what is his humility?
> Revenge! And if a Christian wrong a Jew
> What should his sufferance be?

By Christian example, why, revenge!
The villainy you teach me
I will execute: and it shall go hard
But I will better the instruction.   (III. i. 71 sq.)

Not content with that, Shakespeare in the trial scene gives Shylock a truly tremendous argument:

DUKE: How shalt thou hope for mercy, rendering none?
SHY.: What judgment shall I dread, doing no wrong?
You have among you many a purchased slave,
Which, like your asses and your dogs and mules,
You use in abject and in slavish parts,
Because you bought them: shall I say to you,
Let them be free, marry them to your heirs?
Why sweat they under burthens? let their beds
Be made as soft as yours, and let their palates
Be seasoned with such viands? You will answer
'The slaves are ours': so do I answer you:
The pound of flesh, which I demand of him,
Is dearly bought: 'tis mine and I will have it.
If you deny me, fie upon your law!
There is no force in the decrees of Venice.
I stand for judgment: answer, shall I have it?   (IV. i. 87–103)

Shall I not do as I will with mine own? It is the morality of a whole society, to which Antonio and his friends belong no less than Shylock, which Shylock challenges here, and by anticipation blunts the edge of Portia's great plea for mercy. As Hazlitt put it, in his tempestuous way, 'the appeal to the Jew's mercy, as if there were any common principle of right and wrong between them, is the rankest hypocrisy, the blindest prejudice.' The world where mercy prevails is not the world of the play. That is a world where justice is the bulwark of injustice.

This is much more than a dramatic device to gain a momentary sympathy for Shylock; yet it is less, or at least other, than a deliberate posing of a profound moral problem. *The Merchant of Venice* is not a problem play; it is a fairy story, within the framework of which Shakespeare allowed free working to the thoughts of his mind and the feelings of his heart. What an unfettered Shylock might say, this fettered Shylock does say.

In other words, Shylock is both the embodiment of an irrational hatred, and a credible human being. He is neither of these things to the exclusion of the other. And if we ask how can that be? the only answer is that it is so. This was Shakespeare's way of working. If we choose, we may say that there are in the story primitive elements which he could not wholly assimilate to his own conception; but such an explanation, in *The Merchant of Venice* as in *Hamlet,* brings us against the fact that the dramatic impression made by these plays is the impression of an artistic whole. And, indeed, it seems more probable that Shakespeare did not deal in 'conceptions' of the kind that are often attributed to him. He set himself in successive attempts to infuse a general impression of credibility into an old story, and to secure from his audience no more, and no less, than 'that willing suspension of disbelief which constitutes poetic faith.'

One cannot too often emphasize the nature of Shakespeare's dramatic 'method.' It was not chosen by him, neither was it imposed upon his reluctant genius; it was simply the condition of the work he had chosen to do. The situation was given; necessarily, therefore, the 'characters' in a certain primitive sense—much the same sense in which we can speak of 'characters' in a nursery-story like Cinderella or Robin Hood or a Punch and Judy show. They are simply the necessary agents for that situation or that story. Shakespeare proceeded to endow them with poetic utterance, and with character in a quite different sense. He did what he could to make them credible human beings to himself. He gave them, so far as was possible, humanly plausible motives for their acts and situations, although these were often in fact prior to humane psychology. In a word, the method of Shakespeare's drama consists, essentially, in the humanization of melodrama. And each of those terms must have real validity for the Shakespeare critic who is to avoid ascending or descending into some private universe of his own and calling it Shakespeare.

This Shakespeare, who strove to humanize melodrama, and yet was perforce content with the immediate dramatic impression—an 'essential Shakespeare,' if ever there was one—is apparently very difficult for modern criticism to grasp. There is something monstrous about him which must be brought to order. The methods of disciplining him are various. In their extreme form they were practised by the late Mr. J. M. Robertson, and consisted in assigning to somebody else, on 'stylistic' grounds, nearly all that was unpalatable in Shakespeare. In the more circumspect form, practised by the New Cambridge editors, they are a combination of discovering 'old-play-fossils,' which generally contain the parts of Shakespeare which are held to be morally or aesthetically reprehensible, and downright charges of bad workmanship, by standards which are irrelevant. Thus, the New Cambridge edition argues that, since 'everyone of the Venetian *dramatis personae* is either a "waster" or a "rotter" or both, and cold-hearted at that,' the true dramatic contrast between Shylock and Antonio and his friends is blurred.

> For the evil opposed against these curious Christians is specific; it is Cruelty; and yet again specifically, the peculiar cruelty of a Jew. To this cruelty an artist at the top of his art would surely have opposed mansuetude, clemency, charity and specifically Christian charity. Shakespeare misses more than half the point when he makes his intended victims, as a class and by habit, just as heartless as Shylock without any of Shylock's passionate excuse.

The basis of this argument is surely mistaken. To supply the true dramatic contrast to Shylock's insistence upon his bond, not rare Christian charity, but ordinary human decency is enough. The contrast would not be heightened, but made intolerable, if Antonio and his friends were represented as uncanonized saints. Deliberate and conscious cruelty is an outrage upon ordinary human nature. And the careless paganism of Antonio's friends—ordinary 'decent' young aristocrats—is the proper foil to it.

Antonio and his friends are unconscious. They do not realize any more than did the average decent man of Shakespeare's day, that their morality is essentially no finer than Shylock's, or rather that Shylock's is the logical consequence of their own. Because they are unconscious, they are forgiven; where Shylock, being conscious, cannot be. And that is true to live. Logic in morality is intolerable and inhuman, and Antonio's escape from Shylock's revenge by a legal quibble is poetic justice. The impediment of logic and law is broken down by logic and law, and the stream of human life—ordinary, approximate, unconscious, instinctive human life— can flow on. The decency of an age and an average prevails over the design of an isolated bitterness.

There is a morality in *The Merchant of Venice,* though it is not of the formulable kind; nor is it a morality on the level of the deepest insights expressed in the play. Shylock's incrimination of 'Christian' society, Portia's appeal to Christian mercy—these are overtones, as it were, caught from the celestial spheres.

> Sit Jessica. Look how the floor of heaven
> Is thick inlaid with patines of bright gold:
> There's not the smallest orb which thou beholdest
> But in his motion like an angel sings
> Still quiring to the young-eyed cherubins;
> Such harmony is in immortal souls;
> But whilst this muddy vesture of decay
> Doth grossly close us in, we cannot hear it.   (V. i. 58–65)

No one distinctly hears that harmony in the play: and it would be fatal if they did. For this play was never intended to vex us with thoughts beyond the reaches of our souls, but 'to give some shadow of satisfaction to the mind of man in these points where the nature of things doth deny it.' ⟨. . .⟩

The unity of a Shakespeare play (if we may generalize) is seldom what would be described today as a unity of conception. That was precluded, save in rare cases, by the necessities of Shakespeare's peculiar craft. The axiom, which has long been current in Shakespeare criticism, that the situation derives from the character is, in the main, a mistaken one. The reverse is nearer to the truth; for the situations are generally prior to the characters. But that does not mean, as some modern critics assert, that the reverse *is* the truth, and that the characters derive from the situations. They do not. They are largely epiphenomenal to the situations.

   This is difficult to grasp, because it is so simple. There is an element in a
Shakespeare character which derives from the situation; but that element is relatively small compared to the element which floats as it were free of the situation.
On this element Shakespeare lavished himself, because here he was, within limits,
a free agent. A simple example is Antonio's motiveless melancholy at the opening
of *The Merchant*. It is motiveless: because it is motiveless, modern 'scientific' criticism explains it away by a 'cut.' 'We have here,' says Dr. Dover Wilson, 'a dramatic
motive deliberately suppressed at the time of a revision, and the broken line "I am
to learn" shows us where one of the "cuts" involved in this suppression took place.'
On the contrary, I am persuaded that Shakespeare intended Antonio's melancholy
to be motiveless and that the half-line was deliberate. Shakespeare was taking
advantage of that part of Antonio's character which was free to introduce a depth
into his character, and still more a feeling-tone into the play, which he felt the play
could bear, and which would enrich it. That Antonio's character, as fixed by the
situation, does not fully square with this; that he has subsequently to be one who
'rails upon' the Jews, and spits upon a Jewish gaberdine, did not trouble Shakespeare. He had had to learn not to be troubled by such necessities. Antonio would
remain a presence in the responsive imagination, a character whose nature was not
wholly expressed in the acts required of him. It is not otherwise with Shylock.
Shylock's 'free' character is created of sentiments and thoughts which are, on any
cool analysis, incompatible with the acts required of him. The 'bloody-minded
usurer' is the mouthpiece of an oppressed nation and the impassioned critic of
current Christian morality; yet he is, because he has to be, 'the bloody-minded
usurer' as well. And Shakespeare, as we have seen, will exalt and degrade him at
need, either to make uncouthness in the action more plausible, or to wring every
atom of imaginative and dramatic possibility out of the central situation. As Dr.
Bridges wrote, 'He had, as it were, a balance to maintain, and a fine sense of its
equipoise: if one scale descends, he immediately throws something into the other,
and though he may appear to be careless as to what he throws in, he only throws
in such things as he knows he may be careless about. But an examination of those
matters would tend to prove that he did not regard the reader as well as the
audience of his plays.'
   Coherent, in the modern sense of the word, such characters are not. Nor are
they even consistent among themselves, so to speak. At their best, which is often,
they create the inimitable Shakespearian impression of being imagined 'in the round'
and exhibiting in action only one aspect of their rich substance to us; at the worst,
which is rare, they are puzzling and demand from the reader more than the normal
effort towards the willing suspension of disbelief which constitutes poetic faith. Such
a method of character-creation could arise (I think) only out of a sort of consub-
stantiality of the poet with the theatre. It was imposed by the practice of re-writing
time-honoured and time-proven theatrical material: and it is notable that where
Shakespeare had a relatively free hand this imaginative ambiguity is much less
frequent. For in this order we should need to make a distinction between story-

material which was familiar to Shakespeare's audience, and story-material which, though not of Shakespeare's invention, was not familiar to them. The degree of Shakespeare's liberty to adjust his dramatic action to his imaginative need must have varied greatly according to the definiteness of popular expectation.

To determine that variation is, perhaps fortunately, beyond our power. We lack the knowledge, and it is unlikely that we shall ever attain it. But it is worthy of more than passing notice that the two perennially popular plays of Shakespeare— *The Merchant of Venice* and *Hamlet*—are the two of which we can say, most definitely, that his freedom to alter the action was most limited; and that they are also the plays in which the nature of the chief character is most disputed.

John Palmer
SHYLOCK

The political career of Thomas Devereux, Earl of Essex, frequently impinges upon the dramatic career of Mr. William Shakespeare. In 1593 this proud, capricious, brilliant and foolish nobleman was stimulating the Queen's commissioners to suppress the *School of Night*. This affair elicited from Shakespeare the first of his notable comedies, *Love's Labour's Lost*. Eight years later, in 1601, the friends of Essex conspired to stage a revival of *Richard II*, the first of Shakespeare's great tetralogy of histories, which resulted in at least one member of the audience being hanged.[1] Meanwhile, in June 1594, Essex was actively concerned in the persecution of one, Roderigo Lopez, a Jew of Portuguese descent, physician to the Queen, wrongfully accused of plotting to poison Her Majesty for reasons that have ceased to have any great interest for posterity. Essex, who manufactured the evidence, also presided at the trial, an arrangement which greatly simplified the procedure. The unfortunate Jew was hanged, drawn and quartered at Tyburn in the presence of an excited crowd who marvelled that he should dare, in his last moments, to utter the name of Jesus.

The trial and death of Roderigo Lopez was the second *cause célèbre* in a twelvemonth which had for Shakespeare a personal and professional interest. Marlowe and Kyd had been involved in the scandal which led to the suppression of the *School of Night*. The death of Lopez came yet nearer home. It is not unlikely that Shakespeare was personally acquainted with the man. Lopez, a member of the College of Physicians, was the medical attendant of many notable persons, including the Earl of Leicester, patron of the Company of 'servants and players' in which Shakespeare was a 'sharer'. It is not improbable that Shakespeare witnessed the butchery at Tyburn. Quite certainly he heard the case discussed in the taverns of London, where the lamentable theme of Jewry's place in a Christian commonwealth must have been frequently debated among the free spirits of the time. It is not suggested that Shakespeare, in portraying Shylock, had any political or social

From *Comic Characters of Shakespeare* (London: Macmillan, 1946), pp. 53–61, 66–91.

intentions. *The Merchant of Venice* is not a transcript from contemporary life, still less a political morality. It is essentially a fairy-tale or, more precisely, a combination of two fairy-tales. Whether Burbage, in playing Shylock, trimmed his beard to the cut of Lopez or whether the spectators who witnessed the trial of Shylock before the Duke of Venice were prompted to remember the trial of Lopez before the Earl of Essex, is neither here nor there. Gratiano when he declares in his speech to Shylock:

> Thy currish spirit
> Governed a wolf, who hanged for human slaughter,
> Even from the gallows did his fell soul fleet,
> And whilst thou layest in thy unhallowed dam,
> Infused itself in thee

may or may not have been punning on the name Lopez (Lopez = Lupus = Wolf). It is a point for the scholars and we may feel with Horatio when invited by Hamlet to trace the noble dust of Alexander, till he find it stopping a bung-hole, that ' 'twere to consider too curiously, to consider so'. What really matters is the effect on Shakespeare's imagination of this particular fragment of personal experience. He was the likelier, if he had known a Jew with more than one fair daughter (Lopez had three), to find a place for Jessica in his play and to insist, if he had witnessed the savage spectacle at Tyburn, that a Jew, if you prick him, will most certainly bleed. Nor was he likely to forget the indignant mirth of a Christian mob execrating a Jew who in his last agony presumed to call upon Jesus Christ.[2]

The Elizabethan theatre reflected the life and mind of the nation and, when Shakespeare sat down to write *The Merchant of Venice* in 1594, anti-semitism was in fashion. Marlowe had exploited it four years previously with all the resources of his poetic genius and there seemed little more to do or say. Barabbas, the Jew of Malta, embodied in his wicked person all the qualities which a persecuting major-ity commonly attributed to its victims. For four years Marlowe's Jew had held the stage and, during the excitement aroused by the trial of Lopez, between May and December, 1594, his play was twenty times revived. Barabbas was greedy as a pike, cruel as a cat and artful as a wilderness of monkeys. He was sinister and yet ridiculous, impressive in the intensity of his passion and grotesque in the versatility of his performance. He was robbed of one fortune by the State, but remained master of another. He contrived that two Christian suitors for the hand of his daughter should kill one another; and, when his daughter became a Christian, he killed her, too. He strangled a monk and poisoned a whole nunnery. He betrayed the Christian to the Turk and the Turk to the Christian. Finally he fell into a cauldron which he had artfully contrived for his principal benefactor and was boiled alive.

Such was the play about a Jew which held the London stage when Shake-speare was asked to supply his company with another. Charles Lamb, gazing with aversion upon Barabbas, finds him 'a mere monster brought in with a large painted nose to please the rabble ... just such an exhibition as a century or two earlier might have been played before the Londoners by Royal Command when a general pillage and massacre of the Hebrews had been resolved on in the cabinet'. Lamb wrote in the comfortable conviction that such exhibitions had ceased for ever to have any relation to practical politics.

Officially there were no Jews in Shakespeare's England. Edward I had driven them all out in 1290. But there was nevertheless a Jewish question, actual as well as legendary, and, in appreciating *The Merchant of Venice,* we shall do well to remember that Marlowe's Barabbas still held the stage when Shakespeare created Shylock. The fashion was fixed and Shakespeare must seem to follow it. It did not matter how absurd or improbable the plot of his play might be, because the public was ready to believe anything about a Jew. Any horrible mischief which a Jew might contrive would be credited and any device by which the Jew might be foiled of his purpose, however childish or improbable, would be commended.

Then why not use that old story of Gernutus, the Jew of Venice, who in merry jest had induced a Christian merchant to sign a bond for a pound of his flesh and who, in cruel earnest, had claimed the forfeiture? This same Gernutus had for some time been a popular figure. There were shortly to be ballads about him, sung to the tune of 'Black and Yellow':

In Venice town not long ago
A cruel Jew did dwell,
Which livèd all on usury,

As Italian writers tell.
His heart doth think on many a wile
How to deceive the poor;
His mouth is almost full of muck,
Yet he gapes for more.

Nearer to the purpose were the merry tales of Ser Giovanni Fiorentino, one of those Italian books that sold in Elizabethan England like hot cakes, so that Schoolmaster Ascham was moved to warn his pupils: 'These be the enchantementes of Circes, brought out of Italie to marre men's manners in England.' Ser Giovanni had the whole story almost ready for the theatre: a Venetian youth who had won the lady of Belmonte, a merchant who supplied the youth with money borrowed from a Jew, the pound of flesh, the notorious quibble whereby the merchant was rescued in court by the lady, in disguise, even the mystification about a ring which she received from her bridegroom as a reward for saving his friend. All the dry bones of Shakespeare's play, except for the caskets, were waiting here for the man who could make them live upon the stage.

Nor was it necessary for Shakespeare to look very far for his caskets. They had been lying about for centuries—genuine antiques, bequests from the Greek monk of St. Saba in Syria which, after appearing in places of less repute, had turned up in the *Gesta Romanorum,* a collection of tales so popular with the Elizabethans that no less than six editions of an English translation were published between 1577 and 1601.

It is doubtful whether Shakespeare was even put to the trouble of combining the story of the pound of flesh with that of the caskets. For in 1579, fifteen years before he wrote *The Merchant of Venice,* the actor and dramatic author, Stephen Gosson, leaving the stage for the pulpit, published a 'pleasant invective against poets, pipers, players, jesters and such like caterpillars of the commonwealth', in which he trounced the abuses of the theatre and referred incidentally to two plays showing at the Bull Tavern. One of these plays, entitled *The Jew,* he describes as 'representing the greediness of worldly chusers and the bloody minds of usurers'. From this it must presumably be inferred that a play had been produced either in 1579 or before that date, in which the casket theme (the greediness of worldly chusers) and the story of the pound of flesh (the bloody minds of usurers) had already been woven into a single piece. Thus it seems hardly possible to avoid the conclusion that Shakespeare, in writing *The Merchant of Venice,* was working from an old play in which every essential feature of his double plot already figured.[3]

There is no means of assessing the merits of the old play from which Shakespeare very probably derived his comedy. But these fashionable Jew plays were probably all very much alike. Dekker wrote one which has been lost. The illiterate Henslowe alludes in his diary to a 'Venesyon Comoedy' produced in August 1594. Another English Jew play of the period, *Der Jud von Venedig,* has survived in a German text. An English company, strolling on the Continent, performed it before a German audience at Halle in 1611. As in Shakespeare's comedy, a second Daniel comes to judgment. If this, or something like it, was the sort of play which Shakespeare had at his disposal when he wrote *The Merchant of Venice,* we can only marvel at the transformation. For this German manuscript is a bawdy, vulgar and brutal piece of work. The essential features of Shakespeare's plot are there, but the result is what might be expected of an attempt by anyone but Shakespeare to present a fairy-tale in the *Blue Bird* tradition as a contribution to the secular pastime of baiting the Jew.

There is, of course, another side to the picture. The execution of Lopez, while it gratified the Jew-baiters, seems to have provoked indignation and even a searching of hearts among the more reasonable and sensitive citizens of London. Elizabeth, who believed that Lopez was innocent, at first refused to sign his death warrant. She yielded to popular clamour, stimulated by Essex and his friends, but against her better judgment. The feeling inspired by the execution of Lopez in civilised spectators was much the same as that of the pale, fair Briton observed by Heine at Drury Lane who, at the end of the fourth act of Shakespeare's play, several times exclaimed with tears in her eyes: *The poor man is wronged.* In 1596, two years after the production of *The Merchant of Venice,* a book was published in London entitled *The Orator,* a translation from the French of a collection of model speeches or declamations on subjects of historical or contemporary interest. Moral and legal problems were handled in speeches put into the mouths of advocates arguing for or against a particular case. Among the declamations was one which shows that even in Shakespeare's time opinions were divided on the Jewish question. It is a speech such as Shylock might have made in appealing against the sentence of the Venetian Court. The Jew, very ably and convincingly, puts his judges in the wrong, both on moral and legal grounds. What right have these Christians to deny him his pound of flesh? Do they not themselves condemn their debtors to worse forfeits, 'binding all the body into a most loathsome prison or into an intolerable slavery'? Did not the Romans regard it as 'lawful for debt to imprison, beat and afflict with torments the free citizens'? Debtors who fail to keep their contracts must abide the consequences. It is lawful to kill a soldier, if he should come to the wars an hour late, or to hang a thief, though he steal never so little. Is it then so great a matter to take a pound of flesh from one who by breaking his promise has endangered his creditor's solvency and reputation, which to a man of business is more precious than life itself?

The Jew here turns the tables on the Christian and, under the cover of a shrewd defence, carries the war to the enemy. The inclusion of such a homily in a book translated and published in 1596 is convincing proof that Shakespeare, in presenting Shylock to the public in 1594, was not writing for an audience incapable of appreciating the more humane aspects of his comedy.[4]

These, then, are the circumstances in which Shakespeare's comedy stands as a piece of contemporary literature: a topical interest in Jews which had led to the production of several Jew plays on the stage, one of which very possibly combined the story of the pound of flesh with that of the caskets; some lively discussion in the London taverns of the rights and wrongs of a distinguished member of that unhappy race, executed at Tyburn; an audience which expected a stage Jew to be presented as a comical and merciless villain; a possible tendency on the part of more judicious spectators to deplore the barbarity of a public act recently committed and to regard the stage Jew of the period as an inhuman travesty.

Shakespeare, having regard to these circumstances, contrived to write a play in which what the contemporary public wanted to meet a topical occasion was with superb felicity combined with what posterity has accepted on its merits as one of his major achievements as a comic dramatist. Here was the 'mere monster brought in with a large painted nose to please the rabble', claiming his pound of flesh; there were the traditional caskets and here was the lady whose locks hung on her temples like a golden fleece—two fantastical stories, one of them wickedly grotesque and the other prettily fanciful, which had somehow to be brought into harmony with one another and to be presented as humanly credible within the limits of a play. Was ever a more formidable challenge presented to a poet, called on to create a mood and to suggest an environment in which these quaint figures and incidents might be accepted, or to a dramatist, called on to create the characters in which we might believe as beings of a like nature with ourselves? Portia, first to last, is as legendary a figure as Shylock. But these legendary figures behave, within their limits, as recognisable creatures of flesh and blood. Humanity comes creeping, or even breaking, into the composition. The people of the play, within a magic circle drawn by the poet, successfully assert their reality.

Shakespeare has so brilliantly succeeded in this part of his task that the veracity of his characters relative to the play—which is just sufficient to carry his design—has been accepted as absolute. Critics and editors insist on viewing every character and incident in the broad light of common day. Bassanio, legendary Jason of the old story, is removed from the play and, because Shakespeare has made him suffi-ciently real for his purpose, is discussed as though he were a person whom we should hesitate to invite to dinner. He is charged with being a spendthrift and a gold-digger. He sponges on his best friend and marries for money. Antonio, for all his fine speeches and impressive deportment, is a spineless nonentity; Jessica a heartless minx who robs her father. Each character, removed from its context, is submitted to everyday tests of moral worth and social decorum. Shakespeare, in giving to these people just enough reality to make them humanly credible for the purpose of his story, has succeeded to such good purpose that they are brought to judgment as human beings true for all time or in any place.[5] ⟨...⟩

If Shakespeare, in handling the secondary characters and legal incidents of his play, achieved so strong an illusion of reality that they have been discussed for generations and are still discussed to-day as though he were presenting a transcript from the social life of Venice in the sixteenth century, his delineation of Shylock has had results even more remarkable. He set out to write a comedy about a stage Jew involved in a grotesque story about a pound of flesh. But Shylock, to satisfy his author, must seem to act as a recognisably human being would behave in the given circumstances and Shakespeare has *humanised* him to such good purpose that this comic Jew has become, for many brilliant and sensitive critics, a moving, almost a tragic, figure. Some even go so far as to exclaim of Shylock in his anguish: O what a noble mind is here o'erthrown!

How exactly has this come about? Why and when, if ever, does Shylock cease to be a comic character? Going to Shakespeare's text for an answer to these questions we shall perhaps find a clue not only to the nature of Shakespeare's achievement but to the process by which it is attained. ⟨...⟩

There is no better example of interplay between technical craft and creative imagination than the way in which the character of Shylock, apparently predeter-mined by the necessities of the story in which he figures and by the expectations of the audience to which he was presented, assumes the dimensions and habit of a character which exists freely and in its own right. Admittedly his behaviour in the play is settled in advance. But Shakespeare immediately identifies himself with the sort of person who must inevitably behave in that particular way. Shylock, setting forth upon the stage, is at once a man with hands, organs, dimensions, senses, affections, passions, and the plot to which he must conform soon appears to be no more than an opportunity for bringing him to life. The plot determined the kind of character which Shakespeare created; but the character, once created, determines everything he says or does. It is the paradox of great art that limitations arising from the nature of a given subject, the quality of the materials used and the restrictions imposed by necessary conventions merely serve to concentrate the activity of a free spirit on the business in hand. The artist with little or nothing to express complains of the discipline imposed upon him by the laws of his craft, wastes his energy in quarrelling with his tools or devotes more attention to the invention of a new technique than to the exploitation and development of an inherited tradition. Not so the man of genius. Shakespeare, taking Shylock's merry bond for a theme and accepting all the restrictions of the Elizabethan theatre, expressed himself as freely and profoundly as Beethoven when he unlocked his heart and disclosed the entire length, breadth and depth of his genius, in thirty-three variations on a merry waltz by Diabelli.

Shakespeare in presenting Shylock has so artfully combined the necessities of his plot with the revelation of a character that it is difficult, almost impossible, to say of any single incident or speech which of the two purposes is better served. The man lives in every word that he utters. He has a distinct language of his own and every syllable denotes his quality. His first words are of ducats; his introductory conversation with Bassanio might be cross-headed: Any usurer to any client: *Three thousand . . . ducats . . . For three months . . . Antonio shall become bound . . . Antonio is a good man . . . Yet his means are in supposition . . . The man is notwithstanding sufficient . . . Three thousand ducats—I think I may take his bond.* There is nothing here that seems to serve any other purpose than to present the comic Jew and to get the story under way. But the man is already alive. We shall know him again as soon as he opens his lips—a man whose words are stubborn in his mouth, in whose speech there is no ease or warmth or levity, who hammers out his phrases and can find no way of varying them once they are uttered. *Three thousand ducats . . . Antonio bound.* It is the utterance of a man whose mind is concentrated, obsessed, focused upon a narrow range of fixed ideas. Shylock had the trick of compulsive repetition characteristic of the man in whom imagination, such as it is, forever sits on brood. It is the speech of one who is incapable of humour, whose words will always precisely fit his meaning, in whom no play or flight of fancy is possible:

> Ships are but boards, sailors but men. There be land-rats and water-rats, land-thieves and water-thieves—I mean pirates. And then there is the peril of waters, winds and rocks.

Such is the eloquence of Shylock. So literal is his habit of mind that he must interrupt his recitation of the bleak hazards of trade to explain that by water-thieves, a phrase which strikes him as possibly too picturesque to be exactly understood, he means pirates. Contrast with this plain, surly, intensive style of utterance the warm, easy flow of the Venetian gentleman, Salerio, speaking to the same theme:

> My wind, cooling my broth,
> Would blow me to an ague when I thought
> What harm a wind too great might do at sea.

I should not see the sandy hour-glass run
But I should think of shallows and of flats,
And see my wealthy Andrew docked in sand,
Vailing her high-top lower than her ribs
To kiss her burial. Should I go to church
And see the holy edifice of stone,
And not bethink me straight of dangerous rocks,
Which touching but my gentle vessel's side
Would scatter all her spices on the stream,
Enrobe the roaring waters with my silks,
And, in a word, but even now worth this,
And now worth nothing?

Here, then, is Shylock revealed at his first appearance in every phrase that he utters as a certain kind of man and, what is equally to the purpose, as a totally different kind of man from his Christian adversaries. His tricks of speech already project a character, unmistakeably alive, which will be recognisably true to itself in all that follows. The will recur throughout the play till they culminate in those stubborn, reiterated appeals to his bond of a man possessed by a single thought expressed in a phrase that has become almost an incantation.

Meanwhile Shakespeare must come immediately to grips with his story of the comic Jew and the pound of flesh. He grasps the nettle firmly in an aside wherein Shylock discloses his intention and the motives behind it:

How like a fawning publican he looks!
I hate him for he is a Christian:
But more for that in low simplicity
He lends out money gratis, and brings down
The rate of usance here with us in Venice.
If I can catch him once upon the hip,
I will feed fat the ancient grudge I bear him.
He hates our sacred nation, and he rails,
Even there where merchants most do congregate,
On me, my bargains, and my well-won thrift,
Which he calls interest. Cursèd be my tribe,
If I forgive him!

There is no hint in this speech, and there has been as yet no suggestion in the play, that Shylock has any human justification for his monstrous project. For the moment Shakespeare is satisfied with presenting his comic Jew in all the stark, ugly simplicity of the legend with which his audience was familiar. Shylock detests Antonio because he is a Christian; because he lends out money gratis and brings down the rate of usance; because he 'hates the Jews and dislikes their way of doing business'. Shylock, in this first exhibition of his malice, is a comic figure and so he remains in the passages that follow: debating of his present store; delivering the traditional patter of the moneylender about the difficulty of making up the sum required; justifying his practice of usury by citing the trick played by Jacob on Laban over the parti-coloured lambs.

Then comes the first intimation that Shakespeare, having undertaken to supply his audience with a comic Jew committed to a barbarous enterprise, not only intends to make his conduct psychologically credible but has already realised in imagination what it means to wear the star of David:

> SHYLOCK: Signior Antonio, many a time and oft
> In the Rialto you have rated me
> About my moneys and my usances:
> Still have I borne it with a patient shrug,
> For suff'rance is the badge of all our tribe.
> You call me misbeliever, cut-throat dog,
> And spet upon my Jewish gaberdine,
> And all for use of that which is mine own.
> Well then, it now appears you need my help:
> Go to then, you come to me, and you say,
> 'Shylock, we would have moneys'—you say so!
> You that did void your rheum upon my beard,
> And foot me as you spurn a stranger cur
> Over your threshold—moneys is your suit.
> What should I say to you? Should I not say
> 'Hath a dog money? is it possible
> A cur can lend three thousand ducats?' or
> Shall I bend low, and in a bondman's key,
> With bated breath, and whisp'ring humbleness,
> Say this:
> 'Fair sir, you spet on me on Wednesday last—
> You spurned me such a day—another time
> You called me dog: and for these courtesies
> I'll lend you thus moneys'?

That is perhaps the most remarkable speech in the play. It suggests for the first time on any stage that the Jew has a case. The Jew, moreover, puts that case with a deadly logic, sharpened by persecution to the finest edge, and with a passion which no amount of suff'rance can conceal. It reveals a mind so intensely concentrated upon itself, so constricted in its operation, that it can only express itself in repetitions of a rhythmic, almost hypnotic, quality. *You have rated me about my moneys . . . Shylock, we would have moneys . . . moneys is your suit. . . . You call me misbeliever, cut-throat dog. . . . Hath a dog money? . . . You called me dog and, for these courtesies, I'll lend you thus much moneys. And spet upon my Jewish gab-erdine. . . . You that did void your rheum upon my beard. . . . Fair sir, you spet on me on Wednesday last.*

Neither in logic nor in passion can Shylock be assailed and the Christians do not even attempt a rejoinder. Antonio, in fact, calls down upon himself the doom that awaits one side or the other in any conflict that passes the bounds of reason:

> I am as like to call thee so again,
> To spet on thee again, to spurn thee too.
> If thou wilt lend this money, lend it not
> As to thy friends—for when did friendship take
> A breed for barren metal of his friend?—
> But lend it rather to thine enemy,
> Who, if he break, thou mayst with better face
> Exact the penalty.

And so we come to the business of the bond. It is a difficult moment. But note how quickly and easily it is handled. The passages that precede it may be likened to the patter of a conjurer who distracts the attention of his audience as he prepares to play his master-trick. Shylock's speech and Antonio's reply have fixed our attention on the fundamental issue of the play as between Christian and Jew and, before we have recovered our emotional balance sufficiently to realise what is happening, hey presto! the thing is done:

> SHYLOCK: Why, look you, how you storm!
> I would be friends with you, and have your love,
> Forget the shames that you have stained me with,
> Supply your present wants, and take no doit
> Of usance for my moneys, and you'll not hear me:
> This kind I offer
> ANTONIO: This were kindness
> SHYLOCK: This kindness will I show.
> Go with me to a notary, seal me there
> Your single bond, and, in a merry sport,
> If you repay me not on such a day,
> In such a place, such sum or sums as are
> Expressed in the condition, let the forfeit
> Be nominated for an equal pound
> Of your fair flesh, to be cut off and taken
> In what part of your body pleaseth me.
> ANTONIO: Content, in faith—I'll seal to such a bond,
> And say there is much kindness in the Jew.

It is done, too, in a fashion which in no way detracts from the reality of the characters or their relationship. Shylock, in forwarding the plot, is still revealing himself as the kind of man who will later come into court with his knife and scales. There is nothing more sinister-comic in the whole literature of hypocrisy than the two speeches to Antonio. *This is kind I offer. . . . And in a merry sport.* Shylock kind!

Shylock merry! Why, even as he makes his proposal, the secret passion that moves him is strong enough to penetrate and subdue his victim who is, as it were, hypnotised into adopting Shylock's own characteristic trick of repetition. 'This were kindness', says Antonio; 'there is much kindness in the Jew.'

The ease with which Antonio is trapped into the bond with Shylock is a good example of the way in which Shakespeare turns to advantage the limitations imposed upon him by his material. Antonio is predestined to sign a contract which will put his life at the mercy of a mortal enemy whom he has every reason to distrust. That is a tall order. Shakespeare does not evade the difficulty, but uses it to serve perhaps the most striking purpose of his play, which is to contrast the narrow, alert and suspicious character of the Jew, member of a persecuted race, with the free, careless and confident disposition of the Christian sure of his place in the sun. It is a contrast maintained in every scene of the play. Shylock in word and deed is typical, intense and precise; the Christians are impulsive, sentimental and wayward. Shylock trusts in his bond; the Christians trust to luck—whether it be Bassanio staking love and fortune on the choice of a casket or Antonio gambling on the ships which fail to come home. Shylock tells us of his 'bargains' and his 'well-won thrift', but riches fall from a window on to the head of Lorenzo. The characteristic qualities on either side are respectively those of the oppressed and the oppressor. If in Shylock we stand appalled by the warping of mind and spirit which oppression inflicts on those who suffer it, we are not less repelled by the infatuated assumption of Antonio and his friends that to them all is permitted in the best of possible worlds. The point is constantly emphasised in the minutest particulars of dialogue and incident. When Shylock, justifying his bargains, cites the case of Jacob and the parti-coloured lambs:

> This was a way to thrive, and he was blest:
> And *thrift* is blessing if men steal it not;

Antonio rejoins:

> This was a venture, sir, that Jacob served for—
> A thing not in his power to bring to pass,
> But swayed and fashioned by the hand of heaven.

Here, incidentally but in a nutshell, the careful husbandry of the Jew is contrasted with the careless genial improvidence of the Christian. Such touches of character, constantly repeated, not only prepare us for Antonio's easy acceptance of the bond but dispose us to swallow the whole preposterous story as entirely natural to the persons conceived.

From the sealing of the merry bond we pass to the story of Jessica. No incident in the play has so richly contributed to the transformation of Shylock, the comic Jew, into a lamentable victim of Christian bigotry and licence. This metamorphosis reached its literary climax in Heine:

I heard a voice with a ripple of tears that were never wept by eyes. It was a sob that could come only from a breast that held in it all the martyrdom which, for eighteen centuries, had been borne by a whole tortured people. It was the death-rattle of a soul, sinking down dead tired at heaven's gates. And I seemed to know the voice, and I felt I had heard it long ago when in utter despair it moaned out, then as now, 'Jessica, my girl'.

On the stage it attained its theatrical climax, for those who remember it, when Henry Irving returning by the light of a lantern knocked on the door of an empty house. Where, now, is your monster with a large painted nose? This is a patriarch of Israel, wronged in his most sacred affections. Small wonder if, after this, the afflicted Jew grows blind to the quality of Christian mercy.

Alas for those who, seeking to find Shakespeare in one part only of his design, lose or pervert the whole! There is as little warrant for the voice that moaned in Heine's ear as for the Irving interpolation which made of that tragic figure beating on the door a sublime and pathetic incident to wring your hearts.

What are the facts?

Shylock, bidding farewell to his daughter, is more truly comic than at any point of the story so far reached:

> I am bid forth to supper, Jessica.
> There are my keys. But wherefore should I go?
> I am not bid for love—they flatter me.
> But yet I'll go in hate, to feed upon
> The prodigal Christian. Jessica, my girl,
> Look to my house. I am right loath to go—
> There is some ill a-brewing towards my rest,
> For I did dream of money-bags to-night.

This, then, is the voice, the death rattle of a soul sinking down dead tired at heaven's gates. *Jessica, my girl, look to my house.* Heine, in underlining the pathos, has missed the essential quality of the scene. Shakespeare did not write *'Jessica, my girl'*, but *'Jessica, my girl, look to my house'*, and 'house' is the operative word. In claiming for Shylock the heartbroken misery of a loving father bereft of his child the man of sentiment loses the essential genius of the dramatist who created him. It is the house which stands at the core of Shylock's being; Jessica is no more than the daughter of the house:

> Do as I bid you, shut doors after you:
> Fast bind, fast find.

Not only the doors but the windows must be shut:

> Lock up my doors, and when you hear the drum
> And the vile squealing of the wry-neck'd fife,
> Clamber not you up to the casements then,

Nor thrust your head into the public street
To gaze on Christian fools with varnished faces:
But stop my house's ears, I mean my casements,
Let not the sound of shallow fopp'ry enter
My sober house.[6]

Shylock, speaking of his house, is moved almost to poetry. The house is for him a living thing—*Stop my house's ears;* and the word once used, since it stands for one of the few things on which his mind is passionately centred, must be repeated—*'Let not the sound of shallow fopp'ry enter my sober house.'* And that word will be heard again:

Nay, take my life and all, pardon not that.
You take my house, when you do take the prop
That doth sustain my house.

Shylock's farewell to Jessica, which established him for Heine as a tragic figure, leaves him still comic in the play that Shakespeare wrote. Shakespeare has done no more in this scene—but how much it is —than humanise the stage qualities of the comic Jew. Every stroke aims at our sense of comedy. 'Thou shalt not gormandise, as thou hast done with me', he tells Lancelot who is quitting him to serve Bassanio, and, in bidding farewell to this 'huge feeder', he exhibits a malevolence which, like all fixed ideas in a living creature, is at the same time ludicrous and terrible:

Drones hive not with me.
Therefore I part with him, and part with him
To one that I would have him help to waste
His borrowed purse.[7]

Is Shylock, mourning his daughter's flight, any less comic than Shylock bidding his daughter to shut his doors and windows? A careful study of the scene with Salerio and Tubal provokes conclusions profoundly disconcerting to the heirs of the romantic tradition. It is supremely comic in itself and Shakespeare deliberately contrived in advance that the comic element should prevail over its emotional implications. Far from intending us to sympathise with an afflicted father, he has emphasised before the event that Shylock's affection is abnormally possessive and, in depicting the Jew's reaction to her flight, he subordinates even this self-centred affection to the fury of a man of property upon whose well-won thrift an unspeakable outrage has been committed. *My own flesh and blood to rebel. . . . I say, my daughter is my own flesh and blood.* This chimes perfectly with 'Jessica, my girl, look to my house'. His daughter, his own flesh and blood, had abandoned his house and 'she is damned for it'. She has made off, too, with his jewels and his ducats. There was no need for Shakespeare to introduce this incident at all. It detracts from the pleasure which his audience is clearly intended to take in the sweet infidel who holds a candle to her shames and it encourages romantics and realists alike to take a very poor view of Bassanio's friend, Lorenzo. Heine, as we have seen, would have given Lorenzo fifteen years in the penitentiary. But Shakespeare had other fish to fry. Jessica gilds herself with Shylock's ducats so that Shylock may reveal himself more effectively as an essentially comic character:

SHYLOCK: How now, Tubal! what news from Genoa? hast thou found my daughter?

TUBAL: I often came where I did hear of her, but cannot find her.

SHYLOCK: Why there, there, there, there—a diamond gone, cost me two thousand ducats in Frankfort—the curse never fell upon our nation till now, I never felt it till now—two thousand ducats in that, and other precious, precious jewels. I would my daughter were dead at my foot, and the jewels in her ear! would she were hearsed at my foot, and the ducats in her coffin! No news of them? Why, so—and I know not what's spent in the search: why, thou loss upon loss! the thief gone with so much and so much to find the thief, and no satisfaction, no revenge, nor no ill luck stirring, but what lights o' my shoulders, no sighs but o' my breathing, no tears but o' my shedding. (*he weeps*)

That is admittedly a rather terrible scene. But it is undeniably comic, the victim owing more ludicrous as he becomes more poignantly enslaved to his obsession; and the passage that follows in which Shylock alternately rages at the thought of Jessica squandering his ducats and rejoices to hear of Antonio's losses at sea, brings the comedy to a climax. Shylock's responses to Tubal are like the jerking reflexes of a marionette. They give him just that appearance of a human automaton which is one of the most characteristic effects of pure comedy:

TUBAL: Yes, other men have ill luck too. Antonio, as I heard in Genoa—

SHYLOCK: What, what, what? ill luck, ill luck?

TUBAL: —hath an argosy cast away, coming from Tripolis.

SHYLOCK: I thank God, I thank God! Is it true? is it true?

TUBAL: I spoke with some of the sailors that escaped the wrack.

SHYLOCK: I thank thee, good Tubal, good news, good news: ha, ha! Where? In Genoa?

TUBAL: Your daughter spent in Genoa, as I heard, one night, fourscore ducats.

SHYLOCK: Thou stick'st a dagger in me. I shall never see my gold again— fourscore ducats at a sitting! fourscore ducats!

TUBAL: There came divers of Antonio's creditors in my company to Venice, that swear he cannot choose but break.

SHYLOCK: I am very glad of it. I'll plague him. I'll torture him, I am glad of it.

TUBAL: One of them showed me a ring that he had of your daughter for a monkey.

SHYLOCK: Out upon her! thou torturest me, Tubal—it was my turquoise—I had

> it of Leah when I was a bachelor: I would not have given it for a
> wilderness of monkeys.
> TUBAL: But Antonio is certainly undone.
> SHYLOCK: Nay, that's true, that's very true. Go, Tubal, fee me an officer,
> bespeak him a fortnight before. I will have the heart of him if he forfeit,
> for were he out of Venice I can make what merchandise I will.[8]

The conclusion is worth noting. Shylock has lost his daughter. He has been
wounded to the quick of his personal feeling and racial pride. But Shakespeare still
insists on the point from which he started. The Jew hates Antonio because he lends
out money gratis and brings down the rate of usance. He will have the heart of
Antonio, for 'were he out of Venice I can make what merchandise I will'.

Nevertheless it is this scene from which the romantic tradition of Shylock is
mainly derived. For it contains the great speech, so often read and quoted with too
little regard for its context, which has misled so many critics into praising Shakespeare as a champion of tolerance and humanity where they might more pertinently have admired his genius as a dramatist and his imaginative intimacy with all
sorts and conditions of men:

> SHYLOCK: Hath not a Jew eyes? Hath not a Jew hands, organs, dimensions,
> senses, affections, passions? fed with the same food, hurt with the same
> weapons, subject to the same diseases, healed by the same means,
> warmed and cooled by the same winter and summer, as a Christian is?
> If you prick us, do we not bleed? if you tickle us, do we not laugh? if you
> poison us, do we not die?

That sounds like a plea for charity. Taken in its context, however, it is something
less, and at the same time something more. Shylock's theme is not charity but
revenge. He will have Antonio's flesh, if only to bait fish withal:

> He hath disgraced me and hindred me half a million, laughed at my losses,
> mocked at my gains, scorned my nation, thwarted my bargains, cooled my
> friends, heated mine enemies—and what's his reason? I am a Jew.

and he concludes:

> If a Jew wrong a Christian, what is his humility? Revenge. If a Christian
> wrong a Jew, what should his sufferance be by Christian example? Why,
> revenge. The villainy you teach me, I will execute, and it shall go hard but I will
> better the instruction.

Thus, what is commonly received as Shylock's plea for tolerance is in reality his
justification of an inhuman purpose. That does not, however, lessen, but rather
increase its significance. The most dreadful consequence of injustice is that it de-
grades not only the oppressor but the oppressed. Shakespeare is concerned to
present only the human truth of a situation which he has accepted for the purpose

of his play. Shylock, since his motives must be more humanly comprehensible, is presented as a natural product of Christian intolerance, but he does not thereby cease to be a comic character or become an advocate of the humaner virtues. There is something grotesque even in his pleading. *If you tickle us, do we not laugh?* Shakespeare was not here concerned—he never is concerned—with pleading a case in morality. He was presenting Shylock as Shylock lived in his imagination and, in so doing, he showed us how a dramatist, intent only upon his vision, incidentally achieves a moral effect wider in scope and more profound in its implications than a dramatist who consciously devotes himself to an ethical purpose. The comically distorted image of Shylock the Jew is in effect a more telling indictment of Christian oppression, though Shakespeare was not primarily concerned with that aspect of the matter, than the fictitiously sentimentalised presentment of the character created for modern playgoers by Edmund Kean and his successors. Many fine plays have been written by dramatists which expressly indict man's inhumanity to man, but no work of art created with an express political or moral intention is in the last resort so effective, even in the attainment of its purpose, as a work of art which achieves excellence in the form and spirit proper to itself. Critics and actors who, to enhance Shakespeare's hypothetical message, do their best to make Shylock humanly impressive and invite our commiseration for the ruins of a noble nature are likely to discover in the end that they have not only spoiled a comedy but defeated their own object and impaired the moral effect of the play.

There is one other point to be noted in Shakespeare's handling of Jessica. It is often insinuated by commentators who are determined to elevate the issue between Shylock and Antonio, that the Jew was goaded into claiming his pound of flesh by the abduction of his daughter. Here, again, Shakespeare has, in the biblical sense, prevented them. Shakespeare uses the Jessica incident to make Shylock's behaviour in court more acceptable to the audience. We must have seen for ourselves some reason for the Jew's hatred of Antonio made real and visible in dramatic form. Having witnessed the flight of Jessica and Shylock's reaction to it, we shall be more likely to believe in the inexorable dog who sharpens the knife on his sole. But Shakespeare having used the incident to make the Jew's conduct in court seem less improbable suddenly realises that, in so doing, he may have left us with an impression that Shylock was moved to extremity by paternal anguish, and, as though he foresaw the use to be made of this episode by a romantic posterity, he slips in an explicit repudiation of any such interpretation. When the news of Antonio's arrest reaches Belmont and is discussed with Portia, Jessica assures Bassanio:

> When I was with him, I have heard him swear
> To Tubal and to Chus, his countrymen,
> That he would rather have Antonio's flesh
> Than twenty times the value of the sum
> That he did owe him.[9]

Shakespeare here goes out of his way to inform us expressly that Shylock had made up his mind to kill Antonio long before Jessica's flight with Lorenzo—that he had, in fact, been in the habit of delivering at home speeches of the kind which he was shortly to repeat in the court-house:

> If every ducat in six thousand ducats
> Were in six parts and every part a ducat,
> I would not draw them, I would have my bond!

'Shylock no miser' declared Coleridge in a lecture on Shakespeare delivered on February 6th, 1812 to a 'numerous and genteel audience'. He was maintaining that Shakespeare 'drew from the eternal of our nature' and that the miser being but a 'transitory character', peculiar to a certain type of society, could find no place in his imagination. Coleridge would probably have agreed to the obverse of his proposition, namely, that Shakespeare, in depicting a 'transitory character', almost inevitably gave to it a permanent reality. 'Shylock no miser' is a true bill in the sense that he is a man of many parts and qualities. Shakespeare did not, like Jonson, see men as humours walking. He presents us not with character parts or stage types, but with complete and often unaccountable human beings. 'Shylock no miser' is true in the general sense that he is more than a personification of avarice. 'Shylock no miser' is equally true in the more particular sense that, though he dreams of money-bags and wishes his daughter hearsed at his foot with the ducats in her coffin and hates Antonio for bringing down the rate of usance, he would not for any number of ducats forgo his revenge on the merchant and refuses thrice the sum due to him in open court. Shakespeare nevertheless never allows us to lose sight of the fact that the most *abiding* element in his character is hatred of extravagance. He may not love money for its own sake, but it stands for the cardinal virtues in his calendar of sober thrift and respect for material values. That he should be cheated of his hard-won bargains by the easy-handed gentlemen of Venice touches him to the quick. It destroys the very foundations on which he bases his conduct and assesses his own personal worth. Jessica's behaviour is an outrage. That she should make away with his ducats is bad enough. That she should have bartered her turquoise ring—and her mother's ring at that—for a monkey makes sacrilegious nonsense of the thrift that in Jacob was blest by the God of Israel.[10]

Shylock makes only one other appearance before his case is heard and Shakespeare takes this occasion to remind us once again of his principal grievance against Antonio. The Jew meets him in custody:

> Gaoler, look to him. Tell me not of mercy.
> This is the fool that lent out money gratis.

There is no reference here to a lost child or even to his sacred nation; and the essentially comic quality of the Jew's mind and utterance, with its compulsive repetitions, is admirably sustained. The word 'bond' occurs six times:

I'll have my *bond,* speak not against my *bond,*
I have sworn an oath that I will have my *bond:*
Thou call'dst me dog before thou hadst a cause,
But since I am a dog beware my fangs.

I'll have my *bond*—I will not hear thee speak.
I'll have my *bond,* and therefore speak no more.
I'll not be made a soft and dull-eyed fool,
To shake the head, relent, and sigh, and yield
To Christian intercessors . . . Follow not—
I'll have no speaking, I will have my *bond.*

Shakespeare is now ready—and his audience, too—for the confrontation in court by which his comedy will stand or fall. His task was to get the maximum dramatic effect out of an intrinsically improbable situation. So well did he succeed that the scene is theatrically one of the most effective ever put upon the stage. It is, at the same time, a scene which, owing to the skill with which the playwright solved his technical problems and brought his characters imaginatively to life as dramatic persons, has moral implications which exceed the author's immediate purpose. Critics tend to ignore the technical achievement and make too much of the implications, finding here a noble plea for Christian charity or there an exposure of Christian barbarity. The court scene is frequently read or produced as though its prime purpose and title to fame were Portia's very adequate but by no means outstanding discourse upon the quality of mercy, whereas, in fact, that speech is merely one of many in which Shakespeare exploits the dramatic possibilities of the situation.[11]

Shylock, in this scene, achieves his discomfiture by the very qualities which distinguish him most conspicuously as a comic character. He digs with his own hands the pit into which we know that he will most assuredly fall and supplies his enemies with the very weapons by which he is defeated. From the moment in which he enters the court, he stands inexorably upon the letter of the law. The Duke, when the case is opened, entreats him to glance an eye of pity on the losses of Antonio. But Shylock has sworn to have his bond. The Duke asks how he can hope for mercy if he renders none. But Shylock has no need of mercy; Antonio's flesh is dearly bought, 'tis his and he will have it. Portia, finding the bond correct, declares that the Jew must be merciful. But Shylock admits no such compulsion; and, when Portia, echoing the Duke, urges that men should be merciful as they hope for mercy, he exclaims: 'My deeds upon my head, I crave the law.' When Portia begs him to take the money and to forgo the pound of flesh, he charges her by the law to proceed to judgment; he stays upon his bond. The flesh must be cut from the merchant's breast—nearest his heart. So says the bond—those are the very words. Portia asks for a surgeon. But Shylock can find no mention of a surgeon. Is it so nominated in the bond?

Thus, speech by speech, Shakespeare prepares for the moment when Shylock's own insistence upon the letter of the law will be turned against him and when
his repudiation of charity will bring its own retribution. Portia's speech on the
question of mercy is dramatically merely an item in the comic process.

Note, too, how Shylock increases his own discomfiture—again it is the comic
process—by accepting Portia in advance as a worthy representative of the law by
which he stands. Portia has been scolded by some critics for keeping the wretched
Antonio and his friends on tenterhooks. Surely it was most unkind to bring the poor
merchant to the point of baring his breast for the knife when she had it in her
power at any moment to shatter the whole case against him.[12] Shakespeare, by
lending verisimilitude to this impossible scene, has again betrayed his commentators into applying to it the standards of normal behaviour. He sees to it, as a
craftsman, that the scene shall be played for all it is worth and that Shylock shall
in every particular turn the tables on Shylock. The Jew is self-entrapped not only
into supplying the Christian advocate with a plausible justification for strictly rendering the letter of the law against him but into finding for his enemies the very
words with which they taunt him in his overthrow. *Most rightful judge! Most
learned judge! A Daniel come to judgment!* Portia, proceeding to extremes
against Antonio, earns these praises from Shylock in order that they may in poetic justice be used against him. Her behaviour throughout the scene is conditioned by the part which Shakespeare requires her to play in achieving the comic
catastrophe.

Shylock is never more Shylock than when he bears the full burden of this
incredible scene. He has the same tricks of speech, the same obsessions, the same
compulsive habits of thought and expression. The clear stubborn logic of his mind
still enables him to confound his enemies by justifying his own practice from
Christian example. He has rated Christian hypocrisy—*How like a fawning publican
he looks!* He has declared that the Jew, equally with the Christian, knows how to
revenge a wrong and can even better the instruction. He now turns in court on the
men who counsel mercy and try to argue him out of his rights with the same
unanswerable logic:

> You have among you many a purchased slave,
> Which, like your asses and your dogs and mules,
> You use in abject and in slavish parts,
> Because you bought them—shall I say to you,
> Let them be free, marry them to your heirs?
> Why sweat they under burthens? Let their beds
> Be made as soft as yours, and let their palates
> Be seasoned with such viands? You will answer,
> 'The slaves are ours.' So do I answer you—
> The pound of flesh, which I demand of him,
> Is dearly bought, '*tis mine*, and I will have it.

On his own ground, which he claims to share with his persecutors, Shylock is impregnable. He knows, none better, that Christian society is *not* based on the mercy for which the Duke and Portia so ingenuously plead. He asks no more than that the Christians shall apply to his case the principles where by their own affections and affairs are ruled. A man may do what he will with his own. Antonio's flesh is his, legally acquired and dearly bought, and, if he likes to use it to bait fish withal, that is entirely his affair:

> You'll ask me why I rather choose to have
> A weight of carrion flesh than to receive
> Three thousand ducats: I'll not answer that!
> But say it is my humour, is it answered?
> What if my house be troubled with a rat,
> And I be pleased to give ten thousand ducats
> To have it baned? what, are you answered?

He has successfully contrived a situation which enables him to do for once what they are in the habit of doing every day of their lives and he means to make good use of it:

> Some men there are love not a gaping pig,
> Some that are mad if they behold a cat,
> And others when the bag-pipe sings i' th' nose
> Cannot contain their urine: for affection,
> Master of passion, sways it to the mood
> Of what it likes or loathes. Now, for your answer:
> As there is no firm reason to be rendered,
> Why he cannot abide a gaping pig;
> Why he, a harmless necessary cat;
> Why he, a woollen bag-pipe; but of force
> Must yield to such inevitable shame,
> As to offend, himself being offended;
> So can I give no reason, nor I will not,
> More than a lodged hate and a certain loathing
> I bear Antonio, that I follow thus
> A losing suit against him! Are you answered?

Shylock, carrying his hatred to extremes, exposes the injustice and ferocity of the social institutions from which it springs. He appeals to the twin laws of retribution and property on which the society in which he lives is based. Nothing is further from Shakespeare's mind than to convey a lesson. But the lesson is there, product of a perfectly balanced and sensitive mind intent upon the dramatic presentation of human realities. The debated question whether Shakespeare writing certain passages of *The Merchant of Venice* was pleading for toleration or indicting Christian hypocrisy, exalting equity above the law or divine mercy above human justice, does not arise. He presents a situation in which all these issues are involved, characters in which their effects are displayed, arguments appropriate to the necessary incidents and persons of the comedy; and leaves it to his critics to draw the indictment or convey the apology. His purpose was to write a comedy and he is never more intent on this purpose than in the scene whose moral implications have excited so much interest among those who study the play in the light of their own ethical and social standards. Shylock eagerly producing the bond for Portia's inspection—the bond which is to prove his own undoing—is undeniably comic. So is Shylock examining the bond to verify that the flesh must be cut from Antonio nearest his heart. So is Shylock looking in vain for any mention of a surgeon. So is Shylock applauding the wisdom of the judge who is about to ruin him. So, above all, is Shylock promptly asking for the return of his money when he realises that his claim to Antonio's flesh will not be allowed.

And behind all this obvious comedy is the indifferent irony of the comic spirit which, in presenting the human realities of a situation, necessarily exposes the blindness of human beings to their own inconsistencies: Portia, singing the praises of mercy when she is about to insist that the Jew shall have the full rigours of justice according to the strict letter of the law; Antonio, congratulating himself on his magnanimity in the very act of imposing on his enemy a sentence which deprives him of everything he values; Christian and Jew mutually charging one another with an inhumanity which is common to both parties.

How Shylock, imagined by Shakespeare as a comic figure and sustaining his comic character to the last, was yet able to become a depositary of the vengeance of his race (Hazlitt), the ruins of a great and noble nature (Hudson) and the most respectable person in the play (Heine) is now perhaps sufficiently evident. The question when and how, if ever, Shylock ceases to be comic answers itself as we read the play. To the question when? the answer, if we bear in mind that Shakespeare's comedy springs from imaginative sympathy and not from intellectual detachment, is: never for an instant. The question how? should not therefore arise. But alas for logic and the categories! No-one can remain wholly insensible to the emotional impact of the play. The imaginative effort expended by Shakespeare in making his Jew a comprehensibly human figure has imparted to him a vitality that every now and then stifles laughter and freezes the smile on our lips. If these passages are rightly handled by the actor or accorded their just place and value by the reader, the comedy remains intact. If, on the contrary, these passages are thrown into high relief and made to stand out of their context, the comedy is destroyed. Heine maintained that Shakespeare *intended* to write a comedy but was too great a man to succeed.[13] This comes very near the truth, but what really happened was something rather more subtle and difficult to describe. Shakespeare took the comic Jew for a theme, and wrote a true comedy. But it was a comedy after his own pattern and desire—a comedy in which ridicule does not exclude compassion, in which sympathy and detachment are reconciled in the irony which is necessarily achieved by the comic spirit in a serene presentation of things as they are.

Shylock as a comic character held the stage for over a century. Then came an interval of forty years, from 1701 to 1741, when good taste imposed on English audiences a mangled version of the play by Lord Lansdowne, a nonentity whose trimmings and embellishments may be recommended to the curious as an up-standing monument to the complacency with which an eighteenth-century noble-man was able to view the achievements of a barbarian:

> The first rude sketches Shakespeare's pencil drew
> But all the shining master-strokes are new;
> This play, ye critics, shall your fury stand
> Adorn'd and rescu'd by a faultless hand.

Shylock was still a comic character, for whom Lord Lansdowne was good enough to provide fresh occasions for mockery, notably at a banquet where the Jew drinks to his money-bags. Then, in 1741, came Macklin of whom Pope, not without good reason, indited a famous epitaph:

> Here lies the Jew
> That Shakespeare drew.

There is some evidence that it was Macklin who first suggested to an English audience that Shylock was pathetic. 'The Jew's private calamities', says Davies, who saw Macklin at Drury Lane, 'made some tender impressions on the audience'. But Macklin's Shylock was in the comic tradition and it gave birth to a whole generation of comic Shylocks who devoted their considerable talents to building up the gro-tesque figure denounced by Hazlitt: a 'decrepit old man, bent with age and ugly with mental deformity, with the venom in his heart congealed in the expression of his countenance, sullen, morose, gloomy, inflexible, brooding over one idea, that of his hatred, and fixed on one unalterable purpose, that of his revenge'.[14]

All these Shylocks were destroyed in a single night by Edmund Kean on January 26th, 1814. Kean converted Hazlitt and for the next hundred years Hazlitt's judgment was never seriously challenged. All the great actors conspired to per-petuate and adorn the new reading. The nobility of Macready's Shylock was in due course exceeded by the priestly dignity of Henry Irving (1879) and the aristocratic good form of Forbes Robertson.[15] The actor's triumph over the author was by the end of the nineteenth century complete.

Shakespeare has finished with Shylock when he stumbles from the court:

> I am not well. Send the deed after me
> And I will sign it.

The law which he invoked pursues him to the last, and the bond in which Antonio signed away his life is replaced by the deed in which the Jew must sign away his property. Shakespeare, who has used all his art to put Shylock credibly before our eyes in flesh and blood, now takes us back to the pleasant estate of Belmont which, with a skill that will claim your admiration if you look into it at all closely, he has kept so carefully secluded from the harsh realities of the ghetto and the market-place. We hear the music to which the ears of Shylock's house were closed. Music in Shylock's Venice is a vile squeaking of the wry-necked fife or a bag-pipe that sings i' th' nose. Music at Belmont now enters with moonlight to take entire possession:

> LORENZO: How sweet the moonlight sleeps upon this bank!
> Here will we sit, and let the sounds of music
> Creep in our ears—soft stillness and the night
> Become the touches of sweet harmony.
> Sit, Jessica. Look how the floor of heaven
> Is thick inlaid with patines of bright gold,
> There's not the smallest orb which thou behold'st
> But in his motion like an angel sings,
> Still quiring to the young-eyed cherubims;
> Such harmony is in immortal souls!
> But whilst this muddy vesture of decay
> Doth grossly close it in, we cannot hear it.
>
> The man that hath no music in himself,
> Nor is not moved with concord of sweet sounds,
> Is fit for treasons, stratagems, and spoils,
> The motions of his spirit are dull as night,
> And his affections dark as Erebus:
> Let no such man be trusted.

The little candle in Portia's hall throws its beams; so shines a good deed in a naughty world. We are back in the age of innocence when tales are told indoors by candlelight, and beyond the window, Peace ho, the moon sleeps with Endymion! Here we can believe again in the lucky caskets and are caught up in a pretty confusion of rings and posies. Antonio's ships can now come home and the story of Shylock lingers in the memory as an old, unhappy tale.

But it was a tale in which we believed—and to such good purpose that for generations its rights and wrongs, its arguments and incidents and the persons who figured in it, have been seriously debated as matters pertaining to the 'eternal of our nature'.

NOTES

[1] See the present author's *Political Characters of Shakespeare*, pp. 119, 120.
[2] That Shakespeare had Lopez in mind when he set out to portray Shylock is incidentally confirmed by the lines that slip into the mouths of Bassanio and Portia at Belmont. Lopez, prior to his prosecution by the Crown, made some damaging admissions concerning the plot of which he was accused, but pleaded at his trial that he had much belied himself in his confession *to save himself from racking*. The use of torture to obtain evidence was a legally respectable institution under Elizabeth; but we need not necessarily conclude that normally decent people regarded it as morally defensible or even a sensible practice. It has always been the habit of English citizens individually to question or condemn proceedings

and institutions which for some strange reasons they tolerate or even applaud collectively. Shakespeare's personal views on men and things rarely disturb or colour his imaginative presentation of a character or a situation, but they may be occasionally inferred from a casual epithet or metaphor. There is no reason why Shakespeare, when Bassanio is professing his love for Portia, should suddenly think of the rack. The metaphor just occurs to him because it stood for something freshly present in his mind:

BASSANIO: Let me choose!
For as I am, I live upon the rack.
PORTIA: Upon the rack, Bassanio! Then confess
What treason there is mingled with your love.

Ay, but I fear you speak upon the rack
Where men enforcèd do speak anything.

[3] Another exasperating example of the way in which the critic who hopes to surprise Shakespeare at work finds the ground removed from under his feet. How interesting to study in detail the way in which the story of the caskets is dovetailed into the story of the bond as related by Ser Giovanni, if we could be sure that Shakespeare had really done the work! The dramatist rejects passages in the story of the bond which would be ineffective on the stage and replaces them with material from another source. We admire the craft with which the one theme is grafted upon the other and the sure sense of the theatre which prompted the acceptance or rejection of this or that particular feature. All this would provide valuable indications concerning Shakespeare's method and workmanship. But what if all this preliminary work had already been done before Shakespeare put his quill to paper?

[4] The legend of the pound of flesh is not, in fact, either by origin or in some of its post-mediæval developments, directed against the Jews. There is no Jew in the earliest European version of the tale as narrated by Herbert, the troubadour, in 1223; and in what is perhaps the most amusing version of all, which purports to be an incident in the life of Pope Sixtus V as narrated by Leti, his fanciful biographer, the tables are turned with a vengeance. For in this account it is the Christian who claims a pound of flesh from the Jew (a situation which some may regard as possibly more agreeable to the facts of history); and the good Pope, with magnificent impartiality, condemns both parties to death: the Christian, for entering into a contract with intent to murder the Jew, and the Jew, for signing a bond which virtually involved him in the crime of suicide.

[5] Witness the celebrated outburst of Heine: 'Antonio is a poor-spirited creature, with the heart of a worm, whose flesh is really worth nothing else but to bait fish withal.... Bassanio is a downright fortune-hunter; he borrows money to show a more swelling port with and to capture a rich heiress. As for Lorenzo, he is an accomplice in a most infamous burglary and under Prussian law he would have been condemned to fifteen years in the penitentiary. The other noble Venetians, who appear in the scene as the comrades of Antonio, do not seem to hate money very much and for their poor friend, when he is in ill-luck, they have nothing but words.'

[6] Note in this speech a delicious characteristic parenthesis. Having been betrayed into what for his precision is a flight of fancy, he instinctively corrects himself: 'Stop my house's ears, I mean my casements'. We have surprised him once before in this same revealing trick of speech when, after talking of water-rats and water-thieves, he felt it necessary to add: 'I mean pirates.'

[7] Let anyone who is disposed to over-sentimentalise Shylock's relations with his daughter ponder his sly warning: Perhaps I will return immediately. Distrusting her obedience he cautions her that he may be back sooner than she expects.

[8] This particular passage comes nearer in spirit and treatment to the comedy of Molière than any other scene in Shakespeare.

[9] This speech of Jessica's incidentally helps us to understand why she had so little compunction about leaving her father's house.

[10] 'Shylock no miser' inevitably calls to mind Harpagon in Molière's L'Avare. Molière in his characterisation runs more truly to type than Shakespeare. But the comic characters of Molière, though they embody more systematically some master passion of the play, are far from being stage figures with generic labels attached to them. Molière, like Shakespeare, gets his finest comedy from a conflict of inconsistencies. Shylock, preferring a pound of carrion flesh to thrice three thousand ducats—one passion driving out another—, recalls Harpagon who in his desire to cut a figure in the eyes of Mariane, organises a banquet.

[11] The dramatic significance of this speech lies in its inconsistency with the behaviour of the Christians who applaud it. From this point of view it may be regarded as a striking example of the way in which

Shakespeare's habit of presenting things as they are constantly reveals the irony of character and circumstance.

[12] Mr. M. J. Landa in a searching study of the Shylock myth is provoked into a notable outburst on the inhuman conduct of Portia in the trial scene: 'She plays cat and mouse ... hypocrite to boot.' All this, and much more, equally unanswerable, just shows what happens when we allow ourselves to be misled by Shakespeare's theatrical skill into praising or blaming his characters for conduct which, however true and appropriate in its setting, fails to conform with our standard notions of a good companion.

[13] Heine wrote: 'Shakespeare intended perhaps, for the amusement of the "general", to represent a tormented, fabulous creature that thirsts for blood, and of course loses his daughter and his ducats, and is ridiculed into the bargain. But the genius of the poet, the genius of humanity that reigned in him stood ever above his private will and so it happened that in Shylock, in spite of all his uncouth grimacings, the poet vindicates an unfortunate sect, which, for mysterious purposes, has been burdened by Providence with the hate of the rabble both high and low, and has reciprocated this hate—not always by love.'

[14] See Harold Child's note on the *Stage History of the Play;* New Cambridge Edition.

[15] Within living memory there have nevertheless been notable attempts to restore Shakespeare's comic character to the stage. Sir William Poel, in 1898, conveyed to a modern audience some idea how Shylock comported himself in the Elizabethan theatre, and Mr. Michael Sherbrooke in 1914 bravely insisted that Shylock, even at his most terrible, was essentially ludicrous.

Harold C. Goddard

THE MERCHANT OF VENICE

I

The anti-Semitism of the twentieth century lends a fresh interest to *The Merchant of Venice*. It raises anew the old question: How could one of the most tolerant spirits of all time have written a play that is centered around, and seems to many to accept, one of the most degraded prejudices of the ages? "About 1594," says a recent critic of high standing, "public sentiment in England was roused to an outbreak of traditional Jew-baiting; and for good and evil, Shakespeare the man was like his fellows. He planned a *Merchant of Venice* to let the Jew dog have it, and thereby to gratify his own patriotic pride of race." "The bond story," says another contemporary commentator, "has an anti-Semitic edge, and in recent years many secondary schools have wisely removed the play from the curriculum.... Shakespeare simply accepts the Jews as a notoriously bad lot.... I do not see how a Jew can read *The Merchant of Venice* without pain and indignation." And others express themselves to the same effect.

Not all, of course, go that far. There have been many to point out that Shylock is by no means a monster. He has traits that humanize him and excite our sympathy. But few who vindicate Shakespeare do so in a bold or ringing tone. They are timid, or qualified, or even apologetic. The thought of how the Elizabethan crowd at any rate must have taken Shylock makes them shudder. And beyond doubt, whatever the poet intended, most of his audience must have made the Jew an object of ridicule or contempt, or both. Is there danger that modern schoolboys will do the same?

"Shakespeare is a great psychologist," said Goethe, "and whatever can be known of the heart of man may be found in his plays." If it has come to the point where a masterpiece of this great psychologist has to be removed from the schools

From *The Meaning of Shakespeare* (Chicago: University of Chicago Press, 1951), pp. 81–116.

because of the bad passions it may arouse, it would seem to be time to re-examine that oft-examined masterpiece once more.

II

However it may be now, there was a time when anyone who had been through high school knew that *The Merchant of Venice* is an interweaving of three strands commonly known as the casket story, the bond story, and the ring story. The teacher in those days always pointed out the skill with which Shakespeare had made three plots into one, but generally left out the much more important fact that the three stories, as the poet uses them, become variations on a single theme.

The casket story obviously stresses the contrast between what is within and what is without. So, however, if less obviously, do the other two. The bond story is built about the distinction between the letter and the spirit of the law. But what are letter and spirit if not what is without and what is within? And the ring story turns on the difference between the outer form and the inner essence of a promise. When Bassanio rewards the Young Doctor of Laws with Portia's ring, he is keeping the spirit of his vow to her as certainly as he would have been breaking it if he had kept the ring on his finger. In the circumstances literal fidelity would have been actual faithlessness.

Yet in spite of this thematic unity (into which the love story of Lorenzo and Jessica can also be fitted) we find one of the keenest of recent critics asking: "What in the name of all dramatic propriety and economy are the casket scenes doing? They are quite irrelevant to the plot, and . . . for the characterization of Bassanio, a positive nuisance. . . . They are a mere piece of adornment. And the answer to that 'why' is no doubt just that Shakespeare knew that they were effective episodes, and that no audience with the colour of the scenes in their eyes and the beauty of his verse in their ears was going to trouble its heads that they were no more than episodes. Shakespeare was writing for audiences and not for dramatic critics."

Of course Shakespeare the playwright was writing for audiences. But how about Shakespeare the poet?

Drama, as we have said, must make a wide and immediate appeal to a large number of people of ordinary intelligence. The playwright must make his plots plain, his characters easily grasped, his ideas familiar. The public does not want the truth. It wants confirmation of its prejudices. That is why the plays of mere play-wrights have immediate success but seldom survive.

What the poet is seeking, on the other hand, is the secret of life, and, even if he would, he cannot share with a crowd in a theater, through the distorting medium of actors who are far from sharing his genius, such gleams of it as may have been revealed to him. He can share it only with the few, and with them mostly in solitude.

A poet-playwright, then, is a contradiction in terms. But a poet-playwright is exactly what Shakespeare is. And so his greater plays are one thing as drama and another as poetry, one thing on the outside, another within. Ostensibly, *The Merchant of Venice* is the story of the friendship of an unselfish Venetian merchant for a charming young gentleman who is in love with a beautiful heiress; of the noble sacrifice that the friend is on the point of making when nearly brought to disaster by a vile Jew; of the transformation of the lovely lady into lawyer and logician just in the nick of time and her administration to the villain of a dose of his own medicine. Was ever a play more compact with popular appeal? But what if, all the while, underneath and overhead, it were something as different from all this as the contents of the three caskets are from their outward appearance? It would be in keeping. What if the author is putting to the test, not just the suitors of Portia, but other characters as well, even, possibly, every reader or spectator of his play? It would be like him.

The seductive atmosphere of the play lends immediate credence to such an hypothesis. The critic quoted believes that the playwright was counting on it to hypnotize his audience into not noticing irrelevancies. It may be that he was also counting on it for profounder and more legitimate reasons.

The social world of Venice and more especially of Belmont centers around pleasure. It is a golden world—a gilded world we might better say. It is a world of luxury and leisure, of idle talk and frivolity, of music and romance. It has the appearance of genuine grace and culture. Except for a few scenes, the average production of *The Merchant of Venice* leaves an impression of bright costumes, witty conversations, gay or dreamy melody, and romantic love. Gold is the symbol of this world of pleasure. But what is under this careless ease? On what does it rest for foundation? The answer is—on money. Or, if you will, on the trade and commerce that bring the money, and on the inheritance that passes it along. Now this world of trade and commerce, as it happens, does not resemble very closely the world that its profits purchase. Its chief symbol in the play is silver, which in the form of money is the "pale and common drudge 'tween man and man." When the Prince of Arragon opens the silver casket, he finds, within, the portrait of a blinking idiot and verses telling him that he is a fool who has embraced a shadow in mistake for substance.

But there is something even worse than money under the surface of this social world. Exclusiveness—and the hypocrisy exclusiveness always involves, the pretense that that which is excluded is somehow less real than that which excludes. When the Prince of Morocco opens the golden casket he finds not a fool's head, as Arragon finds, but a Death's head—so much deadlier than money is the moral degradation that money so often brings. "All that glisters is not gold."

Dimly, in varying degrees, these Venetians and Belmontese reveal an uneasiness, a vague discontent, an unexplained sense of something wrong. This note, significantly, is sounded in the very first words of four or five of the leading characters.

In sooth, I know not why I am so sad,

says Antonio in the first line of the play. "By my troth, Nerissa, my little body is aweary of this great world," are Portia's first words. "Our house is hell," Jessica announces in her opening speech. And we wonder what cruelty her father has been guilty of, until she goes on to explain that the hell she refers to is tediousness. Melancholy, weariness, tedium—the reiteration of the note cannot be coincidence. And the other characters confirm the conjecture. Over and over they give the sense of attempting to fill every chink of time with distraction or amusement, often just words, to prevent their thinking. Bassanio makes his bow with a greeting to Salanio and Salarino:

> Good signiors both, when shall we laugh? say when?

and Gratiano (after a reference to Antonio's morose appearance, from which he takes his cue) begins:

> Let me play the fool!
> With mirth and laughter let old wrinkles come,
> And let my liver rather heat with wine
> Than my heart cool with mortifying groans.

Gratiano's cure for care is merriment and torrents of talk. He is not the only one in Venice who "speaks an infinite deal of nothing." Launcelot Gobbo, the "witsnapper," is merely a parody and reduction to the absurd of the loquaciousness that infects the main plot as well as the comic relief. Lorenzo condemns as fools those of higher station who, like Launcelot, "for a tricksy word defy the matter," and then proceeds in his very next speech to defy it in the same way. We can feel Shakespeare himself wearying of "wit"—the verbal gold that conceals paucity of thought—and it would scarcely be far-fetched to find a prophecy of his great taciturn characters, like Cordelia and Virgilia, in the declaration: "How every fool can play upon the word! I think the best grace of wit will shortly turn into silence, and discourse grow commendable in none only but parrots."

What is the trouble with these people and what are they trying to hide? Why should the beautiful Portia, with all her adorers, be bored? Nerissa, who under her habit as waiting-maid has much wisdom, hits the nail on the head in *her* first speech in answer to Portia's: "For aught I see, they are as sick that surfeit with too much as they that starve with nothing." What these people are trying to elude is their own souls, or, as we say today, the Unconscious.

Now Shylock is a representative of both of the things of which we have been speaking: of money, because he is himself a moneylender, and of exclusion, because he is the excluded thing. Therefore the Venetian world makes him their scapegoat. They project on him what they have dismissed from their own consciousness as too disturbing. They hate him because he reminds them of their own unconfessed evil qualities. Down the ages this has been the main explanation of racial hatred and persecution, of the mistreatment of servant by master. Our unconsciousness is our foreign land. Hence we see in the foreigner what is actually the "foreign" part of ourselves.

Grasp this, and instantly a dozen things in the play fall into place, and nearly every character in it is seen to be one thing on the outside and another underneath—so inherent, so little mere adornment, is the casket theme. It ramifies into a hundred details and into every corner of the play.

III

Bassanio is a good example to begin with. He fools the average reader and, especially if the play is conventionally cast and handsomely mounted, the average spectator, as completely as the dashing movie star does the matinee girl. Is he not in love with the rich heroine?

Bassanio admits that he has posed as wealthier than he is and has mortgaged his estate

> By something showing a more swelling port
> Than my faint means would grant continuance.

And Antonio abets the deception. As a youth, says Bassanio, when I lost one arrow, I shot another in the same direction and often retrieved both. So now. Lend me a little more to make love to a lady who has inherited a fortune (and who has beauty and virtue) and with good luck I will repay you (out of her wealth) both your new loan and your old ones:

> I have a mind presages me such thrift.

This is not exactly in the key of *Romeo and Juliet*.

If this seem an ungracious way of putting it, note that Bassanio himself describes it as a "plot" to get clear of his debts. But when the young spendthrift is handsome, we forgive him much. In watching the development of the love affair it is easy to forget its inception. And yet, when Bassanio stands in front of the golden casket, clad in the rich raiment that Antonio's (i.e., Shylock's) gold has presumably bought, and addresses it,

> Therefore, thou gaudy gold,
> Hard food for Midas, I will none of thee,

we feel that if Shakespeare did not intend the irony it got in in spite of him. No, gold, I'll have none of thee, Bassanio declares (whether he knows it or not), except a bit from Antonio-Shylock to start me going, and a bit from a certain lady "richly left" whose dowry shall repay the debts of my youth and provide for my future. Beyond that, none.

> *Who chooseth me must give and hazard all he hath.*

It is almost cruel to recall the inscription on the casket Bassanio picked in the light of what he *received* from Shylock and of what he let Antonio *risk* in his behalf.

If it be objected that this is subjecting a fairy tale to the tests of realistic literature, the answer is that it is not the first time that a fairy tale has been a fascinating invention on the surface and the hardest fact and soundest wisdom underneath. Ample justice has been done by his admirers to Bassanio's virtues. It is the economic aspect of his career that has been understressed. Like a number of others in this play the source of whose income will not always bear inspection, like most of us in fact, he was not averse to receiving what he had not exactly earned. Bassanio is the golden casket. He gained what many men desire: a wealthy wife.

I V

Antonio's case is a bit subtler than Bassanio's but even more illuminating. Why is Antonio sad?

Shakespeare devotes a good share of the opening scene of the play to a discussion of that question.

> In sooth, I know not why I am so sad.
> It wearies me; you say it wearies you;
> But how I caught it, found it, or came by it,
> What stuff 'tis made of, whereof it is born,
> I am to learn;
> And such a want-wit sadness makes of me,
> That I have much ado to know myself.

Solanio and Salarino confirm his changed appearance and suggest that he is anxious over his argosies. But Antonio brushes that aside. His ventures are not in one bottom trusted nor all his wealth committed to the present enterprise:

> Therefore, my merchandise makes me not sad.

He denies, too, the charge that he is in love. So Salarino, baffled, concludes that it is a matter of temperament. Antonio was born that way. But this explains nothing and his altered looks give it the lie.

Commentators have commonly either side-stepped the problem or explained Antonio's melancholy as a presentiment of the loss of his friend Bassanio through marriage. That may have accentuated it at the moment, but Antonio has had barely a hint of what is coming when the play opens, while his depression has all the marks of something older and deeper. It is scarcely too much to say that he is a sick man. Later, at the trial, when the opportunity of sacrificing himself is presented, his sadness becomes almost suicidal:

> I am a tainted wether of the flock,
> Meetest for death. The weakest kind of fruit
> Drops earliest to the ground; and so let me.
> You cannot better be employ'd, Bassanio,
> Than to live still, and write mine epitaph.

Only something fundamental can explain such a sentimental welcome to death. The opening of the play is an interrogation three times underscored as to Antonio's sadness.

Later, a similar question is propounded about another emotion of another character: Shylock and his thirst for revenge. Now Shylock is a brainier man than Antonio, and his diagnosis of his own case throws light on Antonio's. The Jew gives a number of reasons for his hatred. Because Antonio brings down the rate of usury in Venice. Because he hates the Jews. Because he rails on Shylock in public. Because he is a hypocrite. Because he is a Christian. Because he has thwarted the Jew's bargains. Because he has heated his enemies. Because he has cooled his friends. And so on, and so on. An adequate collection of motives, one would say. Yet not one of them, or all together, sufficient to account for his passion. They are rationalizations, like Iago's reasons for his plot against Othello, or Raskolnikov's for his murder of the old woman in *Crime and Punishment*. And Shylock comes finally to recognize that fact. In the court scene when the Duke asks his reason for his mad insistence on the pound of flesh, Shylock says he can and will give no reason other than "a certain loathing I bear Antonio." A certain loathing! It matches exactly the certain sadness of Antonio.

But it matches another emotion of Antonio's even more closely. If Shylock loathes Antonio, Antonio has a no less savage detestation of Shylock. His hatred is as "boundless" as was Juliet's love. It appears to be the one passion that like a spasm mars his gentle disposition, as a sudden squall will ruffle the surface of a placid lake.

A kinder gentleman treads not the earth,

says Salarino, and so Antonio impresses us except in this one relation. When Shylock complains,

Fair sir, you spat on me on Wednesday last;
You spurn'd me such a day; another time
You call'd me dog,

we might think it the hallucination of a half-maddened mind. But does Antonio deny the charge? On the contrary he confirms it:

I am as like to call thee so again,
To spat on thee again, to spurn thee too.

That from this paragon of kindliness! It is not enough to say that in those days everybody hated the Jews, for that leaves unexplained why the gentlest and mildest man in the play is the fiercest Jew-baiter of them all. As far as the record goes, he outdoes even the crude and taunting Gratiano. Oh, but Shylock is a usurer, it will be said, while Antonio is so noble that the mere mention of interest is abhorrent to him. Why, then, does not Antonio state his objection to it like a rational being instead of arguing with kicks and saliva? Why is he so heated, as well as so noble?

Unless all signs fail, Antonio, like Shylock, is a victim of forces from far below the threshold of consciousness. What are they?

Shakespeare is careful to leave no doubt on this point, but, appropriately, he buries the evidence a bit beneath the surface: Antonio abhors Shylock because he catches his own reflection in his face.

"What! Antonio like Shylock!" it will be said. "The idea is preposterous. No two men could be more unlike." They are, in many respects. But extremes meet, and in one respect they are akin. It is Antonio's unconscious protest against this humiliating truth that is the secret of his antipathy. "Wilt thou whip thine own faults in other men?" cries Timon of Athens. Shakespeare understood the principle, and he illustrates it here.

The contrast between Shylock and Antonio is apparently nowhere more marked than in the attitude of the two men toward money. Shylock is a usurer. So strong is Antonio's distaste for usury that he lends money without interest. But where does the money come from that permits such generosity? From his argosies, of course, his trade. For, after all, to what has Antonio dedicated his life? Not indeed to usury. But certainly to moneymaking, to profits. And profits, under analysis, are often only "usury" in a more respectable form. Appearance and reality again.

Shakespeare seizes one of the most exciting moments of the play (when the dramatic tension is so high that nobody will notice) to drive home this truth, the instant when Portia, disguised as a Young Doctor of Laws, enters the courtroom.

Which is the merchant here and which the Jew?

she inquires in almost her first words. All she wants, of course, is to have defendant and plaintiff identified. But the Shakespearean overmeaning is unmistakable. Merchant and Jew! Noble trader of Venice and despicable money-changer, at what poles they appear to stand! Yet—which is which? (Editors who punctuate the line

Which is the merchant here? And which the Jew?

miss the point.)

Nor is the distinction between merchant and moneylender the only one, the poet implies, that may be difficult at times to draw. As if to prepare us for Portia's Delphic line, Shakespeare has Gratiano anticipate it in cruder form with respect to Gentile and Jew. Jessica, in boy's clothes, is about to elope with Lorenzo:

I will make fast the doors, and gild myself
With some more ducats, and be with you straight.
                    (*Exit above*)

That "gild," with its clear allusion to the golden casket, not to mention the familiar symbolism of the descent from above, gives us in one word the moral measure of this girl who crowns her deception and desertion of her father by robbing him. As the young thief comes down, Gratiano cries in delighted approval,

Now, by my hood, a Gentile, and no Jew.

Gratiano is thinking of the fascinating boldness of this saucy boy-girl. She's too good to be a Jew, he says, she's one of us. But Shakespeare has not forgotten the stolen ducats. That unusual oath, "by my hood," is enough to suggest that there is something under cover here. Is it her dashing air or her hard heart that entitles Jessica to the name of Gentile? The poet does not say. But he clearly asks. Plainly Jew and Gentile are not to him separate species with distinct virtues and vices. Morocco makes a like point when he says his blood will be found as red as that of the fairest blonde from the north. And Shylock, when he asks, "If you prick us, do we not bleed?" Under the skin, all men are brothers.

And here an interesting fact should be recorded. On July 22, 1598, James Roberts entered in the Stationers' Register *The Marchaunt of Venyce or otherwise called the Jewe of Venyce.* Here is testimony that already in Shakespeare's own day the public was puzzled by the title of the play and had substituted for, or added to, the author's another title more expressive of what seemed to be its leading interest and central figure. The world did not have to wait for Kean and Irving to discover its "hero." Yet the poet knew what he was about when he named it.

Which is the merchant here and which the Jew?

The public needed two titles. Shakespeare is content with two-in-one.

Now Shylock, with his incisive mind, grasps very early this resemblance of Antonio's vocation to his own. Apparently it first strikes him with full force on the occasion when Antonio backs Bassanio's request for a loan. Knowing of old the merchant's antipathy to interest, Shylock is astonished:

Methought you said you neither lend nor borrow
Upon advantage.

Antonio admits it is not his habit.

When Jacob graz'd his uncle Laban's sheep,

Shylock begins. Jacob? What has Jacob to do with it?

And what of him? Did he take interest?

Antonio inquires.

No; not take interest; not, as you would say,
Directly interest.

That "directly"! It is necessary to get the tone as well as the word. The sarcasm of it is the point. There are more ways than one of taking interest, it says. There are many tricks of the trade, many ways of thriving, as Jacob knew in the old days. *And as certain others know nowadays.* But Antonio, quite unaware in his self-righteousness of the fact that he is himself the target, thinks the story Shylock goes on to tell of how Jacob increased his wages by a sly device is told to justify the taking of interest, whereas what the Jew is saying, if a bit less bluntly, is: Look a bit closer, Antonio, and you will see that your profits amount to the same thing as my interest. We are in the same boat.

Antonio, though unaware that he is hit, does scent some danger lurking in the story and insists on a distinction essential to his self-respect:

> This was a venture, sir, that Jacob serv'd for;
> A thing not in his power to bring to pass,
> But sway'd and fashion'd by the hand of heaven,

and, still puzzled over the point of Shylock's illustration, he adds:

> Was this inserted to make interest good?
> Or is your gold and silver ewes and rams?

"I cannot tell," answers Shylock, "I make it breed as fast."

"Your example turns against you, Shylock!" is what Antonio implies. Rams and ewes are very different from silver and gold. It is right and proper that they should multiply, but it is against nature for barren metal to. Antonio's speech is an example of how a man may say one thing with his tongue and quite another with his soul. It is the word "venture" that gives him away. The very term he had applied to his own argosies ("My ventures are not in one bottom trusted")! It is these and not Jacob's lambs that are really troubling him, and his "sway'd and fashion'd" confirms the conjecture, the one an allusion to the winds of heaven as certainly as the other is to the hand of heaven. But this unconscious introduction of the argosies into the argument, by way of self-defense, is fatal to Antonio's contention. For when it comes to generation, cargoes generally resemble gold and silver far more nearly than they do ewes and rams. In so far as they do, Aristotle's famous argument against interest proves to be equally cogent against profits. Antonio and Shylock are still in the same boat.

But Antonio, blind as ever, turns to his friend and says:

> Mark you this, Bassanio,
> The devil can cite Scripture for his purpose.
> An evil soul, producing holy witness,
> Is like a villain with a smiling cheek,
> A goodly apple rotten at the heart.
> O, what a goodly outside falsehood hath!

Considering Antonio's reputation for virtue (what are the smiling villain and goodly apple but the golden casket?), the speech is a moral boomerang if there ever was one. He very conveniently forgets that he no more produced the treasures with which his argosies are loaded than Shylock did his ducats—treasures which he himself boasts a few speeches further on will bring in within two months "thrice three times the value of this bond." Antonio's business is thriving. Usury? God forbid! "Not, as you would say, directly interest."

This does not mean that Antonio is a hypocrite. Far from it. Who does not know an Antonio—a man too good for money-making who has dedicated his life to money-making? Antonio was created for nobler things. And so he suffers from that homesickness of the soul that ultimately attacks everyone who "consecrates" his life to something below his spiritual level. Moreover, Antonio is a bachelor, and his "fie, fie!" in answer to Solanio's bantering suggestion that he is in love may hint at some long-nourished disappointment of the affections. Antonio has never married, and he is not the man to have had clandestine affairs. So he has invested in gentle friendship emotions that nature intended should blossom into love. But however tender and loyal, it is a slightly sentimental friendship, far from being an equivalent of love. Both it and the argosies are at bottom opiates. Those who drown themselves in business or other work in order to forget what refuses to be forgotten are generally characterized by a quiet melancholy interrupted occasionally by spells of irritation or sudden spasms of passion directed at some person or thing that, if analyzed, is found to be a symbol of the error that has spoiled their lives.

Therefore, my merchandise makes me not sad.

By his very denial Antonio unwittingly diagnoses his ailment correctly. This surely is the solution of the opening conundrum of the play, and anger at himself, not a conventional anti-Semitism of which Antonio could not conceivably be guilty, is the cause of his fierce and irrational outbursts against Shylock. Antonio is the silver casket. He got as much as he deserved: material success and a suicidal melancholy.

V

Why did Shylock offer Antonio a loan of three thousand ducats without interest?

On our answer to that crucial question, it is scarcely too much to say, our conception of the Jew and our interpretation of the play will hinge.

The superficial reader or auditor will think this is complicating what is a simple matter. He has probably heard the outcome of the bond story before he ever picks up the book or enters the theater, or, if not, is the willing victim of an actor who has. Where, he will ask, is there any problem? Shylock is a villain. He is out from the first for bloody revenge. Doesn't he say so, in an aside, the moment Antonio enters his presence?

If I can catch him once upon the hip,
I will feed fat the ancient grudge I bear him.

What could be plainer than that? The Jew foresees (as does the actor of his part) that Antonio will not be able to pay on the appointed day, and so, slyly and cruelly, traps the merchant into signing the bloody bond under the pretense that he is joking.

Unfortunately the text contradicts in a dozen places this easy assumption that the Jew is a sort of super-Iago. (We will mention some of them presently.) But apart from this, the idea that as intelligent a man as Shylock could have deliberately counted on the bankruptcy of as rich a man as Antonio, with argosies on seven seas, is preposterous. And if anyone would cite to the contrary his speech about land-rats and water-rats, waters, winds, and rocks, the answer is that that is the merest daydreaming, the sheerest wishful thinking. The bond, whatever else it is, is more of the same. It does indeed reveal a hidden desire on Shylock's part to tear out Antonio's heart, but that is a power-fantasy pure and simple. It is like a child's "I'll kill you!" Such things are at the opposite pole from deliberate plans for murder, even judicial murder.

Shylock's offer to take no interest for his loan was obviously as unexpected to him as it was to Bassanio and Antonio. Just thirty-six lines before he makes it he was considering the rate he should charge:

Three thousand ducats; 'tis a good round sum.
Three months from twelve; then, let me see; the rate—

Then comes the well-known speech beginning

Signior Antonio, many a time and oft
In the Rialto you have rated me . . .

(a significant pun, by the way, on the word "rate"). "You spat upon me, kicked me, called me dog," is the gist of what he says, "and for these courtesies you now expect me to lend you money?"

"No!" cries Antonio, stung by the justice of Shylock's irony, "I want no courtesy or kindness. Friends take no interest from friends. Let this transaction be one between enemies, so that, if I forfeit, you can exact the penalty with a better conscience, and so that I" (he does not say it, but who can doubt that he thinks it?) "may retain my right to spit on you."

How to the heart Antonio is hit is revealed by the stage direction which Shakespeare, as so often, skilfully inserts in the text.

Why, look you, how you storm!

cries Shylock. Antonio's anger is as good as a confession, but, clad in the pride of race and virtue, he does not realize it. How the tables are now turned, how the relation between the two is reversed! Hitherto, Antonio has always been the superior, Shylock the inferior. It is not just that the borrower, being the beggar, is always below the lender. That is a trifle here. The significant thing is that the man who loses his temper is below the man who keeps his self-control. A small man meets anger with anger. A big man meets it with augmented patience and self-restraint. Does Shylock show himself great or small in the situation? And if great, is it genuine greatness of heart, or only the counterfeit greatness of intelligent self-interest?

It is just here that he makes his offer to forget the past, to supply Antonio's wants, as a friend would, without interest. What is back of this obviously unpremeditated and apparently uncharacteristic move on the Jew's part? Is it

1. Fawning?—a sudden realization that he must hold on to Antonio at any price lest in his anger he turn on his heel and depart.

2. Shrewdness?—a calculated attempt to buy off this rich merchant's insults.

3. Thirst for moral revenge?—a move to humiliate his enemy by putting him under obligation to him.

4. Protective coloration?—the instinctive reaction of the animal to delude the pursuer, accompanied, presumably, with an unconscious desire to kill.

5. Bait?—a deliberate device to tempt his foe, when off guard, into signing the bloody bond. Or, finally,

6. Just what it purports to be?—a sincere wish to wipe out the past and be friends.

Shylock is not a *unanimous* man. (Who is?) There are several Shylocks pulling Shylock simultaneously in several directions and (except No. 5) there may be at least a touch of every one of these motives activating him at the moment. Even in the normal man, instinct, reason, and imagination are at cross-purposes. How much more in this torn victim of Gentile insolence! Hence we must discriminate scrupulously between what happens in Shylock's conscious from what happens in his unconscious mind. His capacity to rationalize was shown in his account of his motives for hating Antonio. The tendency will be bound to manifest itself in the present situation.

The reaction to Antonio's anger of the shrewd, intelligent, logical Shylock is least open to question. (Not to imply that he formulated it precisely in his own mind.) Here the man who had always treated him like a cur has approached him as a human being. But, stung by his sarcasm, his foe threatens to revert to his old insults or break off negotiations entirely. This must be prevented at any cost. Friends, Antonio says, never lend at interest. Instantly the Jew sees his opening. His enemy has supplied it! Here is the chance of chances to humble him by compelling him to do just what he does not want to do, accept a loan, namely, on an outward basis of friendship. Such a loan would be heaping coals of fire on his head in the most savage sense of that ferocious metaphor. Here would be revenge at its sweetest, in its most exquisite, prolonged, and intellectual form. What could any interest be, even the most extortionate, compared with this?

But lest this sudden reversal of a lifetime practice be suspect, and its motive exposed, it must be covered with the pretense of a jest. Hence the improvisation of the "merry bond" with the extravagant penalty in case of forfeiture. And to back this up with a more plausible reason, Shylock adds:

> I say,
> To buy his favour I extend this friendship.

But surely this is an afterthought. The interest Shylock will lose will be more than offset by the elimination of Antonio's interference with the Jew's other bargaining, to say nothing of the buying-off of his insults. But this is something thrown in, as it were, a secondary consideration, not the main motive, so much stronger in Shylock is hatred than avarice. And we think the more highly of him for that fact, to the extent that revenge is a spiritual, avarice a material evil.

Somewhat on this order must have been the response of the moneylender Shylock to Antonio's outburst. But what forces moved beneath the surface of this moneylender's mind?

Shakespeare is at pains to make plain the noble potentialities of Shylock, however much his nature may have been warped by the sufferings and persecutions he has undergone and by the character of the vocation he has followed. His vices are not so much vices as perverted virtues. His pride of race in a base sense is pride of race in a high sense inverted, his answer to the world's scorn. His love of sobriety and good order is a degeneration of his religion. His domestic "tyranny"—which it is easy to exaggerate—a vitiated love of family and home. His outward servility, a depraved patience. His ferocity, a thwarted self-respect. Even his avarice is partly a providence imposed by the insecurity of his lot. There is a repressed Shylock.

Now repression inevitably produces a condition of high tension between the conscious and the unconscious, with sudden unpredictable incursions of the latter into the former attended by a rapid alternation of polar states of mind. Dostoevsky is the unsurpassed expositor of this mental condition. What reader of that book, for instance, will not remember the old man in *The Insulted and Injured* who in secret covers with kisses the locket containing the picture of his adored but wayward daughter, but who later, when no longer alone, hurls it on the ground, stamps on it, and curses the one whose image it holds, only to fall sobbing like a child—again clasping and kissing the object he has just been trampling underfoot; or the poverty-stricken captain, father of Ilusha, in *The Brothers Karamazov*, who, when offered money after the insult he has received, is at one instant in a heaven of ecstasy at the thought of the happiness it will buy and at the next is crumpling the notes in his fist and then treading them into the dirt; or Dmitri Karamazov in the same book (more injured by neglect in childhood than by insult) who, when the perfect opportunity to kill his father comes, has actually lifted the weapon to strike the blow when his hand is suddenly stayed by an angelic impulse? Such, declares Dostoevsky in character after character, in book after book, is the psychology of the insulted and injured. Now if ever a man was insulted and injured it is Shylock. When we find him, then, acting in the exact pattern of his Dostoevskian counterparts, it is as if Shakespeare were confirming Dostoevsky, and Dostoevsky Shakespeare. Only very ingenuous persons will think that these two supreme students of the human mind, because they do not express themselves in scientific nomenclature or in the language of the twentieth century, must have been ignorant of truths that psychology is only now beginning to formulate.

Shylock has tried to fuse the usurer with the father of Jessica—but in vain. They will no more mix than oil and water. Troubled dreams about his money bags are proof of this—symptoms of struggle in a divided nature. And so the two Shylocks exist side by side, now the one, now the other asserting sovereignty. The reiterated cry "My daughter! O my ducats!" which the next moment becomes "My ducats, and my daughter!" is an example of this ambivalent state of the man's mind. It is a mark of the near-balance between outraged love and avarice, though it is not without significance that the daughter—the first time at least—is mentioned first. It is the same with the turquoise that he had of Leah when he was a bachelor. First, it is the jewel as a memento of romance, then as a valuable material possession. But there is a still more revealing instance. "Would she were hearsed at my foot and the ducats in her coffin!" That tormented cry is usually taken as meaning, "I would give my daughter's life to get my ducats back." And doubtless that is what Shylock thinks he is saying. But note that it is not Jessica dead and the ducats locked up in his vault. The ducats are in the coffin too! Plainly an unconscious wish to bury his own miserliness. Shylock is ripe for a better life. It takes a Shakespeare to give a touch like that.

Such passages shed an intense light on the offer to Antonio of a loan without interest, followed instantly by the stipulation of the bloodthirsty bond (passed off as a jest). The pattern is identical. When we read the passage for the first time, or see the incident on the stage, we are too excited by the situation and the suspense to look beneath the surface. We are taking the play as drama and consider each scene separately as it comes or as interpreted by an actor who is probably thinking more of its effect on the audience than of the truth of its psychology. But when, later, we read it as poetry, and take the parts in the light of the whole, we see how perfectly the Jew's words and actions here cohere with the rest of his role.

Let us analyze the incident a bit further.

Shylock, the despised usurer, is on the point of lending Antonio, the great merchant, three thousand ducats, presumably at a high rate of interest, when he is suddenly confronted by a storm of anger from a man humiliated by the necessity of borrowing from a Jew (whom he has been in the habit of insulting) and stung by the Jew's recognition of the highly ironical nature of the situation. The merchant's loss of temper brings an inversion of everything. The inferior is suddenly the superior—in all senses. As certainly as when a wheel revolves and what was a moment before at the bottom is now at the top, so certainly what was deep down in Shylock is bound to come to the surface. But what is deep down in Shylock is precisely his goodness. How often the finer Shylock must have dreamed of a different kind of life, of being received into the fellowship of the commercial princes of Venice, treated as a human being, even as an equal. And now suddenly the beginning of that dream comes true. One of the greatest of Venetian merchants does come to him, without insults, asking a favor. How can the Jew's imagination fail, for a moment at least, to round out the pattern of the old daydream? Whatever

the moneylender feels, or fancies he feels, what the dreamer within Shylock experiences is an impulse to be friendly:

> SHY.: I would be friends with you and have your love,
> Forget the shames that you have stain'd me with,
> Supply your present wants, and take no doit
> Of usance for my moneys, and you'll not hear me.
> This is kind I offer.
> BASS.: This were kindness.
> SHY.:   This kindness will I show.

Bassanio's words show that there was no obvious irony in Shylock's tone nor
conspicuous fawning in his manner. Only gross distortion could impart to the Jew's
lines the accent of Iago, an accent they would have to carry if Shylock were a
deliberate villain. On the contrary, little as he may recognize it himself, here is the
instinctive reaction of the nobler Shylock. But, precisely as with all the analogous
Dostoevskian characters, the good impulse is followed instantly by its polar opposite. The wheel goes on revolving. The highest gives place to the lowest. When the
window is opened to the angel, the devils promptly rush in at the unguarded back
door. The daydream of kindness is followed by the daydream of killing. As the
imaginative Shylock pictured himself coming to the aid of a friend, so the primitive
Shylock dreams of shedding the blood of an enemy. In the first fantasy the heart of
one man goes out to unite with the heart of the other. In the second the hand of
the one would tear out the heart of the other. The perfect chiasmus stamps the
two as products of the unconscious. Such a diametrical contradiction is one of its
almost infallible marks.

The opposite hypothesis—that the offer of no interest is a snare and the bond
a deliberate trap—breaks down completely for another reason. If Shylock were
that sort of plotter, however much he might have tried not to show it, he would
have leaped with the eagerness of a villain at the first news that Antonio's argosies
had miscarried. But, as several discerning critics have pointed out, he does nothing
of the sort. When Salarino asks him if he has not heard of Antonio's loss at sea, he
does not cry even to himself, "Ah, now I have him on the hip!" but only "There I
have another bad match," the noun revealing that his mind is still on his daughter,
and it is Salarino himself who has to recall the pound of flesh and ask him of what
possible use it can be to him. Shylock's reply is scarcely what Salarino was fishing

Anyone should be able to corroborate this psychology. Who, in love or
hatred, has not let his deepest feeling or conviction escape in a word or look only
to try the next instant, in shame or fear, to pass the slip off as a jest? So ashamed,
and then so terrified, is the conscious Shylock, first at the friendliness, then at the
ferocity, of the uncomprehended impulses within him. When we say what we think
we do not mean, we may mean it to the nth degree. So the two Shylocks, between
them, mean both the friendliness and the ferocity.

for. Instead of an anticipatory daydream of blood, it is precisely the famous speech, "I am a Jew. Hath not a Jew eyes? . . ," which, more than any other in his role, wrings sympathy even from those who elsewhere grudge him a particle of it.

So, too, a moment later, when Tubal mentions Antonio's ill luck. Shylock takes the news joyfully, to be sure, but casually, in fact almost absentmindedly, his "in Genoa?" showing that his confused thoughts are still in the place where his fellow-Jew has been trying to trace his daughter. Tubal has to keep whipping his thoughts back to Antonio and the impending forfeiture. Indeed, if Tubal had been trying deliberately to forge a link in Shylock's mind between the infidelity of his daughter and the forfeiture of the bond he could not have proceeded more skilfully. He is trying. He does forge it. Jessica—Antonio; Jessica—Antonio; Jessica—Antonio: back and forth from the one to the other Tubal yanks Shylock's mind. Yet the utmost he can extort from it concerning Antonio is "I'll torture him"—not kill him. And when in his very next speech Shylock cries, with regard to the ring his daughter has exchanged for a monkey, "Thou torturest me, Tubal," the echoed word shows that if he lives to torture Antonio it will be because Jessica and Tubal have tortured him. If ever a man egged on revenge it is this other Jew. Indeed it is he rather than Shylock who is acting the role of "Shylock" in this scene, by which of course I mean the Shylock of popular conception. That Shylock needs no one to instigate him. But Shakespeare's Shylock, strangely, does. Those who find a bloodthirsty Jew in this play are right. But they have picked the wrong man.

> TUB.: But Antonio is certainly undone.
> SHY.: Nay, that's true, that's very true. Go, Tubal, fee me an officer; bespeak him a fortnight before. I will have the heart of him, if he forfeit; for, were he out of Venice, I can make what merchandise I will.

"Were he out of Venice"! Here is the proof that, even at this late hour, Shylock is thinking of tearing out Antonio's heart in a metaphorical sense only and has no idea of literal bloodshed. Just five words. But what a difference they make!

It must be something else, then, that turns the Jew from a desire to be rid of Antonio's presence in Venice to the idea of demanding the literal pound of flesh, a desire that only a madman could entertain. Solanio's description of Shylock in the streets gives us the clue:

> I never heard a passion so confus'd,
> So strange, outrageous, and so variable,
> As the dog Jew did utter in the streets . . .

There are scarcely three more illuminating lines in the play, little as their speaker is aware of the light he is shedding. Plainly this proud man, displaying his inmost heart to all beholders (like Katerina Ivanovna in Crime and Punishment coming out in public to die), has been driven to the verge of madness. The combined infidelity and thievery of his own child, culminating in her elopement with a Christian, are what have done it. Tubal and Salarino, as we have seen, precisely when the Jew was in the most suggestible state, implant in his mind what amounts to posthypnotic directions to demand the literal fulfilment of his bond. And no one knows what the street urchins contribute to the same end. But it is the daughter who first releases the flood of despair that helps these later seeds to germinate. Solanio foresees what may come of such passion:

> Let good Antonio look he keep his day,
> Or he shall pay for this.

He is still picturing the distracted creature he saw in the streets, and it suddenly comes over him that that creature is a different one from the man he has formerly known as Shylock, a more ferocious creature that, unlike the other, might stop at nothing. And he does nothing to make him stop. On the contrary, the next time they meet we hear him lashing the Jew's despair on toward madness by intentionally misunderstanding him.

> SHY.: My own flesh and blood to rebel!
> SOLAN.: Out upon it, old carrion! rebels it at these years?
> SHY.: I say my daughter is my flesh and blood.

That "flesh and blood," fitting so exactly the penalty prescribed in the bond, reveals in a flash how much the dereliction of the daughter has to do with the final bloodthirsty intention of the father. Everything, we might almost say.

And we must not forget that Bassanio and Antonio have connived in the elopement of Jessica. Yet the tormented Shylock, pursued by jeering boys, has not even then become fully conscious of his own murderous impulses, for the scene with Tubal, with its "were he out of Venice," comes after that. It is not until he runs on Antonio with the jailer that the Jew, enraged perhaps at seeing his enemy at large, threatens him directly:

> Thou call'dst me dog before thou hadst a cause,
> But, since I am a dog, beware my fangs.

At last Shylock recognizes that the animal within him is gaining ascendancy. "You called me dog. I'll take you at your word, and myself at your own estimate." His repetitions betoken his irrational state:

> I'll have my bond; speak not against my bond:
> I have sworn an oath that I will have my bond . . .
> I'll have my bond; I will not hear thee speak.
> I'll have my bond, and therefore speak no more. . . .
> I'll have no speaking; I will have my bond.

It is as if the revengeful Shylock were afraid that even one reasonable word from Antonio might revive the natural instincts of the kinder Shylock now so near extinction. The repeated "I'll have no speaking" measures the tremendous inner resistance the Jew has had to overcome before he could surrender and become unmitigatedly bad.

What was the nature of this resistance that at last seems to be breaking down? Obviously it was a desire to be just the opposite of what he now feels himself becoming. Though he was rendered coldhearted by his vocation, made cruel by the insults that had been heaped upon him by everybody from the respectable Antonio to the very children in the streets, driven to desperation by his daughter, there is nothing to indicate that Shylock was congenitally coldhearted, cruel, or desperate. On the contrary, it is clear that he had it in him, however deep down, to be humane, kindly, and patient, and his offer to Antonio of a loan without interest seems to have been a supreme effort of this submerged Shylock to come to the surface. If so, here is the supreme irony of this ironical play. If so, for a moment at least, the Jew was the Christian. The symbolism confirms the psychology: Shylock was the leaden casket with the spiritual gold within.

VI

The moment this fact is grasped the court scene becomes something quite different from what it seems to be. It is still a trial scene, but it is Portia who is on trial. Or, better, it is a casket scene in which she is subjected to the same test to which she has submitted her suitors. Can she detect hidden gold under a leaden exterior?

Concerning Portia's own exterior the poet leaves us in no doubt. To the eye she is nothing if not golden, and she does nothing if she does not shine. The praise showered on her within the play itself has been echoed by thousands of readers and spectators and the continued appeal of her role to actresses is proof of the fascination she never fails to exercise. No one can deny her brilliance or her charm, or could wish to detract from them. (If I do not linger on them here, it is because ample justice has been done to them so often.) Yet Portia, too, like so many of the others in this play, is not precisely all she seems to be. Indeed, what girl of her years, with her wealth, wit, and beauty, could be the object of such universal adulation and come through unscathed? In her uprush of joy when Bassanio chooses the right casket there is, it is true, an accent of the humility that fresh love always bestows, and she speaks of herself as "an unlesson'd girl, unschool'd, unpractis'd." There the child Portia once was is speaking, but it is a note that is sounded scarcely anywhere else in her role. The woman that child has grown into, on the contrary, is the darling of a sophisticated society which has nurtured in her anything but unself-consciousness. Indeed, it seems to be as natural to her as to a queen or princess to take herself unblushingly at the estimate this society places on her.

> Who chooseth me shall gain what many men desire.
> Why, that's the lady: all the world desires her;
> From the four corners of the earth they come . . .

says Morocco. And tacitly Portia assents to that interpretation of the inscription on the golden casket. She mocks half a dozen of her suitors unmercifully in the first scene in which we see her, and it never seems to occur to her that any man who could would not choose her. Yet it is not easy to imagine Hamlet choosing her, or Othello, or Coriolanus. (Nor Shakespeare himself, I feel like adding.)

> *Who chooseth me shall get as much as he deserves.*
> I will assume desert,

says Arragon. Portia, likewise, quietly assumes that she somehow deserves the attention and sacrifices of these crowding suitors. Perhaps she does. Yet we cannot help wishing she did not know it, though we scarcely blame her for thinking what everyone around her thinks.

But if Portia is willing to let her suitors take any risk in her pursuit in the spirit of the third inscription,

> *Who chooseth me must give and hazard all he hath,*

there is nothing to indicate that life has ever called on her to sacrifice even a small part of all she has, and when the man of her choice attains her, though she modestly wishes that for his sake she were a thousand times more fair, she also wishes significantly that she were ten thousand times more rich. Bassanio pronounces her

> nothing undervalu'd
> To Cato's daughter, Brutus' Portia.

But it is hard to think Shakespeare would have thought the comparison a happy one. Both Portias were good women. But, granted that, how could they be more different? If it is a question of the poet's later heroines, another comes to mind. When the Prince of Morocco goes out after having chosen the wrong casket, Portia dismisses him and innumerable other uninspected suitors with the line:

> Let all of his complexion choose me so.

Who is judging now by the outside? And we remember Desdemona's

> I saw Othello's visage in his mind.

In view of her father's scheme for selecting her husband, no one will blame Portia for giving Bassanio several hints on the choice of the right casket. Because of her declared intention not to be forsworn, we give her the benefit of the doubt and assume the hints were unconscious ones.[1] Indeed, the fact that she uses the word "hazard" (from the inscription on the leaden casket), not only before Bassanio chooses but before Morocco and Arragon do, all but proves that the suspense and peril of the choice fascinate her at the moment hardly less than her passion for Bassanio. She is not the only girl who has been excited by the adventure of getting married, as well as by being in love with her future husband. Contrast her with Juliet, who did give and hazard all she had for love, and you feel the difference.

This is not to suggest that Portia ought to have been a Juliet, or a Desdemona, and still less that Shakespeare should have made her anything other than she is. Given his sources, it is easy to see why Portia had to be just what she is.

The casket motif, the court scene, and the ring incident taken together comprise a good share of the story. Each of them is intrinsically spectacular, histrionic, or theatrical—or all three in one. Each is a kind of play within a play, with Portia at the center or at one focus. The casket scenes are little symbolic pageants; the court scene is drama on the surface and tragedy underneath; the ring incident is a one-act comedy complete in itself. What sort of heroine does all this demand? Obviously one with the temperament of an actress, not averse to continual limelight. Portia is exactly that.

When she hears that the man who helped her lover woo and win her is in trouble, her character and the contingency fit each other like hand and glove. Why not impersonate a Young Doctor of Laws and come to Antonio's rescue? It is typical of her that at first she takes the "whole device," as she calls it, as a kind of prank. Her imagination overflows with pictures of the opportunities for acting that her own and Nerissa's disguise as young men will offer, of the innocent lies they will tell, the fun they will have, the fools they will make of their husbands. The tragic situation of Antonio seems at the moment the last thing in her mind, or the responsibility of Bassanio for the plight of his friend. The fact that she is to have the leading role in a play in real life eclipses everything else. There is more than a bit of the stage-struck girl in Portia.

And so when the curtain rises on Act IV, Shakespeare the playwright and his actress-heroine, between them, are equipped to give us one of the tensest and most theatrically effective scenes he had conceived up to this time. What Shakespeare the poet gives us, however, and what it means to Portia the woman, is something rather different.

VII

When Shylock enters the courtroom he is in a more rational if not less determined state than when we last saw him. He is no longer unwilling to listen, and the moderate, almost kindly words of the Duke,

We all expect a gentle answer, Jew,

lead us to hope that even at the eleventh hour he may relent.

Shylock's answer to the Duke is one of the most remarkable evidences of Shakespeare's overt interest in psychological problems in any of the earlier plays. The passage is sufficient in itself to refute the idea that it is "modernizing" to detect such an interest on his part. Naturally Shylock does not talk about complexes, compulsions, and unconscious urges, but he recognizes the irrational fear of pigs and cats in the concrete for what it is, a symbol of something deeper that is disturbing the victim. He senses in himself the working of similar forces too tremendous for definition, too powerful to oppose even though he feels them driving him—*against his will and to his shame,* he implies—to commit the very offense that has been committed against him. Imagine Richard III or Iago speaking in that vein! If this be "villainy," it is of another species. Here is the main theme of the play in its profoundest implication. For what is the relation of what is conscious to what is unconscious if not the relation of what is on the surface to what is underneath? Thus Shylock himself—and through him Shakespeare—hands us the key: to open the casket of this play we must look beneath *its* surface, must probe the unconscious minds of its characters.

> You'll ask me why I rather choose to have
> A weight of carrion flesh than to receive
> Three thousand ducats. I'll not answer that;
> But say it is my humour. Is it answer'd?
> What if my house be troubled with a rat
> And I be pleas'd to give ten thousand ducats
> To have it ban'd? What, are you answer'd yet?
> Some men there are love not a gaping pig;
> Some, that are mad if they behold a cat;
> And others, when the bagpipe sings i' the nose,
> Cannot contain their urine: for affection,
> Mistress of passion, sways it to the mood
> Of what it likes or loathes. Now, for your answer:
> As there is no firm reason to be render'd
> Why he cannot abide a gaping pig;
> Why he, a harmless necessary cat;
> Why he, a wauling bagpipe; but of force
> Must yield to such inevitable shame
> As to offend, himself being offended;
> So can I give no reason, nor I will not,
> More than a lodg'd hate and a certain loathing
> I bear Antonio, that I follow thus
> A losing suit against him. Are you answer'd?

(Note, especially, that "losing suit"!)

Antonio recognizes the futility of opposing Shylock's passion with reason. You might as well argue with a wolf, he says, tell the tide not to come in, or command the pines not to sway in the wind. The metaphors reveal his intuition that what he is dealing with is not ordinary human feeling within Shylock but elemental forces from without that have swept in and taken possession of him. And Gratiano suggests that the soul of a wolf has infused itself with the Jew's. Shylock's hatred does have a primitive quality. But Gratiano did not need to go back to the wolves, or even to Pythagoras, to account for it. It is elemental in character because it comes out of something vaster than the individual wrongs Shylock has suffered: the injustice suffered by his ancestors over the generations. As Hazlitt finely remarks: "He seems the depositary of the vengeance of his race." It is this that gives him that touch of sublimity that all his fierceness cannot efface. The bloody Margaret of *Henry VI,* when she becomes the suffering Margaret of *Richard III,* is endowed with something of the same tragic quality. If this man is to be moved, it must be by forces as far above reason as those that now animate him are below it.

And then Portia enters.

VIII

The introduction and identifications over, Portia, as the Young Doctor of Laws, says to Shylock:

Of a strange nature is the suit you follow;
Yet in such rule that the Venetian law
Cannot impugn you as you do proceed.

This bears the mark of preparation, if not of rehearsal. It seems a strange way of beginning, like a partial prejudgment of the case in Shylock's favor. But his hopes must be raised at the outset to make his ultimate downfall the more dramatic. "Do you confess the bond?" she asks Antonio. "I do," he replies.

Then must the Jew be merciful.

Portia, as she says this, is apparently still addressing Antonio. It would have been more courteous if, instead of speaking of him in the third person, she had turned directly to Shylock and said, "Then must you be merciful." But she makes a worse slip than that: the word *must.* Instantly Shylock seizes on it, pouring all his sarcasm into the offending verb:

On what compulsion *"must"* I? Tell me that.

Portia is caught! You can fairly see her wheel about to face not so much the Jew as the unanswerable question the Jew has asked. He is right—she sees it: "must" and "mercy" have nothing to do with each other; no law, moral or judicial, can force a man to be merciful.

For a second, the question must have thrown Portia off balance. This was not an anticipated moment in the role of the Young Doctor. But forgetting the part she is playing, she rises to the occasion superbly. The truth from Shylock elicits the truth from her. Instead of trying to brush the Jew aside or hide behind some casuistry or technicality, she frankly sustains his exception:

The quality of mercy is not strain'd. . . .

"I was wrong, Shylock," she confesses in effect. "You are right"; mercy is a matter of grace, not of constraint:

> It droppeth as the gentle rain from heaven
> Upon the place beneath. . . .

Shylock, then, supplied not only the cue, but, we might almost say, the first line of Portia's most memorable utterance.

In all Shakespeare—unless it be Hamlet with "To be or not to be"—there is scarcely another character more identified in the world's mind with a single speech than Portia with her words on mercy. And the world is right. They have a "quality" different from anything else in her role. They are no prepared words of the Young Doctor she is impersonating, but her own, as unexpected as was Shylock's disconcerting question. Something deep down in him draws them from something deep down—or shall we say high up?—in her. They are the spiritual gold hidden not beneath lead but beneath the "gold" of her superficial life, her reward for meeting Shylock's objection with sincerity rather than with evasion.

A hush falls over the courtroom as she speaks them (as it does over the audience when *The Merchant of Venice* is performed). Even the Jew is moved. Who can doubt it? Who can doubt that for a moment at least he is drawn back from the brink of madness and logic on which he stands? Here is the celestial visitant—the Portia God made—sent expressly to exorcise the demonic powers that possess him. Only an insensible clod could fail to feel its presence. And Shylock is no insensible clod. Can even he show mercy? Will a miracle happen? It is the supreme moment. The actor who misses it misses everything.

And then, incredibly, it is Portia who fails Shylock, not Shylock Portia. The same thing happens to her that happened to him at that other supreme moment when he offered Antonio the loan without interest. Her antipodal self emerges. In the twinkling of an eye, the angel reverts to the Doctor of Laws. "So quick bright things come to confusion." Whether the actress in Portia is intoxicated by the sound of her own voice[2] and the effect it is producing, or whether she feels the great triumph she has rehearsed being stolen from her if Shylock relents, or both, at any rate, pushing aside the divine Portia and her divine opportunity, the Young Doctor resumes his role. His "therefore, Jew" gives an inkling of what is coming. You can hear, even in the printed text, the change of voice, as Portia sinks from compassion to legality:

> I have spoke thus much
> To mitigate the justice of thy plea,
> Which if thou follow, this strict court of Venice
> Must needs give sentence 'gainst the merchant there.

It would be unbelievable if the words were not there. "You should show mercy," the Young Doctor says in effect, "but if you don't, this court will be compelled to decide in your favor." It is as if a mother, having entreated her son to desist from some wrong line of conduct and feeling she had almost won, were to conclude: "I hope you won't do it, but, if you insist, I shall have to let you, since your father told you you could." It is like a postscript that undoes the letter. Thus Portia the lover of mercy is deposed by Portia the actress that the latter may have the rest of her play. And the hesitating Shylock, pushed back to the precipice, naturally has nothing to say but

> My deeds upon my head! I crave the law,
> The penalty and forfeit of my bond.

The rest of the scene is an overwhelming confirmation of Portia's willingness to sacrifice the human to the theatrical, a somewhat different kind of sacrifice from that referred to in the inscription on the leaden casket. If there was any temptation that Shakespeare understood, it must have been this one. It was his own temptation. And, as he tells us in the *Sonnets,* he nearly succumbed to it:

> And almost thence my nature is subdu'd
> To what it works in, like the dyer's hand.

Portia's *was* subdued.

IX

The skill with which from this point she stages and acts her play proves her a consummate playwright, director, and actress—three in one. She wrings the last drop of possible suspense from every step in the mounting excitement. She stretches every nerve to the breaking point, arranges every contrast, climax, and reversal with the nicest sense for maximum effect, doing nothing too soon or too late, holding back her "Tarry a little" until Shylock is on the very verge of triumph, even whetting his knife perhaps. It is she who says to Antonio, "Therefore lay bare your bosom." It is she who asks if there is a balance ready to weigh the flesh, a surgeon to stay the blood. And she actually allows Antonio to undergo his last agony, to utter, uninterrupted, his final farewell.

It is at this point that the shallow Bassanio reveals an unsuspected depth in his nature by declaring, with a ring of sincerity we cannot doubt, that he would sacrifice everything, including his life and his wife, to save his friend.

Who chooseth me must give and hazard all he hath.

It is now, not when he stood before it, that Bassanio proves worthy of the leaden casket. Called on to make good his word, he doubtless would not have had the strength. But that does not prove that he does not mean what he says at the moment. And at that moment all Portia can do to help him is to turn into a jest—which she and Nerissa are alone in a position to understand—the most heart-felt and noble words her lover ever uttered.

POR.: Your wife would give you little thanks for that,
If she were by to hear you make the offer.

This light answer, in the presence of what to Antonio and Bassanio is the very shadow of death, measures her insensibility to anything but the play she is presenting, the role she is enacting.

From this jest, in answer to the Jew's insistence, she turns without a word of transition to grant Shylock his sentence:

A pound of that same merchant's flesh is thine.
The court awards it, and the law doth give it . . .
And you must cut this flesh from off his breast.
The law allows it, and the court awards it.

It is apparently all over with Antonio. The Jew lifts his knife. But once more appearances are deceitful. With a "tarry a little" this mistress of the psychological moment plays in succession, one, two, three, the cards she has been keeping back for precisely this moment. Now the Jew is caught in his own trap, now he gets a taste of his own logic, a dose of his own medicine. Now there is no more talk of mercy, but justice pure and simple, an eye for an eye:

POR.:   as thou urgest justice, be assur'd
Thou shalt have justice, more than thou desir'st.

Seeing his prey about to elude him, Shylock is now willing to accept the offer of three times the amount of his bond, and Bassanio actually produces the money. He is willing to settle on those terms. But not Portia:

The Jew shall have all justice; soft! no haste:
He shall have nothing but the penalty.

Shylock reduces his demand: he will be satisfied with just his principal. Again Bassanio has the money ready. But Portia is adamant:

He shall have merely justice, and his bond.

When the Jew pleads again for his bare principal, she repeats:

Thou shalt have nothing but the forfeiture,

and as he moves to leave the courtroom, she halts him with a

Tarry, Jew:
The law hath yet another hold on you.

All this repetition seems enough to make the point clear. But that the "beauty" of the nemesis may be lost on no one in the courtroom (nor on the dullest auditor when *The Merchant of Venice* is performed) Shakespeare has the gibing Gratiano on the spot to rub in the justice of the retribution: "O learned judge!" "O upright judge!" "A second Daniel, a Daniel, Jew!" "A second Daniel!" over and over. Emily Dickinson has spoken of "the mob within the heart." Gratiano is the voice of that mob, and he sees to it that a thrill of vicarious revenge runs down the spine of every person in the theater. So exultant are we at seeing the biter bit.

Why are we blind to the ignominy of identifying ourselves with the most brutal and vulgar character in the play? Obviously because there is a cruel streak in all of us that is willing to purchase excitement at any price. And excitement exorcises judgment. Only when we are free of the gregarious influences that dominate us in an audience does the question occur: What possessed Portia to torture not only Antonio but her own husband with such superfluous suspense? She knew what was coming. Why didn't she let it come at once? Why didn't she invoke immediately the law prescribing a penalty for any alien plotting against the life of any citizen of Venice instead of waiting until she had put those she supposedly loved upon the rack? The only possible answer is that she wanted a spectacle, a dramatic triumph with herself at the center. The psychology is identical with that which led the boy Kolya in *The Brothers Karamazov* to torture his sick little friend Ilusha by holding back the news that his lost dog was found, merely in order to enjoy the triumph of restoring him to his chum at the last moment in the presence of an audience. In that case the result was fatal. The child died from the excitement.

To all this it is easy to imagine what those will say who hold that Shakespeare was first the playwright and only incidentally poet and psychologist. "Why, but this is just a play!" they will exclaim, half-amused, half-contemptuous, "and a comedy at that! Portia! It isn't Portia who contrives the postponement. It is Shakespeare. Where would his play have been if his heroine had cut things short or failed to act exactly as she did?" Where indeed? Which is precisely why the poet made her the sort of woman who would have acted under the given conditions exactly as she did act. That was his business: not to find or devise situations exciting in the theater (any third-rate playwright can do that) but to discover what sort of men and women would behave in the often extraordinary ways in which they are represented as behaving in such situations in the stories he inherited and selected for dramatization.

X

"Logic is like the sword," says Samuel Butler, "—those who appeal to it shall perish by it." Never was the truth of that maxim more clearly illustrated than by Shylock's fate. His insistence that his bond be taken literally is countered by Portia's insistence that it be taken even more literally—and Shylock "perishes." He who had been so bent on defending the majesty of the law now finds himself in its clutches, half his goods forfeit to Antonio, the other half to the state, and his life itself in peril.

And so Portia is given a second chance. She is to be tested again. She has had

her legal and judicial triumph. Now it is over will she show to her victim that quality
which at her own divine moment she told us "is an attribute to God himself"? The
Jew is about to get his deserts. Will Portia forget her doctrine that mercy is mercy
precisely because it is not deserved? The Jew is about to receive justice. Will she
remember that our prayers for mercy should teach us to do the deeds of mercy
and that in the course of justice none of us will see salvation? Alas! she will forget,
she will not remember. Like Shylock, but in a subtler sense, she who has appealed
to logic "perishes" by it.

Up to this point she has been forward enough in arrogating to herself the
function of judge. But now, instead of showing compassion herself or entreating the
Duke to, she motions Shylock to his knees:

Down therefore and beg mercy of the Duke.

"Mercy"! This beggar's mercy, though it goes under the same name, has not the
remotest resemblance to that quality that drops like the gentle rain from heaven.
Ironically it is the Duke who proves truer to the true Portia than Portia herself.

DUKE: That thou shalt see the difference of our spirits,
I pardon thee thy life before thou ask it.

And he suggests that the forfeit of half of Shylock's property to the state may be
commuted to a fine.

Ay, for the state; not for Antonio,

Portia quickly interposes, as if afraid that the Duke is going to be too merciful, going
to let her victim off too leniently. Here, as always, the aftermath of too much
"theatrical" emotion is a coldness of heart that is like lead. The tone in which Portia
has objected is reflected in the hopelessness of Shylock's next words:

Nay, take my life and all! Pardon not that!
You take my house when you do take the prop
That doth sustain my house. You take my life
When you do take the means whereby I live.

Portia next asks Antonio what "mercy" he can render. And even the man
whom Shylock would have killed seems more disposed than Portia to mitigate the
severity of his penalty: he is willing to forgo the half of Shylock's goods if the Duke
will permit him the use of the other half for life with the stipulation that it go to
Lorenzo (and so to Jessica) at his death. But with two provisos: that all the Jew dies
possessed of also go to Lorenzo-Jessica and that

He presently become a Christian.

Doubtless the Elizabethan crowd, like the crowd in every generation since
including our own, thought that this was letting Shylock off easily, that this *was*
showing mercy to him. Crowds do not know that mercy is wholehearted and has

nothing to do with halves or other fractions. Nor do crowds know that you cannot make a Christian by court decree. Antonio's last demand quite undoes any tinge of mercy in his earlier concessions.

Even Shylock, as we have seen, had in him at least a grain of spiritual gold, of genuine Christian spirit. Only a bit of it perhaps. Seeds do not need to be big. Suppose that Portia and Antonio, following the lead of the seemingly willing Duke, had watered this tiny seed with that quality that blesses him who gives as well as him who takes, had overwhelmed Shylock with the grace of forgiveness! What then? The miracle, it is true, might not have taken place. Yet it might have. But instead, as if in imitation of the Jew's own cruelty, they whet their knives of law and logic, of reason and justice, and proceed to cut out their victim's heart. (That that is what it amounts to is proved by the heartbroken words,

I pray you give me leave to go from hence.
I am not well.)

Shylock's conviction that Christianity and revenge are synonyms is confirmed. "If a Christian wrong a Jew, what should his sufferance be by Christian example? Why, revenge." The unforgettable speech from which that comes, together with Portia's on mercy, and Lorenzo's on the harmony of heaven, make up the spiritual argument of the play. Shylock asserts that a Jew is a man. Portia declares that man's duty to man is mercy—which comes from heaven. Lorenzo points to heaven but laments that the materialism of life insulates man from its harmonies. A celestial syllogism that puts to shame the logic of the courtroom.

That Shakespeare planned his play from the outset to enforce the irony of Portia's failure to be true to her inner self in the trial scene is susceptible of something as near proof as such things can ever be. As in the case of Hamlet's

A little more than kin, and less than kind,

the poet, over and over, makes the introduction of a leading character seemingly casual, actually significant. Portia enters The Merchant of Venice with the remark that she is aweary of the world. Nerissa replies with that wise little speech about the illness of those that surfeit with too much (an observation that takes on deeper meaning in the retrospect after we realize that at the core what is the trouble with Portia and her society is boredom). "Good sentences and well pronounced," says Portia, revealing in those last two words more than she knows. "They would be better if well followed," Nerissa pertinently retorts. Whereupon Portia, as if gifted with insight into her own future, takes up Nerissa's theme:

If to do were as easy as to know what were good to do, chapels had been churches, and poor men's cottages princes' palaces. It is a good divine that follows his own instructions: I can easier teach twenty what were good to be done, than be one of the twenty to follow mine own teaching.

If that is not a specific preparation for the speech on mercy and what follows it, what in the name of coincidence is it? The words on mercy were good sentences, well pronounced. And far more than that. But for Portia they remained just words in the sense that they did not teach her to do the deeds of mercy. So, a few seconds after we see her for the first time, does Shakespeare let her pass judgment in advance on the most critical act of her life. For a moment, at the crisis in the courtroom, she seems about to become the leaden casket with the spiritual gold within. But the temptation to gain what many men desire—admiration and praise—is too strong for her and she reverts to her worldly self. Portia is the golden casket.

XI

The last act of *The Merchant of Venice* is often accounted a mere epilogue, a device whereby Shakespeare dissipates the tension aroused by the long court scene of Act IV. It does dissipate it, but the idea that it is a mere afterpiece is superficial.

To begin with, the moonlight and the music take up the central theme and continue the symbolism. At night what was concealed within by day is often revealed, and under the spell of sweet sounds what is savage in man is tamed, for "music for the time doth change his nature." It is not chance that in the first hundred lines and a little more of this scene (at which point the music ceases) Portia, Nerissa, Lorenzo, and even Jessica utter words that might well have been out of their reach by day or under other conditions. Lorenzo's incomparable lines on the harmony of heaven seem, in particular, too beautiful for the man who called Jessica "wise" and "true" at the very time when she was robbing her father. But under the influence of love and moonlight this may be his rare moment. Over and over Shakespeare lets an unsuspected depth in his characters come out at night. However that may be, the passage lends a sort of metaphysical sanction to the casket metaphor. Moonlight opens the leaden casket of material reality and lets us see

> how the floor of heaven
> Is thick inlaid with patines of bright gold.

But the garden by moonlight is only a glimpse, a prelude, or rather an interlude, and with the return of the husbands and Antonio, the poetry and romance largely disappear, the levity is resumed, the banter, the punning, the sexual allusions, including some very frank ones on Portia's part, until the secret of the impersonations is revealed and everything is straightened out. What a picture it is of the speed with which so-called happy people rush back to the idle pleasures of life after a brief compulsory contact with reality. Privilege was forced for a moment to face the Excluded. It makes haste to erase the impression as quickly and completely as it can. Similarly, for theatergoers, the fifth act erases any earlier painful impressions.

The story came out all right after all! Nothing need cloud the gaiety of the after-theater supper

In spite of this fifth act, there has been much discussion of the dissonance which the Shylock story introduces into what is otherwise a light and diverting play, much quoting of authorities on the question of what is, and what is not, permissible in a comedy. There is nothing to indicate that Shakespeare's imagination ever allowed itself to be shackled by such prescriptions or definitions. Indeed in this case, as so often, I think he gives us a direct hint how his drama should be taken.

Those who stress the matter of construction have often pointed out that the playwright meticulously prepares for a scene in this play that he never presents— the masque at which Lorenzo was to make Jessica his torchbearer. After whetting our appetites, the whole matter is dismissed in one line (with an explanatory second line) when Antonio announces:

> No masque to-night: the wind is come about;
> Bassanio presently will go aboard.

Just so the winds of life are forever coming about and calling off life's revels at the last moment. In that sense no comedy is true to life in which the seeds of tragedy are not concealed. Every performance of *The Merchant of Venice* might well be heralded with the cry: *No comedy tonight. The winds are come about.* And so the scene Shakespeare prepared for and left out is not left out after all. Those who think the playwright showed slipshod craftsmanship here should look a bit deeper at the poet's intention.

XII

The authority of imaginative literature resides in the fact that its masterpieces, whenever or wherever written, confirm one another. Anyone who doubts that the overtones and undertones of *The Merchant of Venice* were intended by their author, anyone who doubts that Shylock might have been transformed if Portia had been true to herself, should read Chekhov's "Rothschild's Fiddle." Here is another story written around the same economic theme. Here is the same contrast of inner and outer, the same two major characters, the Christian money-maker and the despised Jew, the same hatred of the Jew by the Christian because he is an unconscious symbol of his own wasted life—but with the other ending: mercy, forgiveness, spiritual transformation, even a hint of immortality. Though the chances against it are as great as in Shakespeare's play, the miracle does take place, a double miracle, in both Christian and Jew. "The gods are to each other not unknown." Not the only case where Shakespeare and Chekhov agree.

Such harmony is in immortal souls.

Shakespeare could not have used Chekhov's ending. His work is a play to be presented before a crowd, not just a story to be read by individuals—and the crowd demands the obvious. It is (ostensibly) a comedy—and the crowd demands a happy ending. But the conclusion of a poem, unlike the conclusion of a play, is not always to be found at the end. And in this sense the conclusions of the English and Russian versions of this theme are at one.

It is the crowning virtue of a work of art, as it is of a man, that it should be an example of its own doctrine, an incarnation of its own main symbol. A poem about fire ought to burn. A poem about a brook ought to flow. A poem about childhood ought not just to tell about children but ought to be like a child itself, as are the best of Blake's *Songs of Innocence*. "Rothschild's Fiddle" and *The Merchant of Venice* both meet this test. "Rothschild's Fiddle," as its title indicates, is a story about money and music. Or, better, about death and music, for, just as in *The Merchant of Venice*, money and death are equated. A coffin and a violin are its focal symbols. But they are more than that. The story is itself a coffin within which the author compels each reader to lie down, either to be buried within it (if he is one thing) or (if he is another) to be awakened and lifted out of it by strains of music. In precisely the same sense *The Merchant of Venice* is a casket. In fashioning it its author proceeded like the Maker of all things: he put the muddy vesture of decay—that is, the gilt and glitter—on the outside where no one can miss it and left the heavenly harmony in the overtones for those to hear who can. If this be deception, it is divine deception.

The metaphor that underlies and unifies *The Merchant of Venice* is that of alchemy, the art of transforming the base into the precious, lead into gold. Everything in it comes back to that. Only the symbols are employed in a double sense, one worldly and one spiritual. By a kind of illuminating confusion, gold is lead and lead is gold, the base precious and the precious base. Portia had a chance to effect the great transformation—and failed. But she is not the only one. Gold, silver, and lead in one, the play subjects every reader or spectator to a test, or, shall we say, offers every reader or spectator the same opportunity Portia had. Choose—it says—at your peril. This play anti-Semitic? Why, yes, if you find it so. Shakespeare certainly leaves you free, if you wish, to pick the golden casket. But you may thereby be revealing more of yourself than of his play.

And what is true of an individual is true of an age. Poetry forever makes itself over for each generation. *The Merchant of Venice* seems expressly written for a time like our own when everywhere the volcano of race hatred seems ready to erupt. But even when we see this we may still be taking it too narrowly. Its pertinence for us is no more confined to the racial aspect than are our hatreds and exclusions. What inspired Shakespeare to introduce into this gay entertainment, with all its frivolity and wedding bells, prototypes of those two giants of the twentieth century, Trade and Finance (each so different at heart from its own estimation of itself), to let them look in each other's eyes, and behold—their own reflections?

Which is the merchant here and which the Jew?

How came he to inject so incongruously into it that haunting figure that has grown steadily more tragic with the years until it has thrown his supposed comedy quite out of focus? More sinned against than sinning, this villain-victim now strikes us as more nearly the protagonist, a far-off forerunner of King Lear himself. Beside him, the gentleman-hero of the piece shrinks to a mere fashion-plate, and his sad-eyed friend to a mere shadow. It is as if, between the passing darkness of feudalism and the oncoming darkness of capitalism, the sun broke forth briefly and let the poet store up truth for the future. When the Old Corruption goes, there is always such a glimpse of clear sky before the New Corruption assumes the throne. Not that Shakespeare was interested in economic evolution or foresaw its course. Poetic prophecy does not work in that way. Goethe reveals its secret rather when he says: "If a man grasp the particular vividly he also grasps the general without being aware of it at the time, or he may make the discovery long afterward." It is in this sense that Shakespeare wrote *The Merchant of Venice* for us even more than for his own age. Its characters are around us everywhere. Its problems still confront us—on an enormously enlarged scale.

At a time like our own when economic problems sometimes threaten to eclipse all others, their relation to moral and spiritual problems gets forgotten. But to divorce the two is to leave both insoluble. *The Merchant of Venice* not only does not make this error itself, it corrects it for us. It offers precisely the wisdom that we need, a wisdom that goes deeper than the doctrine of any economic school or sect. Shylock made his money by usury, Antonio his by trade, Portia got hers by inheritance, Bassanio by borrowing and then by marriage, Jessica by theft and later by judicial decree. The interplay of their lives makes enthralling drama. But to those not content to stop with the story it propounds questions that have a strangely contemporary ring: How are these various modes of acquiring and holding property related? Are they as unlike as they seem? And, coming closer home: Am I myself possibly, thanks to one or more of them, living in a golden world?

Those who might be compelled to answer "yes" to this last question will generally be protected from asking it. Some instinct of self-preservation—or fear of death—will keep them from seeking where they might discover, could they understand them, grounds sounder, in their opinion, than its supposed anti-Semitism for withdrawing *The Merchant of Venice* from the schools.

"There are certain current expressions and blasphemous modes of viewing things," says Thoreau, "as when we say 'he is doing a good business' more profane than cursing and swearing. Let not the children hear them." The author of *The Merchant of Venice*, I suspect, would have understood and agreed. He knew what he was doing when he named his play and when he made its merchant the victim of a melancholia so intense it verged on the suicidal.

"God won't ask us whether we succeeded in business."

NOTES

[1] Who selected the song that is sung while Bassanio meditates we shall never know. It of course gives away the secret. And in that connection there is a point I have never happened to see noted. The verses inside the golden casket begin with a rhyme on long *o* (gold); those inside the silver casket on a rhyme on short *i* (this). The song sung while Bassanio is making up his mind begins with a rhyme on short *e* (bred). But *bred* (as someone has pointed out) is a full rhyme with *lead!*

[2] "It is a sad but sure truth that every time you speak of a fine purpose, especially if with eloquence and to the admiration of bystanders, there is the less chance of your ever making a fact of it in your own poor life."—Carlyle, quoted in John Buchan's *Pilgrim's Way* (Boston, 1940), p. 136.

Graham Midgley

THE MERCHANT OF VENICE:
A RECONSIDERATION

The problem of *The Merchant of Venice* has always been its unity, and most critical discussions take this as the centre of their argument, asking what is the relative importance of its two plots and how Shakespeare contrives to interweave them into a unity; the two plots being the Shylock plot and what is called the love or romance plot. Is the play, we are asked to decide, primarily a love comedy, as most of Shakespeare's mature comedies are, in which the story of the Jew and his bond is but a necessary cog in a more important machine, or is the play a study of the personality of the Jew, with the love-story merely a useful way of engineering the entry of Antonio into the dreadful bond? Moreover, where does Shakespeare mean our sympathies to lie—with the Jew as an oppressed and persecuted sufferer forced to vengeance by the heartless society which surrounds him, or with the ladies and gentlemen of Venice who so splendidly thwart the machinations of the diabolic Jew? If we insist on analysing the play with these two plots as our central consideration, we find ourselves in trouble. We find Shakespeare working out a remarkably steady alternation of scene between Venice and Belmont and then, as if to cap this alternating structure, giving the whole of Act IV to Venice and the trial scene, and the whole of Act V to Belmont, with Shylock apparently forgotten. Whatever else he might do, Shakespeare does not throw away his fifth act and, if we are working on the Shylock-lovers pattern, it would appear that the farewell and lasting impression on the audience, which the fifth act can give, is meant by Shakespeare to be, not the end of Shylock and the misery of his defeat, but the love theme, the happiness of the united lovers and the lyrical beauty of Belmont by moonlight. Shylock is forgotten completely by the lovers beneath the stars, and the main theme is the triumph of love. If this is the truth, then Shylock has been allowed to become far too imposing a figure in the previous four acts of the play (where he should have been little more than the equivalent of such characters as Don John or Malvolio in the other love comedies), and this fifth act is a desperate attempt to

From *Essays in Criticism* 10, No. 2 (April 1960): 119–33.

redress a lost balance. If, on the other hand, we accept Shylock as the central point of interest, the play collapses beautifully but irrelevantly in a finely-written act given over to a secondary theme. It is possible to show, however, that the construction becomes more meaningful if we accept an entirely different theme and two different points of interest. If we do this, the problem of divided interest between Shylock and the lovers becomes an irrelevant one, or at least relevant in a different way, and the play becomes something far more interesting than a fairy tale with unfortunate deeper intrusions, or a tragic downfall of a Jew, disfigured by lovers' adventures and tedious casket scenes.

Other critics have faced up to the problem, but their solutions are not completely convincing. At the one extreme is the critic who rejects any serious consideration of the play as beside the point, like Granville-Barker to whom the play was a 'fairy tale' and who saw 'no more reality in Shylock's bond and the Lord of Belmont's will than in Jack and the Beanstalk'.[1] Professor Nevill Coghill wishes us to interpret the play as an allegory of 'Justice and Mercy, of the Old Law and the New', with the trial scene as the central point of the debate and the last act the act of reconciliation, where we find 'Lorenzo and Jessica, Jew and Christian, Old Law and New, united in love; and their talk is of music, Shakespeare's recurrent symbol of harmony'.[2] Some see the theme as one of contrast between seeming and reality or, as Professor C. S. Lewis, between the *values* of Bassanio and Shylock, 'between the crimson and organic wealth in his veins, the medium of nobility and fecundity, and the cold, mineral wealth in Shylock's counting house'.[3] Professor J. W. Lever contrasts love which 'comprehends the generous give and take of emotion, the free spending of nature's bounty, and the increase of progeny through marriage', with usury which, he writes, is the 'negation of friendship and community'.[4] Sir E. K. Chambers, with an attractive simplicity, found a conflict between Love and Hate, Shylock representing Hate and Antonio and Portia embodying Love.[5] Most of these solutions are only partial, most of them failing to explain great parts of the play's subject matter and attitude. All of them are trying to find a synthesis of a wrong opposition.

I would suggest that the two focal points of the play are Shylock and, not the lovers or the romance theme, but Antonio, and that the world of love and marriage is not opposed by Shylock, but rather paralleled by Venetian society as a whole, social, political and economic. The scheme of the play is, if I may reduce it to ratio terms: As Shylock is to Venetian society, so is Antonio to the world of love and marriage. The relationship of these two to these two worlds is the same, the relationship of an outsider. The play is, in effect, a twin study in loneliness. The fact that these two outcasts, these two lonely men, only meet in the cruel circumstances they do, adds an irony and pathos to the play which lift it out of the category of fairy tale or romance. Indeed, seen from any angle, *The Merchant of Venice* is not a very funny play, and we might gain a lot if, for the moment, we ceased to be bullied by its inclusion amongst the Comedies. This thesis has much to offer in our understanding of the play. It reinstates Antonio to a position in the play more commensurate with the care and interest Shakespeare seems to have known in his creation (and the play is, after all, called *The Merchant of Venice*): it does not force us into having to condemn Shylock if we accept the values of the love world, for it offers us different oppositions and asks us to make different moral judgments, different in kind as well as direction: and finally, it seems to make more impressive sense of the construction of the play, especially of Acts IV and V.

An examination of the characters of Shylock and Antonio as parallel studies is a preliminary task which should throw light on the reconsideration of the play as a whole.

Examinations of Shylock have too often been obscured by a scholarly heap of secondary considerations arising from the fact that he is a Jew. It is surprising how much of the work on *The Merchant of Venice* turns out on inspection to be on the lines of 'The Jew in Elizabethan England', 'The Elizabethan Jew in Drama', or 'The Jew in Elizabethan Drama'. We are urged, in seeing the play, not to forget that the audience had probably never seen a Jew; we are reminded that this is an Elizabethan play and that Shakespeare could count on a stock response to a Jew figure, shaped by age-old memories of the Hugh of Lincoln and baby-killing kinds; we are advised not to be influenced by our reactions to anti-Semitism in our own day into making a sentimental figure out of Shylock which Shakespeare could never have understood. Comparisons with Marlowe's Jew are made, and the body of the unfortunate Dr. Lopez is always exhumed as an important exhibit. To work through this mass of material is to feel at once that the play is being smothered, and when, for example, one is asked to accept as superbly clever hypocrisy a speech of Shylock's which rings with obvious sincerity and feeling, one begins to rebel and return to the play and what the play says. In my opinion it is not of much importance that Shylock is a Jew, and all the 'background work' on Jews and Judaism strikes me as quite irrelevant. The important thing is that he is a Jew in a Gentile society, that all he is and all he holds dear is alien to the society in which he has to live. He is an alien, an outsider, tolerated but never accepted. His being a Jew is not important in itself: what is important is what being a Jew has done to his personality. He is a stranger, proud of his race and its traditions, strict in his religion, sober rather than miserly in his domestic life, and filled with the idea of the sanctity of the family and family loyalty. Around him is the society of Venice, a world of golden youth, richly dressed, accustomed to luxury, to feasting, to masking, of a comparatively easy virtue and of a religious outlook which, though orthodox, hardly strikes one as deep, a society faithful and courteous in its own circle and observing a formal politeness of manner and address, but quite insufferable to those outside its own circle, where Shylock is so obviously placed. By that society Shylock is treated as dirt. Antonio never denies the treatment he has given this proud man:

Signior Antonio, many a time and oft
On the Rialto you have rated me
About my moneys and my usances:

Still have I borne it with a patient shrug,
For suffrance is the badge of all our tribe.
You call me misbeliever, cut-throat dog,
And spit upon my Jewish gaberdine,
And all for use of that which is mine own.   (I.iii.101)

Antonio's only response is:

I am as like to call thee so again,
To spit on thee again, to spurn thee too.
If thou wilt lend this money, lend it not
As to thy friends; for when did friendship take
A breed of barren metals?   (I.iii.125)

And all the repressed humiliation and sense of injustice which lies beneath Shylock's
proud and patient bearing, bursts out in:

He hath disgraced me and hindered me half a million; laughed at my losses,
mocked at my gains, scorned my nation, thwarted my bargains, cooled my
friends, heated mine enemies; and what's the reason? I am a Jew. Hath not a
Jew eyes? hath not a Jew hands, organs, dimensions, senses, affections, passions? fed with the same food, hurt with the same weapons, subject to the
same diseases, healed by the same means, warmed and cooled by the same
summer and winter, as a Christian is? If you prick us, do we not bleed? if you
tickle us, do we not laugh? if you poison us, do we not die?   (III.i.48)

With this side of the man in mind, let us follow him swiftly through the play.
    Our first meeting with him is in the arranging of the bond. He is faced with
insolent rudeness on the part of those who come in fact to beg a favour, with the
peremptory snaps of Bassanio:

Ay sir, for three months. . . .
May you stead me? will you pleasure me? shall I know
your answer?
Your answer to that. . . .   (I.iii.2)

He is drawn into a discussion on usury, attacked for lending money on interest, and
the only reply to his quite sensible defense is Antonio's supercilious:

              Mark you this, Bassanio,
The devil can cite scripture for his purpose,
An evil soul, producing holy witness,
Is like a villain with a smiling cheek,
A goodly apple rotten at the heart.
O what a goodly outside falsehood hath!   (I.iii.93)

Shylock is stirred to remind Antonio, in words already quoted, of his former cruel behaviour to him, to call attention to the almost forgotten fact that Antonio *is* begging a favour, but he is again rejected by Antonio with cold scorn. Can we blame him if a scheme of revenge forms in his mind?

Later Lorenzo elopes with Jessica, the two of them rejoicing callously in the tricking and robbing of the Jew. Jessica's elopement, added by Shakespeare to his source, is no mere romantic addition, but the crucial point in Shylock's development. In this deed a blow is struck at all that Shylock holds dear, his pride of race, the sober decency of his household life and the dear sanctity of the family and family bonds. The mixing of ducats with his daughter in his cries of despair is because his ducats, as his daughter, are part of his family pride, the only bulwarks against the general scorn of the society he lives in, as he exclaims later when his estates are ordered to be confiscated:

> Nay, take my life and all; pardon not that:
> You take my house when you do take the prop
> That doth sustain my house; and take my life
> When you do take the means whereby I live.   (IV.i.370)

When he first appears in the court his mood is not one of rage or mad vindictiveness: rather of cold and controlled intent on revenge. He speaks quietly, deliberately and logically, but quite unwavering in his intent. Against the calm insults of the Duke and the more hysterical reviling of Gratiano, he maintains this calm:

> Repair thy wit, good youth, or it will fall
> To cureless ruin.   (IV.i.141)

And behind this calm front, the burning sorrow of Jessica's shame is still there:

> The pound of flesh which I demand of him
> Is dearly bought.   (IV.i.99)

Dearly bought by Jessica's shame, surely, for which he holds Antonio scapegoat, rather than the miserable 3,000 ducats. There we may leave Shylock for the moment, postponing a fuller discussion of the trial scene until Antonio, the dramatic antagonist of Shylock, is also established as his spiritual companion, adrift like him in a hostile society.

Antonio is in no way rejected externally or consciously by the people he has to live with. He is respected, rich, with easy access to economic, legal and social circles, and Venice is always on his side. His loneliness is within and not without, as Shylock's. Antonio is an outsider because he is an unconscious homosexual in a predominantly, and indeed blatantly, heterosexual society. Against such a statement I am aware that a great amount of scholarly opposition could be mustered, studies of friendship in Renaissance thought and Elizabethan literature, evidence of an extremer vocabulary of endearment between men than could be used nowadays without risk of misunderstanding, studies of Shakespeare's sonnets and the theme of friendship there. All this may be very true, but my first bare formulation stands. The fact which strikes one above all about Antonio is his all-absorbing love of Bassanio, his complete lack of interest in women—in a play where this interest guides the actions of all the other males—and his being left without a mate in a play which is rounded off by a full-scale mating dénouement. Moreover, his relationship with Bassanio has very special facets which need a special interpretation. We first meet Antonio in a state of deep melancholy—not the pretty heigh-ho sadness of Portia which is (purposefully?) to be contrasted with it in the next scene—but a deeper and completely unaffected melancholy:

> In sooth, I know not why I am so sad,
> It wearies me, you say it wearies you;
> But how I caught it, found it, or came by it,
> What stuff 'tis made of, whereof it is born,
> I am to learn;
> And such a want-wit sadness makes of me,
> That I have much ado to know myself.   (I.i.1)

It is soon established that its cause is not worry over his business affairs, and the first clue comes in the exchange with Solanio:

> SOL.: Why then you are in love.
> ANT.:   Fie! Fie!   (I.i.46)

This is more than a simple contradiction or negative. There is a reproach here either for something being mentioned which ought not to be mentioned—Antonio thinking Solanio refers to his love for Bassanio—or for something being mentioned which Antonio finds repugnant to his nature—thinking Solanio suggests some love-affair with a woman. Whichever it may be, Antonio, a few lines later, perfectly sums up his place in the society in which he moves:

> I hold the world but as the world, Gratiano,
> A stage, where every man must play a part,
> And mine a sad one.   (I.i.77)

The cause of this sadness which Antonio has refused to acknowledge even to himself is revealed as soon as Antonio and Bassanio are alone together, for Antonio's first words are:

> Well, tell me now what lady is the same
> To whom you swore a secret pilgrimage.   (I.i.119)

It was, apparently, Bassanio's first mention of the possibility of his wooing and marriage some time previously, which had cast Antonio into this gloomy sadness. This is not, I think, a forcing of the text, for all the previous writing about Antonio has been to establish that sadness, to stress its apparent causelessness, except in that inexplicably angry 'Fie! Fie!' Now, added to this, comes this sudden rush to the heart of the matter, where Antonio seeks to know more of the thing which has ruined his happiness, and then, knowing, he does the only thing his love can do, sacrificing himself as fully as possible for his beloved. The description of the parting of these two brings out these motives in Antonio quite clearly:

> I saw Bassanio and Antonio part,
> Bassanio told him he would make some speed
> Of his return: he answered, 'Do not so,
> Slubber not business for my sake, Bassanio,
> But stay the very riping of the time,
> And for the Jew's bond which he hath of me—
> Let it not enter into your mind of love:
> Be merry, and employ your chiefest thoughts
> To courtship, and such fair ostents of love
> As shall conveniently become you there.'
> And even there (his eye being big with tears),
> Turning his face, he put his hand behind him,
> And with affection wondrous sensible
> He wrung Bassanio's hand, and so they parted.   (II.viii.36)

Solanio's reaction is clearly meant to be ours:

> I think he only loves the world for him.

Perhaps that is why, knowing Bassanio was going, Antonio could say earlier:

> I hold the world but as the world, Gratiano,
> A stage where every man must play a part,
> And mine a sad one.

We are not to see Antonio again until disaster has overtaken him, his fortune gone and his death at the hands of the Jew for his friend's sake apparently inevitable. His attitude to that fate and what he makes of it have been neglected in criticism, which has concentrated its interest on Shylock and Portia, relegating Antonio to the rank of another bystander. The first piece of evidence is the letter which he sends to Bassanio:

> Sweet Bassanio, my ships have all miscarried, my creditors grow cruel, my estate is very low, my bond to the Jew is forfeit, and (since in paying it, it is impossible that I should live) all debts are clear'd between you and I, if I might but see you at my death: notwithstanding, use your pleasure—if your love do not persuade you to come, let not my letter.   (III.ii.314)

The last words indicate Antonio's mood. The death is, in a way, welcome, for it is his greatest, if his last, opportunity to show his love, and to escape from the world where his part is a sad one. This is why he never questions Shylock's claim, never fights against the outrage of it. Death he accepts—as long as Bassanio is there:

These griefs and losses have so bated me
That I shall hardly spare a pound of flesh
To-morrow to my bloody creditor.
Well, gaoler, on—pray God Bassanio come
To see me pay his debt, and then I care not.   (III.iii.32)

In the trial scene his attitude is of resignation, and almost of an eagerness for death:

Let me have judgment, and the Jew his will.   (IV.i.83)

Most heartily I do beseech the court
To give the judgment.   (IV.i.238)

and there are two important exchanges with Bassanio, the first when Bassanio tries to encourage Antonio with hope and big words, and Antonio replies in terms which only make sense if they refer to a bigger problem in his life than the immediate legal one:

I am a tainted wether of the flock,
Meetest for death—the weakest kind of fruit
Drops earliest to the ground, and so let me;
You cannot better be employ'd, Bassanio,
Than to live still and write mine epitaph.   (IV.i.114)

What would have been, but for Portia's intervention, his last farewell to Bassanio is a wonderful drawing-together of all the threads which make up the complex character and motives of Antonio at this point:

Give me your hand, Bassanio, fare you well,
Grieve not that I am fall'n to this for you:
For herein Fortune shows herself more kind
Than is her custom: it is still her use
To let the wretched man outlive his wealth,
To view with hollow eye and wrinkled brow
An age of poverty: from which ling'ring penance
Of such misery doth she cut me off.
Commend me to your honourable wife,
Tell her the process of Antonio's end,
Say how I lov'd you, speak me fair in death:
And when the tale is told, bid her be judge
Whether Bassanio had not once a love:
Repent but you that you shall lose your friend
And he repents not that he pays your debt.
For it the Jew do cut but deep enough,
I'll pay it instantly with all my heart.   (IV.i.261)

Death is welcome in that it cuts short what would be a wretched existence; it is also welcome as a final and supreme expression of love which Antonio can leave with Bassanio, which he impresses on him and cannot help contrasting with that other love which is always at the back of his mind when he speaks to Bassanio, the love for Portia. Bassanio's reply could not be nearer to what Antonio longs to hear:

> Antonio, I am married to a wife
> Which is as dear to me as life itself,
> But life itself, my wife, and all the world,
> Are not with me esteem'd above thy life.
> I would lose all, ay sacrifice them all
> Here to this devil, to deliver you.   (IV.i.284)

But we know that Bassanio speaks for the nonce. Portia speaks the real truth of the world which is to conquer:

> Your wife would give you little thanks for that
> If she were by to hear you make the offer.

And so the trial scene moves to its climax and resolution, and from now on Antonio hardly speaks, with the result that, reading the play, we tend to forget him—a mistake which leads to a maimed interpretation of the Fifth Act.

What now remains to be done is to look again at the play as a whole, accepting these two interpretations of Shylock and Antonio, to see how it achieves a unity and meaning denied it by the Shylock-romance antithesis.

The parallel between Shylock and Antonio is the framework of the play. Both are not fully at home in the society in which they are forced to live, for different reasons. Shylock is accepted only because of his wealth and economic usefulness: otherwise in all the things which a man needs for happiness with his fellows, friendship, respect, social intercourse, sympathy, cooperation, he is denied and spurned. Antonio has all these things, but the thing he most desires is denied him, again by the society around him, not denied to him as violently as to Shylock, because Antonio's lack is secret and personal, and those around him neither know nor understand that in fact he lacks anything. Yet for all these differences, there is the basic kinship in the Jew and the Merchant, the kinship of loneliness.

Each, then, has to make a gesture against being overwhelmed, and each has to make it through the channel open to him or dear to him. The Jew makes his offer of friendship, he tries to escape from his isolation by means of the only common link between himself and his enemies, his wealth. Antonio makes his gesture of sacrifice in entering upon the bond, through the only thing which really means anything to him, his love.

Each makes his gesture and each is defeated, for as the people around Shylock violently and cruelly reply to his gesture with renewed attacks on his home and beliefs, finally overcoming him completely through the congregated social and legal powers of that society, at the same time they condemn Antonio to the loneliness his death would have ended. The violence of the defeat differs, of course, as the very positions of Shylock and Antonio differ. Shylock's fate is more violent and cruel because he outwardly opposes a whole society and outrages its pride and its code: Antonio's fate is private and quiet, as his opposition and loneliness are private and quiet. But their defeat is nevertheless a common one, and each is left holding an empty reward, each is left with cold comfort. Shylock is stripped of half of his wealth, the one thing which gave him standing in Venice, and is given in return the formal badge of entreé, to become a member of the society in which he has always been an outcast—he is to be made a Christian. The hollowness of the gesture and its real meaninglessness are obvious in the words of the play:

> DUKE: Get thee gone, but do it.
> GRAT.: In christ'ning shalt thou have two godfathers,—
> Had I been judge, thou shouldst have had ten more
> To bring thee to the gallows, not to the font.   (IV.i.393)

Antonio is rewarded with the return of his ships and money, and his receiving of this news is marked by such a flat unexcitement that we realise he speaks the whole truth and nothing more nor less, when he tells Portia:

> Sweet lady, you have given me life and living;
> For here I read for certain that my ships
> Are safely come to road.   (V.i.286)

'Life and living' in a world where he is destined to play a part, and that a sad one. The defeat of Shylock has been in a way the cause of his defeat, for it has deprived him of the one great gesture of love which would have ended his loneliness and crowned his love with one splendid act. Now he is left with his wealth and his loneliness, surrounded by the lovers and received by Portia at Belmont with words as full of warmth and feeling as those receiving Shylock into the fold of the Church:

> Sir, grieve you not,—you are welcome notwithstanding.

The climax of this parallel which is built up throughout the play, is reached in the parallel action of Act IV and Act V. Act IV covers the rejection and defeat of Shylock, quite explicitly, quite completely. It also covers the defeat of Antonio, but not so explicitly, and Act V is needed to bring out fully and unmistakably what has actually been done to him before the Duke and the court. In Act IV all the powers which oppose Shylock are drawn together into the court room, the glittering youth of Venice, with their friendship and solidarity, and above all the Duke and the magnificoes, embodiments of the law and social code which has rejected Shylock all his life, which, in bitter revenge, he now tries to use for his own ends, but which will turn and destroy him. Shylock is doomed and the net closes round him quite inescapably. He is thrust out from the court as he has always been thrust out, and the visual symbol is more powerful than any reading can be—the Duke on his throne, the magnificoes in all the haughty pomp and robes of state, the gentlemen and ladies grouped together hand in hand or arm in arm, a great, splendid and friendly phalanx filling one side of the stage, while at the other, beaten and alone, the Jew leaves the stage. Antonio's act is still to come, and I would stress it as his act, though he hardly speaks, rather than an attempt to restore the play safely to the romance comedy world from which it seemed to have been in danger of escaping—the interpretation forced on us if we accept the old reading of the play. Now it is not the state, the law, the social solidarity of Venice which is built up into the symbol of the rejecting power. The Act opens with:

> The moon shines bright. In such a night as this,
> When the sweet wind did gently kiss the trees,
> And they did make no noise, in such a night
> Troilus methinks mounted the Trojan walls,
> And sigh'd his soul towards the Grecian tents
> Where Cressid lay that night.   (V.i.1)

and this lyrical note of romance sets the key for the whole act:

> How sweet the moonlight sleeps upon this bank!   (V.i.54)

Against this background move the lovers, Lorenzo and Jessica, lying entranced in the moonlight, Portia hastening back to her husband, Nerissa to hers—even Launce-lot has found a dark-skinned lover. The talk is all of husbands and wives, of reunion, of welcomes home, of going to bed—for with three pairs of happy united lovers, this night is to see the consummation of their marriages. Antonio is welcomed to Belmont, but welcome him as they may, he is alone, and the words of welcome are formal and polite, spoken by people who have more important things to think about:

> Sir, you are welcome to our house:
> It must appear in other ways than words,
> Therefore I scant this breathing courtesy ...
> Sir, grieve you not,—you are welcome notwithstanding.

And then he is forgotten. Again one needs to see the scene to realize this fully. From the moonlit garden into the glow of the candle-lit house the lovers pass two by two, Portia with her Bassanio, Lorenzo with his Jessica, and lastly, rushing to their bed, Gratiano and Nerissa—and Antonio is left behind to walk from the stage alone, the stage to which he had likened his world, where he must play a part, and that a sad one. Visually one cannot escape the parallel between the lonely Shylock creeping from the stage, leaving the triumphant ranks of Venice, and this lonely Antonio walking from the stage, following without joy the triumphant pairs of lovers. The sad irony of the whole play is that these two never really meet. Indeed, they are pitched *against* each other, each retiring defeated into his own loneliness again, while Venice goes about its business, and the nightingales of Belmont sere-nade three happy marriage beds.

NOTES

[1] Prefaces to *Shakespeare*. Second Series, p. 67.
[2] *Shakespeare Quarterly*, I, 'The Governing Idea', pp. 9–17
[3] *Proceedings of the British Academy*, 1942, 'Hamlet: The Prince or the Poem', p. 146.
[4]*Shakespeare Quarterly*, III, p. 383.
[5]*Shakespeare: A Survey*, p. 112.

John Russell Brown

THE REALIZATION
OF SHYLOCK:
A THEATRICAL CRITICISM

One of the prime mysteries of Shakespeare's plays is their actability. When characters have been delineated and their traits numbered, when dramatic structure has been analyzed as form or 'imitation', when the linguistic and musical subtlety of the dialogue has been assessed and themes or meanings have been deduced, the quality which makes his plays eminently actable may yet escape definition. If we are optimistic and untempted by the unknown we may presume that an actor will find instinctively how he can best speak Shakespeare's lines, and leave the matter there: but our appreciation will be the poorer, and the actor, when instinct fails him, will be left to founder insecurely. Moreover, our judgment of the meaning or force of a whole play may be affected: the author who wrote successful titanic parts like Titus Andronicus or Richard the Third knew his actors' resources well and could calculate when to restrain them, when to let them have full scope; he would expect a groan, a silence or a movement, if well placed, to alter the emphasis of an entire scene. But this is to speak too crudely: a knowledge of the actor's opportunities—as complex and far-ranging as the human voice and body which are his instruments—was continuously at Shakespeare's service; those who wish to understand his writings, as well as those who perform them, must try to assess their actability in the finest detail.

The importance of such considerations is well shown by *The Merchant of Venice*. Ever since 14 February 1741, when Charles Macklin persuaded the management of Drury Lane to restore Shakespeare's text in place of George Granville's adaptation and to allow him to play Shylock, this comedy has nearly always been revived for the same purpose—to give some actor the chance of playing the lead. For that is what Shylock is: although he appears in but five of its twenty scenes and not at all in the last act, he can dominate every other impression and display the powers of many kinds of actor. He takes the final curtain-call, without Portia or

From *Early Shakespeare* (Stratford-upon-Avon Studies 3), edited by John Russell Brown and Bernard Harris (New York: St. Martin's Press, 1961), pp. 187–209.

Bassanio, without Antonio, the merchant of Venice. This tradition is so strong that
it is easy to forget how strange it is: how odd that a villain—the one who threatens
the happiness of the others—should so run away with a play that is a comedy by
other signs, and that makes only a passing, unconcerned allusion to him at its
conclusion. But the records are unequivocal: in the theatre it is his play. Fortunately
the records are also unusually detailed, so that we are able to reconstruct the
different ways in which Shylock has been given life and observe the qualities in
Shakespeare's text which make this a star part. And from this inquiry, other
questions arise: have ambitious actors misrepresented Shakespeare's play? is one
interpretation, one reading of the actor's opportunities, more faithful than another?
is a fully realized Shylock incompatible with a well proportioned *Merchant of
Venice*, one that is satisfactorily concluded?

At first the part seemed to have been written especially for Macklin, as
Kemble's *Memoirs* (1825) affirm:

> His acting was essentially manly—there was nothing of trick about it. His
> delivery was more level than modern speaking, but certainly more weighty,
> direct and emphatic. His features were rigid, his eye cold and colourless; yet
> the earnestness of his manner, and the sterling sense of his address, produced
> an effect in Shylock, that has remained to the present hour unrivalled.
>
> (i. 440)

It was thought that Shakespeare had drawn Shylock 'all shade, not a gleam of light;
subtle, selfish, fawning, irascible, and tyrannic', and that Macklin's voice was:

> most happily suited to that sententious gloominess of expression the author
> intended; which, with a sullen solemnity of deportment, marks the character
> strongly; in his malevolence, there is a forcible and terrifying ferocity.[1]

He cast his performance between two extremes, sullen and malevolent, and the
two were linked by weight and power in his deportment and his eyes:

> There was, beside his judgment which went to the study of every line of it,
> such an iron-visaged look, such a relentless, savage cast of manners, that the
> audience seemed to shrink from the character.   (*Memoirs*, pp. 405–6)

His performance began sullenly:

> when Shylock and Bassanio entered, . . . there was an awful, a solemn si-
> lence. . . . He approached with Bassanio. . . . Still not a whisper could be heard
> in the house. Upon the entrance of Anthonio, the Jew makes the audience
> acquainted with his motives of antipathy against the Merchant. Mr. Macklin had
> no sooner delivered this speech, than the audience suddenly burst out into a
> thunder of applause, and in proportion as he afterwards proceeded to exhibit
> and mark the malevolence, the villainy, and the diabolical atrocity of the

character, so in proportion did the admiring and delighted audience testify their approbation. . . .[2]

Macklin himself spoke of the first scenes as 'rather tame and level' but:

> I knew where I should have the pull, which was in the third act, and reserved myself accordingly. At this period I threw out all my fire; . . . the contrasted passions of joy for the Merchant's losses, and grief for the elopement of Jessica, open a fine field for an actor's powers, . . .[3]

For this scene with Salerio and Solanio, and then with Tubal, he 'broke the tones of utterance' and ensured that his 'transitions were strictly natural' (Kirkman, i. 264). But for the trial he reverted to what he called 'a silent yet forcible impression' (*Memoirs*, p. 93):

> Macklin . . . 'stood like a TOWER,' as Milton has it. He was 'not bound to *please*' any body by his pleading; he claimed a right, grounded upon LAW, and thought himself as firm as the Rialto.[4]

The kind of detail that impressed an audience can be judged from this account in a letter by a German visitor, Georg Lichtenberg, who saw Macklin in 1775:

> Shylock is not one of those mean, plausible cheats who could expatiate for an hour on the virtues of a gold watch-chain of pinchbeck; he is heavy, and silent in his unfathomable cunning, and, when the law is on his side, just to the point of malice. Imagine a rather stout man with a coarse yellow face and a nose generously fashioned in all three dimensions, a long double chin, and a mouth so carved by nature that the knife appears to have slit him right up to the ears, on one side at least, I thought. He wears a long black gown, long wide trousers, and a red tricorne, after the fashion of Italian Jews, I suppose. The first words he utters, when he comes on to the stage, are slowly and impressively spoken: 'Three thouand ducats.' The double 'th', which Macklin lisps as lickerishly as if he were savouring the ducats and all that they would buy, make so deep an impression in the man's favour that nothing can destroy it. Three such words uttered thus at the outset give the keynote of his whole character. In the scene where he first misses his daughter, he comes on hatless, with disordered hair, some locks a finger long standing on end, as if raised by a breath of wind from the gallows, so distracted with his demeanour. Both his hands are clenched, and his movements abrupt and convulsive. To see a deceiver, who is usually calm and resolute, in such a state of agitation, is terrible.[5]

Macklin's imitators cheapened this portrait, presenting a Shylock 'bent with age and ugly with mental deformity, . . . sullen, morose, gloomy, inflexible, brooding over one idea, that of his hatred, and fixed on one unalterable purpose, that of his revenge' (Hazlitt, iv. 320–4). If this mood was relieved it was by laughter at Shylock's expense, especially in the Tubal scene which often excited 'a mixture of mirth and

indignation'.[6] But then, on 26 January 1814, Edmund Kean played the Jew at Drury
Lane with 'terrible energy'; like Macklin he established a reputation overnight and
founded a new tradition.

His Shylock was not so easy to imitate, for it depended on most unusual gifts.
His voice had a range 'from F below the line to F above it', its natural key being that
of B♭. His hard guttural tone upon G was said to be 'as piercing as the third string
of a violon-cello', and his mezzo and pianissimo expressions as 'soft as from the
voice of a woman.' This instrument he learned to control so that it gave sudden and
thrilling effects: he could give 'the yell and choaked utterance of a savage':

At times he gave 'a torrent of words in a breath', yet with 'all the advantages of
deliberation'. His pauses could give a 'grandeur', speaking 'more than the words
themselves':[7]

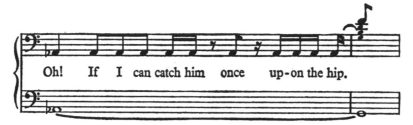

Kean was fond of 'abrupt transitions . . . mingling strong lights and shadows with
Caravaggio force of unreality'. He gave an irregular performance, always seeking
'points' for passion and power. This might have degenerated into trickery, but he
'vigilantly and patiently rehearsed every detail' until his artistic sense was satisfied;
and he acted with his whole being, watching the effect of passion as well as its
sudden expression:

> a strong emotion, after discharging itself in one massive current, continues for
> a time expressing itself in feebler currents. . . . In watching Kean's quivering
> muscles and altered tones you felt the subsidence of passion. The voice might
> be calm, but there was a tremor in it; the face might be quiet, but there were
> vanishing traces of recent agitation.[8]

His arms, hands and large black eyes were, with his voice, eloquent of intelligence,
spirit and power.

Kean's first scene as Shylock started, as Macklin's did, slowly, but added dignity
and a crushing, sardonic humour:

From the first moment that he appeared and leant upon his stick to listen gravely while moneys are requested of him, he impressed the audience, . . . 'like a chapter of Genesis'. [Then followed] the overpowering remonstrant sarcasm of his address to Antonio, and the sardonic mirth of his proposition about the 'merry bond' . . .   (Lewes, p. 11)

As he spoke of Laban and his flock (I. iii. 72–91), he seemed 'borne back to the olden time':

> Shylock is in Venice with his money-bags, his daughter, and his injuries; but his thoughts take wing to the east; his voice swells and deepens at the mention of his sacred tribe and ancient law, . . .

But he can rapidly change:

> The audience is then stirred to enthusiasm by the epigrammatic point and distinctions with which he gives the lines:
>
>> Hath a *dog* money? Is it possible
>> A *cur* can lend three thousand ducats?[9]

In Shylock's second scene, taking leave of Jessica, Kean revealed yet another facet of his powers, for in his calling 'Why, Jessica! I say' there was a 'charm, as of music'.[10] But his chief triumph was, like Macklin's, in III. i. This became the crucial test for all succeeding Shylocks; Squire Bancroft, discussing one particular failure at the end of the century, noted that:

> The fact of rushing on the stage in a white-heat frenzy, with nothing to lead up to its passion, I take it, is the main difficulty.

He had seen only Kean's son, Charles, assay it satisfactorily, and he closely reproduced his father:

> Apropos of which, Mr. Wilton often spoke to me; he having once, when quite a young actor, played Tubal to the Shylock of Edmund Kean. The great actor did not appear at rehearsal, but sent word that 'he should like to see the gentleman who was to be the Tubal at his hotel'. Mr. Wilton obeyed the summons, and spoke always of the kindness with which Kean instructed him, after saying, 'We'll run through the scene, Mr. Wilton, because I'm told that if you don't know what I'm going to do I might frighten you!' Mr. Wilton described the performance as *stupendous!* and said that, although prepared beforehand, at night Kean really frightened him.[11]

For this scene Kean could use his flashing transitions; he showed, with alternate force:

> Shylock's anguish at his daughter's flight; his wrath at the two Christians who make sport of his anguish; his hatred of all Christians, generally, and of Antonio

in particular; and then his alternations of rage, grief, and ecstasy, as Tubal
relates the losses incurred.   (Doran, p. 430).

In the speech beginning 'He hath disgraced me, and hindered me half a million;...'

He hurried you on through the catalogue of Antonio's atrocities and unpro-
voked injuries to him, enforcing them with a strong accentuation, and a high
pitch of voice; and when he had reached the *climax*, he came down by a
sudden transition to a gentle, suffering tone of simple representation of his
oppressor's manifest un-reason and injustice, on the words

'I am a *Jew!*'[12]

In the trial scene was noted:

His calm demeanor at first; his confident appeal to justice; his deafness, when
appeal is made to him for mercy; his steady joyousness, when the young
lawyer recognizes the validity of the bond; his burst of exultation, when his
right is confessed; his fiendish eagerness, when whetting the knife;—and then,
the sudden collapse of disappointment and terror, with the words,—'Is *that*—
the LAW?'...

Then, his trembling anxiety to recover what he had before refused: his
sordid abjectness, as he finds himself foiled, at every turn; his subdued fury;
and, at the last, (and it was always the crowning glory of his acting in this play),
the withering sneer, hardly concealing the crushed heart, with which he replied
to the jibes of Gratiano, as he left the court.   (Doran, pp. 430–1)

To this account must be added the return of his sardonic humour, in lines like:

An oath, an oath, I have an oath in heaven:
Shall I lay perjury upon my soul?   (228–9)

or in, 'I cannot find it; 'tis not in the bond' (262), which, according to *The Examiner*,
was accompanied with a 'transported chuckle.' There was in Kean's performance,
as the same journal noted, a 'union of great powers with a fine sensibility': for
Macklin's malevolence he had found sardonic intellect and fiery spirit, for his sullen
strength, family love and racial pride, both being subjected to suffering and pain; the
whole impressed by a series of instantaneous, forceful effects. So he reversed a
tradition and, for Hazlitt, Kean's Jew was:

more than half a Christian. Certainly, our sympathies are much oftener with
him than with his enemies. He is honest in his vices; they are hypocrites in their
virtues.[13]

Irving's Shylock at the Lyceum on 1 November 1879 was the next to be
generally accepted as an original reading. He accentuated earlier suggestions of
dignity, was venerable, lonely, grieved, austere: he moved with pride and grace; his
humour was coldly cynical, rather than sardonic; his thought was meditative, not

sullen, and his anger was white and tense; in defeat he called forth pity and awe. When he first played the role he bent all his effort toward gaining sympathy, but later he allowed his Shylock to become more 'hard, merciless, inexorable, terrible'.[14] Irving's elevated tone was established in that early, 'tame and level' scene: his first lines were spoken half-turned away from Bassanio, in a subdued monotone, and the whole was played more deliberately than was customary, even in the sneers and expressions of anger. In III. i, to Salerio and Solanio, he spoke wildly at first, but then with the 'calm tone of desperate resolve'.[15] He eliminated the 'almost incessant movement [and] explosive vociferation' that was customary, but gave a 'lightning flash' at 'To bait fish withal' (56); and, after a pause of suspense, 'there ensued the torrid invective ... uttered at first in an almost suffocated voice, ... but presently in the fluent tones of completely liberated passion' (Winter, pp. 187–9). With Tubal he played for pathos: there was a break-down after 'would she were hearsed at my foot....' (93–4), and the speech finished ('no tears but of my shedding') with sobs; on 'I will have the heart of him, if he forfeit', he tore open his robe, repeatedly striking his breast.

But unlike other Shylocks, Irving made his strongest effects in the Trial Scene. Here his dignity had full scope: he entered in dead calm, as 'a priest going to the altar', or as 'a figure of Fate—pitiless, majestic, implacable'.[16] Yet he was also a 'lethal monster, sure of his prey, because bulwarked behind the pretence of religion and law' (Winter, p. 196); there was a:

> momentary flashing out of a passionate delight, where Portia's words to Antonio, 'You must prepare your bosom for his knife,' seem to put within his grasp the object of his hate.

And both these impressions contrasted finely and surprisingly with:

> the total collapse of mind and body, when at a glance the full significance of the words—'This bond doth give thee here no jot of blood' (306)—burst upon his keen intellect. In these words, and what follows, he seems to receive his death-blow. ... We feel the prop is in effect gone 'that doth sustain his life'. But he keeps a firm front to the last, and has a fine curl of withering scorn upon his lip for Gratiano, as he walks away to die in silence and alone.[17]

Yet this was not all: he moved slowly and with difficulty away, as if opposing a fatal weakness by an act of will; at the door he nearly fell, to recover and 'with a long, heavy sigh' to disappear (Winter, p. 195).

After Macklin, Kean and Irving, no one has so completely captured the public's imagination with an original Shylock. Most actors have moved somewhere within the earlier limits while frankly comic interpretations, or a woman in the role, have been short-lived eccentricities; occasionally there have been clear failures. Lewis Casson, Ernest Milton and John Gielgud have probably been the most assured and independent. Casson, performing with the Old Vic Company in 1927, stripped Shylock of romance, dignity and moral stature; this gave a 'new comic quality in his lighter scenes', and in the trial held attention without relying on purely 'theatrical effects'.[18] St. John Ervine in *The Observer* complained that this Shylock lacked the 'magnificence of baffled rage and the courageous abandon of a man whose life is filled with despair'. But to this Casson replied that he could find neither of these qualities in Shakespeare's text: instead of dying for his religion and oath or remaining scornful to the end, Shylock replies, 'I am content,' and to Casson that was 'contemptible' conduct.[19] He acted within an every-day and even petty idiom: his first scene was the 'ordinary bluff of commerce, common to all tired businessmen'; he dined with Antonio, against his religious scruples, to satisfy mere 'spite'. Casson believed that what is mean, malicious, cunning, cruel and cowardly—traits found in almost every man—draws Shylock on to his 'abominable acts', and this process he tried to portray. The performance was continuously interesting (especially to experienced playgoers), but not compelling; and it did not establish a tradition.

Ernest Milton, five years later, likewise avoided easy theatricality; he played the opening scenes lightly, but with a studied Jewishness, and then, on discovering that Jessica has fled, 'the lamp he is carrying falls from his hand and fate suddenly and savagely transforms him'.[20] From this point he showed more power, but without spectacular strokes, and the final prolonged moment before he leaves the court, as he looks round and 'shows his teeth in a snarl of impotent but silent hatred',[21] was one that could be successfully attempted only by an actor who had played with consistent and minute truth, and with progressive tension.

John Gielgud came to the role in 1938, influenced by a highly acclaimed Chekhov season. He thus saw his problem as that of acting 'in style', appropriate to Shakespeare's language and period, while still acting 'in character'; and as he rehearsed he came to believe that Shakespeare himself had 'obviously calculated' on this attempt, and given full scope for it.[22] As with Casson's, some critics complained that his Shylock fell 'rather from the pavement to the gutter, than from the mountain to the abyss';[23] but Gielgud had added intensity, throughout. He provoked *The New Statesman* to give a detailed account (reprinted here by courtesy of the journal):

> Mr. Gielgud is riveting as the Jew, ... most careful not to sentimentalise the part. ... When he is on the stage you can feel the whole house motionless under the painful weight of his realism. In the trial scene he obliged us to suspend disbelief in the impossible story, and when he stropped his knife upon his shoe, we were appalled, not by fear for Antonio, but by the sight of hatred turned to madness. His appearance throughout was extraordinary—gummy, blinking eyes, that suggested some nasty creature of the dark, and loquacious hands with as many inflections as his voice. 'But stop my house's ears,' 'I had it of Leah when I was a bachelor,' 'I am not well'—the intensity with which he delivered such phrases lingers in the memory.

Shylock could sustain Chekhovian attention to detail, and could evoke pathos without sentimentality, intensity without theatricality.

*   *   *

Literary critics might complain that these various Shylocks tell more about the 'pitiful ambition' of the actors who invented them than about Shakespeare's play. They could cite, in evidence, the 'No, no, no!' which Kean added after his '. . . would she were hearsed at my foot, and the ducats in her coffin!', or Irving's interpolated scene of Shylock's return at night after Jessica's escape, to knock at his closed door and wait as the curtain fell.[24] But as surely as such additions alter Shakespeare's play, so surely did the interpretations they serve arise from that play: all these Shylocks, despite their contradictions, exist only in and through *The Merchant of Venice*; nothing else could inspire them or support them. The text itself shows how they exploit opportunities given to the actor by Shakespeare.

Shylock's entry is delayed until the third scene, when the audience has already seen Antonio, Bassanio and Portia. The heroine leaves the stage with tripping doggerel:

Come Nerissa. Sirrah, go before.
Whiles we shut the gates upon one wooer, another knocks at the door.

and Shylock enters with Bassanio, or, rather Bassanio with Shylock, for the Jew but echoes him:

SHYLOCK: Three thousand ducats; well.
BASSANIO: Ay, sir, for three months.
SHYLOCK: For three months; well.
BASSANIO: For the which, as I told you, Antonio shall be bound.
SHYLOCK: Antonio shall become bound; well.
BASSANIO: May you stead me: will you pleasure me? shall I know your answer?
SHYLOCK: Three thousand ducats for three months and Antonio bound.
BASSANIO: Your answer to that.

While this is pedestrian exposition on the printed page, it is not so when acted. Of course, repetition without variation would deflate the 'strongest' scene; but no actor would be guilty of that in this situation. Shylock first contrasts in slow movement and speech with the departing Portia and Nerissa; thus a distinct impression is made at once and the very flatness of the words arouses curiosity. Then as Bassanio becomes more impatient—'Ay, sir, . . .' and 'as I told you'—Shylock's repetitions, in his own tempo and intonation, assure the audience that this man has his own time and his own thoughts; he even neglects the three urgent questions to repeat earlier points yet again. And in distinguishing his delivery from Bassanio's, the actor can find many suggestions from the text. As Lewis Casson played him, he is a canny businessman by flat repetitions drawing his client out to show how much he needs the money. For Macklin, the echoing would be sullen and heavy, a slow savouring of 'it now appears you need my help' (l. 115). With Kean they would show a sharper satisfaction on the twice repeated 'Antonio bound', supported by 'I will feed fat the ancient grudge I bear him' (l. 48), and:

Fast bind, fast find;
A proverb never stale in thrifty mind.   (II. v. 54–5)

The reptitions need 'sub-texts', or 'under-meanings', in order to sustain the introduction of the new character, and the text abundantly supplies them. Probably the
stronger they are, the closer they will be to Shakespeare's intention. The ambiguous
'well's' (variously printed as exclamations or questions by editors) can serve to
allow two under-meanings to each speech: the repetition of Bassanio's words can
thus be so private with hatred that the 'well' is a necessary declension towards
conversation; or the repetition could be falsely bland and the 'well' spoken aside,
voicing the private satisfaction. In any case the effect of thus introducing Shylock
with thoughts and feelings not directly expressed in the words themselves is to
awaken a precise curiosity, an intense focus, as the audience watches for explicit
statement.

    If so far only the privacy of Shylock's thoughts has been fully established, the
diologue at once proceeds to further complication:

SHYLOCK: Antonio is a good man.
BASSANIO: Have you heard any imputation to the contrary?
SHYLOCK: Oh, no, no, no, no: . . . .

The emphatic reply suggests that the Jew is surprised at being misunderstood, or
pretends to be, and this is used to add to the impression of guile which may already
be implicit in the way in which he made Bassanio talk. At once he explains patiently:

. . . no, no: my meaning in saying he is a good man is to have you understand
me that he is sufficient. . . .

Shylock's intellectual superiority is nicely established by this elaboration, and by the
ironic tone of 'good' and 'sufficient'. And the impression is strengthened by the ease
with which he proceeds to make the rich merchant seem a bad security, by his
pedantic and humorous enumeration of risks, his parenthetic explanation, and his
final show of modesty—'I think I may take his bond.' Bassanio's short-phrased and,
perhaps, short-tempered reply—'Be assured you may'—enhances Shylock's control by contrast; and the repetitive rejoinder:—'I will be assured I may'—gives
opportunity for re-impressing the ominous under-meanings of the opening.

    So far the dramatic issues have been most strongly expressed through con-
trasts and a controlled manner of speaking, but then Shylock is stung by a chance
word of Bassanio's:

SHYLOCK: . . . May I speak with Antonio?
BASSANIO: If it please you to dine with us.

Possibly the invitation is diffident, for it implies a show of familiarity with someone
the speaker despises; but, however it is spoken, Shylock's reply has contrast enough
in its forceful vocabulary and phrasing, and in the sudden, scornful particularization

of 'Yes, to smell pork; to eat . . .' The projected bargain is forgotten, apparently by a stronger impulse:

> . . . to eat of the habitation which your prophet the Nazarite conjured the devil into. I will buy with you, sell with you, talk with you, walk with you, and so following, but I will not eat with you, drink with you, nor pray with you. What news on the Rialto?

His sharp, piled-up phrases culminate in his first allusion to religious observances in 'pray with you'; then, as if by force or a recall to immediate concerns, there is a sudden anti-climax in 'What news on the Rialto?' and, quickly, the feigned ignorance of 'Who is he comes here?' The *power* of Shylock is first shown in this sudden gust of utterance so firmly subdued; and its cause is not money or personal animosity, but race and religion. As Bassanio briefly identifies Antonio and joins him, Shylock is left alone for a soliloquy which, at last, expresses directly what has hitherto been suggested under the lines, by 'sheer acting'; Shakespeare has prepared for this moment the audience's curiosity and expectation.

Yet as Shylock speaks now with greater control of verse, all is not made plain. His hatred, avarice and cunning become unequivocal, but there is a confusion about the grounds of hatred. The first statement is quick, as if unstudied:

> I hate him for he is a Christian.

But the second, while claiming to be more important, has a show of reason which makes it sound considered rather than passionate:

> But more for that in low simplicity
> He lends out money gratis and brings down
> The rate of usance here with us in Venice.

His next phrase, 'If I can catch him once upon the hip', is both an everyday idiom and a possible allusion to Jacob's wrestling with the angel (Gen., xxxii); certainly it is no casual thought, for it awakens, in 'I will feed fat the ancient grudge I bear him', the physical idea of devouring as a beast, linked with the solemn connotations of 'ancient'. Then racial consciousness is uppermost again with 'He hates our sacred nation'; and, as this new intensity echoes in tempo and words the first rush of feeling, so it also is followed more reasonably, with parenthesis and enumeration:

>   . . . and he rails,
> Even there where merchants most do congregate,
> On me, my bargains and my well-won thrift,
> Which he calls interest.

The soliloquy concludes sharply:

>   Cursed be my tribe,
> If I forgive him!

The actors were all, in their partial interpretations, responding to the opportunities of the text: the Shylock who confronts Antonio has had opportunities for inviting an intense and precise scrutiny, of suggesting cunning, avarice, deliberation, power and control—and a hatred that is private and considered, and also irrational and uncontrolled. And in all this he towers—in force, intellectual fineness and quick sensation—over Bassanio, the romantic hero.

With Antonio present he still dominates the scene and calls the tune. As Bassanio recalls him from soliloquy he makes a sudden transition to blandly assumed simplicity and forgetfulness. He can taunt Antonio by reminding him that he breaks his principles in asking for money on interest. He can test the importance of the loan by making Antonio listen to a detailed story of Laban and Jacob, his ancestors, and at the same time show his isolation by being himself absorbed in it. When Antonio turns aside to talk to Bassanio, he can draw him back, simply by mentioning 'Three thousand ducats'. Moreover he shows that he has a keener awareness of the situation than Antonio: the Christian's assumed and brief courtesy—'shall we be beholding to you?'—is answered with sharp mockery and imitation, and a scornful reminder that he has been kicked and spat upon; he even imitates the fawning reply which Antonio seems, somewhat naïvely, to expect. The Christian deals shortly with Shylock to good purpose, because he hates his avarice and cruelty and because he is thinking of his friend, but little is said or done to draw the audience's attention to this; the handling of the scene makes the audience follow Shylock, for he most fully, consecutively and immediately responds to the situation.

Antonio now drops his pretence to Shylock and, dilating on truly generous friendship as his love for Bassanio allows him to do, asks for the loan 'as to an enemy'. The two men are irreconcilable, but, whereas Antonio sounds annoyed, Shylock is self-possessed and knows that, in 'a merry sport', he can now propose his bond for the forfeit of a pound of flesh if the debt is not repaid in three months. He seems to have arranged the *impasse* purposely: the audience will have been reminded by his mockery that he seeks to catch Antonio 'on the hip' and will now intently watch his hypocritical finesse and relish:

> Why, look you, how you storm!
> I would be friends with you and have your love.

The ploy works and, after more mockery, he leaves the stage, ostentatiously busy with mundane considerations. He has given a new direction and uncertainty to the action, and the brief comments that follow his privately triumphant exit only accentuate the danger by suggesting that Antonio and Bassanio underestimate the inflexible hatred and the cunning management of this man.

Shylock is allowed to grow in the audience's knowledge independently of the other major characters, for while he is often spoken of during the next two acts, he is seen only with minor characters until just before the trial. With Launcelot and Jessica he appears in a new setting, his own household. He easily dominates this scene, still isolated ('Who bids thee call?'), sarcastic at Antonio's expense (expecting his 'reproach'), concerned with his race ('By Jacob's staff, I swear'); and, in a short time, much is added to his realization on the stage—chiefly his concern and affection for his daughter. Characteristically there are no long, gentle speeches to enforce this, but the lines demand its enactment. Hatred of the Christian is expressed by his willingness to 'eat pork' to further it and by an allusion to fabulous tales of Jews eating Christian flesh:

> I am not bid for love; they flatter me:
> But yet I'll go in hate, to feed upon
> The prodigal Christian.

From this build-up of hatred there is a sudden transition:

> Jessica, my girl,
> Look to my house.

Its rapid contrast, the simplicity of 'my girl' at the line-ending, the suspicion implied in 'Look to my house', show Shylock exposed, touched, in need for the first time. This must be the right reading, for now he can express fear:

> I am right loath to go:
> There is some ill a brewing towards my rest,
> For I did dream of money-bags to-night.

The 'money-bags' turns the subject to one in which the audience may laugh at Shylock as a mere miser, but only after the sudden transition to tenderness and fear has brought them more closely at one with him than before. Macklin's solemnity, the musical 'charm' of Kean's voice and Irving's dignity, all found scope here. The scene proceeds to show Shylock concerned that Jessica shall not hear the music of the masque nor 'gaze at Christian fools with varnish'd faces', and watchful for his 'sober house'. And during this the audience is made aware at least twice that his daughter is about to rob him and escape from the home she calls a 'hell'. So now the audience is forced to see that Shylock is limited in knowledge, ignorant about the affection for which he has shown his need. After this disclosure, challenging and therefore reawakening earlier ones, the issues are briskly drawn forward, and Shylock leaves intent on 'Fast bind, fast find'; no other character in the play holds comparable interest for the audience in his own development, as distinct from that of the action and interplay of characters; Shylock alone has such unforeseeable responses.

The opportunities for the actor in the scene with Salerio and Solanio, and then Tubal, are well known, but the points of emphasis need to be distinguished. The disorder of Shylock's first entry, wild with grief and anger is an overwhelming visual contrast to his early control. His immediate and direct approach to the gossiping young men and their freedom to quip and jest at his expense represent loss of cunning and command. His outright self-exposure:

> My own flesh and blood to rebel!... I say, my daughter is my flesh and blood.

shows him impervious to mockery and shame. However much he later laments his loss of money and jewels, all these unguarded, unpremeditated moments show the centre of his grief: his family, home, authority, race. And thus his heart is alarmingly exposed. The two young men turn the talk to Antonio and this provokes the first of the great 'transitions' of the scene, used to such powerful effect by Macklin and Kean; the change is to mocking scorn of Antonio, but this develops to a hope of revenge, and his scorn then returns. Yet now he openly lists Antonio's deeds which he counts injuries, and this halts only for the second, and greater, transition:

> ... cooled my friends, heated mine enemies; and what's his reason? I am a Jew.

Then through the rest of the speech—remarkable for its range of sensation, from laughter to tears and thoughts of death, for its sarcasm and its plea for acceptance as a human being (his reasoning in this respect is much like Henry the Fifth's before Agincourt[25])—he draws away from this fact to a still more sustained threat of villainy and revenge. The mere release of energy, of crowded and baffling impressions, makes this unanswerable; the young men go without reply, quickly responding to a message from Antonio. Shylock stands now, silent, alone, unapproachable; the actor can, and must, hold the whole theatre silent.

Tubal, a fellow Jew, enters and with him Shylock, still unexhausted, has a series of transitions between grief (for the loss of his daughter and his ducats) and pleasure (in the 'good news' of Antonio's losses). He concludes it after Tubal's account of Jessica's exchange of a ring for a monkey. This must be the climax of the scene, not only by its position but also because here alone Shylock remembers an uncommitted past ('I had it of Leah when I was a bachelor') and sees the difference between himself and his daughter: 'I would not have given it for a wilderness of monkeys'. The last phrase may be a wry or helpless jest; certainly 'wilderness' seems to release from his unspoken thoughts, as such a jesting might, a sense of desolation.[26] The overwhelming effect of these feelings upon him is shown in his reaction to Tubal's next piece of news about Antonio: this time, instead of exulting, he makes deliberate and practical plans to 'have the heart of him'. Shylock is now so alone, intemperate, inhuman and assured, that, if the scene were acted slackly, it would be absurd: with almost grotesque earnestness, he twice appoints Tubal to meet him 'at our synagogue'—again words which touch his deepest feelings—and he does not wait for an answer. For this central manifestation of Shylock—a moment of clarity and powerful utterance, an opportunity for Irving's pathos and Kean's terror—Shakespeare has also contrived the impression that he is driven by feelings too deep to be resisted or fully uttered, or even understood. The Jew at once dominates the play and makes it appear unable to contain him; the emotions which seem to drive and threaten him cannot be made fully articulate in its words.

Before the trial, a short scene (III. iii) shows that the manacled Antonio confronting Shylock is resigned to death, if only Bassanio will return. However, this is already known from his letter, and a more important development is the return of Shylock's sardonic humour in this scene, and the emphasis it gives to his inflexible intention to 'have his bond'. By this means, when Shylock enters the court-room silent and alone to listen to the duke's last plea, and when he makes his politely and solemnly phrased reply, the audience can at once recognize the deadly inhumanity underneath, behind his 'performance'. So his long taunting speeches and sharp rejoinders alike show confidence and composure without concealing his savage, fixed intent. Shylock's stature is maintained to the last possible moment (here Irving's dignity had strong effect) and, in contrast, Bassanio's most generous sentiment is lightly mocked by Portia and considered a trifle by Shylock. At first only Antonio is not belittled, but this is through lofty resignation, the acceptance of himself as the 'tainted wether of the flock, Meetest for death'; he seems to live outside the issues of the court-room. In her disguise, of course, Portia withstands Shylock, and with the plea for mercy—more solemn and sustained than any of his speeches—brings before him the antithesis of his hatred: but he is unmoved and, once more, demands the forfeit. His defeat, therefore, comes very suddenly, by a verbal quibble as he is about to kill the silent Antonio; the surprise is instantaneous and as thrillingly dramatic as Claudius' 'Give me some light', or Hal's 'I know thee not'. Portia and Shylock are for the second time opposed and, as it were, spot-lit.

It may at first seem strange that Shylock should be denied any words with which to express his immediate reaction to the reversal in full measure; yet this is the very means by which Shakespeare has drawn almost all the audience's interest to him once more. He collapses physically as Portia elaborates the case against him and then, after Gratiano has had time to taunt him, there is probably a moment of total silence (the break of the verse-line suggests this) before he speaks, incredulously: 'Is that the law?' On the other side they now speak in turn, but he alone faces them and they must wait for his answers; there are more pauses, in some of which Gratiano mocks him or Portia questions. Except for the garrulous Gratiano, his opponents do not speak of their joy in victory, and the reunion of Antonio and Bassanio takes place out of the dramatic focus—this Shylock holds, until he leaves the stage. As the audience waits on his words to satisfy their interest, they will watch closely and see that he is inwardly struggling to understand and come to terms: rapidly he tries two bolt-holes and then a plea for death. But there is no escape and he must listen to his full sentence and the utmost mercy of his enemies, which is a life of poverty and the outward acceptance of his daughter's husband and his enemies' religion. The verbal conclusion of his role is:

> I am content

and

> I pray you, give me leave to go from hence;
> I am not well: send the deed after me,
> And I will sign it.

The speeches are brief but, in the intensified focus, they suggest a renewed control—a dignity (especially in the assurance of fulfilling his word), or a new, hidden purpose (as of suicide or revenge), or an accepted hopelessness. And there is yet the silence in which Shylock leaves, hearing the duke's curt command and Gratiano's jibe: this cannot fail to impress the audience, at least for his physical weakness as he moves slowly and with difficulty, and probably for his restraint and isolation in saying nothing more; and if he turns towards Gratiano for a moment only, there will be an impression of rekindled scorn for such Christians, or of now-impotent hatred. The slow, silent exit is an unmistakable invitation for the actor to reinforce at the conclusion the salient traits of his characterization; and it was surely meant to be powerfully affecting, for Shakespeare immediately changed the subject, providing a contrast in relieved inquiries about dinner-engagements.[27] Shylock departs from the play, as he entered it, with an intense focus upon him; and now there is no doubt that his being is more fully and deeply apprehended than his words alone can suggest; his is a part that must be realized in acting.

By many devices Shakespeare has ensured that in performance Shylock is the dominating character of the play; none other has such emotional range, such continual development, such stature, force, subtlety, vitality, variety; above all, none other has his intensity, isolation, and apparent depth of motivation. The various interpretations that have become famous do not overgo the intended impression but rather fall short, owing to some limitation of the actor.

This dominance often does ill service to the play as a whole. Thematically, of course, it is well balanced: Shylock's desire to 'get as much' as he thinks he 'deserves' contrasts with Bassanio's choice of the casket which enjoins to 'give and hazard' all he has; his claim that the pound of flesh is 'dearly bought; 'tis mine and I will have it' (IV. i. 100) contrasts with Portia's attitude represented by 'Since you are dear bought, I will love you dear' (III. ii. 316) as she parts from Bassanio; his careful avarice contrasts with Antonio's bold generosity; his pursuit of hatred with the pursuit of love and friendship. But the audience's interest is liable to be one-sided: there is nothing in comparable terms to balance Shylock's presence, and the last act can seem dull or trivial without him.

Many courses have been tried in the attempt to make a satisfactory whole in performance. Antonio's friendship for Bassanio, which runs throughout the play, has been given special emphasis in productions from Arthur Bourchier's to Tyrone Guthrie's. But then Antonio's part seems underwritten: he has little variety of mood, he does not state the cause of his melancholy in soliloquy as Shylock does the cause of his hatred, and his parting from Bassanio is only reported by others. In the last act, when he sees Portia claiming the friend for whom he 'only loves the world' (II. viii. 50), his separation has a potential dramatic interest comparable to Shylock's isolation at the end of the trial when he has lost 'the means whereby he lives' (IV. i. 376–7): but this interest is not exploited; the audience's view is directed to the general scene, and Antonio's loss is not given even the passing emphasis of lines like those addressed to Jaques and Don Pedro, isolated characters at the end of the other comedies. It is easy to invent devices for drawing attention to Antonio's plight, but then he remains disconcertingly, because unemphatically, dumb—it looks like an author's mistake.

Other ways of trying to balance the play have included a special emphasis on Portia. Here there is a danger of forcing the early witty scenes and so giving the part an exaggerated gamesomeness: Sybil Thorndike once said that Portia had a 'continual facetiousness' that 'tires me beyond words'.[28] On the other hand, if authority can be gained when she is a lawyer this does help to balance interest in the trial scene. But this is only half an answer, for she makes light of this role in the last act and can do little there to sustain and resolve the interest her adversary has aroused. Of course, it is possible to underplay Shylock throughout; but this is wasteful. Or he can be turned into a comic figure, as Max Reinhardt tried in a German version; but, since he is treated too seriously by the other characters to be comic alone, this involves fantasticating the whole play against the nature of much of its dialogue.

The Merchant of Venice is probably more satisfying as a whole if all the characters are played for all they are worth and the last act presented as if on two levels of acceptance, thus using the unemphasized memory of Shylock to give ironic comment or a sense of perspective. To attempt to use all the opportunities offered to an actor of Shylock would give a balance within the character which it too often lacks; his humanity can counteract his cruelty, his power his isolation, his wrongs his rights. It should be possible to play Shylock so that the audience's tendency to feel for him is balanced by its tendency to turn away from his cruelty and hatred. And if Antonio is played fully, without added emphasis, he can sustain a continuing interest and contrasts in the background, as it were, of more lively and assertive elements. With Portia the problem is to find a graceful style for the wit which will allow her good sense, courage and warm affection to be expressed as well: it must be shown that she knows before the trial that to 'offend and judge' are distinct offices and can scarcely afford a single acceptance, and that deliberate fools lose what they seek by their very wit in pursuing it (II. ix. 61–2 and 80–81); her strong affection for Bassanio must be seen struggling with her modesty, and at the moment of his choosing she must be able to speak the noble and yet fearful description of him as

> young Alcides, when he did redeem
> The virgin tribute paid by howling Troy
> To the sea-monster: I stand for sacrifice;
> The rest aloof are the Dardanian wives,
> With bleared visages, come forth to view
> The issue of the exploit. . . .   (III. ii. 55)

The earlier casket scenes are usually played for incidental comedy extracted from the wooers, but if Portia is their centre the accepted curb on the 'living daughter

... by the will of a dead father' (I. ii. 26–7) can help to make the audience concerned with her fortunes throughout the action.

The need to play all the parts for all they are worth extends to minor characters. For example, Solanio and Salerio have important lines about Antonio and Shylock and must not seem merely talkative and callow; again a graceful style is needed so that their description of Antonio's concern in the first scene may be listened to for its good sense as well as its attempt to enliven their friend—it contains, among other ideas, the knowledge that something of great worth may in an instant be 'worth nothing', a premonition of a whole sequence of crises later in the play. If they are so acted, their baiting of Shylock will suggest a greater reversal and their silence after his cry for vengeance will be the more eloquent. There is little risk that *The Merchant of Venice* will thus become solemn from too much concern; the wit will be lighter if it is graceful, and the speed of the several developments, the variety of moods and tempos, the artificial (or fairy-tale) clarity and transformations of the casket scenes and the trial, all ensure otherwise.

In the fifth act the dominant quality of the dialogue and action is quick and, despite the misunderstandings, delighted and gay. Certainly Antonio remembers how once he 'did lend' his body for Bassanio's wealth, but he is ready, apparently lightly enough, to do so all over again (ll. 249–53). Yet the persistent memory of Shylock in the minds of the audience (quickened, but not allayed, by two thought-less references to him) need not seem extraneous within the whole. For there are other reactions that are evoked behind the dialogue, and can thus join with this memory to give ironic depth to the total scene: Antonio's loneliness is one, the lovers' mutual faith and content behind their quarrels is another. But the reaction most able to answer, or contain, the memory of Shylock is a response to the music played on stage welcoming Portia back to Belmont and, presumably, playing again as the lovers walk off together at the end. Music had been heard earlier at the crucial moment of Bassanio's choice of the caskets and now the opening dialogue of the fifth act between Jessica and Lorenzo likens Belmont's music to that of the spheres, a heavenly harmony which immortal souls cannot hear while they are closed within their 'muddy vesture of decay' (ll. 58–65); behind worldly affairs there is harmony in the heavens, as behind the dialogue of the play and its busy action there is music. When Portia first enters in the last act, she is given time to note the more powerful effect of lights which shine alone and the added sweetness of music played in silence (ll. 89–118), and thus again, with almost pedantic clarity, Shake-speare reminds the audience that behind an earthly harmony lies another that is perfect, that behind the conclusions of the fifth act is a further peace, one which may resolve and contain all apparent discords. If the right, reverently harmonious music plays at the end of the comedy (too often the music chosen is perky or sugary), it may awaken the audience's responses behind the immediate dialogue; and with its image of divine harmony may be blended a perception of the lovers' underlying confidence and Antonio's loneliness, and a memory of pity and terror aroused by Shylock, who had called the music of his enemies a 'shallow foppery'.

Thus the fifth act can suggest a deep perspective stretching away behind the easy, heartening talk of the lovers; in its vast dimensions there is scope for a recollection of the fullest realization of Shylock.

NOTES

[1] F. Gentleman, *Dramatic Censor* (1770), i. 291.
[2] J. T. Kirkman, *Memoirs of Macklin* (1799), i. 258–9.
[3] *Memoirs of Charles Macklin* (1804), p. 93.
[4] J. Boaden, *Memoirs of J. P. Kemble* (1825), i. 440.
[5] *Lichtenberg's Visits to England*, tr. Margaret L. Mare and W. H. Quarrell (1938), p. 40.
[6] R. Hole, 'An Apology for the Character and Conduct of Shylock', *Essays by a Society of Gentlemen, at Exeter* (1816), p. 559.
[7] W. Gardiner, *The Music of Nature* (1832), pp. 48–9.
[8] G. H. Lewes, *On Actors and the Art of Acting* (1875), pp. 2–8.
[9] F. W. Hawkins, *Life of Kean* (1869), i. 129.
[10] J. Doran, *Their Majesties' Servants* (ed. 1897), pp. 429–30.
[11] S. B. and Marie E. Bancroft, *Mr. and Mrs. Bancroft* (8th ed., 1891), p. 212.
[12] Vandenhoff; quoted by H. H. Hillebrand, *Edmund Kean* (1933), p. 346.
[13] *The Chronicle* (6 April 1816).
[14] W. Winter, *Shakespeare on the Stage* (1912), pp. 175 and 178.
[15] L. Irving, *Henry Irving* (1951), p. 341.
[16] *The Theatre* (1879), p. 294.
[17] *Blackwood's Magazine* (Dec. 1879).
[18] *Daily Telegraph* (18 Oct. 1927).
[19] *The Observer* (23 Oct. and 24 Dec. 1927).
[20] *The Times* (29 April 1932).
[21] *Daily Telegraph* (29 April 1932).
[22] Cf. an interview in *The Observer* (3 April 1938).
[23] *The Saturday Review* (30 April 1938).
[24] Cf. A. C. Sprague, *Shakespeare and the Actors: The Stage Business in His Plays 1660–1905* (1944), pp. 22 and 24.
[25] Cf. *Henry V*, IV. i. 105–15.
[26] At the time of writing *The Merchant of Venice*, the connotations of this word for Shakespeare appear to have been desolation and savagery; cf. *2 Henry VI*, III. ii. 360, *Titus Andronicus*, III. i. 54 and 94, *2 Henry IV*, IV. v. 137 and *The Rape of Lucrece*, 544.
[27] Cf. Menenius' attempt at a similar change of subject; *Coriolanus*, IV, ii. 49.
[28] *Evening Standard* (20 Jan. 1930).

Bernard Grebanier

SHYLOCK HIMSELF

It would be fair to say that few great comedies venture so precariously near the borderline of tragedy as does *The Merchant of Venice*. But Shakespeare manages with his own secret magic that the play is triumphantly a comedy—though a serious one, as befits a play with an important idea. ⟨...⟩

Of course, the chief cause of disapprobation for *The Merchant of Venice* has been a well-meant distortion of Shakespeare's intentions by those who read in it, as Stirling does, "a pretty piece of Jew-baiting."[1] "I do not see," says Spencer, "how a Jew can read *The Merchant of Venice* without pain and indignation."[2] Spencer rejoices in the fact that "in recent years many secondary schools have wisely removed the play" from their courses of study.[3]

Calish accuses Shakespeare of having done "a great wrong" to the Jewish people, not in the portrayal of Shylock, but by associating "the word 'Jew' with the usury, the cruelty, the vindictiveness, and the bloodthirsty vengefulness ascribed to him, by emphasizing at every evil point Shylock's race and religion."[4] That the word "Jew" was associated with usury is a result, as we have seen, not of Shakespeare's deliberate imposition, but of a long precedent, some of it based upon historical fact. That Shakespeare emphasizes "at every evil point Shylock's race and religion" is simply not the fact. Nothing was further from Shakespeare's purposes than to hold up Shylock vindictively as the portrait of a Jew; Shylock, as I have intimated, is the portrait of a moneylender. Calish goes on to declare that no Jew is "vengeful or vindictive," and quotes the Bible to show that Jews are expressly forbidden "to practise cruelty" against even "the beast of the field" (Exodus xxiii, 12; Proverbs xii, 10) and the birds (Deuteronomy xxii, 6),[5] and that therefore Shakespeare was deliberately slandering the Jewish people by making Shylock vindictive and vengeful. This is, unhappily, a very foolish argument. These same Biblical passages hold for Christians too; therefore any portrait of a vindictive or vengeful Christian would

From *The Truth about Shylock* (New York: Random House, 1962), pp. 149, 153–62, 164–68, 174–80, 185–213.

have to be held a slander against those of Christian faith. Kittredge has answered this attitude well: "Shakespeare was not attacking the Jewish people when he gave Shylock the villain's role. If so he was attacking the Moors in *Titus Andronicus,* the Spaniards in *Much Ado,* the Italians in *Cymbeline,* the Viennese in *Measure for Measure,* the Danes in *Hamlet,* the Britons in *King Lear,* and the English in *Richard III.*"[6]

Quiller-Couch confessed that as a boy he could find no heart in the play at all, and was "chilled" by it; his view as a mature man did not alter much. With the exception of Antonio and Shylock, who is meant to be cruel, he says, every one of the Venetians is either a "waster" or a "rotter" or both—and cold-hearted wasters and rotters at that.[7] This judgment by a Cambridge editor of Shakespeare is a choice misreading of the play.

On the other hand, many have felt that Shakespeare was defending the Jews in his play. Harry Golden goes so far as to see in it "a satire on the Gentile middle class of Venice." Mr. Golden loves his Shakespeare, and for that one is ready to forgive him his overinterpretation. But he is little short of amazing in his eager distortions to prove his point. Shylock, he is convinced, was intended as the sole sympathetic character in the play. Bassanio's wooing of Portia is purely predatory (herein Golden is at one with Quiller-Couch and many other professional scholars); Golden paraphrases Bassanio's appeal to Antonio for a loan in these words: "Lend me some dough so I can make love to a rich lady who has just inherited a vast fortune"; in his portraiture of Bassanio and Antonio, Shakespeare "was writing an indictment of the hypocrites who vitiated every precept taught them by Christianity." But Golden goes further. Shakespeare has Shylock say: "When you prick us do we not bleed?"; he has Morocco say: "Bring the fairest blond from your northern forests, make the incisions, and you'll find my blood as red as his." Shakespeare's point, according to Golden, is that Morocco, Shylock, and Antonio are all "brothers under the skin." The crowning proof of this is to be found in the Trial Scene. Why should Portia ask, at its opening, "Which is the merchant here and which the Jew?" as though she could not tell at once? [The reason for her question, as we shall see, is really quite simple, much more dramatic, and philosophically far less weighty than the one advanced by Golden.] The reason is, believes Golden, that Shakespeare meant to imply that there were no real differences in character between Antonio and Shylock, that both were made of the same stuff. And by the time the trial is over, this enthusiast observes, the dramatist has left "only Shylock with a shred of dignity."

His love of Shakespeare makes Harry Golden as much a victim of literary strabismus as Shakespeare's detractors. Nevertheless, for all his error and deliberate vulgarity of expression, I respect him more than I do many a seasoned scholar. He is at least wise enough not to believe that Shakespeare was in this play simply writing another potboiler; he at least is sure that Shakespeare had something to say in *The Merchant of Venice.* While many professional scholars are busy diminishing Shakespeare by trying to prove that he was like every other run-of-the-mill Elizabethan, Golden demonstrates anew that a sympathetic reader can discern important matters which scholars tend to believe outside their province. Golden, for all his errors in dates and interpretation, can occasionally hit the nail on the head by saying simply, "Shakespeare was the first writer in seven hundred years who gave the Jew a 'motive.' " Why? Shakespeare did not need to do so, remembers Golden; "certainly his audience didn't expect it."[8] Golden is wrong, of course, in what he believes to be Shylock's motive—Antonio's spitting on him. But my objections to Golden are, after all, of the same order as my objections to eighteenth-century criticism: I approve of the questions he asks; I am merely in total disagreement with his answers.

All platitudes to the contrary, Hazlitt makes good sense when he warns that the library may be a better place to study Shakespeare than the theater. Besides the dangers of foolish novelties there is the equal danger of foolish traditions inherited by the acting profession. The stage, says Hazlitt, "is too often filled with traditional commonplace conceptions of the part, handed down from sire to son, and suited to the taste of the great vulgar and the small."[9]

Ever since Sir Henry Irving portrayed Shylock as a man greatly sinned against, in 1879, that has been the axiomatic conception of the role. No one seemed more bothered then than he would be bothered now at some unpardonable additions introduced into the play to fortify an actor's or director's, not Shakespeare's, meaning. Only George Bernard Shaw was well aware of what Irving was up to. Despite the universal praise bestowed upon the idol of the age, Shaw said: "Sir Henry Irving has never thought much of the immortal William, and has given him more than one notable lesson—for instance, in *The Merchant of Venice* where he gave us not 'the Jew that Shakespeare drew,' but the one he ought to have drawn if he had been up to the Lyceum mark." Returning to the attack, Shaw said later: "In a true republic of art Sir Henry Irving would ere this have expiated his acting versions on the scaffold. He does not merely cut plays, he disembowels them. . . . A prodigious amount of nonsense has been written about Sir Henry Irving's conception of this, that, and the other Shakespearean character. The truth is that he has never in his life conceived or interpreted the characters of any author except himself." His Shylock was not "a bad Shylock or a good Shylock: he was simply not Shylock at all; and when his own creation came into conflict with Shakespear's, as it did quite openly in the Trial Scene, he simply played in flat contradiction of the lines, and positively acted Shakespear off the stage."[10] These words could be reprinted today with reference to other actors in other roles, almost every time Shakespeare is presented.

Irving made of Shylock "a patriarch of Israel, wronged in his most sacred affections." To increase the distortion, he introduced a scene showing Shylock returning "by light of lantern" to knock "on the door of an empty house." Ellen Terry, his Portia, speaking with the tongue of actors, wrote that "for absolute pathos," she had never seen anything to compare with that scene.[11] What matters it that Shakespeare wrote no such scene, and that its intrusion is in violation of everything he tells us about Shylock's relationship to his daughter? William Winter also paid tribute to that "image of the father convulsed with grief."[12]

To be fair, Irving was actually preceded in his sentimental interpretation of Shylock by an English girl at a performance of the play. "When I saw this Play at Drury Lane," the poet Heine (d. 1856) reported, "there stood behind me in the box a pale, fair Briton, who at the end of the Fourth Act, fell to weeping passionately, several times exclaiming, 'The poor man is wronged!' It was a face of the noblest Grecian style, and the eyes were large and black. I have never been able to forget those large and black eyes that wept for Shylock! When I think of those tears I have to rank *The Merchant of Venice* with the Tragedies." It need not be said that despite the largeness and blackness of her eyes, the pale fair Briton has had less effect upon stage traditions of Shylock than Irving. But she did succeed in convincing the impressionable German that the play was tragic.

And tragic it has been held to be by many a critic since. Hudson said of Shylock that his character is "essentially tragic."[13] If you participate in Shakespeare's own sympathies for him, says Raleigh, you see Shylock as "a sad and human figure," who makes you deplore the verdict at the end, so that Portia "seems little better than a clever trickster." Shylock's "very hatred has in it something of the nobility of patriotic passion." He is at the end sent off to "insult and oblivion," and the memory of him gives to the beautiful last act an "air of heartless frivolity."[14] Unconsciously, Raleigh is echoing Irving's own exposition of his interpretation. He said that he conceived Shylock as "the type of persecuted race, almost the only gentleman in the play, and the most ill-used." Encouraged by these words, Packard goes off the deep end on the subject: Shylock may be grasping, "but what a scrambling after money do we detect among the others, what eager hunt after heiresses . . . and what a shameful desertion of a friend by all the Venetian Christian merchants for the sake of three thousand ducats." Did Bassanio ever return the money which he borrowed for his fortune-seeking trip? Packard asks. [Bassanio certainly makes every attempt to do so, and at the earliest possible moment—with Portia's backing, too. As for the other friends the play expressly states that they attempt to come to Antonio's rescue, but Shylock refuses to accept their money once the day of repayment is past.] Lorenzo is nothing more than an infamous burglar, Packard continues, whereas Shylock loves Jessica "more than ducats and jewels." Shylock is "distinguished by dignity. He feels and acts as one of a noble but long oppressed nation." In "intelligence and culture he is far above the Christians with whom he comes in contact." The proof of these assertions would be far to seek and, I am sure, impossible to find. ⟨. . .⟩

Calish believes that Shylock speaks "as the representative of his people, voicing the wrongs, the insult, the humiliation" visited upon them. This commentator would place Shylock, "a figure of tragic . . . power . . . by the side of Lear, Hamlet, Othello."[15] Honigmann, too, finds the moneylender a spokesman for and an avenger of the Jews' wrongs.[16] Coe is sure that Shakespeare meant to represent Shylock "as the underdog."[17] Even that staunch insister upon Shakespeare's anti-Semitic intentions, E. E. Stoll, finds that Shylock is "given now and then a touch of almost incompatible tenderness."[18] (Here, one fears, Stoll's usual intransigent prosiness of evaluation falls into the opposite extreme only because he seems unaware that Shakespeare [*unlike* many many other Elizabethan dramatists!] does not, with the exception of the early *Titus Andronicus,* deal in monsters.) And Granville-Barker adds another unwarranted sentimental touch by averring that when Launcelot Gobbo leaves his employ to serve Bassanio, Shylock demonstrates that he has "a niggardly liking for the fellow," and "is even hurt a little by his leaving."[19] Harbage goes further in the way of absurdity by declaring that "Shylock is no miser.... The ultimate satisfaction he craves is spiritual; we cannot picture him fondling his gold."[20] As a point of fact that is precisely what we cannot *help* picturing him doing; it is Shakespeare who gives us the cue, when Shylock murmurs:

> I did dream of money-bags tonight.   (II, v, 18)

It is perhaps Goddard who has drawn the sentimental picture of Shylock which is in most ludicrous defiance of the facts of Shakespeare's play. Shylock, he says, is by nature "humane, kindly," and is "the leaden casket with the spiritual gold within." "If ever man was insulted and injured it is Shylock"; he acts "in the exact pattern of his Dostoevskian counterpart.... It is as if Shakespeare were confirming Dostoevsky." Shylock as usurer cannot fuse with Shylock as father of his beloved daughter: "they will no more mix than oil and water." These "two Shylocks exist side by side." Thus, too, Shylock, who at first dreams of being accepted as an equal by Antonio when the latter comes to borrow money, suddenly, because of Antonio's storming at him [*sic!*], "now dreams of shedding the blood of an enemy." At the beginning Shylock "has no idea of literal bloodshed"; does he not say to Tubal concerning Antonio, "were he out of Venice, I can make what merchandise I will"? Apparently Goddard wishes us to understand that this means that the extremest desire Shylock entertains is to have Antonio exiled from Venice! But ah! the sleight-of-hand which selected quotation is capable of! For the full sentence tells us something a little less mild about Shylock's purposes:

> Go, Tubal, fee me an officer. Bespeak him a fortnight before. *I will have the heart of him if he forfeit,* for were he out of Venice, I can make what merchandise I will.   (III, i, 131–4)

Goddard traces the evolution of Shylock's desire for revenge in these steps: At first Shylock intends charging Antonio interest, as is usual with the moneylender. Next he is stung by Antonio's sarcasms. Then he sees his opportunity when Antonio speaks of friends' never lending money to friends at interest. "Here is the chance of chances to humble him (Antonio) by compelling him to do just what he does not want to do, accept a loan ... on an outward basis of friendship. Such a loan would be heaping coals of fire on his head in the most savage sense.... Here would be revenge at its sweetest, in its most exquisite, prolonged, and intellectual form."[21]

After that, when Antonio "storms" at him, and only then, does Shylock think of revenge

A good number of other scholars refuse to believe that Shylock has any nefarious purposes in suggesting a pound of flesh as the forfeit. Walley is of that opinion.[22] And Campbell outlines the attitude of this school of thought by insisting that it is only *after* the bond has been signed that Shylock plots Antonio's death. "To regard him as already scheming to murder" Antonio is to "belittle Shakespeare's artistry." Shakespeare makes it "the subsequent events"—the elopement of Jessica, the merrymaking over his distress—which drives Shylock to seek revenge.[23] Neilson and Hill are of the same opinion: when Shylock's terms are offered in merry sport "there is no real reason to accuse him of diabolical insincerity"; he means what he says when he offers to be friends. What "goads him" later is Jessica's elopement "with a Christian," who is "aided and abetted by Antonio's friends. . . . He is a father terribly wronged."[24]

It is my unpleasant duty to report that despite the authority of some of the names supporting the views of Shylock as a tragic figure, more sinned against than sinning, a wronged father, a feeling man thwarted in his longing for friendship, etc., I am bound to consider those views, in the light of the play Shakespeare wrote, as totally meaningless. In one sentence Mark Van Doren routs all this irrelevance when he justly and powerfuly remarks that Shylock's voice "comes rasping into the play like a file; the edge of it not only cuts but tears."[25] That one stroke more accurately depicts Shakespeare's moneylender than all the opinions we have quoted.

But if the sentimental notion of Shylock as the victim of the play is annoying in its blindness to what Shakespeare has actually written, the insensitive conception of him as a comic figure is almost intolerable in its obtuseness.

The chief spokesman for this view has been E. E. Stoll, who in a long and subtle argument filled with learned and copious illustration from other writers, insists that there is absolutely nothing sympathetic about Shylock, and that Shakespeare intended him as the comic butt. Stoll would be very convincing if one did not trouble to re-read the play; his proof is based on the scholarly misconception, a favorite with Stoll, that Shakespeare is never at any time wiser or more farseeing than his fellow-Elizabethans. Shylock is, according to him, an example of Shakespeare's "thoroughly Elizabethan taste for comic villainy." Both Barrett Wendell and Brander Matthews had been of the opinion that the character was taken as comic by the Elizabethan audience, but did not insist that this was Shakespeare's intention.[26] The chief prop for Stoll's argument is that the Restoration thought Shylock comic. Although there were no performances of the play during that period, Thomas Jordan, an actor, published a ballad in 1664 with this description of Shylock:

> His beard was red; his face was made
>   Not much unlike a witches.
> His habit was a Jewish gown
>   That would defend all weather;

> His chin turn'd up, his nose hung down,
>   And both ends met together.[27]

Stoll comments that the Restoration stage was "still swayed by the tradition of Alleyn and Burbage," both of whom have been credited with enacting the role of Shylock in Shakespeare's day. From which Stoll argues that it is "highly probable" that Shakespeare's Shylock wore red hair and beard and a "bottle-nose."[28] ⟨...⟩

Yet other scholars have hastened to follow Stoll's lead in portraying Shylock as a comic figure, and even twist comic values out of passages that are not in the least comic. Rosenberg says that Shylock is "a bogey," and when he "alludes to his dead wife Leah, the audience is intended to howl him down with laughter." (!!) At his exit line, "I am not well," Rosenberg continues, "the audience is assumed to jeer at his adolescent refusal to take his come-uppance like a man."[29] (Yet Mr. Rosenberg's book is a very thoughtful and honest one as a whole. On the subject of Shylock himself, however, he proves how a scholar can sacrifice his very humanity—without which there is no sense in talking about Shakespeare at all—merely to be consistent with an *a priori* theory.) Stoll had already said, "Shylock's being unwell is received as would be a similar plea from a bully at school, just worsted in a fight."[30]

Spencer believes that Shylock's is "much like the villain's role in Victorian melodrama, who plots, gloats, curses, and ha-ha's his way through to the final scene, when he is exposed, foiled, disgraced, and ridiculed, till he expires, leaves town, or at best slinks off stage with a futile imprecation." He is a "semifarcical villain."[31]

When Shylock says of Antonio that he hates him because he is a Christian and lends out money gratis, it is, says Spivack, as if in our own time "a caricatured villain of a commissar turned to the front seats in order to say of the hero, 'I hate him because he believes in God, and even more because he believes in human liberty and free enterprise.'"[32] Palmer goes still further: "Shylock bidding farewell to his daughter is more truly comic than at any part of the story so far reached." And "there is something grotesque even in his pleading 'If you tickle us, do we not laugh' etc."; Shylock never ceases to be a comic character, "never for an instant."[33] Sen Gupta tries to strike a medium between two views: he sees Shylock as tragic in so far as he hates Antonio, and comic in so far as he is greedy and miserly.[34]

It is hard to believe that the most torpid of readers unencumbered by a "scholarly" theory could possibly come away from his reading of The Merchant of Venice with the feeling that Shylock is comic. Whatever the predispositions of the Elizabethan audience, Shakespeare's humanity has shielded his moneylender from that. Indeed, Shylock is not amusing at any moment of the play. There is one time in which he figures in a comic scene, his dialogue with Tubal. But there it is Tubal who is comic; Shylock is torn between misery over his lost ducats and exaltation in the prospect of triumphing over Antonio, and the comedy turns upon the way Tubal alternately depresses his friend's spirits and raises them. On the other hand, to insist that Shakespeare has made Shylock a believable human being instead of a caricature, is not thereby to imply that he has sentimentalized him as a man sinned against. ⟨...⟩

Shylock, beyond dispute, figures as the villain of our story. He is not, as some innocently assume, the "merchant" of the title. The 1600 edition of the play has a title-page which makes that plain; it reads "The most excellent Historie of the *Merchant of Venice*. With the extreame crueltie of *Shylocke* the Jewe towards the sayd Merchant, in cutting a just pound of his flesh: and the obtayning of *Portia* by the choyse of three chests."

But another school of critics would make Shylock out to be a villain depicted without any mitigating touches of humanity, that is to say, a villain without any other motive than love of villainy. To see things thus is to be in the quandary of Launcelot Gobbo—"Thus when I shun Scylla, your father, I fall into Charybdis, your mother." (III, v, 13). Spedding and Stoll agree that Shylock is "a cur and a devil,"[35] fiercely thirsting for Christian blood. Fripp finds that revenge "is part of his religion."[36] Quiller-Couch is sure that Shakespeare meant to make him "a cruel, crafty, villainous Hebrew."[37] Murry thinks his hatred of Antonio "is represented as deep, irrational and implacable."[38] Spencer believes that Shakespeare "Simply accepts the Jews as a notoriously bad lot," for he "never drew a noble Jew."[39] (It happens to be true that outside of Tubal, he never drew another one!) Frank Harris says that Shakespeare loathed Shylock "more than any character in all his plays."[40] Stirling attempts to have it both ways: Shakespeare, he says, had an ambivalent attitude towards Shylock, partly anti-Semitic and partly sympathetic.[41]

Mark Van Doren again makes sense when he says what is undeniable, that Shylock's creator has not "made the least inch of him lovely." But Shylock is not a monster. "He is a man thrust into a world bound not to endure him."[42] This truth is in accord with the total view I myself entertain regarding Shylock's character, though I am not sure that Van Doren and I come to that particular conclusion with the same thoughts in mind.

In love and friendship ⟨. . .⟩ *The Merchant of Venice* luxuriates. Only Shylock, a creature who nourishes but hate, is cut off from these tender and ennobling emotions. And when he disappears from the play in the fourth act, the air is never again tainted with the fumes of hatred.

While the others are joined throughout the drama in the sweet ties of love and friendship, Shylock remains isolated in an enveloping atmosphere that knows neither friendship nor love.

What has made him so? Nothing connected with his being Jewish, nothing connected with his being persecuted or a member of a persecuted race. Shakespeare nowhere implies that what is forbidding, unloving, and unloveable in his character is a result of his being a Jew.

His daughter Jessica is proof enough of that. She has "Jewish blood" in her veins, yet is not only capable of great love but also can inspire it. In his love for her Lorenzo has been allotted some of the most beautiful lines of the play to express it. Portia, Bassanio, and their friends treat her with the greatest cordiality and accept her as an equal. It never occurs to anyone to gloat over her deceiving her father or to congratulate her on escaping with some of his ducats and jewels.

Nor will it do to explain their kindness to her on the grounds that she has become a Christian. ⟨...⟩

Indeed, far too much has been made of Shylock's being Jewish. Some of the scholars look for his fundamental traits in that fact—in spite of what Shakespeare's play has to say. Shylock's "love of race is as deep as life," says Raleigh,[43] although the evidence is all to the contrary. Schücking lists the "peculiar" Jewish qualities of Shylock: "a keen intellect, a well-controlled though a passionate temperament, . . . a strict adherence to the letter of the law, . . . an insatiable avarice, and an uprightness governed by purely external standards."[44] I should certainly deny that a keen intellect and a well-controlled but passionate temperament are in the monopoly of the Jews, just as I should just as emphatically deny that a strict adherence to the letter of the law, an insatiable avarice, and a purely external morality are not as often found among Christians. Shakespeare, in fact, drew a portrait far more repelling than Shylock's, of a man of strict adherence to the letter of the law and an uprightness governed by purely external standards in the person of the Christian Angelo of *Measure for Measure.*

Doubtless a wrong impression concerning Shylock has been conveyed to moderns because of the frequency with which he is referred to as "the Jew" in the play. He is so called simply because he is not a Venetian. The word *Jew* occurs in 60 lines; the word *Moor* occurs in 55 lines of *Othello* and refers to one of the noblest, purest characters Shakespeare ever drew, a great general revered in the Venetian state. The way it occurs makes it perfectly clear that though Othello is set apart by the word, it is not an insult which is intended; here the word *Moor* is merely a designation signifying that he is not a native Venetian—just as, in the same play, Cassio is set apart from the Venetians by the appellation, "Florentine." ⟨...⟩

In the 60 lines in which the word *Jew* appears there are only four in which the word has anything but a sort of national designation. [It may be worthy of note that if Shylock were called *a* Jew instead of *the* Jew (as he is), it might be possible to say that he appears as someone typical of his race. But he is always "the Jew."] It is in this not-meaningful way the term is almost always used:

Hie thee, gentle Jew.   (I, iii, 178)

To be ruled by my conscience, I should stay with the Jew my master.
                                                                        (II, ii, 24)

Young man, you, I pray you, which is the way to master Jew's?   (II, ii, 35)

I am Launcelot, the Jew's man.   (II, ii, 94)

What sum owes he the Jew?   (III, ii, 299)

Go one, and call the Jew into the court.   (IV, i, 14)

Which is the merchant here, and which the Jew?   (IV, i, 174)

There is no heat or color involved in the term in any of these passages. In the four lines out of the 60 where this is not the case, the word *Jew* is used, in the way ( ) said Elizabethans often loosely used it, to mean any nonbeliever; in this sense its nearest synonym would be "atheist." Launcelot Gobbo uses the word thus three times:

My master is a very Jew.   (III, ii, 112)

I am a Jew, if I serve the Jew any longer.   (119)

[to Jessica] Most beautiful pagan, most sweet Jew!   (II, iii, 10–11)

and Gratiano (the only real anti-Semite in the play) once, in reference to Jessica,

Now, by my hood, a Gentile and no Jew.   (II, vi, 51)

[Since this is Gratiano speaking, it is possible to understand him as meaning to be patronizing here. If so, he is no more condescending than thousands of Jews have been toward Christians.] Of course, Shylock, as "the Jew" is several times spoken of caustically; but in those cases, an adjective is required (e.g., "harsh Jew," "this currish Jew"); the noun itself has no force as an insult, except to the degree that calling anyone "a non-Christian" would be an insult.

Now, in point of fact, Shakespeare has made Shylock not very much of a Jew at all. Every once in a while Shylock does wrap himself in the cloak of his religion, just as many a money-hungry Christian will wrap himself in the folds of Christianity—in both cases only to serve his own irreligious ends. God and the Bible are ever on the tongue of the unscrupulous politician. Men utterly remorseless in their rigid consecration to the doctrine that "Business is business" are often pillars of their church—indeed, find it highly profitable to be so. It is precisely the same with Shylock.

He also does not hesitate to capitalize on the persecutions visited upon his co-religionists—but when he does so, it is craftily, deliberately, with much feigned indignation, and, again for his own particular ends.

In order to apprehend this truth about him fully, it is necessary that we understand *the actual root of his hatred for Antonio. It has nothing to do with the difference in their religions, nothing to do with persecution.* Shakespeare could hardly have been at more pains than he has been to reveal what has poisoned Shylock's heart against the merchant. *At least five times during the course of the play Shylock himself,* now consciously, now unconsciously, *explicitly states the source of his hatred.* In his very first soliloquy, he tell us:

I hate him for he is a Christian,
But *more* for that in low simplicity
He lends out money gratis, and brings down
The rate of usance here with us in Venice.   (I, iii, 43–6)

As the day of repayment approaches he says in anger to Solanio and Salarino:

A bankrupt, a prodigal, who dare scarce show his head on the Rialto; a beggar, that was us'd to come so smug [well-dressed] upon the mart; let him look to his bond. *He was wont to call me usurer;* let him look to his bond. *He was wont to lend money for a Christian courtesy;* let him look to his bond.

(III, i, 46–50)

and a minute later:

He hath ... hindered me [kept me from making] *half a million.*   (55–6)

and soon to Tubal:

Go, Tubal, fee me an officer; bespeak him a fortnight before. I will have the heart of him, if he forfeit, for, *were he out of Venice, I can make what merchandise I will.*   (131–4)

After that, when Antonio has been taken into custody, Shylock says to Salarino and the Gaoler, sneeringly:

Gaoler, look to him; tell not me of mercy.
This is the fool that lent out money gratis!   (III, iii, 1–2)

Moreover, Antonio knows perfectly well, however Shylock may have pretended otherwise, the reason for Shylock's hatred:

his reason well I know:
I oft deliver'd from his forfeitures
Many that have at times made moan to me;
Therefore he hates me.   (21–4)

Of course Shylock throws up a lot of dust in masking this basis for his fury against Antonio: it is only in the apartness of a soliloquy or in the confidence to an associate or in the uncensored outpouring of wrath that he allows himself to speak out the clear truth. But, as we shall soon see, even while he is attempting to cover the truth, it pierces through his pretences.

It is this hatred of Antonio for jeopardizing his profits from moneylending—the hatred of a banker for a man whose generosity is causing business to diminish—which constitutes Shylock's function in the dramatic representation of Shakespeare's ruling idea in the play. ⟨...⟩

Shylock is isolated from love and friendship, and insulated against them, because he has nothing of himself to spare for them. Whatever affections he owns are expended upon the accumulation of money and the making of money from money. He bullies his daughter and starves his servant. Shakespeare, never the creator to put the case weakly, makes this greed for money all the more deplorable in that Shylock is a man of no mediocre qualities. He has dignity, strength, purposefulness, tenacity, courage, an excellent mind, a cuttingly wry sense of humor. It is a great injustice to the man Shakespeare has depicted to imagine him "servile and repulsive,"[45] "fawning,"[46] or "sneaking and underhanded"[47]—as many commentators and actors have depicted him. It is an equally grave injustice to him to conceive him, as so many others have done, as suffering from racial persecution. He is too strong-minded, too conscious of personal dignity for that. It is he who looks down upon the Christians, not they on him. He stands on too much of an eminence to feel persecuted, and he who does not feel persecuted, is not persecuted. Shakespeare has so presented him that we are bound to feel the great waste that such a man, framed for noble ends, should be debased by his ruling greed. Without the disease of greed, it is easy to imagine Shylock as walking like a king among men. But this one, terrible obsession channels all his best traits into the service of villainy. And for that he comes to grief in the end. The gods are just, Shakespeare always feels, and of our vices make instruments to plague us.

I am aware that to assert so unconventional an interpretation of Shylock entitles me to no more credence than is to be accorded the time-honored views of him as a pathetic, comic, or conventionally villainous Hebrew, without the proof. The proof is in the play.

Shylock appears in but five scenes of *The Merchant of Venice*. Let us trace what Shakespeare shows us of him, step by step, from the beginning. One of the chief causes of confusion concerning his character comes from the failure of commentators to consider Shylock's speeches in the order in which they occur. If I commence by seizing upon the "Many a time and oft" and "Hath not a Jew eyes?" passages (I, iii, 107 and III, i, 61), I might convincingly enough make out Shylock to be a tragic representative of his race. On the other hand, if I choose to commence with Gratiano's slurs in the trial scene (IV, i, 364, 379, 398), I might convincingly enough make out Shakespeare's purposes to be anti-Semitic. But if I honestly wish to discover Shakespeare's intentions, I will begin with no preconceptions concerning Shylock's character, and start gauging him from the moment we first meet him in the play. If we are to understand him, we must be patient; we shall be wise to take the advice of the King in *Alice's Adventures in Wonderland:* "Begin at the beginning and go on till you come to the end: then stop."

We first meet Shylock in I, iii. [His name has been said, variously, to be a transliteration of Shalach or Shelach (Genesis X, 24), "cormorant," or of Shiloh, the sanctuary of Jehovah. The former seems likely since in the next chapter we meet with the origin of Jessica's name, Iscah or Jeska, "she who looks out." Tubal and Chus are found in these Biblical passages too.] Bassanio has already broached the subject of the loan. From the very outset we see the moneylender standing firm and as unyielding as solid rock. Bassanio is edgy, Shylock absolutely noncommittal: he may lend the money and then again he may not. In these lines which open the scene, it is Shylock who is in control of the situation:

SHYLOCK: Three thousand ducats. Well.
BASSANIO: Ay, sir, for three months.
SHYLOCK: For three months. Well.

BASSANIO: For the which, as I told you, Antonio shall be bound.
SHYLOCK: Antonio shall become bound. Well.
BASSANIO: May you stead me? Will you pleasure me? Shall I know your answer?
SHYLOCK: Three thousand ducats for three months, and Antonio bound.

Shakespeare, as ever, is remarkable in his ability to cause us to hear the very tone in which his characters speak: the calm, deliberately unemotional voice of Shylock, giving not the slightest intimation of his intentions, and the nervous, high-strung anxiety of Bassanio. Nor does Shylock do anything to make Bassanio more comfortable: he is enjoying too much keeping him dangling:

BASSANIO: Your answer to that.
SHYLOCK: Antonio is a good man.

There is something in his voice so arrogant that Bassanio hotly demands:

Have you heard any imputation to the contrary?

To which Shylock rejoins, with the loftiness of an adult quieting a child:

Ho, no, no, no, no! My meaning in saying he is a good man is to have you understand me that he is sufficient.

And then he begins to enumerate the risks, with the precision and carefulness of the man who is used to counting every penny—the risks of ships, seas, human fallibility, pirates, winds, rocks; and ends, once more without in any way hinting that he will oblige:

The man is, notwithstanding, sufficient. Three thousand ducats; I think I *may* take his bond.

That he deliberately stresses the "may" to embarrass Bassanio further is proved by the latter's next line:

Be assured you may.

Which only calls forth a further piece of haughtiness from Shylock:

I *will* be assured I may, and that I may be assured, I will bethink me.

In other words, Don't try to rush me; I mean to think this over.

We have progressed only 30 lines from his first appearance, and it is already too late for us ever to expect a cringing, fawning, imposed-upon Shylock. Whatever we hear him say later, we are bound to interpret in terms of the Shylock we already know.

It is now that Bassanio invites him to meet Antonio over dinner, and that he replies haughtily in words that have been so much and so blindly overinterpreted: he will not go to smell pork.

I will buy with you, sell with you, talk with you, walk with you, and so following; but I will not eat with you, drink with you, nor pray with you.

These certainly sound like the words of a pious Jew. But how seriously are we to take them? Presently we shall learn that he does indeed go to eat and drink with the Christians, and for reasons which do him no credit. Since he has no intention of refusing the invitation, how are we to take his words? In the same spirit as everything else he has thus far said: to make Bassanio uncomfortable.

Antonio now appears, and while Bassanio is greeting him, Shylock has his first soliloquy.

[Shakespeare's predecessors had used the soliloquy either to inform the audience of certain facts and situations, or for only the crudest kind of self-revelation by a character (akin to the silly confidences made in mid-Victorian melodramas by the villains to the audience, while they twirled their mustaches). But Shakespeare found a new use for the soliloquy. As we listen to one of his characters thinking aloud, he invites us to inspect the working of the man's soul. Often, as later in Browning's dramatic monologues, while we hear the character attempting to rationalize or justify his conduct, we understand him better than he is able to understand himself.[48]

This is particularly true of Shylock's first soliloquy. Indeed, I believe that it is the earliest example of Shakespeare's putting the soliloquy to this exciting dramatic use.

Here Shylock expresses his burning hatred for Antonio for the first time. He would like to pretend to himself that that hatred is based upon lofty, religious grounds. But the truth will out in spite of him:

I hate him for he is a Christian,
But *more for that in low simplicity*
He lends out money gratis and brings down
The rate of usance here with us in Venice.
If I can catch him once upon the hip,
I will feed fat the ancient grudge I bear him.

[How, after these words, is it possible to construe, as some critics have amiably done, the bond later proposed as really offered in the spirit of friendship?]

He hates our sacred nation, and he rails
Even there where merchants most do congregate,
On me, *my bargains, and my well-won thrift,*
Which he calls interest. Cursed be my tribe
If I forgive him!

I have italicized the pertinent passages to show that underneath all his pretenses to himself, it is only Antonio's disdain of interest which rankles. Shakespeare is here, as always, fascinating in his psychological presentation. [Surely one of the chief reasons why Shakespeare is so universally admired. But some scholars will not tolerate that. E. E. Stoll: "It is poetically, dramatically, not psychologically, that the characters are meant to interest us."[49] This is again a run-of-the-mill Shakespeare. In a few moments we shall have occasion to remark that in a play we must understand what the characters *are* chiefly by what they *do*. But it is surely absurd to deny that the characters are supposed to hold any psychological interest for the audience. What they *do* gives the psychological key to what they *are*. In a great play what they *are* is certainly, in the end, more important to the audience than the story in which they figure. An offshoot of that doggedly dehumanized sort of scholarship is the frequently heard argument that the characters in a play ought never to be discussed as though they were live figures. Palmer: "Critics and editors insist on viewing every character . . . in the broad light of common day: . . . each character is submitted to everyday tests of moral worth and social decorum." And Palmer believes this a literary crime.[50] But why should we not do precisely what he forbids? If literature worthy of the name is, as it should be, an imitation of human beings in their interrelationships, to what other criteria are we to submit their character traits if not to those of life itself? It is a gross error to lose sight of the play as the author has written it; but it is equally in error to insist that the characters in that play need not be life-like. For what other purpose is literature created? I have found it useful even to ask college students, "How would Beatrice behave in Desdemona's situation?" "How Portia in Ophelia's?" The validity of such questions is proved by the readiness with which they can be answered.]

See how Shylock twists and turns, trying to posture to himself as indignant on grounds purely impersonal and larger. Antonio, according to him, hates the Jews. How does he show it? Not by railing against them but by railing against Shylock. What does he rail against Shylock for? His religion? No. For his taking of exorbitant interest—and, at that, *where other merchants can hear*. All this Shylock chooses to construe as an insult to all the Jews, and on those grounds he vows vengeance. But, for all that, the real basis for his fury has revealed itself. A perfect example of an all-too-human self-justification.

It is part of Shakespeare's profundity that Shylock should not accurately know himself. What miser ever faced the truth about himself, or failed to call his penuriousness by some better-sounding name like thrift or self-restraint? That is why the greed of a Jonsonian miser is not really credible, and Shylock's is. This inability to face what he really is will make itself dramatically vocal when we meet him for the last time, in the trial scene.

Now Shylock forces Bassanio to press him again for an answer, pretends still to be mulling over the loan, and then feigns seeing Antonio for the first time—Ah, how do you do? We were just talking about you. ("Your worship was the last man in our mouths.") Still the condescending Shylock.

Up to this point in the play Antonio, when we have met him, has had nothing to say about Shylock. It is in this scene that we are first given to know how he feels about the moneylender. He speaks to him coldly; this is merely a business matter, and he is quite prepared to pay the interest he disapproves of, since Shylock, of course, will ask for it. His voice is neither friendly nor hostile; Shylock, in responding, lines his words with irony:

> ANTONIO: Shylock, albeit I neither lend nor borrow
> By taking nor by giving of excess,
> Yet to supply the ripe wants of my friend,
> I'll break a custom. (*to Bass.*) Is he yet possess'd
> How much ye would?
> SHYLOCK: Ay, ay, three thousand ducats.
> ANTONIO: And for three months.
> SHYLOCK: I had forgot; three months; you told me so.

But he still refuses to indicate whether or not he will lend the money. Moreover, this is too good an opportunity to miss. I thought, says he, you make it a practice never to ask or give interest on a loan? I never do, Antonio replies.

Now that he has Antonio at a disadvantage, Shylock cannot let slip the occasion to justify the taking of interest. By citing the enterprise of Jacob while serving Laban, he attempts to confute the Aristotelian argument that money, being inanimate, is put to unnatural uses when it is employed only to multiply itself. Again Shylock demonstrates the characteristic precision of his mind: This Jacob was the third in line from Abraham—let's see, wasn't he? Yes, he was the third. Antonio, knowing this man, cuts in: Did Jacob take interest? Shylock does not like such a forthright question:

> No, not take interest, not, as you would say,
> Directly interest.

But Jacob was not above a little trickery to insure his own welfare; it was a way to profit, and profit is a blessing when it isn't stolen. Antonio blasts through the sophistry: was the Scriptural passage written to justify the taking of interest,

> Or is your gold and silver ewes and rams?

Shylock answers him and Aristotle wryly:

> I cannot tell; I make it breed as fast.

Antonio seems well aware that Shylock is a religious hypocrite; in disgust he observes that the Devil knows how to cite Scripture for his purpose:

> O, what a goodly outside falsehood hath!

Unperturbed, Shylock goes back to considering the loan. No hint from him whether it is to be granted. No, not yet—let them wait. Thus, Antonio is compelled to ask again: Will you lend this money? It is here that Shylock delivers one of his celebrated speeches. It is odd that despite its fame, it has never been seen to reveal Shakespeare's psychological cunning.

Shylock has intimated nothing of his intentions concerning the ducats asked for. First he must make Antonio—him who condemns interest—smart, now that he comes asking for a loan. So, for the hated one's benefit, Shylock cloaks himself in the dignity of race. But again, in despite of himself, he reveals that he is not complaining of persecution, only justifying his taking of interest. Many a time and oft Antonio has berated him on the Rialto (where merchants most do congregate!)— about what? His religion? No:

About my moneys and my usances.

But this Shylock deliberately confuses as though it were an insult to all Jews:

Still have I borne it with a patient shrug,
For sufferance is the badge of all our tribe.

We may well imagine that Antonio, no fool, is experiencing a queasiness at this smug sanctimoniousness. Shylock, thoroughly enjoying himself at the others' discomfort, now accuses Antonio of having spat upon his "Jewish" gaberdine. For what? His religion? No, despite his intention of capitalizing on the persecution of the Jews, Shylock finds himself saying:

And all for use of that which is mine own.

It is the need of justifying his greed which rankles in him. And having a first-rate intelligence and great powers of expression, he hurls at his enemy one of the loftiest pieces of sarcasm ever penned:

Well, then, it now appears you need my help.
Go to, then! You come to me, and you say,
"Shylock, we would have moneys;" you say so—
You, that did void your rheum upon my beard
And foot me as you spurn a stranger cur
Over your threshold; moneys is your suit.
What should I say to you? Should I not say,
"Hath a dog money? Is it possible
A cur can lend three thousand ducats?" Or
Shall I bend low and in a bondman's key,
With bated breath and whispering humbleness,
Say this:
"Fair sir, you spat on me on Wednesday last;
You spurn'd me such a day; another time
You call'd me dog; and for these courtesies
I'll lend you thus much moneys"?

The indignation is superb, and it is a callous audience that will fail to be overwhelmed by it. But coming after what has preceded it, it can have but one purpose in Shylock's mind. He has been doing his best to make Bassanio and Antonio squirm. This speech is his crowning effort to humiliate them.

But at this point we have a difficulty. He has charged Antonio with spitting upon him because of his taking interest. Scholars have hastened to ascribe to that contemptuous and contemptible behavior of Antonio the cause of Shylock's hatred. Yet, when we shall presently consider Antonio's character traits, we shall find nothing in his behavior which could possibly be consonant with such conduct. He is at every point a gentle, mild, loving, and modest man. Nowhere up to the very trial scene (Act IV) does he ever say a single thing that is vaguely anti-Semitic about Shylock—not even after he has been taken into custody and his life is in peril. It will not do to say that Antonio's spitting upon Shylock would in that age have been no blot upon his character. That explanation would do very well for a rather vulgar man like Gratiano. Shakespeare proves himself in the play totally alien to bigotry: why should he not have made his hero above it? ⟨...⟩

Of the world's dramatists, no one believed more firmly than Shakespeare in having characters reveal themselves by what they *do*. For instance, in the scene we have been examining, the salient fact about Shylock is that he has kept Antonio and Bassanio in suspense, has done all he could to aggravate their embarrassment in having to come to him for a loan, and has refused to alleviate their discomfort by even a hint that he might lend the money. This, as far as we have progressed in it, is the basic action of the scene. Now Shylock has *said* that Antonio has spit upon him. But if we were asked to believe that this is the truth, it would be Shakespeare's practice to show us Antonio *conducting himself* elsewhere in the play *in a manner consistent with such an act.*

As an analogy: In order to justify his knavery to himself, Iago pretends to believe that Othello has been sleeping with Emilia, Iago's wife. [The "unscholarly" lover of Shakespeare will perhaps be astonished to learn that because Iago *says* this, many scholars believe him, and proceed to discuss Iago's "motives" as though Othello's having cuckolded him were an established fact!] If Shakespeare wished us to entertain even the possibility that such a state of affairs existed, it would have been his practice to show onstage this relationship between Othello and Emilia. In that play such a liaison would constitute too powerful an excuse for Iago to be left even in question by the dramatist. As it is, in the play Shakespeare wrote Othello is hardly aware of Emilia's existence, and she is in considerable awe of him.

Now, since we nowhere see Antonio behaving in a way that would make it possible for us to think of him as spitting on anyone, is it not possible that Shylock is making the charge against him—just as Iago makes his charge against Othello—without really believing a word of it, only to erect a false justification for himself, and, most of all, because he gauges that Antonio's pride will not permit the merchant to defend himself?

If, for the sake of argument, we grant that this is indeed the case—if Antonio is aware of what Shylock is up to, trying further to annoy him—should we expect Antonio to deny hotly, "When did I ever spit on you?" If your enemy approached you and accused you of committing incest with your sister, and you were, more-over, an only child, would you be behaving with any dignity to exclaim, outraged, "Why I haven't got a sister!" Would it not be more consonant with manly pride to answer coolly, "With which sister do you mean?"

It is in a similar spirit that I understand Antonio's making response to the charge. At the moment he is revolted at Shylock's attempts to ennoble the taking of interest; he is disgusted at being kept dangling—after all, he and Bassanio have not come to ask a favor but to engage in a distasteful commercial transaction. We may be sure that if this loan were for his own needs, not his friend's, he would have turned on his heel before this. Instead, he masters his ire, and answers coldly and with unconcealed contempt for Shylock's brazen hypocrisy: Very well, I'll do the same things all over again; for we are not talking as friends; we ask for a loan at your usual rates; when did a friend ever ask interest for a loan?

> I am as like to call thee so again,
> To spit on thee again, to spurn thee too.
> If thou wilt lend this money, lend it not
> As to thy friends; for *when did friendship take*
> *A breed* [increase] *for* [for the use of] *barren metal of his friend?*

There is no point, Antonio is implying, in your talking to me as though we were meeting as intimates. Your attitude toward taking interest makes this purely a matter of business: let's keep it on that level.

> But lend it rather to thine enemy,
> Who, if he break, thou mayst with better face
> Exact the penalty.

Shylock is satisfied that he has pushed Antonio to the limits of annoyance, and so his tone swiftly changes: But why do you take on so? I'm perfectly willing to be your friend, lend you the money, and not take a cent of interest. My offer is kind. (Up to this moment he has made no offer!)

Bassanio who, though silent, has necessarily been more upset by the talk than Antonio could be, since he is the cause of it all, with relief cries, "This were kindness."

And now Shakespeare comes to the knottiest problem in the plot he has inherited from Fiorentino. Stipulating for the illusion of flesh-and-blood reality in his plays, how was he to make it credible that Antonio would sign a bond which places his life in jeopardy? His solution was brilliant. Some sort of consideration will be necessary to make the contract legal. Shylock refuses any financial security, since he is acting as a friend. Well then, let us mention as the consideration something absolutely absurd, just to show my complete confidence in your word. Let us make it something as ludicrous as, say, a pound of your flesh. What is important in this speech is that the bond is framed "in a merry sport," as he puts it. [The whole effect has been ruined by fawning, sniveling Shylocks I have seen—precursors of Uriah

Heep—when they approach close to Antonio at "an equal pound / Of your fair flesh" and with a gesture seem to be cutting it off in anticipation of the event! That should be enough to scare off anyone from signing the bond!]

Innocently Antonio accepts the terms as framed in a merry sport, and is ready to believe that Shylock desires to be friendly. He considers the offer very decent of Shylock ("there is much kindness in the Jew"). Naturally, Bassanio, oversensitive because of his role in this affair, expresses alarm. But Antonio reassures him: No need for alarm; my ships come back laden a good month before the money is due. Shylock, gleeful at the success of his ruse, feigns shock at Bassanio's suspicions in a tone which is anything but humble: What creatures these Christians are, who judge others by their own unfeeling ways! Tell me, what should I do with a pound of his flesh, if I seriously hoped to have it? (With mixed insolence and ever-present greed) he says further: a pound of man's flesh

> Is not so estimable, *profitable* neither,
> As flesh of muttons, beefs, or goats.

I'm willing to act like his friend: let him take the offer or leave it. But in all fairness, don't do me the injustice of ascribing sordid motives to what I am willing to do generously.

Antonio is unworried, and Shylock once more emphasizes that this is to be a "merry bond." Antonio's farewell acknowledges that Shylock's behavior is princely:

> Hie thee, gentle[51] Jew.

Before we meet Shylock again, we learn interesting things about him. His household is a joyless one, and he wishes it to be so. Launcelot Gobbo, his poor idiot of a servant, is becoming skin and bones from starvation. This amiable halfwit is the only companion Shylock's daughter is permitted to have; at the prospect of his leaving Shylock's employ she is unhappy:

> I am sorry thou wilt leave my father so.
> *Our house is hell,* and thou, a merry devil,
> Didst rob it of some taste of tediousness.   (II, iii, 1–3)

That she does not exaggerate will be evident enough in a scene which shortly follows. But apparently the little pleasure she can have in talking to Launcelot must be snatched in secret too. She cuts short their conversation with:

> And so farewell. I would not have my father
> See me in talk with thee.   (8–9)

In a handful of lines Shakespeare has vividly sketched the gloomy and prisonlike atmosphere of Shylock's home.

Jessica turns out to be something less than an ideal daughter, satisfactory as she is in her devotion to Lorenzo. But there is no reason why she should love her father. It is clear from the outset that she has never known tenderness or love from him.

When one considers how careful Shakespeare has been to make this relationship clear, the sentimental vagaries of commentators are truly astounding. They build up the notion of a Shylock who, after lavishing affection on his daughter, is treacherously betrayed by her. They tell us that Jessica "is bad and disloyal, unfilial, a thief, frivolous, greedy, without any more conscience than a cat and without even a cat's redeeming love of home. Quite without heart, on worse than an animal instinct—pilfering to be carnal—she betrays her father."[52] "Shylock as well as Lear has reason to know 'how sharper than a serpent's tooth it is to have a thankless child.' "[53] She was a "pert, disobedient hussy"; "her conduct I regard as in a high degree reprehensible; and those who have the care of families must, I think, feel as I do. [Those who have the care of families had better expend some affection and understanding on their daughters, unless they wish to be treated by them as Shylock is treated by Jessica!] She was a worthless minx, and I have no good word to say of her. . . . Why should she, a maiden of Israel, leave her poor old father, Shylock, alone in the midst of his Christian enemies?"[54] [Her poor old father Shylock, in Shakespeare's play, at least, *is* the enemy threatening the life of Antonio and the peace of mind of Bassanio and Portia.] Her father "is intolerably wronged by Jessica."[55] Margaret Webster sums up this groundless school of thought, by blandly asserting that Shylock loves his daughter, "though Heaven knows why, for she is a little baggage."[56]

Apparently only Graham has noticed that "there is not one line in the entire play in which Shylock directly expresses affection for his daughter."[57] That is indeed the truth, and we have no right to ascribe to Shylock tender emotions which Shakespeare has not endowed him with. [Packard, who grants that Shylock may be a man of "ungentle feeling," takes that as a demonstration "that there is a side of Jewish life that Shakespeare never knew—the domestic." (Shakespeare probably never crossed the English Channel: where was he to have studied Jewish life, domestic or public?) All Jews, Packard insists, are gentle with their children; all Jewish children are devoted to their parents. "Jewish life presents a beautiful picture. Seated about the fire at eventide, the father and husband opens unto his own the burdensome history of the day. The Torah, from which he draws his consolation, is ever at his side. . . . Temperate, patient, gentle, regular in habits, how could the home life of the Jew be otherwise than pleasant?" Shylock's home is not really a Jewish home.[58] It is doubtless futile to argue with anyone who sees his own people in so beatific a light. But just as I deny that Jews are characterized by miserliness, so do I deny that they tend more than others to gentleness and affection. Jews who have children are surely like other people who have children: probably, a minority of them love their children with tenderness and intelligence; probably, a minority of them love their children not at all; probably, a majority of them love their children with indulgence and without intelligence—like other human beings. Some of them will reap love for love lavished; some of them will reap hate for love lavished; some of them will reap indifference for indifference; and some of them will quite unjustifiably reap love for indifference—these being the human averages of children's affections. It is too late in the day to insist that all parents (of whatever people) know how to love. It may also be hoped that there are some Jewish fathers rather better than Packard's roseate picture of them— some who will spare their families the opening of the burdensome history of the day, and report only its felicities.] Though somewhat overstating the case, Murry is nearer the fact than most critics when he says of Jessica that she is "a princess held captive by an ogre."[59]

The next time we meet Shylock (II, v) he is before his house. He assures poor Launcelot, him whose ribs are showing from hunger, that he will not be able to gobble up everything in sight at Bassanio's, as he has done at Shylock's household. (In Shylock's diseased mind every scrap of bread is begrudged his servant.) Shylock is about to go to Bassanio's for dinner. The very invitation shows that Antonio and Bassanio are ready to accept his proffered friendship. And Shylock means to go, despite his earlier high-sounding talk about not eating with Christians. His reason for going? The more he eats of Bassanio's feast, the less Bassanio will have. ("I'll go in hate to feed upon the prodigal Christian.") How well Shakespeare understood every aberration of human nature! Though extreme, Shylock's point of view is of one piece with his embracing the philosophy of cutthroat competition: the less others have, the richer he himself can feel.

But he has a premonition of something unpleasant in the stars: he dreamt last night of money-bags, and is "right loath to go." Launcelot, appropriating the lofty airs that he feels are owing to his new uniform, says grandly, misusing "reproach" for "approach":

I beseech you, sir, go. My young master doth expect your reproach.

Shylock seizes upon the malapropism, and retorts with concentrated malice masked as wry humor:

So do I his.

This quibble is like a sword-thrust: it should be enough to raise goose flesh. It means only one thing: Shylock has every intention of collecting the pound of flesh, and has a plan for making sure he will have it.

Now foolish Launcelot emits what is meant to be a hint to Jessica, but might easily have prevented her intended elopement if Shylock had had any notion of it: there's going to be a masque tonight. At the very mention of purposed merriment, Shylock's hatred of all that is delightful and gay is aroused:

What, are there masques? Hear you me, Jessica.
Lock up my doors; and when you hear the drum
And the vile squealing of the wry-neck'd fife [fifer],
Clamber not you up to the casements then,

Nor thrust your head into the public street
To gaze on Christian fools with varnish'd faces,
But stop my house's ears, I mean my casements.
Let not the sound of shallow foppery enter
My sober house.

He has no use for music. He does not want even the echo of it to penetrate his
house. Obviously Shakespeare will later mean us to take quite seriously Lorenzo's
dictum:

The man that hath no music in himself,
Nor is not mov'd with concord of sweet sounds,
Is fit for treasons, stratagems, and spoils. . . .
Let no such man be trusted.   (V, i, 83–8)

It certainly applies to Shylock. And luckless Jessica! She is not to dare watch the fun
in the streets by looking out the window or even from behind it. Her eyes and ears
are to be sealed against the most innocent pleasure. Small wonder that she will
leave her father's house without regret.

Launcelot goes off, and Shylock reflects that he is glad to be rid of such a huge
feeder (poor, starved Launcelot!); he is, moreover, delighted to think of how he will
now help to waste Bassanio's substance. Then, before he himself departs, he
threatens Jessica: she had better obey every article of his commands:

Perhaps I will return immediately.

Clearly her life under her father's roof is an endless series of commands and
warnings against disobedience—not the sort of existence to evoke love or even
duty.

This scene demonstrates how far from the point those stray who insist that it
is only Jessica's elopement which turns a benevolent Shylock into a hating one. She
has not yet eloped, and we have seen him full of malevolence against Bassanio and
Antonio, most of all in that blood-chilling "So do I his."

Irving, as we have already related, interpolated a scene in which Shylock is
seen returning amidst the revelry of the masques, lantern in hand, knocking in vain
at the door of his empty house for a beloved daughter who has wantonly deserted
him. Shakespeare surely had enough imagination to write such a scene, if it had
been to his purpose. He was careful not to write it, for the very simple reason that
we are not to feel particularly sorry for Shylock when Jessica takes wing—rather,
to feel relief that she has escaped from prison. Nevertheless, Quiller-Couch, Cambridge editor of Shakespeare, can speak of Shylock's returning "from a gay abhorrent banquet to knock on his empty and emptied house."[60] (That "emptied" is a
rather deliberate exaggeration.)

Before we meet Shylock again (in Shakespeare's version), the elopement has
taken place. I suspect that neither the dramatist nor his audience understood her

taking money and jewels with her to be conduct as heinous as modern interpreters have construed it. Her life with Shylock has been a stunted one, what she has appropriated has not left him impoverished. Even today Europeans generally expect that when a girl of means is married, her father will provide a suitable dowry. It is more than likely that we were intended to feel that Jessica has done little more than take with her the marriage-portion that ought to have been hers. (In the probable source for the Jessica-Lorenzo story, we shall see, the girl in that tale also helps herself to her father's possessions when she elopes.)

After the elopement we hear Salarino and Solanio discussing the effects of it upon Shylock. Their picture of his running through the streets shrieking

> My daughter! O my ducats! O my daughter!
> Fled with a Christian! O my Christian ducats!
> Justice! the law! my ducats, and my daughter!
> A sealed bag, two sealed bags of ducats,
> Of double ducats, stolen from me by my daughter!
> And jewels, two stones, two rich and precious stones,
> Stolen by my daughter! Justice! find the girl;
> She hath the stones upon her, and the ducats.

is deliberately grotesque. But it has some of the ring of truth in it too. The emphasis upon the ducats and the stones sounds like the Shylock we know. Likewise does his wish, not so much to have his daughter back for herself, but to find her so that he can retrieve his ducats and his jewels.

In the scene in which we next meet Shylock (III, i), there is more talk of ships wrecked at sea and the possibility that they could be Antonio's (the talk began in II, viii, 25–32). Shylock comes in, and he is in a terrible rage:

> You knew, none so well, none so well as you, of my daughter's flight,

he storms at Solanio and Salarino. The latter tries to moderate Shylock's fury: Shylock must have been aware that Jessica was of an age to think of marriage. But he will not be mollified:

> My own flesh and blood to rebel!

Salarino denies that Jessica is a replica of her father, and does so in language that exonerates him from any charge of anti-Semitism:

> There is more difference between thy flesh and hers than between jet and ivory; more between your bloods than there is between red wine and rhenish.

He changes the subject to ask whether Shylock has heard anything of Antonio's ships. The question but adds fuel to Shylock's passion:

There I have another bad match. A bankrupt, a prodigal, who dare scarce show his head on the Rialto; a beggar, that was us'd to come so smug upon the mart; let him look to his bond.... He was wont to lend money for a Christian courtesy; let him look to his bond.

In wine and in wrath the truth will out. Shylock's list of Antonio's offenses this time significantly omits any reference to spitting on Jewish gaberdines or to insults against the Jews. No, in his fury it does not occur to him to mask the real sources of his fury: Antonio's elegant appearance, Antonio's wasting of money, Antonio's lending money without interest. These are the crimes for which he hates the merchant.

When Salarino asks of what use the forfeiture could be to Shylock, Shylock responds in a way that again is a tribute to Shakespeare's psychological insight. Now that he has been called on to state his grievances, Shylock once more tries to pass off the reasons for his thirst for revenge as better than they are. But, in spite of his tone of injured innocence, he reveals that it is only matters of money which cause his hatred:

He hath disgrac'd me, and *hind'red me half a million;* laugh'd at *my losses,* mock'd at *my gains,* scorn'd my nation, thwarted *my bargains ...*

The reference to his "nation" is almost parenthetical—as though he had thought of something that must be slipped in to justify the rest. Again, despite himself, Shylock makes it plain that the only thing Antonio has done to injure him has been to lend out money gratis.

From the indictment he soars into one of the most movingly written orations ever penned:

And what's his reason? I am a Jew. Hath not a Jew eyes? Hath not a Jew hands, organs, dimensions, senses, affections, passions; fed with the same food, hurt with the same weapons, subject to the same diseases, healed by the same means, warmed and cooled by the same winter and summer, as a Christian is? If you prick us, do we not bleed? If you tickle us, do we not laugh? If you poison us, do we not die? And if you wrong us, shall we not revenge? If we are like you in the rest, we will resemble you in that. If a Jew wrong a Christian, what is his humility? Revenge. If a Christian wrong a Jew, what should his sufferance be by Christian example? Why, revenge. The villainy you teach me, I will execute, and it shall go hard but I will better the instruction.

As we have already said, the author who composed these lines must of necessity have stood far above all possibility of nurturing anti-Semitic feelings—else how could he have conceived the passage? It is noble, manly, superbly convincing. But when we have recovered from the power of its appeal (which Shylock fully intended to be powerful) and ask ourselves why Shylock has said all this and why just now, we are forced to realize that it is all an elaborate piece of self-justification for villainy intended. His accusations of injustices visited upon the Jews by Christians in general are meant by implication to apply to Antonio in particular, even though we have not seen Antonio wronging anyone or revenging himself on anyone. By the very force of his eloquence Shylock is convincing himself (and has convinced many critics!) that he proposes to take reprisals for the persecutions of his people.

Antonio's friends leave, Tubal comes in, and we are witnesses to a wonderfully written scene. Tubal has just arrived from Genoa; he has often heard of Jessica but did not encounter her. Shakespeare now fortifies our previous knowledge of Shylock's inner drive. Shylock is talking to an intimate (we cannot think of his having a true friend, nor does Tubal behave like one), and he speaks without pretense:

> Why, there, there, there, there! A diamond gone, cost me two thousand ducats in Frankfort! *The curse never fell upon our nation till now. I never felt it till now.*

At last the whole truth. Shylock has never felt hurt before. But any wrong to him is a wrong to all Jews. What are the injustices meted out to his co-religionists compared with the loss of two thousand ducats by him? He goes on, and his diseased passion for accumulation vents itself with increasing violence:

> Two thousand ducats in that; and other precious, precious jewels. *I would my daughter were dead at my foot, and the jewels in her ear! Would she were hears'd at my foot, and the ducats in her coffin!*

These shocking sentiments are scarcely in harmony with the long-suffering and loving paterfamilias of the sentimental school of critics. They are among the most horrifying sentences in literature. Confronted with them even the critic who finds Shylock *molto simpatico* would be compelled to admit that it is not that he loved Jessica less but loves his ducats more. And he continues to lament his losses—though surely the bulk of his vast hoard has remained untouched:

> No news of them? Why so? *And I know not what's spent in the search. Why, thou loss upon loss! the thief gone with so much, and so much to find the thief. . . .*

Not a word about missing his beloved daughter, but much on the subject of missing his ducats. And why is it, he cries, that I am the only man to have all this misfortune? Tubal raises his spirits by beginning to say that he has heard in Genoa of Antonio's ill luck. Eagerly Shylock demands to know more. Yes, Tubal says, Antonio is said to have lost a fleet coming from Tripolis. "I thank God, I thank God!" Shylock cries with exaltation. He laughs with delight:

> Good news, good news! Ha, ha! Here in Genoa!

[Here occurs what is perhaps the only crucial phrase in the play to be disputed. The original editions all have "Here in Genoa." But Rowe, remembering that the scene was in *Venice,* thought "here" a typographical error for "where." Most editions have followed his emendation, and read, "Where? In Genoa?" Furness, however, points

out that "Here in Genoa," may very well mean "Here in Italy." As he explains it,
Shylock is laughing aloud "at the thought that the loss which is reported as fallen on
Anthonio has happened, not far off, in England, but is known 'here' in Italy, 'in
Genoa.' "[61] I am not only fully in accord with Furness' interpretation; I also believe
that the word "here" means more than he thinks, as the ensuing discussion indicates.
Brown would emend the word to "heard," so that the line would read "heard in
Genoa!"[62] If emendation is necessary I much prefer this suggestion, which is in
consonance with my interpretation of the line.]

That last brief phrase for what it implies should make us pause to consider one
aspect of the plot about which few commentators have troubled their heads.

Unless we are willing to conceive that Shylock originally suggested taking a
pound of Antonio's flesh purely as a gesture of friendship—an interpretation in
violence with his first soliloquy and everything he had been thinking before Jessica
ever eloped—we must surely feel that a man of his particular purposefulness would
never have stipulated for such terms if he had merely hoped or had left it to chance
to bring Antonio within his power. At the time the bond was signed, there was not
even a wisp of doubt that Antonio could comfortably repay the money long before
it was due. I have already remarked that there is something terribly ominous about
Shylock's turning Launcelot's malapropism, "My young master doth expect your
reproach," with a wry, "So do I his." Nobody ever depended less than Shakespeare
upon accident for dramatic effect. His leading characters are always people either
of strong will or wilfullness; and his strongest strokes as a storyteller are always
closely related to character-traits of the persons involved, not to external, accidental influences. [Even Morocco and Arragon make a choice of the wrong caskets
and Bassanio of the right one, because of their own temperaments.] It would be
most unlike Shakespearean practice that Shylock, once he has proposed a contract
with such terms in it, win power of death over Antonio through the operation of
fate.

At the end of the play (V, i, 276–77) it turns out that Antonio's ships have
come safely to port richly laden, after all. What has happened to Antonio, then, in
the interval between his signing of the bond and Shylock's bringing him to trial?

Obviously, it chanced that nearly all of Antonio's ready money, at the time
Bassanio asked for a loan, was invested in his ventures abroad, else there had been
no need of borrowing the money from Shylock. What could Shylock do, under
these circumstances, to insure his collecting the forfeiture? Only one thing: ruin
Antonio's credit. In II, viii, Salarino reported talking with a Frenchman, who had told
him of an Italian ship wrecked in the English Channel. Shylock has seized upon this
piece of gossip, attributed the loss to Antonio, and broadened it to include the rest
of Antonio's ships. [I am indebted for the basis of my interpretation of this part of
the story to these intelligent words of Hudson: Shylock looks forward to

> the bankruptcy of Antonio. This would seem to infer that Shylock has some
> hand in getting up the reports of Antonio's "losses at sea"; which reports, at

least some of them, turn out false in the end. Further than this, the Poet leaves us in the dark as to how those reports grew into being or gained belief. Did he mean to have it understood that the Jew exercised his cunning and malice in plotting and preparing them? It appears, at all events, that Shylock knew they were coming before they came. . . . He would hardly grasp so eagerly at a bare possibility of revenge, without using means to turn it into something more. This would mark him with much deeper lines of guilt. Why, then, did not Shakespeare bring the matter forward more prominently? Perhaps it was because the doing so would have made Shylock appear too deep a criminal for the degree of interest which his part was meant to carry in the play. In other words, the health of the drama as a work of *comic* art required his criminality to be kept in the background. He comes very near overshadowing the other characters too much, as it is.[63]]

Shylock, it is plain, has the means to spread such rumors abroad. (We have just learned that his agents have been trying to track down Jessica and his ducats abroad.) To be most effective, such rumors had better come from distant places— England or France, for instance. I therefore take his exulting cry, "Good news, good news! Ha, ha! Here [or, as Mr. Brown prefers, "heard"] in Genoa!" to mean, "So at last! These rumors have at last reached Italy, near home!"

To continue with the scene: Tubal, apparently unable to allow Shylock his moment of joy, cuts in with the information that

Your daughter spent in Genoa, as I heard, in one night fourscore ducats.

The very thought of which brings Shylock back to his misery over his losses:

Thou stick'st a dagger in me, I shall never see my gold again. Fourscore ducats at a sitting! Fourscore ducats!

This amusingly inscrutable Tubal continues to play on Shylock as on an instrument: Antonio, he learns from the creditors, is sure to become bankrupt. Once more Shylock rejoices: he is very glad of it; he will plague and torture Antonio. Once more Tubal turns aside Shylock's pleasure:

One of them showed me a ring that he had of your daughter for a monkey.

Shakespeare does not deal in monsters, and he here gives Shylock the one softening touch allotted him in the whole play:

It was my turquoise; I had it of Leah when I was a bachelor. I would not have given it for a wilderness of monkeys.

It is a wonderfully simple human touch, and it reminds us that Shylock, before he gave in to his passion for accumulating money, was once a human being too. Tubal goes back to Antonio's losses, and Shylock eagerly looks forward to his pound of flesh: to be sure of it he arranges a fortnight in advance that an officer arrest Antonio on the day the bond is due.

In the next scene (III, ii) we are in Belmont, and rejoice to watch Bassanio's choosing the right casket. But he and Portia have barely time to revel in the happy fulfillment of their wishes when news comes from Venice that Antonio's ships have been lost and his credit has been ruined. His friends have managed to get together the money owing, but Shylock refuses to accept it, now that the day of repayment is past. Twenty merchants, the Duke of Venice, and leading citizens have pleaded with him in vain; Shylock refuses to accept anything but his pound of flesh. No one can drive him from his malicious stand that he will have only the forfeiture—which he calls demanding justice (275–86).

It takes a little time to get a large sum of money together. No one has seriously expected that Shylock would insist upon the terms of the bond. On but one day after the contract's expiration, we are to suppose, Antonio's friends have approached Shylock with the money, and he has refused them on the technicality of the date. No one, naturally, was prepared that he take such a position, particularly when he is notorious for his love of gold. But Jessica tells the others that she has often heard her father say

> That he would rather have Antonio's flesh
> Than twenty times the value of the sum
> That he did owe him.   (289–91)

(We do not like Jessica for saying this. On the other hand, we should like her less if she approved of her father's murderous intentions; she has chosen to be human rather than dutiful.)

In the next scene (III, iii) we are back in a street of Venice. Antonio, in the custody of the Gaoler, and Salarino are pleading with Shylock to be merciful. But he will allow them to speak hardly a syllable. He is absolutely intransigent. Now that he has Antonio completely in his power, now would be the time, if there were any truth in his allegations that he has endured indignities at Antonio's hands, to speak them out. With what crushing force could he now hurl at Antonio that business of spitting upon him and kicking him out of doors—if that had been the truth. But it was not the truth; he seems even to have forgotten his inventions. In his adamantine sense of power he does not try to conceal his motives as other than they are:

> Gaoler, look to him; tell not me of mercy,
> *This is the fool that lent out money gratis!*

After a few words of scornful abuse, he leaves. Antonio is well aware that Shylock hates him only because he has often rescued people who were in debt to Shylock. He is also fairly convinced that the bond is legally unassailable.

We come now to the great scene of the play, the Trial Scene (IV, i), the last in which Shylock appears. Before Shylock's entry, the point is made again that the Duke has done all he could to urge Shylock to accept the sum of money he advanced and renounce the forfeiture, but without success. The Duke now realizes that the moneylender is

> A stony adversary, an inhuman wretch
> Uncapable of pity, void and empty
> From any dram of mercy.

Shylock comes into court, and the Duke goes out of his way to speak gently and without animosity to him, in the hope of softening his cruelty. We all really believe, he says, that you are only pretending to claim the forfeiture so that at the last minute your mercy and pity will appear all the greater; we expect you not only to renounce the stipulation but also to overlook a portion of the sum due you, considering Antonio's losses; surely you will not behave as only Turks and Tartars do; we all expect a civilized answer to what I ask. But the Duke has underestimated his man. Shylock is like rock, and challenges the city to deny its legal processes.

> You'll ask me why I rather choose to have
> A weight of carrion flesh than to receive
> Three thousand ducats.

This sounds like a prologue (an arrogant and insulting one, to be sure) to a rehearsal of wrongs suffered as Antonio's victim. Now is the time, if ever there was time, for him to justify what he wishes to do, to tell the whole world of his injuries and persecutions. What a triumphant moment for him to do himself justice! But he has nothing to say of the old charges of anti-Semitism. He has nothing to say because they were false.

Moreover, no one has asked him why he chooses a pound of flesh rather than accept three thousand ducats. It is his own intelligence which makes him realize the enormity of his choice in the world's eyes. Perhaps this is the first time he has asked himself the question. Well, and what is his explanation? He has none.

> I'll not answer that;
> But say it is my humour. Is it answer'd?
> What if my house be troubled with a rat
> And I be pleas'd to give ten thousand ducats
> To have it ban'd? What, are you answer'd yet?

His insolence to the Duke would be astonishing in anyone other than this proud, strong, powerful man, who has never in his life known what it is to fawn or cringe. There is not even a hint of respect for the Duke's authority in what he says, as he continues: Some men can't stand roasted pig, some can't tolerate cats, some can't listen to the sound of bagpipes without becoming ill,

> *So can I give no reason, nor I will not,*
> More than a lodg'd hate and a certain loathing
> I bear Antonio, that I follow thus
> A losing suit against him. Are you answer'd?

His last line adds sarcasm to his insolence. But again, despite himself, Shylock declares the truth: he can give no reason and therefore will give no reason for wishing to kill Antonio.

Now, it might be asked: If indeed Shylock has so overpowering a greed for money as has been thus far depicted, why has he not accepted the offer of Antonio's friends to pay him a liberal amount in addition to the money he has loaned the merchant? Why will he refuse Portia's offer of thrice the amount of the loan? Why would he rather have, as Jessica has reported, Antonio's flesh than "twenty times" the sum?

The answer to these questions lies in the very nature of hate. The genesis of Shylock's hatred for Antonio was money. But hate is a cancer that grows and feeds on a man until it devours all of him. When hate becomes an obsession, its origin becomes forgotten, and only the hate itself becomes real. William Blake's "A Poison Tree" is a magnificent poetic exposition of the life-history of a hatred:

> I was angry with my friend:
> I told my wrath, my wrath did end.
> I was angry with my foe:
> I told it not, my wrath did grow.
>
> And I watered it in fears
> Night and morning with my tears,
> And I sunnèd it with smiles
> And with soft deceitful wiles.
>
> And it grew both day and night,
> Till it bore an apple bright,
> And my foe beheld it shine,
> And he knew that it was mine,
>
> And into my garden stole
> When the night had veiled the pole;
> In the morning, glad, I see
> My foe outstretched beneath the tree.

The hater has become a murderer, and his hate has destroyed both the man he hates and himself.

Iago is in a situation parallel to Shylock's. All through *Othello* he is full of reasons for his unremitting hatred of the Moor. When in the last scene, after all the facts have been made known, Othello says:

> Will you, I pray, demand that demidevil
> Why he hath thus ensnared my soul and body?

Iago now has the opportunity, if he has been wronged, at least to explain his terrible vengeance: he can speak of his (pretended) convictions that Othello has slept with Emilia, of his having been unfairly superseded by Cassio, etc. But no. He has the brains to realize that there is nothing he can say to account for his monstrous villainy. Moreover, he is unable, now that he is forced to confront it, to understand his hate himself. And so, he too replies that he can give no reason and therefore will give no reason for his villainy:

> Demand me nothing. What you know, you know.
> From this time forth I never will speak word. (V, ii, 301–4)

These are, indeed, the last words he speaks in the play: he is probably as bewildered as everyone else at his conduct, and he is left to contemplate what is to him probably an insolvable puzzle.

Thus, too, Shylock, eaten up with hate, can really give no reason for desiring Antonio's death. This cancerous hatred, nourished by greed, is all that is left of him.

And here we shall leave Shylock for the moment. Presently he, creature of cold hate and greed, bolstering that hate and greed with a demand for the strict letter of the law, will have to confront his great opponent, Portia, the personification of all he despises in life—generosity, warmth, compassion, and love—Portia, with whom mercy is to be preferred far above mere justice.

In Shakespeare's play generosity, compassion, love, and mercy will triumph, as Shakespeare was convinced that they could and should triumph in life.

They could have triumphed, no doubt. Money need not have poisoned the wellsprings of human existence if Christ's teachings had meant anything to Christians.

Alas! in the course of time it is not Portia and Shakespeare, but Shylock, who has won out. Nowadays if a man, pillar of his church, synagogue, or mosque, lends his brother a hundred dollars, he will probably expect him to pay him six per cent interest. "Why shouldn't he pay it to me?" he will say in self-justification, "since he will have to pay as much if he goes to a bank? Business is business."

Yes, most of the world has adopted Shylock's philosophy, which is the philosophy of banks. No one expects compassion from a bank.

NOTES

[1] B. Stirling, *The Populace in Shakespeare* (New York, 1949), p. 55.
[2] H. Spencer, *The Art and Life of William Shakespeare* (New York, 1940), p. 240.
[3] Ibid., p. 239.
[4] E. N. Calish, *The Jew in European Literature* (Richmond, Va., n.d.), p. 75.
[5] Ibid., p. 78.
[6] G. L. Kittredge, *The Merchant of Venice* (Boston, 1945), p. x.
[7] A. Quiller-Couch, *Shakespeare's Workmanship* (London, 1918), p. 98.
[8] H. Golden, *Only in America* (New York, 1958), pp. 169, 172, 174, 176–7.
[9] W. Hazlitt, *The Characters of Shakespeare's Plays* (London, 1906), p. 212.
[10] In *The Saturday Review*, Dec. 14, 1895, Sept. 26, 1896.

[11] E. Terry, *The Story of My Life* (London, 1908), p. 186.

[12] W. Winter, *Shadows of the Stage* (New York, 1892), p. 183.

[13] Quoted by H. H. Furness, *The Merchant of Venice* (Philadelphia, 1888), pp. 430, 449.

[14] W. Raleigh, *Shakespeare* (London, 1907), pp. 149, 150–1.

[15] E. N. Calish, op. cit., pp. 72, 84.

[16] In *Shakespeare-Jahrbuch*, XVIII, pp. 200 seq.

[17] C. N. Coe, *Shakespeare's Villains* (New York, 1957), p. 52.

[18] E. E. Stoll, *Shakespeare Studies* (New York, 1942), p. 452.

[19] H. Granville-Barker, *Prefaces to Shakespeare, Second Series* (London, 1948), p. 67. These are Shylock's actual words in that scene:

> Well, thou shalt see, thy eyes shall be thy judge,
> The difference of old Shylock and Bassanio—
> ... Thou shalt not gormandize,
> As thou hast done with me....
> And sleep and snore, and rend apparel out....

Actually poor Launcelot has been so much starved that his ribs are sticking out ("I am famished in his service; you may tell every finger I have with my ribs."—II, ii, 113–4). And when Launcelot leaves the stage, Shylock muses:

> The patch [i.e., fool] is kind enough, but a huge feeder;
> Snail-slow in profit, and he sleeps by day
> More than the wild-cat. Drones hive not with me;
> Therefore I part with him, and part with him
> To one that I would have him help to waste
> His borrowed purse.   (II, v, 1–5; 46–51)

[20] A. Harbage, *As They Liked It* (New York, 1947), p. 194.

[21] H. C. Goddard, *The Meaning of Shakespeare* (Chicago, 1951), pp. 6, 94, 99, 100–01.

[22] H. R. Walley, "Shakespeare's Portrayal of Shylock," in *Essays in Dramatic Literature*, ed. by H. Craig (Princeton, 1935), p. 235.

[23] O. J. Campbell, *The Living Shakespeare* (New York, 1949), p. 265.

[24] W. A. Neilson and C. J. Hill, *The Complete Plays and Poems of William Shakespeare* (Cambridge, Mass., 1942), p. 116.

[25] M. Van Doren, *Shakespeare* (New York, 1939), p. 101.

[26] E. E. Stoll, op. cit., pp. 255–336, especially pp. 256–67.

[27] Quoted by T. Lelyveld, *Shylock on the Stage* (Cleveland, 1960), p. 11.

[28] E. E. Stoll, op. cit., pp. 255, 271.

[29] E. Rosenberg, *From Shylock to Svengali* (Stanford, 1960), pp. 3, 35, 37.

[30] E. E. Stoll, op. cit., p. 322.

[31] H. Spencer, op. cit., pp. 245–6.

[32] E. Spivack, *Shakespeare and the Allegory of Evil* (New York, 1958), p. 146.

[33] J. Palmer, *Comic Characters of Shakespeare* (London, 1953), pp. 75, 80, 88.

[34] S. C. Sen Gupta, *Shakespearian Comedy* (Oxford, 1950), p. 143.

[35] E. E. Stoll, op. cit., p. 288.

[36] E. I. Fripp, *Shakespeare, Man and Artist* (Oxford, 1938), Vol. I, p. 416.

[37] A. Quiller-Couch, Introduction to *The Merchant of Venice*, New Cambridge edition, p. xxviii.

[38] J. M. Murry, *Shakespeare* (London, 1954), p. 197.

[39] H. Spencer, op. cit., p. 240.

[40] F. Harris, *The Man Shakespeare* (New York, 1909), p. 196.

[41] B. Stirling, op. cit., p. 59.

[42] M. Van Doren, op. cit., pp. 104, 105.

[43] W. Raleigh, op. cit., p. 150.

[44] L. L. Schücking, *Character Problems in Shakespeare's Plays* (New York, 1948), pp. 88, 89.

[45] L. L. Schücking, op. cit., p. 89.

[46] E. E. Stoll, op. cit., p. 275.

[47] L. L. Schücking, op. cit., p. 91.

[48] B. Grebanier, *The Heart of Hamlet* (New York, 1960), p. 194.

[49] E. E. Stoll, *Shakespeare's Young Lovers* (Toronto, 1937), p. 20.

[50] J. Palmer, op. cit., p. 61.

[51] The usual connotation of "gentle," a word used by his contemporaries to describe Shakespeare himself, was "well-born," "civilized."
[52] A. Quiller-Couch, Introduction to *The Merchant of Venice*, p. xx.
[53] A. Harbage, op. cit., p. 126.
[54] H. Giles, *Human Life in Shakespeare* (London, 1868), p. 147.
[55] A. Quiller-Couch, Introduction to *The Merchant of Venice*, p. xxi.
[56] M. Webster, *Shakespeare Today* (London, 1957), p. 194.
[57] C. B. Graham, "Standards of Value in *The Merchant of Venice*," *Shakespeare Quarterly*, IV, No. 2 (April 1953), p. 150.
[58] M. Packard, op. cit., pp. 51–3.
[59] J. M. Murry, *Shakespeare*, p. 194.
[60] A. Quiller-Couch, Introduction to *The Merchant of Venice*, p. xx.
[61] H. H. Furness, op. cit., p. 131.
[62] J. R. Brown, *The Merchant of Venice* (Cambridge, Mass., 1955), p. 75.
[63] Quoted by H. H. Furness, op. cit., p. 432.

Barbara K. Lewalski

BIBLICAL ALLUSION
AND ALLEGORY IN
THE MERCHANT OF VENICE

Perhaps no other play in the Shakespeare canon has provoked greater controversy regarding its fundamental moral and religious attitudes than has *The Merchant
of Venice*. As everyone knows, acrimonious critical debates have long been waged
concerning whether Shakespeare's attitude in the play is humanitarian or antisemitic, whether Shylock is presented as the persecuted hero or as a crude monster and
comic butt, whether Antonio and Bassanio are portrayed as worthy Christians or
as crass hypocrites.

Recently, however, some critics have in part transcended the controversies
arising out of the literal story by concentrating upon certain allegorical and symbolic
aspects of the play, reflecting in this approach the modern critical emphasis upon
Shakespeare's use of Christian themes and imagery and his debt to the medieval
tradition. In a most illuminating essay, Nevill Coghill[1] discusses several of
Shakespeare's comedies, including *MV*, in terms of the medieval comic form described by Dante—a beginning in troubles and a resolution in joy, reflecting the
fundamental pattern of human existence in this world. Moreover, he traces in *MV*
the direct influence of the medieval allegorical theme of the "Parliament of Heaven",
in which Mercy and Justice, two of the four "daughters of God", argue over the fate
of mankind after his fall. In somewhat similar vein, Sir Israel Gollancz[2] sees the play
as Shakespeare's largely unconscious development of certain myths implicit in the
original sources—the myth of the Parliament of Heaven, and the related Redemption myth in which Antonio represents Christ, Shylock, Evil, and Portia, Mercy and
Grace. These suggestions shed considerable light upon the trial scene, but they
hardly provide a comprehensive account of the entire play.[3] The question of the
extent and manner in which allegory may organize the total work has yet to be
investigated, and constitutes the subject of the present inquiry.

The overingenuity and the religious special pleading that has marred some
"Christian" criticism of Shakespeare make manifest the need for rigorous standards

From *Shakespeare Quarterly* 13, No. 3 (Summer 1962): 327–35, 338–43.

of evidence and argument in such investigations. The present study does not claim that all of Shakespeare's plays approach as closely as *MV* appears to do to the themes and methods of the morality play. Nor does it imply anything about Shakespeare's personal religious convictions, since the religious significances dealt with in the play are basic to all the major Christian traditions and were available to any Elizabethan through countless sermons, biblical commentaries, and scripture annotations. Nor, again, does it assume Shakespeare's direct contact with medieval allegory, since the general Elizabethan assimilation and perpetuation of this tradition is clearly evidenced in Spenser, Marlowe, and many other poets. The study does, however, uncover in *MV* patterns of Biblical allusion and imagery so precise and pervasive as to be patently deliberate; it finds, moreover, that such language clearly reveals an important theological dimension in the play and points toward consistent and unmistakable allegorical meanings.

The allegorical aspects of *The Merchant of Venice* can, I believe, be greatly illuminated by the medieval allegorical method exemplified by Dante. Indeed, though it omits *MV*, a recent study by Bernard Spivack has persuasively argued the utility of the Dante comparison in comprehending the allegorical origins and characteristics of many Shakespearian villains.[4] In contrast to personification allegory wherein a particular is created to embody an insensible, Dante's symbolic method causes a particular real situation to suggest a meaning or meanings beyond itself. In *MV* Shakespeare, like Dante, is ultimately concerned with the nature of the Christian life, though as a dramatist he is fully as interested in the way in which the allegorical dimensions enrich the particular instance as in the use of the particular to point to higher levels of meaning. The various dimensions of allegorical significance in *MV*, though not consistently maintained throughout the play and not susceptible of analysis with schematic rigor, are generally analogous to Dante's four levels of allegorical meaning: a literal or story level; an allegorical significance concerned with truths relating to humanity as a whole and to Christ as head of humanity; a moral or tropological level dealing with factors in the moral development of the individual; and an anagogical significance treating the ultimate reality, the Heavenly City.[5] Moreover, comprehension of the play's allegorical meanings leads to a recognition of its fundamental unity, discrediting the common critical view that it is a hotchpotch which developed contrary to Shakespeare's conscious intention.

The use of Biblical allusion to point to such allegorical meanings must now be illustrated in relation to the various parts of the work.

Antonio and Shylock

At what would correspond in medieval terminology to the "moral" level, the play is concerned to explore and define Christian love and its various antitheses.[6] As revealed in the action, Christian love involves both giving and forgiving: it demands an attitude of carelessness regarding the things of this world founded upon a trust in God's providence; an attitude of self-forgetfulness and humility founded upon recognition of man's common sinfulness; a readiness to give and risk everything, possessions and person, for the sake of love; and a willingness to forgive injuries and to love enemies. In all but the last respect, Antonio is presented throughout the play as the very embodiment of Christian love, and Shylock functions as one (but not the only) antithesis to it.

Antonio's practice of Christian love is indicated throughout the play under the metaphor of "venturing", and the action begins with the use of this metaphor in a mock test of his attitude toward wealth and worldy goods. The key scripture text opposing love of this world to the Christian love of God and neighbor is Matt. vi. 19–21, 31–33:

> Lay not up treasures for your selves upon the earth, where the moth and canker corrupt, & where theeves dig through, and steale. / But lay up treasures for your selves in heaven. . . . / For where your treasure is, there will your heart be also / . . . Therefore take no thought, saying, what shall we eate? or what shall we drink? or wherewith shall we be clothed? / . . . But seeke ye first the kingdome of God, and his righteousnesse, & all these things shalbe ministred unto you.[7]

In language directly alluding to this passage, Salerio suggests that Antonio's melancholy may result from worry about his "ventures" at sea: "Your mind is tossing on the ocean, / There where your argosies [are]", and Solanio continues in this vein: "had I such venture forth, / The better part of my affections would / Be with my hopes abroad" (I.i.8–9, 15–17).[8] Gratiano repeats the charge—"You have too much respect upon the world: / They lose it that do buy it with much care" (I.i.74–75)—a speech also recalling Matt. xvi.25–26, "Whosoever will save his life, shall lose it. . . . / For what shall it profite a man, though he should winne the whole worlde, if he lose his owne soule?" Yet the validity of Antonio's disclaimer, "I hold the world but as the world Gratiano" (I.i.77)—that is, as the world deserves to be held—is soon evident: his sadness is due not to worldly concern but to the imminent parting with his beloved friend Bassanio. After witnessing this parting Salerio testifies, "I think he only loves the world for him" (II.viii.50).

Gratiano's second playful charge, that Antonio's melancholy may be a pose to feed his self-importance, to seem a "Sir Oracle" with a wise and grave demeanor (I.i.88–102), recalls the passage in I Cor. xiii. 4–5 where Paul characterizes Christian love in terms of humility and self-forgetfulness: "Love suffereth long: it is bountifull: love envieth not: love doth not boast it selfe: it is not puffed up: / It disdaineth not: it seeketh not her owne things." But this charge against Antonio is quickly dismissed by Bassanio as "an infinite deal of nothing" (I.i.114–118).

The quality of Antonio's love is then shown in the positive forms of charity and benevolence, according to the following requirements of scripture:

> Give to every man that asketh of thee: and of him that taketh away thy goods, aske them not againe. / And if ye lende to them of whom yee hope to receive,

what thanke shal ye have? for even the sinners lend to sinners, to receive the like / Wherefore   doe good, & lend, looking for nothing againe, and your reward shall be great (Luke vi.30, 34–35).

Greater love then this hath no man, then any man bestoweth his life for his friendes (John xv. 13).

Though his first loan to Bassanio has not been repaid, Antonio is willing to "venture" again for his friend "My purse, my person, my extremest means" (I.i.138), even to the pledge of a pound of his flesh. And when this pledge (and with it his life) is forfeit, he can still release Bassanio from debt: "debts are clear'd between you and I" (III.ii.317). Furthermore, Antonio lends money in the community at large without seeking interest, and often aids victims of Shylock's usurious practices (I.iii.39–40; III.iii.22–23).

Shylock's "thrift" poses the precise contrast to Antonio's "ventures." His is the worldliness of niggardly prudence, well-characterized by his avowed motto, "Fast bind, fast find,— / A proverb never stale in thrifty mind" (II.v.53–54). He locks up house and stores before departing, he begrudges food and maintenance to his servant Launcelot, he demands usurious "assurance" before lending money. This concern with the world poisons all his relations with others and even his love for Jessica: the confused cries, "My daughter! O my ducats! O my daughter!" after Jessica's departure (II.vii.15), reveal, not his lack of love for his daughter, but his laughable and pitiable inability to determine what he loves most. Shylock also manifests pride and self-righteousnes. He scorns Antonio's "low simplicity" in lending money gratis (I.iii.38–39), despises the "prodigal" Bassanio for giving feasts (II.v.15), and considers the "shallow fopp'ry" of the Christian maskers a defilement of his "sober house" (II.v.35–36).

The moral contrast of Shylock and Antonio is more complex with reference to that most difficult injunction of the Sermon on the Mount—forgiveness of injuries and love of enemies. Recollection of this demand should go far to resolve the question as to whether an Elizabethan audience would regard Shylock's grievances as genuine:[9] presumably an audience which could perceive the Biblical standard operating throughout the play would also see its relevance here. The text is Matt. v. 39, 44–47:

Resist not evill: but whosoever shall smite thee on thy right cheeke, turn to him the other also / . . . Love your enemies: bless them that curse you: do good to them that hate you, and pray for them which hurt you, and persecute you. / That ye may be the children of your Father that is in heaven: for hee maketh his sunne to arise on the evill, & the good, and sendeth raine on the just, and unjust. / For if ye love them, which love you, what reward shall you have? Doe not the Publicanes even the same? / And if ye be friendly to your brethren onely, what singular thing doe ye? doe not even the Publicanes likewise?

Antonio at the outset of the play is rather in the position of the publican described as friendly to his brethren only—he loves and forgives Bassanio beyond all measure, but hates and reviles Shylock.[10] For evidence of this we have not only Shylock's indictment, "You call me misbeliever, cut-throat dog, / and spet upon my Jewish gaberdine, / . . . And foot me as you spurn a stranger cur" (I.iii.106–107, 113), but also Antonio's angry reply promising continuation of such treatment: "I am as like to call thee so again, / To spet on thee again, to spurn thee too" (I.iii.125–126). Indeed, the moral tension of the play is lost if we do not see that Shylock, having been the object of great wrongs, must make a difficult choice between forgiveness and revenge—and that Antonio later finds himself in precisely the same situation.

Ironically, Shylock poses at first as the more "Christian" of the two in that, after detailing his wrongs, he explicitly proposes to turn the other cheek—to "Forget the shames that you have stain'd me with, / Supply your present wants, and take no doit / Of usance for my moneys" (I.iii.135–137). Of course it is merely pretence: Shylock had declared for revenge at the first sight of Antonio (I.iii.41–42), and, according to Jessica's later report, he eagerly planned for the forfeit of Antonio's flesh long before the bond came due (III.ii.283–287). And in this fixed commitment to revenge, this mockery of forgiveness, lies I believe the reason for the often-deplored change from the "human" Shylock of the earlier scenes to the "monster" of Act IV. At the level of the moral allegory Shylock undergoes (rather like Milton's Satan) the progressive deterioration of evil; he turns by his own choice into the cur that he has been called—"Thou call'dst me dog before thou hadst a cause, / But since I am a dog, beware my fangs" (III.iii.6–7). Conversely, Antonio in the trial scene suffers hatred and injury but foregoes revenge and rancor, manifesting a genuine spirit of forgiveness—for Shylock's forced conversion is not revenge, as will be seen. Thus, his chief deficiency surmounted, Antonio becomes finally a perfect embodiment of Christian love.

The Shylock-Antonio opposition functions also at what the medieval theorists would call the "allegorical" level; in these terms it symbolizes the confrontation of Judaism and Christianity as theological systems—the Old Law and the New—and also as historic societies. In their first encounter, Shylock's reference to Antonio as a "fawning publican" and to himself as a member of the "sacred nation" (I.iii.36,43) introduces an important aspect of this contrast. The reference is of course to the parable of the Pharisee and the Publican (Luke xviii.9–13) which was spoken "unto certayne which trusted in themselves, that they were ryghteous, and despised other".[11] Shylock's words are evidently intended to suggest the Pharisee's prayer, "God I thank thee that I am not as other menne are, extorcioners, unjust, adulterers, or as this Publicane: / I fast twyce in the weeke, I geve tythe of al that I posesse", and his scornful reference to Antonio's "low simplicity" relates Antonio to the Publican who prayed with humble faith, "God be merciful to me a sinner". The contemporary interpretation of this parable is suggested in Tomson's note:[12] "Two things especially make our prayers voyde and of none effect: confidence of our owne ryghteousnesse, and the contempts of other. . . . we [are] despised of God, as proude & arrogant, if we put never so little trust in our owne workes before God." Through this allusion, then, the emphasis of the Old Law upon perfect legal righteousness is opposed to the tenet of the New Law that righteousness is impossible to fallen man and must be replaced by faith—an opposition which will be further discussed with reference to the trial scene.

Also in this first encounter between Antonio and Shylock, the argument about unsury contrasts Old Law and New in terms resembling those frequently found in contemporary polemic addressed to the usury question. Appealing to the Old Testament, Shylock sets forth an analogy between Jacob's breeding of ewes and rams and the breeding of money to produce interest.[13] Antonio, denying the analogy with the query, "is your gold and silver ewes and rams?" echoes the commonplace Christian argument (based upon Aristotle)[14] that to take interest is to "breed" barren metal, which is unnatural. Antonio's remark, "If thou wilt lend this money, lend it not / As to thy friends, for when did friendship take / A breed for barren metal of his friend? / But lend it rather to thine enemy" (I.iii.127–130), prescribes Shylock's course of action according to the dictum of the Old Law— "Unto a stranger thou mayest lend upon usury, but unto thy brother thou shalt not lend upon usury" (Deut. xxiii.20). However, according to most exegetes, the Gospel demanded a revision of this rule. Aquinas declares, "The Jews were forbidden to take usury from their brethren, i.e., from other Jews. By this we are given to understand that to take usury from any man is evil simply, because we ought to treat every man as our neighbor and brother, especially in the state of the Gospel, whereto all are called."[15] Furthermore, the Sermon on the Mount was thought to forbid usury absolutely by the words, "Lend, looking for nothing againe", a text which is glossed as follows in the Geneva Bible—lend, "not only not hoping for profite, but to lose ye stocke, and principall, for as much as Christ bindeth him selfe to repaie the whole with a most liberall interest."

At this same encounter, Shylock's pretense of following the Christian prescription regarding forgiveness of injuries again contrasts Old Law and New as theological systems, for it recalls the fact that Christ in the Sermon on the Mount twice opposed the Christian standard to the Old Law's demand for strict justice: "Ye have heard that it hath bene saide, An eye for an eye, & a tooth for a tooth. /[16] But I say unto you, Resist not evill: but whosoever shall smite thee on thy right cheeke, turne to him the other also / . . . Ye have hearde that it hath bene saide, Thou shalt love thy neighbour, & hate thine enemie. / But I say unto you, Love your enemies" (Matt. v.38–39, 43–44). Later, some of the language of the trial scene alludes again to the differing demands of the two dispensations with regard to forgiveness of enemies:

> BASS: Do all men kill the things they do not love?
> SHY: Hates any man the thing he would not kill?
> BASS: Every offense is not a hate at first!
> SHY: What! wouldst thou have a serpent sting thee twice?" (IV.i.66–69)

And the Duke reiterates this opposition almost too pointedly when he tenders Shylock the mercy of the Christian court, observing that Shylock could recognize from this "the difference of our spirit" (IV.i.364).

This allegorical dimension encompasses also the historical experience of the two societies, Jewish and Christian. After Jessica's departure, Shylock explicitly assumes unto himself the sufferings of his race: "The curse never fell upon our nation till now, I never felt it till now (III.i.76–78). This curse is that pronounced upon Jerusalem itself—"Behold, your habitation shalbe left unto you desolate" (Matt. xxiii.38). First Shylock's servant Launcelot leaves the "rich Jew" to serve the poor Bassanio; then his daughter Jessica[17] "gilds" herself with her Father's ducats and flees with her "unthrift" Christian lover; and finally, all of Shylock's goods and his very life are forfeit to the state. Shylock's passionate outcries against Antonio (III.i.48ff.) also take on larger than personal significance: they record the sufferings of his entire race in an alien Christian society—"he hath disgrac'd me . . . laugh'd at my losses, mock'd at my gains, scorned my nation, thwarted my bargains, cooled my friends, heated mine enemies—and what's his reason? I am a Jew!" This is followed by the eloquent plea for recognition of the common humanity Jew shares with Christian, "Hath not a Jew eyes? . . .", and it concludes with the telling observation that despite the Christian's professions about "humility" and turning the other cheek, in practice he is quick to revenge himself upon the Jew. The taunts of Salerio, Solanio, and Gratiano throughout the play give some substantiation to these charges.

Yet overlaying this animosity are several allusions to Shylock's future conversion, suggesting the Christian expectation of the final, pre-millennial conversion of the Jews. The first such reference occurs, most appropriately, just after Shylock's feigned offer to forego usury and forgive injury. Antonio salutes Shylock's departure with the words, "Hie thee gentle Jew"—probably carrying a pun on gentle-gentile—and then prophesies, "The Hebrew will turn Christian, he grows kind" (I.iii.173–174). "Kind" in this context implies both "natural" (in foregoing unnatural interest) and "charitable"; thus Antonio suggests that voluntary adoption of these fundamental Christian principles would lead to the conversion of the Jew. The second prediction occurs in Lorenzo's declaration, "If e'er the Jew her father come to heaven, / It will be for his gentle daughter's sake" (II.iv.33–34)—again with the pun on gentle-gentile. As Shylock's daughter and as a voluntary convert to Christianity, Jessica may figure forth the filial relationship of the New Dispensation to the Old, and Lorenzo's prediction may carry an allusion to Paul's prophecy that the Jews will ultimately be saved through the agency of the Gentiles.[18] At any rate, the final conversion of the Jews is symbolized in just such terms in the trial scene: because Antonio is able to rise at last to the demands of Christian love, Shylock is not destroyed, but, albeit rather harshly, converted. Interestingly enough, however, even after Portia's speeches at the trial have reminded Antonio and the court of the Christian principles they profess, Gratiano yet persists in demanding revenge. This incident serves as a thematic counterpoint to the opposition of Old Law and New, suggesting the disposition of Christians themselves to live rather according to the

Old Law than the New. Such a counterpoint is developed at various points through-out the play—in Antonio's initial enmity to Shylock, in the jeers of the minor figures, in Shylock's statements likening his revenge to the customary vengeful practices of the Christians and his claim to a pound of flesh to their slave trade in human flesh (IV.i.90–100). Thus the play does not present arbitrary, black-and-white moral estimates of human groups, but takes into account the shadings and complexities of the real world.

As Shylock and Antonio embody the theological conflicts and historical inter-relationships of Old Law and New, so do they also reflect, from time to time, the ultimate sources of their principles in a further allegorical significance. Antonio, who assumes the debts of others (rescuing Bassanio, the self-confessed "Prodigal", from a debt due under the law) reflects on occasion the role of Christ satisfying the claim of Divine Justice by assuming the sins of mankind. The scripture phrase which Antonio's deed immediately brings to mind points the analogy directly: "This is my commandement, that ye love one another, *as I have loved you.* /[19] Greater love hath no man than this, that a man lay down his life for his friends" (John xv.12–13). And Shylock, demanding the "bond" which is due him under the law, reflects the role of the devil, to whom the entire human race is in bondage through sin—an analogy which Portia makes explicit when she terms his hold upon Antonio a "state of hellish cruelty". The dilemma which that delightful malaprop Launcelot experi-ences with regard to leaving Shylock, whom he terms the "devil incarnation" (II.ii.1–30), springs directly from the implications of this analogy. According to 1 Pet. xiii.18–19, one must serve even a bad master "for conscience toward God": thus Launcelot's conscience bids him stay and the fiend bids him go. But on the other hand, to serve the devil is obviously damnation; so he concludes, "in my conscience, my concience is but a kind of hard conscience to offer to counsel me to stay with the Jew", and determines flight. Similarly, Jessica declares, "Our house is hell" (II.iii.2), thus placing her departure in the context of a flight from the devil to salvation. As E. E. Stoll points out,[20] the identification of Jew and Devil is repeated nine times in the play, and was a commonplace of medieval and Elizabethan antisemitic literature. Yet it seems to function here less to heap opprobium upon the Jew than to suggest the ultimate source of the principles of revenge and hatred which Shylock seeks to justify out of the Law. Again the meaning is clarified by a Biblical quotation—Christ's use of the same identification in denouncing the Jews for their refusal to believe in him and their attempts to kill him—"Ye are of your father the devill, and the lustes of your father ye will doe: Hee hath bene a murtherer from the beginning" (John viii.44). ⟨...⟩

The Trial

The trial scene climaxes the action at all the levels of meaning that have been established. As has been suggested, it portrays at the moral level Shylock's degra-dation to a cur and a monster through his commitment to revenge, and by contrast,

Antonio's attainment of the fullness of Christian love through his abjuration of revenge. Allegorically, the scene develops the sharpest opposition of Old Law and New in terms of their respective theological principles, Justice and Mercy, Righteousness and Faith; it culminates in the final defeat of the Old Law and the symbolic conversion of the Jew.

Throughout the first portion of Act IV, until Portia begins the dramatic reversal with the words, "Tarry a little, there is something else—" (IV.i.301), the action is simply a debate between Old Law and New in terms of Justice and Mercy—but that debate is carried forth in a dual frame of reference. The phrase in the Lord's Prayer rendered by both the Bishops and the Geneva Bibles as "Forgeve us our dettes, as we forgeve our detters", is alluded to twice in this scene, making the debtor's trial in the court of Venice a precise analogue of the sinner's trial in the court of Heaven. The Duke inquires of Shylock, "How shalt thou hope for mercy rend'ring none?" (IV.i.88), and Portia reiterates, "Though justice be thy plea, consider this, / That in the course of justice, none of us / Should see salvation: we do pray for mercy, / And that same prayer, doth teach us all to render / The deeds of mercy" (IV.i.194–198). In his *Exposition of the Lord's Prayer* a contemporary clergyman, William Perkins,[21] works out a similar analogy: "For even as a debt doth binde a man, either to make satisfaction, or els to goe to prison: so our sinnes bindes us either to satisfie Gods justice, or else to suffer eternall damnation." Shylock is referred for this analogy not only to the Lord's Prayer but also to his own tradition: Portia's language (IV.i.180ff.) echoes also certain Old Testament psalmists and prophets whose pleas for God's mercy were explained by Christian exegetes as admissions of the inadequacies of the Law and testimonies of the need for Christ.[22] For example the striking image, "Mercy . . . droppeth as a gentle rain from Heaven upon the place beneath", echoes Ecclesiasticus xxv.19, "O how fayre a thyng is mercy in the tyme of anguish and trouble: it is lyke a cloud of rayne that commeth in the tyme of drought." This reference should also remind Shylock of the remarkable parallel to the Lord's Prayer contained in a passage following close upon this one: "He that seeketh vengeance, shal finde vengeance of the Lord. . . . / Forgeve thy neyghbour the hurt that he hath donne thee, and so shal thy sinnes be forgeven thee also when thou prayest / . . . He that sheweth no mercie to a man which is lyke himselfe, how dare he aske forgevenesse of his sinnes" (Ecclus. xxiii.1–24).[23]

Through these allusions, Antonio's predicament in the courtroom of Venice is made to suggest traditional literary and iconographical presentations of the "Parliament of Heaven" in which fallen man was judged. Both sides agree that Antonio's bond (like the sinner's) is forfeit according to the law, and that the law of Venice (like that of God) cannot be abrogated. Shylock constantly threatens, "If you deny me, fie upon your law" (IV.i.101), and Portia concurs, "there is no power in Venice / Can alter a decree established" (IV.i.214–215). The only question then is whether the law must be applied with strictest justice, or whether mercy may somehow temper it. In the traditional allegory of the Parliament of Heaven,[24] Justice and

Mercy, as the two principal of the four "daughters" of God, debate over the judgement to be meted out to man; Launcelot Andrewes in his version of the debate[25] aligns these figures with the Old Law and the New respectively—"Righteousnesse, she was where the Law was (for, that, the *rule* of *righteousnesse*) where the Covenant of the Old Testament was, *doe this and live* (the very voyce of Justice)", whereas "The Gentiles they claim by *Mercy, that* is their virtue." So in the trial scene Shylock as the embodiment of the Old Law represents Justice: "I stand for Judgment . . . I stand here for Law" (IV.i.103, 142), whereas Portia identifies herself with that "Quality of Mercy" enthroned by the New Law. Also, another conception of the Heavenly Court is superadded to this by means of several references during the trial to Shylock as Devil (IV.i.213, 283). The scene takes on something of the significance of the trial described in the medieval drama, the *Processus Belial,* in which the Devil claims by justice the souls of mankind due him under the law, and the Virgin Mary intercedes for man by appealing to the Mercy of God.[26]

In either formulation, the demands of Justice and Mercy are reconciled only through the sacrifice of Christ, who satisfies the demands of justice by assuming the debts of mankind, and thus makes mercy possible. Therefore it is not surprising that the courtroom scene also evokes something of the crucifixion scene—as the moment of reconciling these opposed forces, as the time of defeat for the Old Law, as the prime example of Christian Love and the object of Christian Faith. Both plot situation and language suggest a typical killing of Christ by the Jew. Antonio, baring his breast to shed his blood for the debt of another, continues the identification with Christ occasionally suggested at other points in the play. Shylock's cry, "My deeds upon my head" (IV.i.202) clearly suggests the assumption of guilt by the Jews at Christ's crucifixion—"His blood be on us, and on our children" (Matt. xxvii.25)—and his later remark, "I have a daughter— / Would any of the stock of Barrabas / Had been her husband, rather than a Christian" (IV.i.291–293) recalls the Jews' choice of the murderer Barrabas over Christ as the prisoner to be released at Passover (Matt. xxvii.16–21). A similar fusion of the symbols of debtor's court and crucifixion occurs in a Christmas sermon by Launcelot Andrewes on Gal. iii.4–5:

> If one be in debt and danger of the *Law,* to have a *Brother* of the same bloud . . . will little avail him, except he will also come *under the Law,* that is, become his Surety, and undertake for him. And such was our estate. As debtors we were, by vertue of . . . the *handwriting* that was against us. Which was our *Bond,* and we had forfeited it. . . . Therefore Hee became bound for us also, entred bond anew, took on Him, not only our *Nature,* but our *Debt.* . . . The debt of a Capitall Law is Death.[27]

Throughout the action thus far described, Shylock has persistently denied pleas to temper justice with mercy—to forgive part of the debt, to accept three times the value of the debt rather than the pound of flesh, or even to supply a doctor "for charity" to stop Antonio's wounds. His perversity is rooted in his explicit denial of any need to "deserve" God's mercy by showing mercy to others, for he arrogates to himself the perfect righteousness which is the standard of he Old Law—"What judgment shall I dread doing no wrong?" (IV.i.89). Accordingly, after Portia's "Tarry a little", the action of the scene works out a systematic destruction of that claim of righteousness, using the laws of Venice as symbol. Shylock is shown first that he can claim nothing by the law: his claim upon Antonio's flesh is disallowed by the merest technicality. This reflects the Christian doctrine that although perfect performance of the Law would indeed merit salvation, in fact fallen man could never perfectly observe it, any more than Shylock could take Antonio's flesh without drawing blood. According to Paul, Romans iii.9–12, "all, both Jewes and Gentiles are under sinne, / . . . There is none righteous, no not one. / . . . there is none that doth good, no not one. / Therefore by the workes of the Law shal no flesh be justified in his sight". Next, Shylock is shown that in claiming the Law he not only gains nothing, but stands to lose all that he possesses and even life itself. He becomes subject to what Paul terms the "curse" of the Law, since he is unable to fulfill its conditions: "For as many as are of the workes of the Lawe, are under the curse: for it is written, Cursed is every man that continueth not in all things, which are written in the booke of the Lawe, to do them" (Gal. iii.10).

The names applied to and assumed by Portia during the trial reinforce these meanings. When Portia gives judgment at first in Shylock's favor, he cries out, "A Daniel come to judgment: yea, a Daniel! / O wise young judge", in obvious reference to the apocryphal Book of Susanna, wherein the young Daniel confounded the accusors of Susanna, upholding thereby the justice of the Law. The name, Daniel, which means in Hebrew, "The Judge of the Lord", was glossed in the Elizabethan Bibles as "The Judgment of God".[28] But the name carries other implications as well, which Shylock ironically forgets. Portia has assumed the name "Balthasar" for the purposes of her disguise, and the name given to the prophet Daniel in the Book of Daniel is Baltassar—a similarity hardly accidental.[29] According to Christian exegetes, Daniel in this book foreshadows the Christian tradition by his explicit denial of any claim upon God by righteousness, and his humble appeal for mercy: "O my God, encline thyne eare, & hearken, open thyne eyes, beholde howe we be desolated . . . for we doo not present our prayers before thee in our owne righteousnesse, but in thy great mercies" (Daniel ix.18).[30] These implications greatly enrich the irony when Gratiano flings the title back in Shylock's face—"A second Daniel, a Daniel, Jew" (IV.i.329).

Shylock's "forced conversion" (a gratuitous addition made by Shakespeare to the source story in *Il Pecorone*) must be viewed in the context of the symbolic action thus far described. Now that Shylock's claim to legal righteousness has been totally destroyed, he is made to accept the only alternative to it, faith in Christ. Paul declares (Gal. ii.16), "A man is not justified by the workes of the Lawe, but by the fayth of Jesus Christ", and a note in the Bishops Bible explains, "Christ hath fulfylled the whole lawe, and therefore who so ever beleeveth in him, is counted just before God, as wel as he had fulfylled ye whole law him selfe." Thus the stipulation for

Shylock's conversion, though it of course assumes the truth of Christianity, is not antisemitic revenge; it simply compels Shylock to avow what his own experience in the trial scene has fully "demonstrated"—that the Law leads only to death and destruction, that faith in Christ must supplant human righteousness. In this connection it ought to be noted that Shylock's pecuniary punishment under the laws of Venice precisely parallels the conditions imposed upon a Jewish convert to Christianity throughout most of Europe and also in England during the Middle Ages and after. All his property and goods, as the ill-gotten gain of usury, were forfeit to the state upon his conversion, but he was customarily allotted some proportion (often half) of his former goods for his maintenance, or else given a stipend or some other means of support.[31]

There is some evidence that Shylock himself in this scene recognizes the logic which demands his conversion, though understandably he finds this too painful to admit explicitly. His incredulous question "Is that the law" (IV.i.309) when he finds the law invoked against him, shows a new and overwhelming consciousness of the defects of legalism. Also, he does not protest the condition that he become a Christian as he protested the judgment (soon reversed) which would seize all his property: his brief "I am content" suggests, I believe, not mean-spiritedness but weary acknowledgement of the fact that he can no longer make his stand upon the discredited Law.

Indeed, Portia's final tactic—that of permitting the Law to demonstrate its own destructiveness—seems a working out of Paul's metaphor of the Law as a "Schoolmaster to bring us to Christ, that we might be made righteous by faith" (Gal. iii.24). The metaphor was utilized by all the major Christian theological traditions, and received much the same interpretation in all of them:

> The law was our pedagogue in Christ. . . . So also did he [God] wish to give such a law as men by their own forces could not fulfill, so that, while presuming on their own powers, they might find themselves to be sinners, and, being humbled, might have recourse to the help of grace. (Aquinas)[32]

> Another use of the law is . . . to reveale unto a man his sinne, his blindnes, his misery, his impietie, ignoraunce, hatred and contempt of God, death, hel, the judgment and deserved wrath of God to the end that God might bridle and beate down this monster and this madde beaste (I meane the presumption of *mans* own righteousness) . . . [and drive] them to Christ. (Luther)[33]

> Some . . . from too much confidence either in their own strength or in their own righteousness, are unfit to receive the grace of Christ till they have first been stripped of every thing. The law, therefore, reduces them to humility by a knowledge of their own misery, that thus they may be prepared to pray for that of which they before supposed themselves not destitute. (Calvin)[34]

And, from the contemporary sermon literature the following commentaries are typical:

> The law . . . was given because of transgression . . . out of the which they might learn the will of God, what sin, right, or unright is; and to know themselves, to go into themselves, and to consider, how that the holy works which God requireth are not in their own power; for the which cause all the world have great need of a mediator. . . . Thus was the law our schoolmaster unto Christ. (Myles Coverdale)[35]

> The law . . . shewes us our sinnes, and that without remedy: it shewes us the damnation that is due unto us: and by this meanes, it makes us despaire of salvation in respect of our selves: thus it inforceth us to seeke for helpe out of our selves in Christ. The law is then our schoolemaster not by the plaine teaching, but by stripes and corrections. (Perkins)[36]

Thus Shylock, as representative of his entire race, having refused the earlier opportunity to embrace voluntarily the principles of Christianity, must undergo in the trial scene the harsh "Schoolmastership" of the Law, in order to be brought to faith in Christ.

The Ring Episode and Belmont

The ring episode is, in a sense, a comic parody of the trial scene—it provides a means whereby Bassanio may make at least token fulfillment of his offer to give "life itself, my wife, and all the world" (IV.i.280) to deliver Antonio. The ring is the token of his possession of Portia and all Belmont: in offering it Portia declared, "This house, these servants, and this same myself / Are yours . . . I give them with this ring, / Which when you part from, lose, or give away, / Let it presage the ruin of your love, / And be my vantage to exclaim on you" (III.ii.170–174). So that in giving the ring to the "lawyer" Balthasar—which he does only at Antonio's bidding—Bassanio surrenders his "claim" to all these gifts, even to Portia's person, and is therefore taunted at his return with her alleged infidelity. But Belmont is the land of the spirit, not the letter, and therefore after Bassanio has been allowed for a moment to feel his loss, the whole crisis dissolves in laughter and amazement as Antonio again binds himself (his soul this time the forfeit) for Bassanio's future fidelity, and Portia reveals her own part in the affair. At the moral level, this pledge and counter pledge by Bassanio and Antonio continue the "venture" metaphor and further exemplify the willingness to give all for love. At the allegorical level, despite the lighthearted treatment, Bassanio's comic "trial" suggests the "judgment" awaiting the Christian soul as it presents its final account and is found deficient. But Love, finally, is the fulfillment of the Law and covers all defects—Bassanio's (Everyman's) love in giving up everything, in token at least, for Antonio, and Antonio's (Christ's) love toward him and further pledge in his behalf.

Belmont functions chiefly at the anagogical level (if one may invoke the term): it figures forth the Heavenly City. Jessica points to this analogy explicitly—"It is very meet / The Lord Bassanio live an upright life / For having such a blessing in his lady, / He finds the joys of heaven here on earth" (III.v.67–70). Here Gentile and Jew,

Lorenzo and Jessica, are united in each other's arms, talking of the music of the spheres:

How sweet the moonlight sleeps upon this bank!

· · · · · · · · · · · · · · · · · ·

    Look how the floor of heaven
Is thick inlaid with patens of bright gold,
There's not the smallest orb which thou behold'st
But in his motion like an angel sings,
Still quiring to the young-eye'd cherubins;
Such harmony is in immortal souls.   (V.i.54, 58–63)

And Portia's allusion upon returning, "Peace!—how the moon sleeps with Endymion, / And would not be awak'd" (V.i.108–109) also suggests eternity, for Diana, enamoured of Endymion's beauty, caused him to sleep forever on Mount Latmos. In Belmont all losses are restored and sorrows end: Bassanio wins again his lady and all Belmont; Antonio is given a letter signifying that three of his argosies are returned to port richly laden; and Lorenzo receives the deed naming him Shylock's future heir. Lorenzo's exclamation, "Fair ladies, you drop manna in the way of starving people", together with the reference to "patens" in the passage quoted above, sets up an implied metaphor of the heavenly communion. Here all who have cast their bread upon the waters in the "ventures" of Christian love receive the reward promised:

Whoever shall forsake houses, or brethren, or sisters, or father, or mother, or wife, or children, or landes, for my names sake, hee shal receive an hundredth folde more, and shal inherite everlasting life (Matt. xix.29).

NOTES

[1] "The Basis of Shakespearean Comedy", *Essays and Studies* III (London, 1950), pp. 1–28. See also Northrop Frye, "The Argument of Comedy", *English Institute Essays*, 1948 (N. Y., 1949), pp. 58–73.
[2] *Allegory and Mysticism in Shakespeare*, reports of lectures edited by A. W. Pollard (London, 1931), pp. 13–68.
[3] As J. R. Brown points out, "Introduction", *The Merchant of Venice*, Arden edition (London, 1955), p. li. All subsequent references to the text are to this edition.
[4] *Shakespeare and the Allegory of Evil: The History of a Metaphor in Relation to his Major Villains* (N. Y., 1958) pp. 50–99.
[5] H. Flanders Dunbar, *Symbolism in Medieval Thought* (New Haven, 1929), pp. 19, 497. Cf. Dante, "Letter to Can Grande della Scala", in *Dante's Eleven Letters*, ed. G. R. Carpenter (N. Y., 1892).
[6] Many critics have suggested that the play is essentially concerned with the contrast and evaluation of certain moral values—such as money, love, and friendship; appearance and reality; true love and fancy; mercy and justice; generosity and possessiveness; the usury of commerce and the usury of love. See Brown, Arden ed., pp. xxxvii–lviii; M. C. Bradbrook, *Shakespeare and Elizabethan Poetry* (London, 1951), pp. 170–179; Cary B. Graham, "Standards of Value in the *Merchant of Venice*", *Shakespeare Quarterly*, IV (N. Y., 1953), 145–151; C. R. Baskervill, "Bassanio as an Ideal Lover", *Manly Anniversary Studies*, pp. 90–103. All these, however, may be subsumed under the central concern, Christian Love.

[7] Unless otherwise indicated, scripture quotations are from the *Geneva Bible* (London, 1584); 1st ed., 1560). Richmond Noble, *Shakespeare's Biblical Knowledge* (London, 1935), notes that all of Shakespeare's Biblical allusions are drawn from one or more of the following versions—*Geneva, Geneva-Tomson* (1st ed., 1576), and the *Bishops Bible* (1st ed., 1568), and that the first two, being quartos, had the widest circulation during the period. For this play, the Geneva renderings seem on the whole closest, though occasionally the phraseology suggests that of the *Bishops Bible,* which Shapeskeare may have recalled from the church services.

[8] In these speeches they testify to their own failure to come up to the standard of Christian perfection achieved by Antonio. Shylock's later speech concerning Antonio's "sufficiency" also alludes to the imagery of this Biblical passage in describing the transiency of worldly goods: "Ships are but boards, sailors but men, there be land-rats, and water-rats, water-thieves and land-thieves" (I.iii.19–21).

[9] For the argument that Shylock could have been nothing but a monster and comic butt to an Elizabethan audience steeped in antisemitism, see E. E. Stoll, *Shakespeare Studies* (N. Y., 1927), pp. 255–336. This argument has been challenged on the ground that there was little ordinary antisemitism in England in Shakespeare's time, because few Jews resided there, and also on the ground that Shylock is, for a part of the play, at least, made human, complex, and somewhat sympathetic. See H. R. Walley, "Shakespeare's Portayal of Shylock", *The Parrott Presentation Volume* (Princeton, N. J., 1935), pp. 211–242, and J. L. Cardozo, *The Contemporary Jew in Elizabethan Drama* (Amsterdam, 1926).

[10] Hence Shylock's reference to Antonio as a "Fawning publican" may allude to the passage cited above (Matt. v. 47) as well as, more obviously, to the parable of the Pharisee and the Publican.

[11] *Bishops Bible* (London, 1572).

[12] *The New Testament.* . . . Englished by L. Tomson (London, 1599).

[13] Again they refer to their characteristic metaphors: Shylock argues that Jacob's trick to win the sheep from Laban (Gen. xxx.31–43) was justifiable "thrift", whereas Antonio (citing a later verse. Gen. xxxi.9, referring the trick to God's inspiration) declares that it was rather a "venture . . . / A thing not in his power to bring to pass, / But sway'd and fashion'd by the hand of heaven."

[14] *Politics,* I.10. 1258[b]. 1–8. Cf. Francis Bacon, "Of Usury", *Essays* (1625), "They say . . . it is against Nature, for *Money* to beget *Money.*"

[15] *Summa Theologica* II–II, Ques. 78, Art. 1, in *The Political Ideas of St. Thomas Aquinas,* ed. Dino Bigongiari (N. Y., 1953), p.149. As R. H. Tawney points out in *Religion and the Rise of Capitalism* (N. Y., 1953), p. 135, the arguments of the schoolmen were in constant circulation during the sixteenth century, and the medieval view regarding usury was maintained by an overwhelming proportion of Elizabethan writers on the subject (pp. 128–149). See Sir Thomas Wilson, *Discourse upon Usury* (1572), Miles Mosse, *The Arraignment and Conviction of Usurie* (1595), H. Smith, *Examination of Usury* (1591).

[16] Christ refers to Exod. xxi.24; Levit. xxiv.20; Deut. xix.21.

[17] It has been plausibly argued that Jessica's name derives from the Hebrew Jesca, a form of Iscah, daughter of Haran (Gen. xi.29), glossed by Elizabethean commentators as "she that looketh out" (Gollancz, p. 42, G. L. Kittredge ed., *Merchant of Venice,* Ginn, 1945, p. ix). A direct play upon this name seems to occur in II. v.31–32, where Shylock directs Jessica, "Clamber not you up to the casements then / Nor thrust your head into the public street", and Launcelot prompts her to "look out at window for all this (II.v.40) to see Lorenzo. Her departure thus signifies a breaking out of the ghetto, a voluntary abandonment of Old Law for New. This significance is continued in III.v.1–5, when Launcelot quips that Jessica will be damned since (according to Mosaic Law, Exod. xx.5) the "sins of the father are to be laid upon the children," and she replies (ll. 17–18), "I shall be sav'd by my husband"—reecting Paul's promise in the New Law, I Cor. vii.14, "the unbeleeving wife is sanctified by the husband". Shylock's name is probably taken from Shalach, translated by "cormorant" (Levit. xi.17, Deut. xiv.17)—an epithet often applied to usurers in Elizabethean English. The name "Tubal", taken from Tubal Cain (Gen. x.2, 6) is glossed in Elizabethan Bibles as meaning "worldly possessions, a bird's nest of the world" (Gollancz, pp. 40–41; Kittredge, p. ix).

[18] See Richard Hooker's paraphrase of this prophecy, *Of the Laws of Ecclesiastical Polity* Bk. V, Appen. I, *Works,* ed. John Keble (Oxford, 1845), II, 587–588.

[19] Italics mine.

[20] *Shakespeare Studies,* pp. 270–271.

[21] Cambridge, 1605, p. 410.

[22] See Psalms 103, 136, 143. With reference to such passages, Henrie Bullinger declares (*Fiftie Godlie and Learned Sermons,* trans. H. I., London, 1587, p. 403), "The ancient Saints which lived under the old

testament, did not seeke for righteousness and salvation in the works of the lawe, but in him which is the perfectnes and ende of the law, even Christ Jesus."

[23] Bishops Bible.

[24] For a resumé of this tradition see Samuel C. Chew, The Virtues Reconciled (Toronto, 147).

[25] "Christmas 1616", XCVI Sermons, 3rd Edn. (London, 1635), p. 104.

[26] See John D. Rea, "Shylock and the Processus Belial", Philological Quarterly, VIII (Oct., 1929), 311–313.

[27] "Christmas 1609", XCVI Sermons, p. 28.

[28] See glossary, Geneva Bible.

[29] The slight variation may be due to imperfect memory: the king whom Daniel served was named Balthasar.

[30] Bishops Bible. A note on this passage declares that it shows how "the godly flee only unto gods mercies and renounce theyr owne workes when they seeke for remission of their sinnes." Cf. Bullinger, Fiftie Sermons, p. 434: "And although they did not so usually call upon God as wee at this day doe, through the mediatour and intercessour Christe Jesus... yet were they not utterly ignorant of the mediatour, for whose sake they were heard of the Lord. Daniel in the ninth Chapter of his prophecie maketh his prayer, and desireth to bee hearde of God for the Lordes sake, that is, for the promised Christ his sake."

[31] James Parkes, The Jew in the Medieval Community (London, 1938), pp. 101–146; Michael Adler, Jews of Medieval England (London, 1939), pp. 280–334; Cecil Roth, A History of the Jews in England (Oxford, 1949), p. 96.

[32] Summa Theologica, II.I. Ques. 98. Art. 2, in Basic Writings, ed. Anton Pegis (N. Y., 1944), p. 809.

[33] A Commentarie of M. Doctor Martin Luther upon the Epistle of S. Paul to the Galathians (London, Thomas Vautroullier, 1575), n.p.

[34] Institutes of the Christian Religion, II, Chap. 7, trans. John Allen (Philadelphia, Pa., 1936), I, 388.

[35] "The Old Faith", trans. by Myles Coverdale from H. Bullinger. 1547, Writings and Translations, ed. George Pearson (Cambridge, 1844), pp. 42–43.

[36] A Commentarie, or Exposition upon the first five chapters of the Epistle to Galatians (London, 1617), p. 200. See also, John Donne, Sermon 17, Sermons, ed. E. Simpson and G. Potter, VI (Berkeley, Calif., 1953), 334–345; John Colet, An Exposition of St. Paul's Epistle to the Romans, 1497, trans. J. H. Lupton (London, 1873), pp. 1–18.

Alan C. Dessen

THE ELIZABETHAN
STAGE JEW AND
CHRISTIAN EXAMPLE

There will be no final solution to the Shylock problem. Learned journals will continue to publish articles invoking Elizabethan attitudes toward Jews and the distinction between the Old Law and the New Law. Meanwhile, no amount of contextual information (or even evidence in the text) will prevent actors and directors from presenting *The Merchant of Venice* as "The Tragedy of Shylock," the story of a persecuted Jew in a Christian society. Teachers, students, and general readers, often torn between their instinctive responses and what they are told to believe, will continue to be disturbed by Shakespeare's apparent lapse in tolerance. After all, they will ask, how could a poet not of an age but for all time create such a narrow, inhumane, Jewish villain? In spite of the efforts of many astute critics, no Moses will appear to lead the modern reader or theatergoer to that promised land where *The Merchant of Venice* will fit comfortably with the post–World War II sensibility.

There are many reasons, both obvious and subtle, for this discomfort. On the simplest level, Shakespeare, unlike Dickens, has had no opportunity to answer the charges leveled against him, either by a direct statement (like Dickens's letter to Eliza Davis) or through a favorably depicted character in a later work (such as Mr. Riah in *Our Mutual Friend*).[1] The creator of Aaron, Richard of Gloucester, and Iago, moreover, probably had his own distinctive view of villainy and evil and may not have shared our need for clear "motivation." Thus, in at least two productions I have seen, directors have sought to make Shylock's vindictive posture in Act IV more understandable for the audience by presenting it as a reaction to Jessica's elopement. But Shakespeare has forestalled such an interpretation (which might satisfy our sense of psychological progression) by including passages which show decisively that the Jew's animosity toward Antonio antedates the bond of flesh (e.g., Shylock's long aside in I.iii.36–47 and Jessica's comment in III.ii.283–89). Furthermore, Shakespeare (like Dickens) might wonder why a villain who happens to be

From *Modern Language Quarterly* 35, No. 3 (September 1974): 231–45.

a Jew should elicit such discomfort or angry responses while other villains who happen to be Moors or English kings or Italian ancients are deemed acceptable. Indeed, one *could* argue in the defense of the author that contemporary reactions to *The Merchant of Venice* tell us more about ourselves than about the comedy.

My purpose here is neither to minimize the problem facing the modern reader nor to offer another neat solution. The problem is a real one, with roots in our cultural assumptions that differ sharply from those of the Elizabethans, and no such solution exists. Rather I hope to shed some light on Shylock and his play by slightly changing the question being considered and then (with apologies) advancing some more contextual information. Thus, if we can assume that Shylock *is* a villain like Aaron or Richard III or Iago, the crucial question yet remains: what is the dramatic function of his villainy? Is Shakespeare's presentation of this noteworthy figure an end in itself, a display of despicable Jewish traits for the edification of the audience (a position held implicitly by many who are made uncomfortable by the play)? Or does this display, which obviously does draw upon racial or religious stereotypes, serve some larger purpose that transcends such an easy, limited target? Is Shylock under attack because he is Jewish or is his Jewishness included in this comedy to call attention to its essential themes?

Two studies devoted to the other famous stage Jew of the 1590s offer some help in answering such questions. Thus, G. K. Hunter has demonstrated that "symbolic Jewishness," as understood by the sixteenth century, had little to do with race or theology but corresponded to a state of mind or set of values to be found in Christian society. Citing George Herbert's "Self-Condemnation," Hunter observes that

> Herbert is at one with a long patristic tradition in seeing Jewishness as a moral condition, the climactic 'Jewish choice' being that which rejected Christ and chose Barabbas, rejected the Saviour and chose the robber, rejected the spirit and chose the flesh, rejected the treasure that is in heaven and chose the treasure that is on earth. . . .[2]

Similarly, Douglas Cole argues that the evil in Marlowe's Barabas lies in "his 'Jewishness'—Jewishness understood partly in the literal or racial sense, but more pervasively in the figurative sense, the sense that evokes a spiritual condition characterized by lack of faith and love." Cole points out that the epithets "Jew" and "Turk" were "applied not only to opponents of Christianity but also to those Christians who acted as the non-Christian was imagined to behave, especially in manifestations of infidelity, usury, and greed."[3] For example, in *The Wonder of a Kingdom* Dekker can describe a Christian pawnbroker, who has destroyed a family through his wiles, as a "christian Iew" (IV.ii.55).[4]

One particularly suggestive passage has not, to my knowledge, been cited in this context. So Princess Elizabeth in 1556, when informed of various plots in her behalf, wrote to her sister the queen:

When I revolve in mind (most noble Queen) the old love of pagans to their princes, and the reverent fear of the Romans to their senate, I cannot but muse for my part, and blush for theirs, to see the rebellious hearts and devilish intents of Christians in name, but Jews in deed, towards their anointed King. . . .[5]

The key phrase—"Christians in name, but Jews in deed"—pinpoints that habit of mind which could conceive of Jewishness as a spiritual or moral condition lurking behind the façade of orthodox profession. What might appear to be a racial slur in a modern context can here function as an ethical indictment of false Christians with the Jew invoked as a constant, a symbol of the unchristian qualities cited by Hunter and Cole.

It would seem but a short step from this formulation to the dramatic presentation of both Jewish and non-Jewish figures who, whatever their professed faith, share the same values. Few Elizabethan plays, however, take this step; rather, the typical brief appearance of the stage Jew employs his legendary or grotesque attributes in a simplistic way to depict total villainy. Thus, in *The Tragical Reign of Selimus* (1592) the "cunning Iew," Abraham, is brought on stage twice as an expert poisoner, "a man so stout and resolute, / That he will venture any thing for gold";[6] later plays, like *The Travels of the Three English Brothers* (1607), provide similar examples of minor Jewish villains. We can only speculate about the lost play, *The Jew*, mentioned by Gosson in 1579, which represented "the greedinesse of worldly chusers, and bloody mindes of usurers";[7] the obvious Jew (the bloody-minded usurer) need not have been the only such worldly chooser in a play concerned with "Jewish" values in Christian society. Many of the morality plays of the 1560s and 1570s were, like *The Jew*, concerned with the impact of materialistic values upon Christian society. To set up their dramatic sermons, however, such moral dramatists apparently did not resort to the stage Jew but instead brought on stage obvious ethical alternatives embodied in contrasting figures like Worldly Man and Heavenly Man (*Enough Is as Good as a Feast*) or Lust and Just (*Trial of Treasure*). In *All for Money* (1577), Thomas Lupton displays Judas, Dives, and a host of venal figures but no designated stage Jew. At the end of George Wapull's *The Tide Tarrieth No Man* (1576), Faithful Few tells the audience:

For better it were vnchristened to be,
Then our Christianity for to abuse:
The Iewish Infidell to God doth more agree,
Then such as Christianity do so misuse.[8]

Throughout much of this play a figure named Christianity is forced to bear the "titles" of Riches and Policy owing to the worldly values of nominally Christian figures like Greediness the usurer. Although there is no evidence that Greediness was portrayed as a stage Jew, he is a worldly chooser whose values allegorically undermine Christianity, a figure less pleasing to God (according to Faithful Few) than the "Iewish Infidell."

At least three extant Elizabethan plays, however, *do* use the obvious stage Jew to indict false Christians. The earliest and simplest example is Robert Wilson's *Three Ladies of London* (1581),[9] a morality play which follows by only a few years *The Jew* mentioned by Gosson. At the heart of this allegorical analysis of contemporary society are the rise to power of Lady Lucre and the resulting subjection of Lady Love and Lady Conscience. The only scenes not set in London involve Mercadorus, a merchant who worships Lucre, and Gerontus, a Jewish money-lender. At their first meeting, when the merchant postpones payment of a long-standing debt, Gerontus observes that if Jews should deal so with each other, no one would trust them, yet "many of you Christians make no conscience to falsifie your fayth and breake your day" (D3^V). When Mercadorus is brought to trial in Turkey for his debt, the judge cites the law which provides that all debts will be canceled for any man who forsakes his faith, king, and country to worship Mahomet. Gerontus the Jew is horrified when the merchant starts to take such an oath and, after offering increasingly better terms, finally cancels the debt entirely; Wilson's Jew would rather lose the money than have others charge that, because of his insistence, a Christian was forced to renounce his faith. When Mercadorus then announces that he will not forsake Christ "for all da good in da world," the Turkish judge (as neutral observer) provides the obvious moralization: "One may iudge and speake truth, as appeeres by this, / Iewes seeke to excell in Christianitie, and Christians in Iewisnes" (FI^r). In this simple dramatic lesson, Wilson uses his stage Jew to indict a Christian (in name) corrupted by the worship of Lucre. Through the heavy-handed paradoxes,"Jewishness" and "Christianity" are shown to be values not limited to racial or ethnic groups but determined by deeds.

Marlowe's Malta is many leagues from Wilson's London, yet his use of the stage Jew sets up an analogous indictment of a Christian society. Thus, at the outset of the play Barabas states openly that he would rather be hated as a rich Jew than pitied as a poor Christian; commenting sardonically upon Maltese hypocrisy, he observes: "For I can see no fruits in all their faith, / But malice, falsehood, and excessive pride, / Which methinks fits not their profession" (I.i.114–16).[10] In the following scene Marlowe reinforces this critique by placing the Elizabethan audience in the awkward position of watching a stage Jew (with his red wig and bottle-nose) ironically achieve moral stature at the expense of Ferneze and his Christian supporters. Thus, the moral posturing of the Maltese spokesmen (e.g., "Excess of wealth is cause of covetousness, / And covetousness, O, 'tis a monstrous sin" [I.ii.123–24]) and the ironically revealing echoes of the Gospels ("And better one want for a common good, / Than many perish for a private man" [98–99]) are played off against Barabas's apt rejoinders (e.g., "Will you then steal my goods? / Is theft the ground of your religion?" [94–95]). Here in the second scene, before the many horrors that follow, Barabas *is* more sinned against than sinning. Our first exposure to Maltese society thereby supports the Jew's critique that the reality ("malice, falsehood, and excessive pride") belies Christian "profession."

Nor does Marlowe give us much opportunity to upgrade our estimate of Christian Malta. A few scenes later, Del Bosco persuades Ferneze to break his treaty with the Turks because "Honor is bought with blood and not with gold" (II.ii.56). There is no mention, however, of returning the money extorted from the Jews. The reference to honor, blood, and gold is soon followed by the setting up of the slave market, an institution that could not have existed if the treaty had been kept (II.ii.21–23). Each slave's price, we are told, "is written on his back" (II.iii.3), a situation that also applies to many of the Christians in the play who can be manipulated once their price is known. By the end of Act II, we can at least understand Barabas's argument that "it's no sin to deceive a Christian" (II.iii.310), for, in practice, he is merely following Christian example. Again, the best Christian to be found in the play is a converted Jew, Abigail. But her dying request ("Convert my father, that he may be sav'd, / And witness that I die a Christian") only elicits the friar's sardonic rejoinder: "Ay, and a virgin, too; that grieves me most" (III.vi.39–41). In spite of the crescendo of horrors associated with Jew and Turk that begins in Act III, Marlowe is leaving us with no firm sense of a true Christian alternative in Malta.

Marlowe's most provocative use of his stage Jew occurs in IV.i, a scene which epitomizes the distinctive dramatic flavor of this play. After Abigail learns the circumstances of her lover's death, she determines to become a Christian because "there is no love on earth, / Pity in Jews, nor piety in Turks" (III.iii.47–48). The failure of this alternative (for Abigail and for Malta) is demonstrated by the revealing interaction between the two visual symbols of Maltese Christianity, Friar Jacomo and Friar Barnardine. When the two friars confront Barabas with his role in the deaths of Mathias and Lodowick, the Jew takes advantage of the price written on their backs. Posing as a repentant sinner ("I am a Jew, and therefore am I lost"), he asks: "Is 't not too late now to turn Christian?" (IV.i.56, 49). After tantalizing the friars with an elaborate catalogue of his wealth, Barabas concludes: "All this I'll give to some religious house, / So I may be baptiz'd and live therein" (74–75). The subsequent competition between the two friars is both intense and petty: "O, Barabas, their laws are strict. . . . They wear no shirts, and they go barefoot, too" (81–83). Such a dangling of wealth before the eyes of these two representatives of Christianity has suddenly blotted out all memory of the Jew's involvement in the deaths of two young men and has made a mockery of the vows of poverty supposedly basic to a friar's profession. The subsequent skirmish between Jacomo and Barnardine is but the first indication of the effect of that monstrous sin, covetousness. Ironically, the Christian ideal of giving up all worldly goods to a religious house in order to pursue one's salvation is here placed in the mouth of a Machiavellian Jew who uses that profession to subvert the two obvious symbols of Christianity. Something is rotten in the state of Malta.

The most revealing insights into spiritual values in Malta are yet to come. The Jew and the Turk, who (as Abigail noted) lack any semblance of pity or piety, have no difficulty strangling the sleeping Friar Barnardine (an act that not only demonstrates the villainy of the murderers but also symbolizes the lack of force in Maltese Christianity which, in its own way, is sleeping if not defunct). A moment later the murderous attack is acted out again, but this time the audience is offered the stage spectacle of a friar attacked not by the obvious infidels but by a fellow Christian, Friar Jacomo. Although perhaps unrealistic from our modern vantage point, this dramatic duplication acts out a second and more insidious threat—not from the grotesque outsiders but from forces within Malta, from the "Jewish" or "infidel" values shared by the Christians who duplicate the villainy of the Jew and the Turk.

Marlowe spares no opportunity to drive home his sardonic point. Once Friar Jacomo has been apprehended for the "murder," both Jew and Turk moralize about such crimes:

> ITHAMORE: Fie upon 'em! Master, will you turn Christian, when
>   holy friars turn devils and murder one another?
> BARABAS: No, for this example I'll remain a Jew.
> Heaven bless me! what, a friar a murderer?
> When shall we see a Jew commit the like?
> ITHAMORE: Why, a Turk could ha' done no more.   (IV.i.189–94)

Here Marlowe with characteristic irony points to the failure of Maltese Christianity to provide a positive alternative to Barabas's Jewishness. That Barabas and Ithamore, not Friar Jacomo, are the true murderers is only a matter of timing. Why then should infidels "turn Christian" if the Christian model held up for emulation is of such dubious value? What fruits *are* to be found in Maltese faith, especially if holy friars can turn devils? Jacomo's dilemma in no way exonerates Barabas or makes the Jew's crimes palatable. Rather, Marlowe is stressing the essential similarity between the acknowledged Jew and the "Jewish" Christian who prides himself upon his assumed superiority. As Barabas puts it later in the play at the peak of his success: "This is the life we Jews are us'd to lead; / And reason, too, for Christians do the like" (V.ii.115–16). Throughout the play Barabas can justify his way of life in this sardonic fashion by appealing to Christian example. "Jewish" values—in both infidel *and* orthodox—are destroying sleeping Christianity in Malta.

The Maltese Christians, of course, see no such relationship between their values and Barabas' Jewishness. Rather, in another curious scene they heave the Jew's apparently dead body over a wall, thereby (they assume) ridding themselves forever of this enemy within. But in near-allegorical fashion Barabas rises from his "death" to lead the Turks into Malta. Ferneze's naïve account of the downfall of the Jew and his cohorts ("the heavens are just: / Their deaths were like their lives; then think not of 'em" [V.i.55–56]) is not very encouraging, for what Barabas stands for will not be eliminated that easily. As the fate of the two friars has shown, Jewishness cannot be purged from Malta until a true Christian example is available, an example not to be found in murders or broken treaties or slave markets or pat assumptions about moral superiority and heavenly justice.

Barabas's subsequent fall into a trap of his own making is a fitting end for such a lurid stage villain. But Ferneze's acceptance of "a Jew's courtesy" or treason (V.v.107–109) says little for Maltese moral superiority, while the governor's final words ("let due praise be given / Neither to fate nor fortune, but to heaven"

[122–23]) sound a hollow note for an audience well aware that Christian success at the end of this play is based upon superiority in treachery. Where then is the answer to Barabas's series of challenges to Christian Malta ranging from the soliloquy of I.i to the gibes of IV.i? The obviously villainous stage Jew has gone to his deserved end, but the Christians who have survived have learned little if anything from the events of the play. The cauldron, that self-constructed trap with hellish overtones,[11] awaits them as well. Without resorting to the simplistic moral extremes of *The Tide Tarrieth No Man* or *The Three Ladies of London,* Marlowe has used his stage Jew to indict a society which is truly Christian in name but not in deed.

The Merchant of Venice, in contrast, is a romantic comedy, not a sardonic tragedy, so Shakespeare's presentation of his stage Jew is somewhat different in tone and over-all effect. Nonetheless, in the middle of the play at the end of his best-known speech, Shylock throws down a challenge to Christian Venice quite similar to Barabas's indictment of Christian Malta:

> if you prick us do we not bleed? if you tickle us do we not laugh? if you poison us do we not die? and if you wrong us shall we not revenge?—if we are like you in the rest, we will resemble you in that. If a Jew wrong a Christian, what is his humility? revenge! If a Christian wrong a Jew, what should his sufferance be by Christian example?—why revenge! The villainy you teach me I will execute, and it shall go hard but I will better the instruction. (III.i.58–66)[12]

Barabas, we should remember, had justified his villainy by arguing that "Christians do the like." Here Shylock, in similar fashion, defends his pursuit of Antonio's pound of flesh by appealing to "Christian example." According to this argument, the villainy about to be executed by the Jew has been taught him by vengeful Christians who in their practice show little humility or sufferance. Shylock's promise to "better the instruction" is therefore the statement not only of a stage villain but also of a good student who has mastered his lesson.

Faced with such an indictment at the beginning of Act III, an audience would think back to the "Christian example" to be found in the first two acts. Admittedly, there is no precise equivalent in this play for Ferneze's hypocrisy in I.ii or the Maltese breaking of faith with both Jews and Turks, but in terms suitable to a romantic comedy Shakespeare has provided analogous evidence. Thus, although Antonio exhibits a selfless love for Bassanio ("I think he only loves the world for him" [II.viii.50]), that merchant is also characterized by his intense loathing for Shylock, an unchristian passion which is described at length by the Jew (I.iii.101–24) and reaffirmed by Antonio ("I am as like to call thee so again, / To spet on thee again, to spurn thee too" [125–26]). Launcelot Gobbo's decision to leave Shylock, in which he chooses the devil ("Budge!") over his conscience ("Budge not!" [II.ii.18–19]), provides another negative example, albeit in low comic terms, while the clown also contributes a comically confused account of the Christian source of Jessica's virtues ("if a Christian [did][13] not play the knave and get thee, I am much deceived" [II.iii.11–12]). The misguided choices by Morocco and Arragon of the gold and silver caskets provide striking negative examples of false or confused values. Perhaps most revealing is the Venetian casket scene (II.vi) in which Jessica throws down to the waiting Lorenzo some of her father's treasure and goes off to "gild myself / With some moe ducats" (49–50). Gratiano's reaction to Jessica's behavior—"Now (by my hood) a gentle, and no Jew" (51)—suggests that for at least one character "Christian example" can include theft, elopement, and betrayal so long as a Christian profits. As with Antonio, Launcelot, Morocco, and Arragon, such confused thinking often lurks beneath the surface of Christian profession in this play. Thus, Shylock's indictment at the beginning of Act III cannot be easily dismissed.

Since Shakespeare's play *is* a comedy, this challenge to Christian society does not remain unanswered. In the next scene, in fact, Bassanio chooses the leaden casket, thereby demonstrating his willingness to venture all he has in a love that transcends gain and possession. Moreover, when the news of Antonio's plight reaches Belmont, both Bassanio and Portia forgo their own personal fulfillment to aid a friend and benefactor. Nonetheless, at the start of the famous trial scene Shylock can still forcefully attack the hypocrisy of Christian Venice, this time using as evidence the institution of slavery:

> You have among you many a purchas'd slave,
> Which (like your asses, and your dogs and mules)
> You use in abject and in slavish parts,
> Because you bought them,—shall I say to you,
> Let them be free, marry them to your heirs?
> Why sweat they under burthens? let their beds
> Be made as soft as yours, and let their palates
> Be season'd with such viands? you will answer
> "The slaves are ours,"—so do I answer you:
> The pound of flesh (which I demand of him)
> Is dearly bought, 'tis mine and I will have it:
> If you deny me, fie upon your law!
> There is no force in the decrees of Venice:
> I stand for judgment,—answer, shall I have it?   (IV.i.90–103)

As in Marlowe's II.iii, Shakespeare uses slavery to call attention to the gap between Christian profession and Christian practice, especially by having Shylock apply such terms as "ours," "mine," and "dearly bought" to human beings or human flesh. After listening to this blunt account of the slavery practiced in Venice, we do not condone Shylock's vindictive treatment of Antonio but we *are* made aware of "Jewish" values in a supposedly Christian society. In his possessive attitude toward his enemy's flesh, this stage Jew is bettering the instruction provided by the Venetians while calling attention to Christians in name but not in deed on and off stage.

Although Portia's legalistic maneuvers soon turn the tables on Shylock, this reversal offers no real answer or alternative example. As many readers have noted, Portia merely out-shylocks the Jew, meeting and defeating him on his own terms.

In her famous speech she has argued that mercy was the most admirable of human qualities, "an attribute to God himself" (191). Since thus far in the play there has been little evidence of such tolerance or forgiveness, Shylock's refusal to show mercy was consistent with his claim of following Christian example. Now Shakespeare reverses the situation, so that the Jew is suddenly subjected to the justice or mercy of Christian society. With the tables turned, the audience can note what kind of example will be set by the Christians who profess to believe in the New Law of Christ, not the Old Law of strict justice. Will the Venetians live up to Portia's ideal of mercy or will they prove to be Jews in deed?

The answers that Shakespeare provides to such questions deserve our attention. First, the Duke announces:

> That thou shalt see the difference of our spirit
> I pardon thee thy life before thou ask it:
> For half thy wealth, it is Antonio's,
> The other half comes to the general state,
> Which humbleness may drive unto a fine.   (364–68)

Shylock is thereby penalized financially (for him, a serious penalty, tantamount to death [370–73]) but is granted his life, in striking contrast to the Jew's treatment of Antonio. The Duke's initial judgment thus combines retribution and mercy in a manner not accounted for in Shylock's indictment.

Antonio too betters the instruction provided by Shylock. When Portia asks, "What mercy can you render him Antonio?" (374), the merchant asks the Duke and court "to quit the fine for one half of his goods" (thereby giving back to the Jew "the prop / That doth sustain my house") but only on several conditions, most notably "that for this favour / He presently become a Christian" (376–86). In spite of innumerable scholarly explanations based upon Elizabethan evidence (including the dying words of Marlowe's Abigail—"Convert my father, that he may be sav'd"), this enforced conversion consistently offends modern readers and playgoers and will continue to do so. Nowhere in the play is the cultural distance between us and the 1590s more apparent. But in fairness to both Antonio and Shakespeare, note what the merchant has done. Like the Duke, he has given back to Shylock something which had been forfeited according to the strict letter of the law (his life, his wealth). Although moments earlier Antonio had been helpless before Shylock's knife (and therefore could easily harbor a desire for revenge), he responds not in kind but in the spirit of Portia's lesson. The Jew's earlier argument ("if you wrong us shall we not revenge?—if we are like you in the rest, we will resemble you in that") has been answered in deed, even though the modern sensibility may not be fully satisfied with that answer.

The Christian example set by the Duke and Antonio, however qualified, is heightened by a third set of reactions to Shylock's new situation. Thus, in response to Portia's question directed at Antonio, Gratiano interjects: "A halter gratis, nothing else for Godsake!" (375). Earlier, before the Duke had granted the pardon, Gratiano had instructed Shylock:

> Beg that thou may'st have leave to hang thyself,—
> And yet thy wealth being forfeit to the state,
> Thou hast not left the value of a cord,
> Therefore thou must be hang'd at the state's charge.   (360–63)

As Shylock leaves the stage, Gratiano states: "In christ'ning shalt thou have two godfathers.— / Had I been judge, thou shouldst have had ten more, / To bring thee to the gallows, not to the font" (394–96). Clearly there is little difference between Shylock's attitude toward Antonio and Gratiano's attitude toward Shylock. Shakespeare, in effect, provides us with a "Jewish" Christian or a Christian Shylock, a figure who has learned little from Portia's speech on mercy or from Antonio's subjection to the bond of flesh. In his vindictiveness, Gratiano (who earlier for dubious reasons had deemed Jessica "a gentle, and no Jew") calls attention to the persistence of values previously identified with Shylock and serves as a foil to set off the Christian example provided by the Duke and Antonio.

These three reactions to Shylock in his new role as a figure vulnerable to the law have too often been neglected. Even though modern audiences troubled by Shylock's fate will not let the actions of the Duke and Antonio pass without challenge, this disposal of the Jew's life and goods does reaffirm the higher values of this comedy. At least some of the figures on stage have listened and learned. In similar fashion, Portia's twitting of Bassanio about the ring in Act V sets up an analogous situation in which mercy and understanding are again pitted against the strict letter of the law. Even though the two husbands may be technically guilty of violating the troths sworn on the rings, both are forgiven in a Belmont characterized by moonlight and harmony, not by profit and retributive justice. In a deft, light-hearted fashion, this comedic ending offers one last demonstration of that forgiveness and understanding rarely found early in the play. Both Act IV and Act V thereby provide Christians in deed to offset the less than Christian example associated with a wide range of figures typified by but not limited to Shylock.

What then are we to conclude about the stage Jew as presented by Wilson, Marlowe, and Shakespeare? Although initially the three plays seem to have little in common, in each the same distinctive stage figure has served a comparable function—not merely to vilify Jews and Judaism but to challenge the professions of supposedly Christian London or Malta or Venice. Indeed, with the proper allowances, there is an interesting continuity from Wilson's "Iewes seeke to excell in Christianitie, and Christians in Iewisnes" to Barabas's "This is the life we Jews are us'd to lead; / And reason, too, for Christians do the like" to Shylock's "The villiany you teach me I will execute, and it shall go hard but I will better the instruction." In the morality play, the episodes involving Gerontus and Mercadorus provide a didactic *exemplum* which functions as one part of a full-scale attack upon materialistic London. In his sardonic tragedy, Marlowe makes more extensive use of his villainous Jew but his emphasis is the same—the failure of a Christian society to live up to its professed ideals. Of the three examples, Shakespeare's comedy is the only one to provide a positive, accessible Christian alternative, even though Gratiano, for one, fails to appreciate it. Significantly, in all three instances there *is* a common denominator, for Wilson, Marlowe, and Shakespeare all use this conventional figure as a means to a larger end, whether that end be moralistic, ironic, or comedic.

By viewing Gerontus, Barabas, and Shylock as dramatic kinsmen, the modern reader can grasp the convention that stands behind them and informs them. In morality play, tragedy, or comedy, the stage Jew could function as a dramatic scalpel with which the Elizabethan dramatist could anatomize the inner reality of a society Christian in name but not necessarily in deed. The fact remains that Shakespeare *did* choose as his villain what seems to us an objectionable stereotype, but by recognizing the stage Jew as a potential theatrical device (and not a direct expression of authorial bigotry) we may be able to sidestep Shakespeare's alleged anti-Semitism and instead appreciate the artistry with which he has incorporated such a stock figure into the world of romantic comedy. Admittedly, recourse to dramatic conventions and to Elizabethan concepts of symbolic Jewishness will be of dubious value to a director at a Shakespeare festival; but readers may find some reassurance in the knowledge that Marlowe and Shakespeare, although perhaps building upon Elizabethan prejudices, were still using the stage Jew as a potent dramatic weapon against Christian hypocrisy and complacency. Perhaps then another reason for the discomfort caused by Shylock is our unconscious awareness of our own failure to answer his challenge. If so, we may have one more example of how, for Shakespeare, the play's the thing to catch the conscience of his audience.

NOTES

[1] For an account of the correspondence with Mrs. Davis and the relevant passages in *Our Mutual Friend*, see Edgar Johnson, *Charles Dickens: His Tragedy and Triumph* (New York, 1952), II, 1010–12.

[2] "The Theology of Marlowe's *The Jew of Malta*," *Journal of the Warburg and Cartauld Institutes*, 27 (1964), 214.

[3] *Suffering and Evil in the Plays of Christopher Marlowe* (Princeton, 1962), p. 132.

[4] See *The Dramatic Works of Thomas Dekker*, ed. Fredson Bowers, III (Cambridge, 1958), 621, and Jacob Lopes Cardozo, *The Contemporary Jew in the Elizabethan Drama* (Amsterdam, 1925), p. 116.

[5] *The Letters of Queen Elizabeth*, ed. G. B. Harrison (London, 1935), p. 22.

[6] Edited for the Malone Society by W. Bang and W. W. Greg (London, 1908), lines 1684–88. Dates attached to this and subsequent plays are drawn from Alfred Harbage, *Annals of English Drama, 975–1700*, rev. S. Schoenbaum (London, 1964).

[7] *The School of Abuse*, reprinted for the Shakespeare Society (London, 1841), p. 30. Hermann Sinsheimer uses the German manuscript of *The Jew of Venice* (apparently a version of a play performed by English actors on the Continent) as the basis for some interesting speculations about *The Jew*. See *Shylock: The History of a Character* (New York, 1963), pp. 58–61.

[8] Ed. Ernst Rühl, *Shakespeare-Jahrbuch*, 43 (1907), lines 1852–55.

[9] Edited for the Tudor Facsimile Texts by John S. Farmer (1911).

[10] *The Jew of Malta*, ed. Richard W. Van Fossen, RRDS (Lincoln, Nebr., 1964). Throughout my discussion I am indebted to the Cole and Hunter essays already cited and to Eric Rothstein, "Structure as Meaning

in *The Jew of Malta," Journal of English and Germanic Philology*, 65 (1966), 260–73, and David M. Bevington, *From "Mankind" to Marlowe* (Cambridge, Mass., 1962), pp. 218–33.

[11] For a valuable discussion of the cauldron and hell, see Hunter, pp. 233–35.

[12] Citations are from the New Arden edition, ed. John Russell Brown (London, 1955). *The Merchant of Venice* in general and Shylock in particular have elicited an enormous response from critics, historians, and apologists, a wealth of material to which I am greatly indebted. The many studies of the Jew in Elizabethan literature (e.g., the works by Cardozo and Sinsheimer cited above) often do link Shylock to Gerontus and Barabas but, on the other hand, do not deal with symbolic Jewishness and dramatic convention in the manner of this essay. Similarly, some of the many essays and chapters on Shylock, the trial scene, and the larger issues of this comedy do advance arguments similar to my analysis but none, to my knowledge, deals with such issues and events (especially the reactions of the Duke, Antonio, and Gratiano after the reversal in IV.i) within the context or framework established here. In general terms, I would like to acknowledge a particular debt to Brown's edition and to J. W. Lever, "Shylock, Portia and the Values of Shakespearian Comedy," *Shakespeare Quarterly*, 3 (1952), 383–86, and Barbara K. Lewalski, "Biblical Allusion and Allegory in *The Merchant of Venice," Shakespeare Quarterly*, 13 (1962), 327–43.

[13] I use F2's "did" rather than Q's or F1's "do" because I take "get" of line 12 to mean "beget." For me, this reading is confirmed by Launcelot's expansion of this passing comment in III.v.1–16. For the alternate argument, see Brown's note on p. 46.

Lawrence Danson
THE PROBLEM OF SHYLOCK

Launcelot Gobbo's debate between his conscience and the fiend (2.2.1–30) may be in our minds as we try to come to terms with the question of Shylock. It sometimes seems that all our conclusions on the subject must turn to "confusions" faced with the mystery of Shylock's dramatic creation. In Launcelot's debate "the fiend gives the more friendly counsel" to run from the Jew; while "conscience is but a kind of hard conscience" to bid him stay with his intractable master. The temptation to put one's heels at the fiend's commandment and run from the problem is strong.

In some ways we are better off than earlier generations, but in others worse, in the effort to see Shylock steadily and to see him whole. Behind us is the work of scholars, who have given us perspective on Elizabethan attitudes toward Jews and usury, on problems of literary genetics, source-influence, conventions of characterization and dramatic construction. But behind us also is Hitler. And with us constantly are our own convictions about religion and humanity—convictions we will not lightly jettison even in the name of supposedly objective fact. Shylock bedevils the characters of the play, but he also bedevils our efforts as readers, audience, actors, or critics.

In modern times those efforts have generally taken one of two different directions—so different that their implications for the play's overall interpretation lead to the situation I mentioned in the Introduction to this book, the two-faced Janus of the present state of critical understanding. One direction is toward Shylock's social redemption, the idea of him as a potentially good man twisted by malignant social and religious prejudice. This approach to Shylock leads, of course, to the view (to simplify it only somewhat) that *The Merchant of Venice* is a deeply ironic play about hypocritical Christians. The other direction, frequently taken in the name of historical accuracy, dismisses as mere sentimentality any efforts toward

From *The Harmonies of* The Merchant of Venice (New Haven: Yale University Press, 1978), pp. 126–69.

Shylock's justification. In this view *The Merchant of Venice* is a typical romantic comedy, which only by historical accident has a Jew occupying the position otherwise filled by (say) a killjoy steward.

Among Shylock's defenders two tendencies seem most significant: the sociological, which exonerates Shylock on the basis of environmental pressures, and the racial, which assimilates him to the whole appalling history of anti-Semitism. In practice the two tendencies are closely related, in spite of a potential conflict between them: the first arises from a "realistic" bias, while the latter generalizes from the particular in the manner of allegory. The sociologically-redeemed Shylock must be a figure of considerable individualism and psychological depth, capable (as he is, for instance, in Harold C. Goddard's description of him) of exhibiting those unconscious motivations produced by environmental pressures: "It is clear that he had it in him, however deep down, to be humane, kindly, and patient, and his offer to Antonio of a loan without interest seems to have been a supreme effort of this submerged Shylock to come to the surface."[1] One can disagree with details of this description—whether, say, Shylock's offer of the loan was ever intended as anything but a trap—without, however, disagreeing with what basically it implies about Shylock's mode of characterization. The discovery of "submerged" psychological depths in Shylock is testimony to the extraordinary degree of "felt life" that generations of critics, actors, and audiences have found in him.

The curious thing is how easily this realistic, individualizing notion of characterization can coexist with the notion that Shylock is, in the actor Henry Irving's words, the "representative of a race." Shylock proves, according to John Palmer, that Shakespeare "realised in imagination what it means to wear the star of David."[2] Of course no racial slur is intended in these formulations—though a Jew may feel that with such friends he doesn't need enemies. We can put aside for the moment our own sense of "what it means to wear the star of David" and appreciate the source, in Shakespeare's method of characterization, for this tendency to see a generalized or representative figure in Shylock. In the two tendencies I am describing we have, in effect, both the beginning and the end of Shylock's own self-defining (although theologically and morally misleading) utterance, both his "*I am*" and his "a *Jew*."

This extraordinary doubleness of characterization, which allows Shakespeare's creations to be deeply individualized while simultaneously and (at their best) without strain representative or typical, is one of the certifiable Shakespearean miracles—as well as one of the greatest difficulties for his critics. In his discursive mode the critic must separate, or even worse, choose between, modes and purposes which in Shakespeare's medium are held in easy combination. The combination—and the deceptive ease of it—can be seen even in the names he gives his characters: the same figure can be called either "Shylock" or "the Jew," "Antonio" or "the Merchant" without our feeling that the character is being called on, in the different instances, to perform different dramatic functions. The ease with which, when it is to the purpose, the generic can substitute for the personal is a distinctive mark of Shakespearean dramaturgy: Lear or the King, Hal or the Prince, Benedick or the Married Man.

It is, as I have said, Shylock's defenders who have, even if unintentionally, most clearly shown this doubleness of characterization. Henry Irving described his great Victorian Shylock as "a representative of a race which generation after generation has been cruelly used, insulted, execrated." To him, Shylock was "the type of a persecuted race; almost the only gentleman in the play and the most ill-used."[3] But, of course, Irving's "representative" and "type" was a theatrical success precisely because he was also intensely realized and individual.

Now it was almost inevitable that the Shylock of the modern stage, being conceived at once as "the type of a persecuted race" and as an individual, should have become a "gentleman" and not a villain. The Elizabethan Shylock was also, perforce, both a type and an individual; but he was not necessarily a gentleman— any more, I will argue, then he was *necessarily* a villain. The question for us is whether Shylock's typifying function justifies exonerating him as an individual, or whether there is not at work in such exoneration a subtle kind of sentimentality. The modern stage director may eschew Victorian theatrical mannerisms and give us, in place of the larger-than-life Shylock, a Jewish businessman of dignified bearing who modestly toys with a penknife during the trial scene; but when this figure makes his final exit to the strains of the Kaddish the same question of sentimentality arises. Does Shylock earn for himself the right, within Shakespeare's play, to be associated with that magnificent prayer, or is the audience being manipulated to respond with an emotion in excess of the facts?

In Heinrich Heine's romantic vision Shylock achieved his apotheosis. Heine's treatment of him draws on both the typical and the individual in the character; but it culminates in so obviously self-indulgent a rhapsody that the entire process is made suspect. On the one hand, "the two chief persons of the drama are so individualized that one might swear they are not the work of a poet's fancy, but real human beings, born of woman." On the other, however, "they are more alive than the ordinary creatures that nature makes": they are immortal. Hence it is that Heine, a "wandering hunter after dreams," while touring Venice, "looked around everywhere on the Rialto to see if [he] could not find Shylock." It was the Day of Atonement, so Heine "determined to seek [his] old acquaintance in the Synagogue":

Although I looked all around the Synagogue, I nowhere discovered the face of Shylock. And yet I felt he must be hidden under one of those white talars, praying more fervently than his fellow-believers, looking up with stormy, nay frantic wildness, to the throne of Jehovah, the hard God-King! I saw him not. But towards evening, when, according to the Jewish faith, the gates of Heaven are shut, and no prayer can then obtain admittance, I heard a voice, with a ripple of tears that were never wept by eyes. It was a sob that could only come from a breast that held in it all the martyrdom which, for eighteen centuries, had been borne by a whole tortured people. It was the death-rattle of a soul sinking down tired at heaven's gates. And I seemed to know the voice, and I felt that I had heard it long ago, when, in utter despair it moaned out, then as now, "Jessica, my girl!"[4]

This was not the only intense experience Heine had on account of *The Merchant of Venice*. He describes seeing the play at Drury Lane, where

> there stood behind me in the box a pale, fair Briton, who at the end of the Fourth Act, fell to weeping passionately, several times exclaiming, "The poor man is wronged!" It was a face of the noblest Grecian style, and the eyes were large and black. I have never been able to forget those large and black eyes that wept for Shylock![5]

Modern theatergoers are discouraged from such public effusions; and critics try, in public, to keep their minds more directly on their work. But the essential emotion behind the pale, fair Briton's cry can still be heard, and coming from the most sophisticated sources. According to Graham Midgley, Shylock "is a stranger, proud of his race and its traditions, strict in his religion, sober rather than miserly in his domestic life, and filled with the idea of the sanctity of the family and family loyalty." It is dislocating to read in a modern critic this description of Shylock as Victorian paterfamilias; and equally disturbing is the fact that Midgley's Venetians would have been at home in Scott Fitzgerald's Princeton:

> Around [Shylock] is the society of Venice, a world of golden youth, richly dressed, accustomed to luxury, to feasting, to masking, of a comparatively easy virtue and of a religious outlook which, though orthodox, hardly strikes one as deep, a society faithful and courteous in its own circle and observing a formal politeness of manner and address, but quite insufferable to those outside its own circle, where Shylock is so obviously placed.[6]

What we see here is one of the chief potential difficulties with efforts to rehabilitate Shylock: not just that they may, through faults of excess, falsify Shakespeare's portrait of the Jew, but that they risk unbalancing all the rest of the play's characters as well.

Hazlitt, commenting on Kean's performance in 1814, put the matter in a way that most succinctly shows the problem: "our sympathies are much oftener with him than with his enemies. He is honest in his vices; they are hypocrites in their virtues."[7] And this reversal of ordinary expectations, which makes "enemies" of the play's Christians and an "honest" man—or as Henry Irving thought, a "gentleman"—of a Jew, is still frequently encountered, both in and out of the theater.

The supposed "moral emptiness" of the Venetians is most resoundingly condemned by Sir Arthur Quiller-Couch (whose phrase I have just quoted) in his introduction to the New Cambridge edition. With the problematic exceptions of Antonio and Shylock, "Q" finds that "every one of the Venetian *dramatis personae* is either a 'waster' or a 'rotter' or both, and cold-hearted at that" (p. xxiii). In this scheme of the play, Antonio becomes "the indolent patron of a circle of wasters, 'born to consume the fruits of this world,' heartless, or at least unheedful, while his life lies in jeopardy through his tender, extravagantly romantic friendship for one of them" (p. xxi).

But Quiller-Couch's sense of fair play is most outraged by Jessica: "bad and disloyal, unfilial, a thief; frivolous, greedy, without any more conscience than a cat and without even a cat's redeeming love of home. Quite without heart, on worse than an animal instinct—pilfering to be carnal—she betrays her father to be a light-of-lucre carefully weighted with her sire's ducats" (p. xx). Quiller-Couch concludes this remarkable tirade by recalling (without acknowledging the source) a famous mimed episode interpolated into the play by Henry Irving: "So Shylock returns from a gay abhorrent banquet to knock on his empty and emptied house." And like Heine's pale Briton, "Q" pronounces, "Shylock is intolerably wronged" (p. xxi).

The wholesale condemnation of the lovers in a Shakespearean comedy is a remarkable situation to encounter. Not even the critical hostility to Bertram in *All's Well That Ends Well* or to Proteus and Valentine in *The Two Gentlemen of Verona* approaches either the vigor or the breadth of the reaction to the Venetians. And this reaction, it should be noted, is solely against the characters and not against the play, as it tends to be with *All's Well* and *Two Gentlemen*. The critical view that condemns Salerio, Solanio, Gratiano, and Nerissa, that proclaims Bassanio a shallow fortune hunter, Antonio an infatuated homosexual, Jessica a worse than catlike cat, and Portia herself a vindictive hypocrite—that critical view simultaneously professes admiration for the play as a whole. The outraged feeling that the poor man is intolerably wronged, while it may attest to the vigor of Shakespeare's characterization, has led to the creation of a tribe of heartless fops where one had expected the cast of a romantic comedy which celebrates harmony and love, human and divine.

If an excess of sympathy for Shylock runs the danger of unbalancing the play, there is danger from the opposite extreme as well. E. E. Stoll, ever the scourge of the critical sentimentalist, is still, half a century after the publication of his *Shakespeare Studies,* the most persuasive voice from that side. Against what one senses is the special-pleading of Shylock's defenders Stoll opposes his brisk commonsense, against their wishful rhetoric his certainty of historical fact:

> Shylock was both money-lender and Jew. In him are embodied two of the deepest and most widely prevalent social antipathies of two thousand years, prevalent still, but in Shakespeare's day sanctioned by the teachings of religion besides. All that was religious in them Shakespeare probably shared like any other easy-going churchman; but all that was popular and of the people was part and parcel of his breath and blood.[8]

I will have occasion to question the accuracy of Stoll's description of contemporary religious teachings. Here one should notice the rigidity of his historical determinism.

If Shakespeare was "of the people," it is implied, then he could not have conceived anything that was not within the ken of that mythical lowest common denominator—leaving us to wonder again who wrote Shakespeare's plays. Surely it makes more sense to assume that Shakespeare was *not* "like any other easy-going churchman"; but rather that in matters of religion, as in matters of dramaturgy, Shakespeare was the exception, examining afresh what to less remarkable minds were the merest axioms.[9]

Stoll's treatment of the "news from Genoa" (3.1.72ff.) is typical of his method with *The Merchant of Venice*, a method that rules out not only sentimentality but sympathy as well. If you find pathos in the loss of Shylock's ring, the turquoise he had of Leah when a bachelor (he "would not have given it for a wilderness of monkeys")—then there (according to Stoll) goes "More Elizabethan fun running to waste!" After all, "the invitation to hilarity … is plain and clear": "Tubal pulls the strings of a puppet already in motion. The situation is thus instinct with comedy, pathos could not possibly live in its midst" (pp. 312, 313, 315). Why not? Because "In comedy … things must be simple and clear-cut; a character which is to prove laughter cannot be kept, like Buridan's ass, in equilibrium, exciting, at the same time, both sympathy and hatred. For the audience will keep its equilibrium too" (p. 319).

The equilibristic trick may not be easy, but the fact is that Shakespeare frequently demands of his audience just that sort of balancing act. There are probably as many audience laughs in *Hamlet* as in *Twelfth Night,* partly because in both plays Shakespeare exhibits "the real state of sublunary nature," in which neither emotions nor the objects which excite them have the simple definition and unity of focus demanded by Stoll. Feste's song at the end of *Twelfth Night* is an exemplary expression of Shakespeare's comic vision, which is anything *but* "simple and clear-cut." The singer's name suggests holiday, but his song—coming at the end of a play which is itself about the end of a holiday—returns us with each chorus to "every day." Its final verse balances vast stretches of time ("A great while ago the world begun") against the brevity of our mortal reach ("our play is done"). The knowledge of "play" coexists with the knowledge of striving, and then that striving itself is subsumed under the idea of pleasure: "But that's all one, our *play* is done, / And we'll *strive* to *please* you every day." And throughout, for every "hey ho" there is the answering sound of "the wind and the rain."

Stoll's no-nonsense approach was no doubt once a welcome relief from the atmosphere of misty puffery in which some Romantics had enveloped Shakespeare. If Stoll now in his turn seems old fashioned, I hope it is because we have learned that respect for historical fact need not lead, as in Stoll's method it frequently did, to esthetic impoverishment. It is useful to know that Shylock shares a dramatic kinship with Pantalone; but if we want purity of comic characterization we should stick with the *commedia dell' arte,* which knows how to keep the audience unconflicted, rather than go to Shakespeare who, on the evidence afforded by the critical responses to *The Merchant of Venice*, abounds in provocative confusions.

Neither the pale Briton's wronged Shylock nor the contentious scholar's comic villain is entirely satisfying. The episode of Leah's turquoise is a perfect case in point: neither a simple judgment for or against Shylock is adequate to it, nor will either laughter or tears—whatever difficulties this may make for actor and audience— express the range of emotional responses it legitimately demands. The brevity of the episode—Tubal tells Shylock that one of Antonio's creditors "showed me a ring that he had of your daughter for a monkey," and Shylock responds, "Out upon her!—thou torturest me Tubal,—it was my turquoise, I had it of Leah when I was a bachelor: I would not have given it for a wilderness of monkeys" (3.1.108–113)— is no argument against its complexity. The new information it gives us can not help but modify our response to Shylock. With just the fewest words Shakespeare has created a "biography" for his character: the old man we see was once a young man who courted a woman named Leah—presumably she is dead; she gave him a turquoise ring which he has treasured over the years, only now to find that the daughter born of his marriage to Leah has stolen the ring and traded it for a pet monkey. All this specificity of detail is quite unnecessary to the mere demands of the plot. And it creates difficulties. We cannot respond to a character about whom we know so much as if he were merely "a puppet on a string." These difficulties must be integrated into our sense of the play as a whole, or the episode must be rejected as a theatrical miscalculation.

The specificity of detail is especially important in its context. We have here, after all, another one of the play's various rings: not gold, like Portia's, but none-theless valuable both intrinsically and for its symbolic associations. Shylock's cry of pain must be caused, in part at least, by something other than the monetary associations of his youthful pledge of conjugal fidelity—or why (again) has Shake-speare given us the specific knowledge of the otherwise unnecessary Leah?

Shylock's refusal ever to part willingly with Leah's ring (for I assume that "a wilderness of monkeys" is an expression of such absoluteness) seems on the face of it entirely admirable. But this little speech comes less than fifty lines after his "Hath not a Jews eyes?" speech; and the violently wrenched conclusion to that speech—its lesson of murderous revenge extracted from the assertion of common humanity—ought to put us on guard against subtly false conclusions here as well. We may hear in his "I would not have given it for a wilderness of monkeys" an ironic echo of the casket-motto, "Who chooseth me, *must give* and hazard all he hath." The immediate context of Shylock's poignant expession of fidelity, his hysterical outbursts over the loss of his ducats, certainly establishes an association between his fidelity to Leah and his less-admirable closeness in business dealings. The Shylockian proverb, "Fast bind, fast find" (2.5.53), expresses an attitude toward material wealth, but it is also entirely consonant with his attitude toward everything, including Leah's ring, that is not solely material.

Our suspicions about the "fast bind, fast find" point of view are again con-firmed in act 5 when Bassanio, in the episode of Portia's ring, plays out a comic reprise of his trial before the caskets. In that culminating demonstration we see again that *giving* can be a higher virtue than keeping. Shylock's "fast bind, fast find" proverb is not so much culpable as it is limited; and its limitations can only be perceived in light of the knowledge of another system of value. That corrective system is suggested by Portia's "How far that little candle throws his beams! / So shines a good deed in a naughty world" (5.1.90–91), with its allusion to Matthew 5 : 15–16: "Nether do men light a candel, and put it vnder a bushel, but on a candelsticke, & it giueth light vnto all that are in the house. / Let your light so shine before men. . . ." Shylock's exclusive concern for thrift, closed doors, and shuttered windows is repeatedly contrasted with the outward-going love that seeks to spend itself and shine before others.

Honor, then, is due Shylock insofar as his faithfulness to his covenant with Leah suggests, as it does, the sense of obligation incurred by the Chosen People of the Old Testament covenant. But it is no accident that the portion of Scripture to which Portia alludes in her talk about brightly shining candles immediately precedes Christ's words about his relationship to that covenant: "Thinke not that I am come to destroye the Law, or the Prophetes. I am not come to destroye them, but to fulfil them." The kind of faithfulness Shylock reveals in his grief over the loss of Leah's ring is, from Shakespeare's point of view, the foundation for a higher faith; in a sense, then, the conflict in *The Merchant of Venice* is not between evil and good, but between a Good and a Better. And our response to Shylock must accommodate what is good in him. At the same time, the limited, or unfulfilled, nature of Shylock's faithfulness is made clear by comparison with an unjealous love that sees beyond the letter of the law.

Shylock's few outraged words about Leah's ring are sufficient to indicate the character's complexity, and the hazards therefore of trying to weigh in any crude scale his claims on the audience's sympathy. Simultaneously, the episode suggests the complexity of Shylock's role in the parabolic structure of the play—showing us again that in Shakespeare's mode of characterization there need not be any conflict between the demands of psychological "realism" and those of a character's representative function. It should be entirely possible to react to Shylock as a human being—that is to say, with sympathy—and also to see his treatment by Portia as proper, and to find in the harmonies of the fifth act the play's appropriate conclusion. With the idea of this characteristically Shakespearean doubleness in mind, I would like to continue the examination of Shylock. From the discussion of textual particulars there will also occasionally arise opportunities to discuss some of the historical considerations necessary for an understanding of the character: Elizabethan attitudes toward money-lending; the actual position of Jews in England; and theological matters that would have had a bearing on Shakespeare's creation of the Jew he called Shylock.

Shylock uses language as he uses money: carefully, and as a weapon. The prodigal Christians may squander their words, enjoying the luxury of rhetorical embellishment for its own sake and for the sake of the beauty it gives to life; but Shylock knows the value of a word. Not that he is a linguistic miser: he can spend as well as save. But like the proper businessman he knows the time for each, and the effectiveness of his speaking comes in large part from his canny investment in silence.[10]

His first appearance, at 1.3, is a tour de force in the use of silence to enhance speaking, and in the aggressive use of both. He dangles his few words before the impatient Bassanio, controlling him with the bait, making him leap after the words as though they were the precious ducats themselves:

> SHYLOCK: Three thousand ducats, well.
> BASSANIO: Aye sir, for three months.
> SHYLOCK: For three months, well.
> BASSANIO: For the which as I told you, Antonio shall be bound.
> SHYLOCK: Antonio shall become bound, well.
> BASSANIO: May you stead me? Will you pleasure me? Shall I know your answer?
> [1.3.1–7]

He allows Bassanio to seem to be in command of the scene; Bassanio must drive it forward, enumerating the items of the contract while the apparently absent-minded Shylock lags behind merely repeating them. But the absentmindedness is part of a careful act, and he gives us sufficient indications to know who really is in control. He changes Bassanio's innocuous "Antonio shall be bound" into the more menacingly specific "shall become bound," giving two meanings to "bound," one of which is frighteningly literal. And his coolness, his unnerving ability to maintain the act in the face of Bassanio's increasing loss of self-control, tells us, through the rhetoric of silence, that we are in the presence of a master.

A lesser businessman or a lesser speaker would give way before Bassanio's "May you stead me? Will you pleasure me? Shall I know your answer?" After all, he already has Bassanio where he wants him: Bassanio's eagerness and anger betray his dependence on Shylock. But Shylock sees further profit to be made in holding him off longer:

> SHYLOCK: Three thousand ducats for three months, and Antonio bound.
> BASSANIO: Your answer to that.
> SHYLOCK: Antonio is a good man.
> BASSANIO: Have you heard any imputation to the contrary?
> SHYLOCK: Ho, no, no, no, no: my meaning in saying he is a good man, is to have
>   you understand me that he is sufficient,—   [1.3.8–15]

It is all so carefully built, and so daring. Shylock has invested silence and gained a misunderstanding, which immediately he converts to a pun—for Shylock, though frugal, does occasionally venture a pun, pleased to get two meanings for the price of one. A punster is not necessarily a verbal squanderer; the trick, on the contrary, is to hold fast to the precise values of a word and to demand the full rate. Here Shylock demands the mercantile meaning, "that he is sufficient," along with the moral meaning understood by Bassanio in the phrase "good man." Even the fussy, pedantic way he explains his quibble is part of the act: at the same time that he shows us the wit in what he has accomplished he warns us against dismissing it with a laugh.

Nor should it be dismissed. This splitting off of moral values from mercantile values lies at the heart of Shylock's and Antonio's mutual antipathy. Much of the rest of this scene will be an explicit debate over the practice of lending money at interest. It is this practice that most sharply distinguishes the professional methods of the play's two merchants: Antonio declares "I neither lend nor borrow / By taking nor by giving excess" (1.3.56–57); while Shylock, although he can say simply "I hate him for he is a Christian," adds to that general ground for hatred a particular one: "But more, for that in low simplicity / He lends out money gratis, and brings down / The rate of usance here with us in Venice" (35–40). From the very start, even before Shylock can haggle over the precise word to describe his kind of business (he will call "thrift" what Antonio "calls interest" [1.3.45–46]), from the moment he parcels that word "good" into separate compartments, one containing moral values and another mercantile values, he has already declared himself no harmless businessman but a usurer in the broad Elizabethan sense.

The Elizabethan horror at the idea of taking interest for the loan of money— the practice which, with little regard to the fine points of the trade, was damned under the blanket term "usury"—is not easy for us to understand, living as we do in a society where credit is the universal way. That horror was compounded of many ingredients, some deriving from the realities of a particular economic situation, others from the realm of myth or superstition, and the largest part from a shady area between the real and the imagined. The late sixteenth century, throughout Europe, was a time of rapid economic change and growth which made the necessity for credit overwhelming. But in this area, social fact and social theory were widely out of touch with each other. Writers, both ecclesiastical and lay, depending for their view of economics upon the most venerable of classical and medieval sources, were unanimous in their condemnation of the practice of "usury"—a word which emerges, as one reads the many pamphlets, sermons, even plays condemning the practice, as a sort of catch-all for every problem that seemed to be threatening the traditional fabric of society. R. H. Tawney has called usury "the mystery of iniquity in which a host of minor scandals were conveniently, if inaccurately, epitomized."[11] And the scarcely perceived divergence between the economic realities that demanded the growth of credit and the economic theory that condemned it, produced an exacerbating tension.

Antonio and Shylock refer directly to the theoretical basis for the orthodox view of money-lending: after Shylock has told the story of Jacob and his uncle Laban's sheep. Antonio asks, "is your gold and silver ewes and rams?"—to which Shylock replies, "I cannot tell, I make it breed as fast" (1.3.90–91); and later Antonio describes lending at interest as taking "a breed for barren metal" (1.3.129). The point at issue was widely known; it derived from Aristotle, and is nicely summed up by Bacon (himself a rare skeptic in the matter), "They say ... it is against Nature, for *Money* to beget *Money*."[12] In their debate over Jacob's animal husbandry, Antonio and Shylock examine this proposition. As we might expect, any simple statement about what is or is not "against Nature" was likely to come under close Shakespearean scrutiny.

Before we look at that debate it should be pointed out that the bare theoretical basis would hardly have been capable of sustaining a loathing as deep and long-lasting as that of the Elizabethans for "usury." Antonio puts flesh on the theoretical skeleton when he tells Shylock:

> If thou wilt lend this money, lend it not
> As to thy friends, for when did friendship take
> A breed for barren metal of his friend?
> But lend it rather to thine enemy,
> Who if he break, thou may'st with better face
> Exact the penalty.   [1.3.127–32]

Here, in the mention of "friendship," is a matter less recondite and more viscerally accessible than the Aristotelian theory that money should not "breed." And while itself irreducibly simple, the idea of "friendship" was also the cornerstone of an entire social theory, one with deep religious foundations—the social theory that elaborates Christ's injunction to love thy neighbor as thyself. In Robert Wilson's play *The Three Ladies of London* (1584), Conscience, who has just been ruined by a character called Usury, says:

> But if we should follow Gods law we should not receave above that wee lend.
> For if we lend for reward, how can we say we are our neighbors friend:
> O how blessed shall that man be that lendes without abuse:
> But thrice accursed shall he be that greatly covets us [i.e., use = usury].

The matter is not one of empty pieties, however often practice may have diverged from theory. The relation of the individual to the community (in both its secular and its religious aspects) is what finally is at stake in the condemnation of usury; and on that relationship the words of Archbishop Laud are particularly relevant: "If any man be so addicted to his private, that he neglect the common, state, he is void of the sense of piety and wisheth peace and happiness to himself in vain. For whoever he be, he must live in the body of the Commonwealth, and in the body of the church." R. H. Tawney, who quotes Laud, says of this statement: "To one holding such a creed economic individualism was hardly less abhorrent than religious nonconformity, and its repression was a not less obvious duty; for both seemed incompatible with the stability of a society in which Commonwealth and Church were one."[13]

If "usury" was universally condemned as a threat to society, the fact that the moneylender's services were nonetheless indispensable must have made the problem seem quite literally diabolical. A gesture toward an accommodation with reality was made by Parliament in 1571, when it legalized an interest rate not to exceed ten percent. The ten percent rate had in fact been set once before, by an Act of 1545, but that Act had been repealed—and all interest outlawed by an Edward ian Act of 1552. The Elizabethan Act reinstated the original Act of 1545, and it did so because the abuses which arose from the total ban on taking interest proved to be much more burdensome than the legal ten percent. Still, the deep-seated prejudice against the idea of taking interest prevented passage of more comprehensive legislation which would have regulated the moneylender's increasingly complex business; hence the age was rife with cunning schemes to take wildly excessive profits. The moneylender might, for instance, be as kind as Shylock, offering to "take no doit / of usance for [his] moneys" (1.3.136–37), demanding only a bond— the forfeit of which might mean total ruin for the defaulter.[14]

The Chancellor's court of equity attempted to mitigate the awful abuses caused by the common law's failure to legitimize and regulate the entire area of credit. Nonetheless the dangers of going into debt were very grave—at the same time that the necessity for going into debt was increasingly strong. And this was true at every level of society, but most spectacularly at the top. According to Lawrence Stone,

> After 1585 there was a steady deterioration in the general situation [among the peerage]. The cutting off of favours from the Crown coincided with an epidemic of gambling and high living to force a crisis in the affairs of the nobility. . . . [A]bout two-thirds of the peerage seem to have been in growing financial difficulties in the last twenty years of the reign of Elizabeth. . . . The period 1580 to 1610 in which the nobility first became heavily dependent on credit was the one in which the dangers of borrowing—high interest rates and the potential danger of forfeiting mortgaged estates—were very real.[15]

Behind the fairy-tale atmosphere of The Merchant of Venice, then, can be felt the daily anxieties of an age in which "venturing" was indeed hazardous, and in which the metaphor of "a pound of flesh" might not have seemed so grotesquely foreign to actual experience.

And who in fact were the predatory moneylenders of Shakespeare's age? William Harrison, in The Description of England (1587), is uncommonly honest and direct when he describes "usury" as "a trade brought in by the Jews, now perfectly practiced almost by every Christian and so commonly that he is accounted but for a fool that doth lend his money for nothing."[16] Among the lower classes, moneylending continued to be what it had always been, "not a profession but a bye-employment," as Tawney puts it; "a bye-employment which is intertwined with, and often concealed by, other economic transactions. . . . In country districts the character most commonly advancing money is a yeoman, and next to him comes probably the parson."[17] In the cities, among the wealthy, money-lending was mostly carried on by "a restricted circle of great London merchants, men who first made their money in overseas or retail trading and who then turned to the money-lending business." Lawrence Stone goes on to say that the most favorably placed for this business were the leading mercers, silkmen, jewellers, and goldsmiths. . . . Virtually the whole of this tight little oligarchy was drawn into money-lending between 1580 and 1620. Sixteen goldsmiths and at least forty aldermen are known to have made loans to peers during this period. . . . The other two groups who were prominent in this business during these forty years—though both were of secondary importance compared with the city magnates—were lawyers and government officials.[18]

So where, among all these pillars of society, were the Shylocks and Tubals? Mostly they were in countries like Italy rather than England (which had expelled the Jews in 1290), crowded together in impoverished ghettoes. The continuing popular association of Jew and moneylender—indeed their virtual synonymity—therefore defies easy explanation. As Lawrence Stone's account makes clear, the Elizabethan moneylender was highly visible, well known to all, and unimpeachably a non-Jew. Yet everywhere in the literature of the age the equivalence of moneylender and Jew is affirmed. One reason for this bewildering state of affairs is clear: since *in theory* the business of making barren metal breed more metal was inimical to the right-minded Christian, then ipso facto the userer must, despite the attest of eyes and ears, be Jewish!

Some small historical justification for the connection of Jew and moneylender did exist in England, although it could hardly have played as important a part in popular attitudes as did bad theology and mere prejudice. Before their expulsion from the country, the English Jews lived in an awful double bind. On the one hand, they "enjoyed" the special protection of the king—in return for which they were kept, in Cecil Roth's phrase, as "the royal milch-cow," banned from most other employment except money-lending and then freely milked of their profits by their royal patron. That patronage, and their royally induced role as moneylenders, made the Jews in turn hated by the common people, from whose violent attacks the Jewish community did indeed need the frequent protection of the king whose protection had made them hated in the first place. This extraordinary state of affairs was ended after the disastrous rapacity of Edward I had virtually bankrupted his Jewish communities; then, in 1290, since the Jews had lost their usefulness to him, Edward took the popular and holy course of having them expelled. England's was the first such wholesale expulsion by any European country.[19]

Suffice to sum up this excursus with the lesson that history so awfully teaches, that no imaginary compound has more power to arouse mindless passion than that of the "usurious" Jew. Therefore it should be apparent that Shakespeare has done something extraordinary in allowing Shylock to argue his case as a moneylender as well as he does. His story of the time "When Jacob graz'd his uncle Laban's sheep" (1.3.66), although presented with a purposeful obliquity, is the strongest part of that case. Jacob's biblical example (the story is drawn from Genesis 30 : 31–43) does not necessarily "make interest good," to use Antonio's contemptuous phrase (89); but it does make it more openly problematic than we might have expected.

Antonio's conclusion, that the exemplum only shows how "The devil can cite Scripture for his purpose" (93), is one legitimate response; certainly there is much about Shylock's argument that should be held suspect as a sophistically false analogy.[20] But Antonio's response is not the only legitimate one.

In Shylock's treatment of it, the Old Testament pastoral interlude is made to fly directly in the face of that universally accepted Aristotelian proposition that it is "unnatural" for money to breed money. The story, in the biblical and the Shylockian version, involves some questionable eugenics, but the essence is simple enough: Jacob and Laban agree that for his wages Jacob will take all the newborn lambs "which were streak'd and pied" (1.3.74). (Curiously, Shylock leaves out of his account Laban's own bit of doubledealing: according to Genesis, Laban first removed from Jacob's flock all parti-colored stock, gave them to his own sons, and "set three days' journey betwixt himself and Jacob.") The resourceful Jacob peeled some of the bark off "certain wands," set them "before the fulsome ewes" while the "work of generation" was proceeding, and thus influenced the birth of "parti-colour'd lambs, and those were Jacob's." "This," Shylock concludes, "was a way to thrive, and he was blest: / And thrift is blessing if men steal it not" (1.3.71–85).

Shylock's point, of course, is that if Jacob "was blest" despite the artificial manner in which he had influenced the ostensibly "natural" process of breeding, the moneylender may similarly thrive through *his* artificial means of breeding. Antonio's response is cogent: for one thing, Jacob had been acting only as the agent of a higher power—

> This was a venture sir that Jacob serv'd for,
> A thing not in his power to bring to pass,
> But sway'd and fashion'd by the hand of heaven   [1.3.86–88]

—and anyway, Antonio asks, "is your gold and silver ewes and rams?" (90). But Shylock's responsive shrug of the shoulders, "I cannot tell, I make it breed as fast," wittily prevents the matter from resting where Antonio confidently believes he has settled it. If Jacob's successful venture was fashioned by the hand of heaven, who is to say that Shylock's success is not under similar auspices? A phrase out of Lear's madness may be recalled in this context: "Nature's above art in that respect" (4.6.86); and, from an ostensibly more rational source, Polixenes' answer to Perdita's disdain for streaked gillyvors, that "The art itself is Nature" (*The Winter's Tale*, 4.4.99). Surely usury is in the province of things artful; but how could that artificial generation of money out of money take place except (*pace* Aristotle) through "an art / That Natures makes"? (*The Winter's Tale*, 4.4.91–92).

It is unlikely that Shylock's sly argument would have converted many of the audience from the deep-seated prejudice against the moneylender's trade. Still, it is important that Shylock gets, as it were, a fighting chance. The issue of money-lending, for those who have attended carefully to this initial exchange between the two merchants, can no longer be decided on purely abstract grounds. Shylock is allowed to open the question sufficiently so that he can be judged on the basis of

what he will do in the course of the play, rather than on preconceived notions
alone.

Shakespeare introduces the whole question of usury through Shylock's apparently unintentional pun on the word "good," with its separate mercantile and
moral senses. It is not a particularly amusing pun: Shylock's verbal wit is generally of
the plodding sort. This is true also of the next pun he ventures, when to the list of
perils waiting Antonio's argosies—"there be land-rats, and water-rats, water-
thieves, and land-thieves"—he adds, "I mean pirates" (1.3.20–21; the quarto and
folio spelling, "Pyrats," makes the pun more obvious). But the wit is not intended to
lie in the pun itself, but rather in the larger dramatic situation. By hiding his real
verbal agility under an assumed pedantic specificity, Shylock creates the outward
persona of a fussy, slow-witted old man—at the same time that he gives away the
persona and shows us the glinting hard wit that goes into its creation.

That hardness appears again when, winding up his initial exchange with Bassanio, he rubs Bassanio's nose in another innocently meant word. Shylock has
concluded, "I think I may take his bond," and Bassanio answers,

> Be assur'd you may.
> SHYLOCK: I will be assur'd I may: and that I may be assur'd, I will bethink me,—
> [1.3.24–27]

The *assurances* Shylock demands are of a different order than those gentlemanly
assurances offered by Bassanio. The figure of speech Shylock uses in his neatly
turned line was known to rhetoricians as *antimetabole* or, in George Puttenham's
special vocabulary, "the Counterchange." Puttenham describes it as "a figure which
takes a couple of words to play with in a verse, and by making them to chaunge and
shift one into others place they do very pretily exchange and shift the sense."[21] In
Shylock's use of it, this "pretty" exchanging of positions produces three subtle shifts
of sense; not only does "assurance" move from the realm of clubby sociability to
that of no-nonsense business, but even the reversed order of the repeated "will"
and "may" takes up Bassanio's simple language, converting his "*be* assur'd" into the
more purposefully determined "I *will* be assur'd," and his "you *may*" into a statement implying the opposite of permission: "that I *may* be assur'd, I *will* bethink me."

It is on occasions like this, especially in act 1, scene 3, when Shylock catches the
Christians *au pied de la lettre,* that we see most clearly (as he intends us to see)
the falseness of the assumed persona. The harmless, silly old man is there in the
nervous deliberateness of his speech patterns, in his absent-mindedness (in scene
3 he several times forgets his subject, returns to it, repeats himself, introduces
long-winded digressions), in his pedantic manner of explicating his own plodding
witticisms. But the careful orchestration of these devices into a larger purpose is
apparent even before the aside, "How like a fawning publican he looks!" (1.3.36),
with its revelation of Shylock's implacable refusal to "forgive" Antonio (47). The
apparent meanderings return precisely to the point: despite Bassanio's impatience

with Shylock's assumed slowness, it is the Christians who waste words, Shylock who puts them, like his money, to use.

Shylock continues his masterful act after the entrance of Antonio. In contrast to the decisive, brusque way in which Antonio first addresses him—

Shylock, albeit I neither lend nor borrow
By taking nor by giving of excess,
Yet to supply the ripe wants of my friend,
I'll break a custom: [*To Bassanio.*] is he yet possess'd
    How much ye would?   [1.3.56–60]

—in contrast to this self-satisfied imperiousness, Shylock continues, as he has done with Bassanio, to play to the full the part of the harmless dodderer. He is outrageously absent minded, then humbly apologetic for his failing; when Antonio reminds him that the three thousand ducats are to be loaned for three months, Shylock says, "I had forgot,—three months,—" and adds with barely disguised mockery of Bassanio, "you told me so" (62). He plays with the two needy Christians, holding them off still longer:

Well then, your bond: and let me see,—but hear you,
Me thoughts you said, you neither lend nor borrow
Upon advantage.   [1.3.63–65]

The back-tracking change of subject, just as he is about to get to the bond, is surely calculated to madden Bassanio and Antonio; as also is his next bewildering non sequitur:

When Jacob graz'd his uncle Laban's sheep,—
This Jacob from our holy Abram was
(As his wise mother wrought in his behalf)
The third possessor: ay, he was the third.   [1.3.66–69]

Thus, with every show of slow-witted difficulty, Shylock prepares the way for his nimble rhetoric in defense of usury.

That defense, the story of Jacob, is ended by Shylock with a typical gesture of mock self-deprecation, "I cannot tell. . . ." And again, for a moment, there appears the old man's persona, mumbling over the terms of a business deal he seems barely able to keep in mind: "Three thousand ducats, 'tis a good round sum. / Three months from twelve, then let me see the rate" (98–99). But it is only a momentary pause to set off to even greater dramatic advantage Shylock's strongest, most dazzlingly sustained speech in this scene he has so subtly dominated throughout:

Signior Antonio, many a time and oft
In the Rialto you have rated me
About my moneys and my usances:
Still have I borne it with a patient shrug,

(For suff'rance is the badge of all our tribe);
You call me misbeliever, cut-throat dog,
And spet upon my Jewish gaberdine,
And all for use of that which is mine own.
Well then, it now appears you need my help:
Go to then, you come to me, and you say,
"Shylock, we would have moneys," you say so:
You that did void your rheum upon my beard,
And foot me as you spurn a stranger cur
Over your threshold, moneys is your suit.
What should I say to you? Should I not say
"Hath a dog money? is it possible
A cur can lend three thousand ducats?" or
Shall I bend low, and in a bondman's key
With bated breath, and whisp'ring humbleness
Say this:
"Fair sir, you spet on me on Wednesday last,
You spurn'd me such a day, another time
You call'd me dog: and for these courtesies
I'll lend you thus much moneys"?   [1.3.101–24]

The speech has got to be quoted in its entirety: to parse it out is to lose the astonishing colloquial rhythm, the unmistakeably individualized sound of a human voice speaking, that is so much a part of its effectiveness. The tense actorly quality, as Shylock in effect imitates Antonio as well as (most remarkably) several conceivable versions of himself, is not unmistakable. Even before this speech, Shakespeare has made the role of Shylock an irresistible opportunity for any actor, who will have had to play back and forth between the surface persona and the deeper, harder character who projects it. Now, in this long speech, Shylock becomes himself an actor's actor, using his histrionic skills (as the professional actor does) simultaneously to seduce and attack his audience. This undisguised display of histrionics brings to consciousness for us one of the claims he has all along in this scene been making on our attention: we see now the intense intellectual and emotional concentration he devotes to his role-playing. We sense in Shylock the danger to which any actor is exposed, and the power he attains from that self-willed exposure. The commerce between stage and audience has kept us alert, even before we are fully conscious of what is being done; we are in a state of heightened expectation, not only about what will happen next in the "story," but about how the actor will accomplish his incredible stunt, how far he can go in his audacious playing.

The seeming paradox about Shylock's carefully turned, precisely calculated speech is that it sounds so natural, so much more vitally human than (say) Antonio's less artful directness. There is little previously in Shakespeare's career to match Shylock's virtuoso trick of seeming natural by accepting fully the necessity for role-playing. Only Richard III is Shylock's equal at the game; and though Shylock is, of course, a mere petit bourgeois in villainy compared to Richard, there are significant affinities between them. Richard's declaration of intent in *3 Henry VI*, where with delighted self-satisfaction he boats, "Why, I can smile, and murther whiles I smile, / And cry 'Content' to that which grieves my heart, / And wet my cheek with artificial tears" (3.2.182–84), makes explicit the connection between politic villainy and a certain kind of histrionic skill. And the display of that skill, by Richard or Shylock, pleases us, even despite our moral sense, giving us a vicarious release from dull goodness by our privileged contact with a more flashily attractive, witty evil.

But no one is more pleased than the actor himself. Each is at his best when he is taking the greatest theatrical risk (the power and the danger grow together): Richard in his preposterous wooing of Lady Anne, Shylock in proposing his murderous bond "in a merry sport" (1.3.141). And while Richard openly exults, "Was ever woman in this humor woo'd? / Was ever woman in this humor won?" (*Richard III*, 1.2.227–28), Shylock is more subtle about showing the pleasure he takes in his role. The very manner in which he proposes the bond is a masterpiece of self-conscious villainy; we cannot mistake it as anything other than an act, and yet we are tempted to applaud it for its sheer expertness: it outvillains villainy so far that the rarity redeems it.[22]

Shylock begins by engineering one of his menacing verbal contretemps. Of his willingness to "Supply your present wants, and take no doit / Of usance for my money," he concludes, "This is kind I offer" (136–38). And Bassanio, possibly with an attempt at sarcasm, replies, "This were kindness"—only to have the phrase shot back at him in a manner that converts both the "kindness" and even the innocent "this" into potential threats:

> *This kindness* will I show,
> Go with me to a notary, seal me there
> Your single bond, and (in a merry sport)
> If you repay me not on such a day
> In such a place, such sum or sums as are
> Express'd in the condition, let the forfeit
> Be nominated for an equal pound
> Of your fair flesh, to be cut off and taken
> In what part of your body pleaseth me. [1.3.139–147]

It is another instance of Shylock getting two meanings for the price of one. Here, he demands all the specificity of legal terminology, and at the same time manages to convey by it a disarming indefiniteness: "on such a day / In such a place, such sum or sums. . . ." He is framing an ironclad contract, already sealing off any possible escape clauses; but his language allows it to be taken as a jovial parody of legalism, another bad joke by the harmless old man. It is apparently the joke, not Shylock, that prompts the legal terminology ("forfeit," "nominated") and explicitness ("to be cut off and taken") in which the kindly offer is couched. The whole "merry" business can hardly fool the audience, which has heard in an aside of Shylock's desire to catch Antonio on the hip; and there is no evidence that it fools Antonio, who trusts not to Shylock's reasonable preference for "flesh of muttons, beefs, or goats," but to his own sufficiency: ". . . in this there can be no dismay, / My ships come home a month before the day" (1.3.176–77). But Shylock does not really intend it to deceive anyone. Rather it is a display of sheer power: Can I do this and cannot get a heart? Shylock's last fillip in the scene, "If he will take it, so,—if not, adieu, / And for my love I pray you wrong me not" (165–66), fairly drips with his contempt for the Christian fools who are so helpless before him. Although the terms of his bond seem wordy and loose, in it, as throughout the scene, Shylock magnificently proves his cunning as an investor of speech.

Shylock is as careful of his very presence as he is of his words: "I will buy with you, sell with you, talk with you, walk with you, and so following: but I will not eat with you, drink with you, nor pray with you" (1.3.30–33). And this social exclusivity is reflected in the facts of his actual dramatic career: Shylock appears in only five scenes, in one of which (3.3) he makes his exit after the seventeenth line.

The power of Shylock's stage presence, which is as manifest in the reading as it is in the role's theater history, would therefore appear to be something of a mystery. But part of that mystery can be explained, I think, by the memory we carry throughout the play of Shylock's histrionic mastery in scene three, as that memory is then played off against the reality of Shylock's successive degeneration. Rhetorical tricks, especially his feigned absent-mindedness and contrived repetitions, which in his first appearance were aspects of his dominance, become in later scenes a product of the man himself, not of his persona; they become signs of weakness rather than of strength. And the contrast itself is arresting.

Flashes of the original Shylock, whose witty performance had engaged our attention despite our moral scruples, remain almost to the end of the trial scene. But increasingly those remnants of beleaguered cunning serve only to throw into relief other moments when he loses his tense self-control—at home, for instance, wearily with Jessica:

> I am bid forth to support Jessica,
> There are my keys:—but wherefore should I go?
> I am not bid for love. . . .   [2.5.11–13]

—or in the stuttering rage of "You knew, none so well, none so well as you, of my daughter's flight" (3.1.22–23). Commenting on Macklin's performance in 1775, Georg Lichtenberg gave this description which catches exactly the effect of contrast I am interested in:

> The first words he utters, when he comes on to the stage, are slowly and impressively spoken. . . . Three such words uttered thus at the outset give the

keynote of his whole character. In the scene where he first misses his daughter, he comes on hatless, with disordered hair, some locks a finger long standing on end, as if raised by a breath of wind from the gallows, so distracted was his demeanour. Both his hands are clenched, and his movements abrupt and convulsive. To see a deceiver, who is usually calm and resolute, in such a state of agitation, is terrible.[23]

The fright-wig and some of the accompanying business may be altered to suit contemporary taste, but Lichtenberg's concluding phrase—"To see a deceiver, who is usually calm and resolute, in such a state of agitation, is terrible"—ought to describe our response to any adequate performance of the role.

Act 1, scene 3—the scene in which Shylock establishes his strength—is, of course, an entirely "public" scene, between Shylock and the Christians, with Shylock at every point tensely alert. His next appearance (2.5)—which follows immediately upon our learning, from Lorenzo, of Jessica's intended elopement—is a "private" scene: Shylock with Launcelot and Jessica, concerning himself with domestic affairs, preparing to go forth to supper. And the effect, therefore, is complex. A relatively more relaxed Shylock is here "humanized"; that, and our knowledge of the real "ill a-brewing to [his] rest," engages our sympathy for him. But by the same token, signs of weakness that are beginning to emerge in Shylock qualify the impression we have carried over from his first appearance. And to the extent that his witty performance in that earlier scene has earned our complicity with him, these hints at his degeneration will make us feel cheated, make us question whether we have not indeed been seduced into taking the fool's gold of flashy evil when we should have known from the start the greater desirability of pale and leaden goodness.

The "witty" Shylock is still apparent in the way he converts an invitation to dine *with* Antonio into an occasion "to *feed upon* / The prodigal Christian" (2.5.14–15). But the cannibalistic menace flashes only briefly out of a more pervasive sense of weariness. Losing his train of thought and repeating himself are no longer tactics to tantalize the listener but an unconscious habit:

> I am bid forth to supper Jessica,
> There are my keys:—but wherefore should I go?
> I am not bid for love, they flatter me,
> But yet I'll go in hate, to feed upon
> The prodigal Christian. Jessica my girl,
> Look to my house,—I am right loath to go,
> There is some ill a-brewing to my rest,
> For I did dream of money-bags to-night.   [2.5.11–18]

Even that sharp declension from the idea of dining with someone for love into feeding on someone in hate is undercut by Shylock's petty concern to make the "prodigal Christian" waste / his borrowed purse" (49–50). There is at once something touching about Shylock's attitude towards the defecting Launcelot ("The patch is kind enough") and faintly ridiculous ("but a huge feeder" [45]). The economic advantage from which Shylock derived his confidence in his first appearance degenerates in this scene into the obsessions of the mere miser. The stinginess, which in his first scene he displayed even in his brilliantly sparing use of language, is now ridiculously extended to include a distaste for music and merriment:

> What are there masques? Hear you me Jessica,
> Lock up my doors, and when you hear the drum
> And the vile squealing of the wry-neck'd fife
> Clamber not you up to the casements then
> Nor thrust your head into the public street
> To gaze on Christian fools with varnish'd faces:
> But stop my house's ears, I mean my casements,
> Let not the sound of shallow fopp'ry enter
> My sober house.   [2.5.28–36]

The pedantic explication of a plodding joke—"my house's ears, I mean my casements"—now has no histrionic justification; it remains a pedantic explication of a plodding joke. Shylock's final words in this scene, "Fast bind, fast find,— / A proverb never stale in thrifty mind," *are* stale. Compared to the way he took his exit several scenes earlier, we are left with the image now of a sadly diminished figure. We can sympathize with that figure, but we can also see him more clearly for what he is.

Shylock's next appearance is in act 3, scene 1: it is the extraordinary scene which includes Shylock's "Hath not a Jew eyes" speech, with its perverse conclusion in Shylock's flaunting his superiority in villainy, and the news of Leah's turquoise ring. The rapid changes of mood as Shylock responds to Tubal's news—exulting at Antonio's losses, bemoaning his own—has no doubt its comic aspect, although "absurd" might be a better word if it more readily comprehends other effects produced by the scene. For this is the scene to which Lichtenberg referred when he described the "terrible" effect of Shylock's degeneration from the character as he appeared in act 1, scene 3.

Shakespeare cannily holds off Shylock's entrance until we have had some typically urbane, easy, and cheap talk from Solanio and Salerio. Their shallow concern for Antonio ("it is true, without any slips of prolixity, or crossing the plain highway of talk, that the good Antonio, the honest Antonio;—O that I had a title good enough to keep his name company!—" [3.1.10–14]) is the perfect foil to set off the dazed fury of Shylock's entrance. And their continued baiting of him— driving him, incidentally, to that greatest if most rhetorically deceitful speech of all, "Hath not a Jew eyes"—makes of Shylock's sudden repeated reversals of emotion with Tubal an image of our own complex feelings about him. The laughter is strangled by horror—at what is done to him, but also at what he himself is doing; and at what menacing but also ridiculously petty thing he has conspired with his enemies to make of himself: "I will have the heart of him if he forfeit, for were he out of Venice I can make what merchandise I will" (116–18).

Only one scene separates Shylock's appearance here from his next appearance (3.3). The intervening scene is the one in which Bassanio undergoes the casket trial and wins Portia, in which news comes of Antonio's utter failure to "scape the dreadful touch / Of merchant-marring rocks" (3.2.269–70), and in which Portia grandly offers "To pay the petty debt twenty times over" (306):

> Pay him six thousand, and deface the bond:
> Double six thousand, and then treble that,
> Before a friend of this description
> Shall lose a hair through Bassanio's fault.   [3.2.298–301]

It is in every way an expansive scene, of great expectations expressed in heroic mythical allusions (Portia calls Bassanio the "young Alcides," a "Hercules" [55, 60]; and when he has succeeded at the trial he says, "We are the Jasons, we have won the fleece" [240]); there is music in the scene and rich metaphor and the actual language of multiplication: "I would be trebled twenty times myself, / A thousand times more fair, ten thousand times more rich" (153–54). Like Portia herself, everything about the scene seems striving to "exceed account" (157). And no contrast in the play is more stark than the contrast between this long scene of outward-flowing richness and the short scene following it, which begins with Shylock's, "Gaoler, look to him."

In the seventeen lines before Shylock makes his exit from act 3, scene 3 he reaches his moral, and simultaneously his linguistic, nadir. The technique of verbal repetition, which had once been a source of flexibility for Shylock, is here the enacted symbol of his own imprisonment within the self-defeating system of vengeance. To speak well was, for the Renaissance, the very proof of humanity, the ability that separates man from beast. A textbook of logic (Thomas Wilson's *Rule of Reason* [1551]) gives as its example of "an undoubted true proposition" the definition, "A man is a liuing creature endewed with reason, hauing aptnesse by nature to speake." Sir Philip Sidney expresses the commonplace association, "*Oratio* next to *Ratio*, Speech next to Reason, [is] the greatest gift bestowed vpon mortalitie."[24] Shylock's speech is now reduced to the obsessive repetition of phrases connoting restriction; simultaneously he refuses others the freedom of speaking, revealing himself as one who, although undoubtedly sinned against, has of his own free will given up the outward sign of humanity. Thus his threat, "Thou call'dst me dog before thou hadst a cause, / But since I am a dog, beware my fangs" (3.3.6–7), has an almost literal as well as figurative truth:

SHYLOCK: Gaoler, look to him—tell not me of mercy,—
This is the fool that lent out money gratis.
Gaoler, look to him.
ANTONIO: Hear me yet good Shylock.

SHYLOCK: I'll have my bond, speak not against my bond,—
I have sworn an oath, that I will have my bond:
Thou call'dst me dog before thou hadst a cause,
But since I am a dog, beware my fangs,—
The duke shall grant me justice,—I do wonder
(Thou naughty gaoler) that thou art so fond
To come abroad with him at his request.
ANTONIO: I pray thee hear me speak.
SHYLOCK: I'll have my bond. I will not hear thee speak,
I'll have my bond, and therefore speak no more.
I'll not be made a soft and dull-ey'd fool,
To shake the head, relent, and sigh, and yield
To Christian intercessors: follow not,—
I'll have no more speaking, I will have my bond.
[Exit]
                                                                    [3.3.1–17]

The linguistic degeneration displayed here is the ironically appropriate fate of the
diabolical literalist.

Shylock has only one more scene in the play: the trial. And there too, of
course, his unreasonable and uncharitable literalism is self-defeating. Shylock himself
has established the apparent absoluteness of the alternatives in that trial: "tell not
me of mercy. . . . the duke shall grant me justice." And it is that sense of absoluteness
that makes Portia's procedure so remarkable (approaching, as I have suggested, the
realm of miracle), showing harmony where there had appeared to be only unalterable division.

A merciful justice is extended to Shylock as well as to Antonio, and Shylock
too is accommodated within the final harmony. But these are matters not easily
accepted by a modern audience, and deserve further attention. Certainly there
would be a moral obtuseness displayed by any modern audience not made at least
queasy by the financial penalties imposed on Shylock and—the greatest stumbling
block—by his forced conversion. But setting these matters in the context of
Shakespeare's comic and Christian vision may at least make them understandable.

Antonio's free decision to administer his half of the estate on Shylock's behalf,
with the proviso that at Shylock's death all of it will go to Jessica and Lorenzo, would
have seemed more generous to an Elizabethan audience than it does to us, considering the Elizabethan abhorrence of usury. As a moneylender, all Shylock's
wealth has supposedly been ill-gained; its total confiscation would not have seemed
an unduly severe penalty. It is conceivable, even, that some of Shakespeare's
audience were aware of historical precedent for the confiscation of a convert's
wealth. For there still existed into the early seventeenth century, although in a state
of decline, a curious institution in London called the *Domus Conversorum,* a hostel
for Jewish converts that had originally been established in 1232. According to Cecil

Roth, the *Domus Conversorum* was set up because, "Legally, converts from Juda
ism forfeited to the Crown all their property, as having been acquired by the sinful
means of usury. Destitute as they were, a hostel was indispensable" (p. 43). The
absurdity of the medieval situation—the encouraging (to put it mildly) of conversion, the subsequent reward for which was to be made an impoverished ward of
the state—led to a modification of the law in 1280. The king at that time "waived
for a seven-year period his legal claim on the property of those who left their faith.
From now on they might retain one-half of what they previously owned, though
amassed in sin, the remainder (with certain other income from Jewry, including the
proceeds of the recently instituted poll tax) being devoted to the upkeep of the
Domus Conversorum in London."[25]

So there was historical precedent in England both for the confiscation of the
convert's property and for the remission of one-half of that penalty. There was
historical precedent for enforced conversion as well; but in this matter we must
look to biblical salvation-history as well as to the history of nations. I have said that
Shylock's unyieldingness suggests, even if in a perverted form, the Old Testament
covenant. But the Jew had another claim on the Christian, one which was in fact to
contribute to the eventual recall of the Jews to England in 1655. That claim is the
Jew's unique and necessary position in the scheme of man's salvation.

In Isaiah it is prophesied that "The remnant shall returne, *euen* the remnant of
Iaakob vnto the mighty God" (10:21). And the return of that saving remnant—the
conversion of the Jews—must occur before all things can be accomplished and
God's Kingdom be established.[26] In Romans, St. Paul elaborates on Isaiah's prophecy and on the role of the Jews in salvation-history. The question he is addressing
for the benefit of his Gentile audience is whether the calling of the Gentiles has
entailed the rejection of the Jews; his answer is one of his most elaborate "God
forbids!" Paul cites Isaiah 65:2, "And vnto Israel he saith, All the day long haue I
stretched forthe mine hand vnto a disobedient, and gainsaying people" (Rom.
10:21). God has not rejected the Jews; it is the Jews, rather, who have put their
trust in "the workes of the Law" rather than seeking salvation by faith (Rom. 9:32):
"According as it is written, God hathe giuen them the spirit of slomber: eyes that
they shulde not se, & eares that they shulde not heare vnto this day" (Rom. 11:8).
Because of this deafness, the Law itself has become, as David prophesied, "a snare,
& a net, & a stombling blocke" (11:9)—a verse glossed in the Geneva Bible as
follows: "Christ by the mouth of the Prophet wisheth that which came upon the
Iewes, that is, that as birdes are taken where as they thinke to finde fode, so the
Law which the Iewes of a blinde zeale preferred to the Gospel thinking to haue
saluation by it, shulde, turne to their destruction."

It is not Portia but Shylock himself, in his "blinde zeale" demanding the law, his
deeds upon his head, who makes the law "a snare, & a net, & a stombling blocke."
Shylock demands it, and Portia gives it: "The Jew shall have all justice" (4.1.317).
Bringing destruction upon himself through a vain self-righteousness, and failing to
hear the Gospel message of mercy freely granted, Shylock at his trial plays out the

role of the Jew as it appears in the New Testament version of salvation-history.

That role has a further dimension, a dimension suggested by Shylock's conversion and by the subsequent comic joys of act 5. In St. Paul's version of Jewish history, the falling off of God's Chosen People is one in a series of "fortunate falls," each preparing the way for a greater joy to come. The "obstinacie"—or as the Authorized Version calls it, the "blindness"—of the Jews has come upon them "vntil the fulnes of the Gentiles be come in" (Rom. 11:25). This "secret" Paul imparts to the Gentiles "lest ye shulde be arrogant in your selues," reminding them that "all Israel shalbe saued, as it is written, The deliuerer shal come out of Sion, and shal turne away the vngodlines from Iacob" (25–26). Therefore, says Paul, the Jews of the present day have a complex relationship to the newly-chosen Christians: "As concerning the Gospel, they are enemies for your sakes: but as touching the election, they are beloued for the fathers sakes" (Rom. 11:28).

And all the more to be beloved for the role Israel plays in God's scheme of "fortunate falls":

> For euen as ye in time past haue not beleued God, yet haue now obteined mercie through their vnbelefe, / Euen so now haue they not beleued by the mercie shewed vnto you, that they may also obteine mercie. / For God hathe shut vp all in vnbelefe, that he might haue mercie on all. [Rom. 11:30–32]

Thus salvation was made possible for the believing Gentiles through the unbelief of Israel; and now Israel's unbelief will allow God to show his free mercy to the Jews when in time their unbelief shall pass away. As Adam's disobedience was made the occasion for God's mercy to Adam's descendants, so the Jews, when they have acknowledged the insufficiency of their "blinde zeale" to the law, will discover the mystery of grace. The casting away of the Jews was the reconciling of the rest of the world; and their eventual reception shall be life from the dead for all (Rom. 11:15). As the glossator of the Geneva Bible writes: "The Iewes now remaine, as it were, in death for lacke of the Gospel: but when bothe they & the Gentiles shal embrace Christ, the world shalbe restored to a new life."

In the medieval cycle plays or a miracle play like *The Croxton Play of the Sacrament*, where present time is regarded *sub specie aeternitatis*, a converted Jew could recognize his glorious culminating place in history and rejoice accordingly. Shakespeare's drama, however, while it affords intimations of the Last Things, accepts stricter limits; it shows mankind, however beautifully arrayed, still wearing its muddy vestures of decay. Thus Shylock's response to the court's merciful extortion of his wealth and his religion is the brief, "I am content"—which may be pronounced bitterly or, as I believe it should be, with a profound weariness, the final stage in that successive weakening we have observed in him since his first bold appearance; followed by his anticlimactic exit lines:

> I pray you give me leave to go from hence,
> I am not well—send the deed after me,
> And I will sign it.   [4.1.391–93]

How to react to these proceedings? Gratiano's capering vindictiveness—

> In christ'ning shalt thou have two godfathers,—
> Had I been judge, thou shouldst have ten more,
> To bring thee to the gallows, not to the font   [4.1.394–96]

—is certainly *not* intended as the final commentary. Rather, the final commentary is conveyed more lengthily and obliquely, by all that follows in the play. As the nightmarishly bright light of the courtroom recedes and we awaken into the candlelit peace of Belmont, those whose "spirits are attentive" will hear a "concord of sweet sounds" which, entering into the heart, may give a promise beyond all this world's discords of the "harmony . . . in immortal souls."

NOTES

[1] Harold C. Goddard, *The Meaning of Shakespeare* (Chicago, 1951; rpt. 1960), 1:100.
[2] John Palmer, *Comic Characters of Shakespeare* (London, 1946), p. 71.
[3] Toby Lelyveld, *Shylock on the Stage* (London, 1961), pp. 83, 82.
[4] Quoted from Variorum ed. of *MV*, ed. H. H. Furness (Philadelphia, 1888), p. 452.
[5] Ibid., p. 449.
[6] Graham Midgley, "*The Merchant of Venice*: A Reconsideration," *Essays in Criticism*, 10 (1960): 122–123.
[7] Quoted in Arden ed. (ed. John Russell Brown), p. xxxiv.
[8] Stoll, *Shakespeare Studies* (New York, 1927; rpt. 1942), pp. 294–95.
[9] Cf. Wilbur Sanders, *The Dramatist and the Received Idea* (Cambridge, 1968), p. 40: "In so far as there is an Elizabethan mind, it is as much moulded by the playwrights who sought to educate its sensibility and broaden its horizons, as it moulds those playwrights. The 'orthodoxy' of a period is not an ideological steamroller that subdues all humanity to its ruling passion for the horizontal, but itself the product of the delicate, breathing organism of human society, in which cause and effect are never very sharply distinguished." Sanders' book has interesting material about attitudes toward Jews, adduced in the discussion of *The Jew of Malta;* unfortunately (since it is so challenging a book) Sanders does not discuss *MV* at any length.
[10] That Shylock "hoards" his words has been remarked by Alexander Leggatt, *Shakespeare's Comedy of Love* (London, 1974), p. 137, among others.
[11] R. H. Tawney, *Religion and the Rise of Capitalism* (New York, 1926), p. 151.
[12] To read Bacon's essay "Of Usury," with its sensible evaluation of the pros and cons of legalizing credit, and its economically-grounded decision in favor of a regulated system of lending (with different rates set for small private loans and larger commercial loans), is to realize the profound change of attitudes that was taking place at the end of this Shakespearean period. "It is better to mitigate usury by declaration," Bacon concludes, "than to suffer it to rage by connivance."
[13] Tawney, *Religion and the Rise of Capitalism*, p. 172.
[14] The Act of 1571 essentially acknowledges the point Bacon makes in the conclusion to the essay "Of Usury" (see note 12, above). The Edwardian Act "hath not done so much good as was hoped it should, but rather the said vice of usury, and specially by the way of sales of wares and shift of interest, hath much more exceedingly abounded, to the utter undoing of many gentlemen, merchants, occupiers, and other, and to the importable hurt of the commonwealth . . . [also] there is no provision against such corrupt shifts and sales of wares, as also . . . there is no difference of pain, forfeiture or punishment upon the greater or lesser exactions and oppressions by reason of loans upon usury: Be it therefore enacted . . ." that the Act banning the taking of any interest is repealed, and the Henrician Act (which set a maximum legal rate) is revived. I quote from Joel Hurstfield and Alan G. R. Smith, eds., *Elizabethan People: State and Society* (London, 1972), pp. 67–68. Hurstfield and Smith also extract a section from Miles Mosse's *Arraignment and Conviction of Usury* (1595), one of many pamphlets attesting to the abiding moral abhorrence of interest-taking: Mosse (writing almost a quarter century after the Act quoted above) still insists that much of what is called "interest" is nonetheless really "usury." Cf., Shylock

who (taking the semantic distinction still further) describes as "well-won thrift" what Antonio calls "interest" (1.3.45–46).

[15] Lawrence Stone, *The Crisis of the Aristocracy, 1558–1641* (Oxford, 1965), pp. 542, 543–44.

[16] Ed. Georges Edelen (Ithaca, N.Y., 1968), p. 203.

[17] Intro. to Thomas Wilson, *Discourse upon Usury* (1572), ed. R. H. Tawney (New York, 1925), pp. 21–22.

[18] Stone, *Crisis of the Aristocracy,* pp. 532–33.

[19] Cecil Roth, *A History of Jews in England* (Oxford, 1941; 3rd ed. rev., 1964), p. 90.

[20] The orthodox view of the episode in Genesis, as it is expressed in Elizabethan sermons, is given by Arnold Williams, *The Common Expositor* (Chapel Hill, 1948), pp. 170–71. It is essentially Antonio's view, which I describe below.

[21] Edward Arbor, ed., *The Art of English Poesy* (1589), fascimile of the 1906 rpt. (Kent State, 1970), p. 217.

[22] But some critics have accepted Shylock's "merry sport" at face value: H. B. Charlton, *Shakespearian Comedy* (London, 1938; rpt. 1966), p. 150; Goddard, *Meaning of Shakespeare,* 1:100.

[23] Quoted in John Russell Brown, "The Realization of Shylock: A Theatrical Criticism," *Early Shakespeare,* Stratford-upon-Avon Studies, 3 (London, 1961): 190.

[24] *An Apologie for Poetrie,* in *Elizabethan Critical Essays,* ed. G. Gregory Smith (Oxford, 1904), 1:182. Cf., Ben Jonson: "*Speech* is the only benefit man hath to express his excellency of mind above other creatures. It is the instrument of *Society.*" (*Timber, or Discoveries,* in *Ben Jonson's Literary Criticism,* ed. James D. Redwine, Jr. [Lincoln, Nebraska, 1970], p. 20.) See also Lawrence Danson, *Tragic Alphabet: Shakespeare's Drama of Language* (New Haven, 1974), pp. 2–7.

[25] Roth, *History of Jews in England,* p. 79. Among the observations made by that fantastical traveler, Thomas Coryat, in his visit to the Venetian ghetto in the first decade of the seventeenth century is this: "And as pitiful it is to see that fewe of them [i.e., the Jews] living in Italy are converted to the Christian religion. For this I understand is the maine impediment to their conversion: All their goodes are confiscated as soone as they embrace Christianity: and this I heard is the reason, because whereas many of them doe raise their fortunes by usury . . . it is therefore decreed by the Pope, and other free Princes in whose territories they live, that they shall make restitution of their ill gotten goods, and so disclogge their soules and consciences, when they are admitted by holy baptisme into the bosome of Christs Church. Seeing then when their goods are taken from them at their conversion, they are left even naked, and destitute of their meanes of maintenance, there are fewer Jews converted to Christianity in Italy, than in any other country of Christendome." *Coryat's Crudities* (1611) (Glasgow, 1905), 1: 373–74.

[26] Cf. Harold Fisch, *The Dual Image: The Figure of the Jew in English and American Literature* (New York, 1971), pp. 14–15: "The Jews [according to traditions based on Pauline doctrine] were a deicide nation but they were also a nation which is redeemed, and on whose redemption the fate of mankind hangs." See also an interesting article by Albert Wertheim, "The Treatment of Shylock and Thematic Integrity in *The Merchant of Venice,*" *Shakespeare Studies,* 6 (1970): 75–87. See also G. K. Hunter's "The Theology of *The Jew of Malta,*" *Journal of the Warburg and Cartauld Institutes,* 17 (1964): 211–40.

René Girard
"TO ENTRAP THE WISEST"

The criticism of *The Merchant of Venice* has been dominated by two images of Shylock that appear irreconcilable. It is my contention that both images belong to the play and that far from rendering it unintelligible their conjunction is essential to an understanding of Shakespeare's dramatic practice.

The first image is that of the Jewish moneylender in the late-medieval and modern book of anti-Semitism. The mere evocation of that Jewish stereotype suggests a powerful system of binary oppositions that does not have to be fully developed to pervade the entire play. First comes the opposition between Jewish greed and Christian generosity, between revenge and compassion, between the crankiness of old age and the charm of youth, between the dark and the luminous, the beautiful and the ugly, the gentle and the harsh, the musical and the unmusical, and so on.

There is a second image that comes only after the stereotype has been firmly implanted in our minds; at first it does not make as strong an impression as the first, but it gathers strength later on because the language and behavior of the Christian characters repeatedly confirm the rather brief but essential utterances of Shylock himself on which it primarily rests.

The symmetry between the explicit venality of Shylock and the implicit venality of the other Venetians cannot fail to be intended by the playwright. It is true that Bassanio's courtship of Portia is presented primarily as a financial operation. In his plea for Antonio's financial support, Bassanio mentions first the wealth of the young heiress, then her beauty, then finally her spiritual qualities. Those critics who idealize the Venetians write as if the many textual clues that contradict their view were not planted by the author himself, as if their presence in the play were a purely fortuitous matter, like the arrival of a bill in the morning mail when one really expects a love letter. On every possible occasion Shakespeare pursued the parallel

From *Literature and Society: Selected Papers from the English Institute*, edited by Edward W. Said (Baltimore: Johns Hopkins University Press, 1980), pp. 100–119.

between the amorous venture of Bassanio and the typical Venetian business of Antonio, his commerce on the high seas. Observe, for instance, the manner in which Gratiano, who is just back from Belmont and still flushed with the success of this expedition, addresses Salerio:

> Your hand, Salerio. What's the news from Venice?
> How doth that royal merchant, good Antonio?
> I know he will be glad of our success.
> We are the Jasons, we have won the fleece.
> SAL.: I would you have won the fleece that he hath lost.   (III, ii, 241–46)[1]

The truth is that Bassanio and friends have done exactly that. Even if Antonio's losses turned out to be real, Portia's conquest would more than make up financially for Antonio's ships.

Regarding this symmetry between Shylock and the Venetians, many good points have been made. I will mention only one, for the sole reason that I have not found it in the critical literature on the play. If I am not original, please accept my apologies.

Act 3, scene 2, Bassanio wants to reward his lieutenant for his services, and he tells Gratiano and Nerissa that they will be married simultaneously with Portia and himself, in a double wedding ceremony—at Portia's expense we may assume. "Our feast," he says, "shall be much honored in your marriage." Upon which the elated Gratiano says to his fiancée: "We'll play with them the first boy for a thousand ducats" (III, ii, 214–17).

These young people have ample reason to be joyous, now that their future is made secure by Bassanio's clever stroke with the caskets, and this bet sounds harmless enough, but Shakespeare is not addicted to pointless social chitchat and must have a purpose. Gratiano's baby will be two thousand ducats cheaper than Antonio's pound of flesh. Human flesh and money in Venice are constantly exchanged for one another. People are turned into objects of financial speculation. Mankind has become a commodity, an exchange value like any other. I cannot believe that Shakespeare did not perceive the analogy between Gratiano's wager and Shylock's pound of flesh.

Shylock's pound of flesh is symbolical of Venetian behavior. The Venetians appear different from Shylock, up to a point. Financial considerations have become so natural to them and they are so embedded into their psyches that they have become not quite but almost invisible; they can never be identified as a distinct aspect of behavior. Antonio's loan to Bassanio, for instance, is treated as an act of love and not as a business transaction.

Shylock hates Antonio for lending money without interest. In his eyes, the merchant spoils the financial business. We can read this as the resentment of vile greed for noble generosity within the context of the first image, but we may prefer another reading that contributes to the second image. The generosity of Antonio may well be a corruption more extreme than the caricatural greed of Shylock. As a rule, when Shylock lends money, he expects more money in return, and nothing else. Capital should produce capital. Shylock does not confuse his financial operations with Christian charity. This is why, unlike the Venetians, he can look like the embodiment of greed.

Venice is a world in which appearances and reality do not match. Of all the pretenders to Portia's hand, Bassanio alone makes the right choice between the three caskets because he alone is a Venetian and knows how deceptive a splendid exterior can be. Unlike his foreign competitors who obviously come from countries where things still are more or less what they seem to be, less advanced countries we might say, he instinctively feels that the priceless treasure he seeks must hide behind the most unlikely appearance.

The symbolic significance of choosing lead rather than the gold and silver selected by the two foreigners faithfully duplicates the whole relationship between the true Venetians and the foreign Shylock. When the two alien pretenders reach avidly for the two precious metals, just like Shylock, they look like personifications of greed; in reality they are rather naive, whereas Bassanio is anything but naive. It is characteristic of the Venetians that they look like the very picture of disinterestedness at the precise moment when their sly calculations cause the pot of gold to fall into their lap.

The generosity of the Venetians is not feigned. Real generosity makes the beneficiary more dependent on his generous friend than a regular loan. In Venice a new form of vassality prevails, grounded no longer in strict territorial borders but in vague financial terms. The lack of precise accounting makes personal indebtedness infinite. This is an art Shylock has not mastered since his own daughter feels perfectly free to rob and abandon him without the slightest remorse. The elegance of the décor and the harmony of the music must not lead us to think that everything is right with the Venetian world. It is impossible, however, to say exactly what is wrong. Antonio is sad but he cannot say why, and this unexplained sadness seems to characterize the whole Venetian business aristocracy as much as Antonio himself.

Even in Shylock's life, however, money and matters of human sentiment finally become confused. But there is something comical in this confusion because, even as they become one, money and sentiment retain a measure of separateness, they remain distinguishable from each other and we hear such things as "My daughter! Oh, my ducats! Oh, my daughter! / Fled with a Christian! Oh, my Christian ducats!" (II, viii, 15–16) and other such ridiculous utterances you would never catch in a Venetian mouth.

There is still another occasion upon which Shylock, goaded by his Venetian enemies, confuses financial matters with other passions, and it is the affair of his loan to Antonio. In the interest of his revenge, Shylock demands no interest for his money, no positive guarantees in case of default, nothing but his infamous pound of flesh. Behind the mythical weirdness of the request, we have one spectacular instance of that complete interpenetration between the financial and the human that is characteristic less of Shylock than of the other Venetians. Thus Shylock appears most scandalous to the Venetians and to the spectators when he stops resembling himself to resemble the Venetians even more. The spirit of revenge drives him to imitate the Venetians more perfectly than before, and, in his effort to teach Antonio a lesson, Shylock becomes his grotesque double.

Antonio and Shylock are described as rivals of long standing. Of such people we often say that they have their differences, but this expression would be misleading. Tragic—and comic—conflict amounts to a dissolving of differences that is paradoxical because it proceeds from the opposite intention. All the people involved in the process seek to emphasize and maximize their differences. In Venice, we found, greed and generosity, pride and humility, compassion and ferocity, money and human flesh, tend to become one and the same. This undifferentiation makes it impossible to define anything with precision, to ascribe one particular cause to one particular event. Yet on all sides it is the same obsession with displaying and sharpening a difference that is less and less real. Here is Shylock, for instance, in act 2, scene 5: "Well thou shalt see, thy eyes shall be thy judge, / The difference between Old Shylock and Bassanio" (II, v, 1–2). The Christians too are eager to demonstrate that they are different from the Jews. During the trial scene, it is the turn of the duke, who says to Shylock: "Thou shalt see the difference of our spirits" (IV, i, 368). Even the words are the same. Everywhere the same senseless obsession with differences becomes exacerbated as it keeps defeating itself.

The paradox is not limited to *The Merchant of Venice*. Everywhere in Shakespeare it is an essential component of the tragic and comic relationship. In *The Comedy of Errors*, the endless efforts of the twins to clear up the confusion created by that identity between them which they cannot recognize keeps generating more confusion. The theme of the identical twins, significantly, is borrowed from Plautus, and it is more than an allegory of the process I am talking about; it is its mythical transposition. We have an allusion to this process of undifferentiation, I believe, in a well-known line of *The Merchant*. When Portia enters the court she asks, "Which is the merchant and which is the Jew?" (IV, i, 174). Even if she has never met either Antonio or Shylock, we have a right to be surprised Portia cannot identify the Jewish moneylender at first sight, in view of the enormous difference, visible to all, that is supposed to distinguish him from the gracious Venetians. The line would be more striking, of course, if it came after rather than before the following one: "Antonio and old Shylock both stand forth" (IV, i, 175). If Portia were still unable to distinguish Shylock from Antonio once the two men have come forward together, the scene would explicitly contradict the primary image of Shylock, the stereotype of the Jewish moneylender. This contradiction would stretch the limits of dramatic credibility beyond the breaking point, and Shakespeare refrained from it, but he went as far as he could, I believe, here and elsewhere, to question the reality of a difference he himself, of course, had first introduced into his play. Even the structure of the line, with its two symmetrical questions, suggests the prevalence of symmetry between the two men. The repetition of the interrogative *which* occurs elsewhere in Shakespeare to suggest the

perplexity of observers confronted with items that should be different enough to
be clearly differentiated but no longer are. In *A Midsummer Night's Dream*, for
instance, the undifferentiation of nature, the confusion of the year's four seasons,
precedes and announces the undifferentiation of the four lovers, and the monstrous
undifferentiation of Bottom, at the height of the midsummer madness:

> The spring, the summer,
> The childing autumn, angry winter change
> Their wonted liveries, and the mazed world
> By their increase, now knows not which is which   (II, i, 111–14)

This analysis must lead to Shylock's famous tirade on reciprocity and revenge;
we now have the context in which the meaning and purpose of the passage
become unmistakable:

> . . . if you tickle us,
> Do we not laugh? if you poison us, do we not
> Die? and if you wrong us, shall we not revenge?
> If we are like you in the rest, we will resemble
> You in that. If a Jew wrong a Christian, what
> Is his humility? Revenge. If a Christian wrong
> A Jew, what should his sufferance be by Christian
> Example? Why, revenge. The villainy
> You teach me, I will execute; and it shall go
> Hard but I will better the instruction.   (III, i, 67–76)

The text insists above all on Shylock's personal commitment to revenge. It does not
support the type of "rehabilitation" naively demanded by certain revisionists. But it
unequivocally defines the symmetry and the reciprocity that govern the relations
between the Christians and Shylock. It says the same thing as the line: "Which is the
merchant and which is the Jew?" It is as essential, therefore, as it is striking, and it
fully deserves to be singled out.

   With his caricatural demand for a pound of flesh, Shylock does, indeed,
"better the instruction." What we have just said in the language of psychology can
be translated into religious terms. Between Shylock's behavior and his words, the
relationship is never ambiguous. His interpretation of the law may be narrow and
negative but we can count on him for acting according to it and for speaking
according to his actions. In the passage on revenge, he alone speaks a truth that the
Christians hypocritically deny. The truth of the play is revenge and retribution. The
Christians manage to hide that truth even from themselves. They do not live by the
law of charity, but this law is enough of a presence in their language to drive the law
of revenge underground, to make this revenge almost invisible. As a result, this
revenge becomes more subtle, skillful, and feline than the revenge of Shylock. The
Christians will easily destroy Shylock but they will go on living in a world that is sad

without knowing why, a world in which even the difference between revenge and charity has been abolished.

Ultimately we do not have to choose between a favorable and an unfavorable image of Shylock. The old critics have concentrated on Shylock as a separate entity, an individual substance that would be merely juxtaposed to other individual substances and remain unaffected by them. The ironic depth in *The Merchant of Venice* results from a tension not between two static images of Shylock, but between those textual features that strengthen and those features that undermine the popular idea of an insurmountable difference between Christian and Jew.

It is not excessive to say that characterization itself, as a real dramatic problem or as a fallacy, is at stake in the play. On the one hand Shylock is portrayed as a highly differentiated villain. On the other hand he tells us himself that there are no villains and no heroes; all men are the same, especially when they are taking revenge on each other. Whatever differences may have existed between them prior to the cycle of revenge are dissolved in the reciprocity of reprisals and retaliation. Where does Shakespeare stand on this issue? Massive evidence from the other plays as well as from *The Merchant* cannot leave the question in doubt. The main object of satire is not Shylock the Jew. But Shylock is rehabilitated only to the extent that the Christians are even worse than he is and that the "honesty" of his vices makes him almost a refreshing figure compared to the sanctimonious ferocity of the other Venetians.

The trial scene clearly reveals how implacable and skillful the Christians can be when they take their revenge. In this most curious performance, Antonio begins as the defendant and Shylock as the plaintiff. At the end of one single meeting the roles are reversed and Shylock is a convicted criminal. The man has done no actual harm to anyone. Without his money, the two marriages, the two happy events in the play, could not have come to pass. As his triumphant enemies return to Belmont loaded with a financial and human booty that includes Shylock's own daughter, they still manage to feel compassionate and gentle by contrast with their wretched opponent.

When we sense the injustice of Shylock's fate, we usually say: Shylock is a scapegoat. This expression, however, is ambiguous. When I say that a character in a play is a scapegoat, my statement can mean two different things. It can mean that this character is unjustly condemned from the perspective of the writer. The conviction of the crowd is presented as irrational by the writer himself. In this first case, we say that in that play there is a theme or motif of the scapegoat.

There is a second meaning to the idea that a character is a scapegoat. It can mean that, from the perspective of the writer, this character is justly condemned, but in the eyes of the critic who makes the statement, the condemnation is unjust. The crowd that condemns the victim is presented as rational by the writer, who really belongs to that crowd; only in the eyes of the critic are the crowd and the writer irrational and unjust.

The scapegoat, this time, is not a theme or motif at all; it is not made explicit by the writer, but if the critic is right in his allegations, there must be a scapegoat effect at the origin of the play, a collective effect probably, in which the writer participates. The critic may think, for instance, that a writer who creates a character like Shylock, patterned after the stereotype of the Jewish moneylender, must do so because he personally shares in the anti-Semitism of the society in which this stereotype is present.

When we say that Shylock is a scapegoat, our statement remains vague and critically useless unless we specify if we mean the scapegoat as theme or the scapegoat as structure, the scapegoat as an object of indignation and satire or the scapegoat as a passively accepted delusion.

Before we can resolve the critical impasse to which I referred at the beginning of my presentation we must reformulate it in the terms of this still unperceived alternative between the scapegoat as structure and the scapegoat as theme. Everyone agrees that Shylock is a scapegoat, but is he the scapegoat of his society only or of Shakespeare's as well?

What the critical revisionists maintain is that the scapegoating of Shylock is not a structuring force but a satirical theme. What the traditionalists maintain is that scapegoating, in *The Merchant of Venice*, is a structuring force rather than a theme. Whether we like it or not, they say, the play shares in the cultural anti-Semitism of the society. We should not allow our literary piety to blind us to the fact.

My own idea is that the scapegoat is both structure and theme in *The Merchant of Venice*, and that the play, in this essential respect at least, is anything any reader wants it to be, not because Shakespeare is as confused as we are when we use the word *scapegoat* without specifying, but for the opposite reason: he is so aware and so conscious of the various demands placed upon him by the cultural diversity of his audience; he is so knowledgeable in regard to the paradoxes of mimetic reactions and group behavior that he can stage a scapegoating of Shylock entirely convincing to those who want to be convinced and simultaneously undermine that process with ironic touches that will reach only those who can be reached. Thus he was able to satisfy the most vulgar as well as the most refined audiences. To those who do not want to challenge the anti-Semitic myth, or Shakespeare's own espousal of that myth, *The Merchant of Venice* will always sound like a confirmation of that myth. To those who do challenge these same beliefs, Shakespeare's own challenge will become perceptible. The play is not unlike a perpetually revolving object that, through some mysterious means, would always present itself to each viewer under aspects best suited to his own perspective.

Why are we reluctant to consider this possibility? Both intellectually and ethically, we assume that scapegoating cannot be and should not be a theme of satire and a structuring force at the same time. Either the author participates in the collective victimage and he cannot see it as unjust or he can see it as unjust and he should not connive in it, even ironically. Most works of art do fall squarely on one side or the other of that particular fence. Rewritten by Arthur Miller, Jean-Paul Sartre or Bertolt Brecht, *The Merchant* would be different indeed. But so would a

Merchant of Venice that would merely reflect the anti-Semitism of its society, as a comparison with Marlowe's *Jew of Malta* immediately reveals.

If we look carefully at the trial scene, no doubt can remain that Shakespeare undermines the scapegoat effects just as skillfully as he produces them. There is something frightening in this efficiency. This art demands a manipulation and therefore an intelligence of mimetic phenomena that transcends not only the ignorant immorality of those who submit passively to victimage mechanisms but also the moralism that rebels against them but does not perceive the irony generated by the dual role of the author. Shakespeare himself must first generate at the grossly theatrical level the effects that he later undermines at the level of allusions.

Let us see how Shakespeare can move in both directions at the same time. Why is it difficult not to experience a feeling of relief and even jubilation at the discomfiture of Shylock? The main reason, of course, is that Antonio's life is supposed to be under an immediate threat. That threat stems from Shylock's stubborn insistence that he is entitled to his pound of flesh.

Now the pound of flesh is a mythical motif. We found earlier that it is a highly significant allegory of a world where human beings and money are constantly exchanged for one another, but it is nothing more. We can imagine a purely mythical context in which Shylock could really carve up his pound of flesh and Antonio would walk away, humiliated and diminished but alive. In *The Merchant of Venice*, the mythical context is replaced by a realistic one. We are told that Antonio could not undergo this surgical operation without losing his life. It is certainly true in a realistic context, but it is also true, in that same context, that, especially in the presence of the whole Venetian establishment, old Shylock would be unable to perform this same operation. The myth is only partly demythologized, and Shylock is supposed to be capable of carving up Antonio's body in cold blood because, as a Jew and a moneylender, he passes for a man of unusual ferocity. This presumed ferocity justifies our own religious prejudice.

Shakespeare knows that victimage must be unanimous to be effective, and no voice is effectively raised in favor of Shylock. The presence of the silent Magnificoes, the élite of the community, turns the trial into a rite of social unanimity. The only characters not physically present are Shylock's daughter and his servant, and they are of one mind with the actual scapegoaters since they were the first to abandon Shylock after taking his money. Like a genuine Biblical victim, Shylock is betrayed "even by those of his own household."

As scapegoating affects more and more people and tends toward unanimity, the contagion becomes overwhelming. In spite of its judicial and logical nonsense, the trial scene is enormously performative and dramatic. The spectators and readers of the play cannot fail to be affected and cannot refrain from experiencing Shylock's defeat as if it were their own victory. The crowd in the theater becomes one with the crowd on the stage. The contagious effect of scapegoating extends to the audience. In *The Merchant of Venice*, at least, and perhaps in many other plays, the Aristotelian catharsis is a scapegoat effect.

As an embodiment of Venetian justice, the duke should be impartial, but at the very outset of the proceedings he commiserates with the defendant and launches into a diatribe against Shylock:

I am sorry for thee. Thou art come to answer
A stony adversary, an inhuman wretch,
Uncapable of pity, void and empty
From any dram of mercy.   (IV, i, 3–6)

These words set the tone for the entire scene. The Christian virtue par excellence, mercy is the weapon with which Shylock is clubbed over the head. The Christians use the word *mercy* with such perversity that they can justify their own revenge with it, give full license to their greed and still come out with a clear conscience. They feel they have discharged their obligation to be merciful by their constant repetition of the word itself. The quality of their mercy is not strained, to say the least. It is remarkably casual and easy. When the duke severely asks: "How shalt thou hope for mercy, rendering none?" (IV, i, 88), Shylock responds with impeccable logic: "What judgment shall I dread, doing no wrong?" (IV, i, 89).

Shylock trusts in the law too much. How could the law of Venice be based on mercy, how could it be equated with the golden rule, since it gives the Venetians the right to own slaves and it does not give slaves the right to own Venetians? How can we be certain that Shakespeare, who engineered that scapegoat effect so skillfully, is not fooled by it even for one second? Our certainty is perfect and it may well be much more than "subjective," as some critics would say. It may well be perfectly "objective" in the sense that it correctly recaptures the author's intention and yet it remains a closed book to a certain type of reader. If irony were demonstrable it would cease to be irony. Irony must not be explicit enough to destroy the efficiency of the scapegoat machine in the minds of those fools for whom that machine was set up in the first place. Irony cannot fail to be less tangible than the object on which it bears.

Some will object that my reading is "paradoxical." It may well be, but why should it be a priori excluded that Shakespeare can write a paradoxical play? Especially if the paradox on which the play is built is formulated most explicitly at the center of that very play. Shakespeare is writing, not without a purpose, I suppose, that appearances, especially the appearances of beautiful language, are "The seeming truth which cunning times put on / To entrap the wisest" (III, ii, 100–101). Shakespeare is writing, not without a purpose, that the worst sophistry, when distilled by a charming voice, can decide the outcome of a trial, or that the most unreligious behavior can sound religious if the right words are mentioned. Let us listen to the reasons given by Bassanio for trusting in lead rather than in silver or gold and we will see that they apply word for word to the play itself:

The world is still deceived with ornament.
In law, what plea so tainted and corrupt

But being seasoned with a gracious voice,
Obscures the show of evil? In religion,
What damned error but some sober brow
Will bless it, and approve it with a text,
Hiding the grossness with fair ornament?
There is no vice so simple but assumes
Some mark of virtue on his outward parts.   (III, ii, 74–82)

This is so appropriate to the entire play that it is difficult to believe it a coincidence.

I see Bassanio's brief intervention during the trial scene as another sign of Shakespeare's ironic distance. As soon as Shylock begins to relent, under the pressure of Portia's skill, Bassanio declares his willingness to pay back the money Shylock is now willing to accept. In his eagerness to be finished with the whole unpleasant business, Bassanio shows a degree of mercy, but Portia remains adamant. Feeling her claws in Shylock's flesh, she drives them deeper and deeper in order to exact her own pound of flesh. Bassanio's suggestion bears no fruit but its formulation at this crucial moment cannot be pointless. It is the only reasonable solution to the whole affair but dramatically it cannot prevail because it is undramatic. Shakespeare is too good a playwright not to understand that the only good solution, from a theatrical standpoint, is the scapegoating of Shylock. On the other hand he wants to point out the unjust nature of the "cathartic" resolution that is forced upon him by the necessity of his art. He wants the reasonable solution to be spelled out somewhere inside the play.

Is it not excessive to say that scapegoating is a recognizable motif in *The Merchant of Venice?* There is one explicit allusion to the scapegoat in the play. It occurs at the beginning of Shylock's trial.

I am a tainted wether of the flock,
Meetest for death. The weakest kind of fruit
Drops earliest to the ground, and so let me.
You cannot better be employed, Bassanio,
Than to live still and write mine epitaph.   (IV, i, 114–18)

Is there a difficulty for my thesis in the fact that Antonio rather than Shylock utters these lines? Not at all, since their mutual hatred has turned Antonio and Shylock into the doubles of each other. This mutual hatred makes all reconciliation impossible—nothing concrete separates the antagonists, no genuinely tangible issue that could be arbitrated and settled—but the undifferentiation generated by this hatred paves the way for the only type of resolution that can conclude this absolute conflict, the scapegoat resolution.

Antonio speaks these lines in reply to Bassanio, who has just asserted he would never let his friend and benefactor die in his place. He would rather die himself. Neither one will die, of course, or even suffer in the slightest. In the city of

Venice, no Antonio or Bassanio will ever suffer as long as there is a Shylock to do the suffering for them.

There is no serious danger that Antonio will die, but he can really see himself, at this point, as a scapegoat in the making. Thus Shakespeare can have an explicit reference to scapegoating without pointing directly to Shylock. There is a great irony, of course, not only in the fact that the metaphor is displaced, the scapegoat being the essence of metaphoric displacement, but also in the almost romantic complacency of Antonio, in his intimation of masochistic satisfaction. The quintessential Venetian, Antonio, the man who is sad without a cause, may be viewed as a figure of the modern subjectivity characterized by a strong propensity toward self-victimization or, more concretely, by a greater and greater interiorization of a scapegoat process that is too well understood to be reenacted as a real event in the real world. Mimetic entanglements cannot be projected with complete success onto all the Shylocks of this world, and the scapegoat process tends to turn back upon itself and become reflective. What we have, as a result, is a masochistic and theatrical self-pity that announces the romantic subjectivity. This is the reason why Antonio is eager to be "sacrificed" in the actual presence of Bassanio.

Irony is not demonstrable, I repeat, and it should not be, otherwise it would disturb the catharsis of those who enjoy the play at the cathartic level only. Irony is anticathartic. Irony is experienced in a flash of complicity with the writer at his most subtle, against the larger and coarser part of the audience that remains blind to these subtleties. Irony is the writer's vicarious revenge against the revenge that he must vicariously perform. If irony were too obvious, if it were intelligible to all, it would defeat its own purpose because there would be no more object for irony to undermine.

The reading I propose can be strengthened, I believe, through a comparison with other plays, notably *Richard III*. When Shakespeare wrote this play, his king's identity as a villain was well established. The dramatist goes along with the popular view, especially at the beginning. In the first scene, Richard presents himself as a monstrous villain. His deformed body is a mirror for the self-confessed ugliness of his soul. Here too we are dealing with a stereotype, the stereotype of the bad king that can be said to be generated or revived by the unanimous rejection of the scapegoat king, the very process that is reenacted in the last act after gathering momentum throughout the play.

If we forget for a while the introduction and the conclusion to focus on the drama itself, a different image of Richard emerges. We are in a world of bloody political struggles. All adult characters in the play have committed at least one political murder or benefited from one. As critics like Murray Krieger and Jan Kott have pointed out, the War of the Roses functions as a system of political rivalry and revenge in which every participant is a tyrant and a victim in turn, always behaving and speaking not according to permanent character differences but to the position he occupies at any moment within the total dynamic system. Being the last coil in that infernal spiral, Richard may kill more people more cynically than his prede-

cessors, but he is not essentially different. In order to make the past history of
reciprocal violence dramatically present, Shakespeare resorts to the technique of
the curse. Everyone keeps cursing everyone else so vehemently and massively that
the total effect is tragic or almost comic according to the mood of the spectator;
all these curses mutually cancel each other until the end, when they all converge
against Richard and bring about his final undoing, which is also the restoration of
peace.

Two images of the same character tend to alternate, one highly differentiated
and one undifferentiated. In the case of *The Merchant of Venice* and *Richard III*
some fairly obvious reasons can be invoked; in both plays, the theme was a sensitive
one, dominated by social and political imperatives regarding which Shakespeare felt
skeptical, obviously, but that he could not attack openly. The method he devised
permitted an indirect satire, highly effective with the knowledgeable few and completely invisible to the ignorant multitude, avid only of the gross *catharsis* Shakespeare never failed to provide.

Some kind of social and political interpretation is unavoidable, I believe, but it
is not incompatible, far from it, with a more radical approach.

Great theater is necessarily a play of differentiation and undifferentiation. The
characters will not hold the interest of the audience unless the audience can
sympathize with them or deny them its sympathy. They must be highly differentiated, in other words, but any scheme of differentiation is synchronic and static. In
order to be good, a play must be dynamic rather than static. The dynamics of the
theater are the dynamics of human conflict, the reciprocity of retribution and
revenge; the more intense the process, the more symmetry you tend to have, the
more everything tends to become the same on both sides of the antagonism.

In order to be good a play must be as reciprocal and undifferentiated as
possible but it must be highly differentiated, too, otherwise the spectators will not
be interested in the outcome of the conflict. These two requirements are incompatible, but a playwright who cannot satisfy both simultaneously is obviously not a
great playwright; he will produce either plays too differentiated, which will be
labeled *pièces à thèse* because they will be experienced as insufficiently dynamic, or
plays too undifferentiated, in order to have a lot of action, or suspense, as we say,
but this suspense will appear pointless and will be blamed for a lack of intellectual
and ethical content.

The successful playwright can fulfill the two contradictory requirements simultaneously, even though they are contradictory. How does he do it? In many
instances he does not seem fully aware of what he is doing; he must do it in the
same instinctive manner as the spectators who passionately identify with one antagonist. Even though the assumed difference between the two always translates
itself into reciprocal and undifferentiated behavior, our view of the conflict tends to
be static and differentiated.

We can be certain, I believe, that such is not the case with Shakespeare.
Shakespeare is fully conscious of the gap between the difference of the static

structure and the nondifference of tragic action. He fills his plays with ironic allusions to the gap between the two and he does not hesitate to widen that gap still further, as if he knew that he could do this with impunity and that in all probability he would be rewarded for doing it; far from destroying his credibility as a creator of "characters" he would increase the overall dramatic impact of his theater and turn his plays into those dynamic and inexhaustible objects upon which critics can comment endlessly without ever putting their finger on the real source of their ambiguity.

In *Richard III* we have examples of this practice no less striking than in *The Merchant of Venice*. Anne and Elizabeth, the two women who have most suffered at the hands of Richard, cannot resist the temptation of power, even at the cost of an alliance with him, when Richard himself diabolically dangles this toy in front of them. After cursing Richard abundantly and discharging in this manner all her moral obligations, Anne literally walks over the dead body of her father to join hands with Richard. A little later Elizabeth walks over the dead bodies of two of her children, symbolically at least, in order to deliver a third one into the bloody hands of the murderer.

These two scenes are structurally close, and they generate a crescendo of abomination that cannot be without a purpose. These two women are even more vile than Richard, and the only character who is able to point out this vileness, thus becoming in a sense the only ethical voice in the whole play, is Richard himself, whose role, *mutatis mutandis,* is comparable to that of Shylock in *The Merchant of Venice*.

It is Shakespeare's genius that he can do such things. And he does them, not to generate irony only, but for the sake of dramatic efficiency. He knows that by doing them, he creates uneasiness among the spectators, he places upon them a moral burden with which they cannot deal in terms of the scapegoat values presented at the outset. The demand for the expulsion of the scapegoat is paradoxically reinforced by the very factors that make this expulsion arbitrary.

I fully agree that, in the case of plays like *Richard III* or *The Merchant of Venice,* an infinite number of readings is possible, and this infinity is determined by "the play of the signifier." I do not agree that this play is gratuitous, and that it is in the nature of all signifiers as signifiers to produce such infinite play. The literary signifier always becomes a victim. It is a victim of the signified, at least metaphorically, in the sense that its play, its *différence,* or what you will, is almost inevitably sacrificed to the one-sidedness of a single-minded differentiated structure à la Lévi-Strauss. The sacrificed signifier disappears behind the signified. Is this victimage of the signifier nothing but a metaphor, or is it mysteriously connected to the scapegoat as such in the sense that it is rooted in that ritual space where the major signifier is also a victim, not merely in the semiotic sense, this time, but in the sense of Shylock or of Richard III? The play of the signifier, with its arbitrary interruption for the sake of a differentiated structure, operates exactly like the theatrical and ritual process, with its conflictual undifferentiation suddenly resolved and returned to static differentiation through the elimination of a victim. Everything I have said suggests that to Shakespeare, at least, all these things are one and the same. The process of signification is one with the scapegoat resolution of the crisis in which all significations are dissolved, then reborn—the crisis that is described at length in *Troilus and Cressida* and designated as the "crisis of Degree." The evidence from ritual as well as from mythology suggests that Shakespeare may well be right. Long before *deciders* acquired its more abstract significance—to decide—it meant to cut with a knife, to immolate a sacrificial victim.

Those who think that the problem of textuality can be disposed of with no regard for the victims to which literary texts allude should have a close look at *The Merchant of Venice*.

NOTES

[1] All citations of *The Merchant of Venice* are to the edition published by J. M. Dent in London in 1894.

Derek Cohen

SHYLOCK AND THE IDEA
OF THE JEW

Current criticism notwithstanding, *The Merchant of Venice* seems to me a profoundly and crudely anti-Semitic play. The debate about its implications has usually been between inexpert Jewish readers and spectators who discern an anti-Semitic core and literary critics (many of them Jews) who defensively maintain that the Shakespearean subtlety of mind transcends anti-Semitism. The critics' arguments, by now familiar, center on the subject of Shylock's essential humanity, point to the imperfections of the Christians, and remind us that Shakespeare was writing in a period when there were so few Jews in England that it didn't matter anyway (or, alternatively, that because there were so few Jews in England Shakespeare had probably never met one, so he didn't really know what he was doing). Where I believe the defensive arguments go wrong is in their heavy concentration on the character of Shylock; they overlook the more encompassing attempt of the play to offer a total poetic image of the Jew. It is all very well for John Russell Brown to say *The Merchant of Venice* is not anti-Jewish, and that 'there are only two slurs on Jews in general';[1] but this kind of assertion, a common enough one in criticism of the play, cannot account for the fear and shame that Jewish audiences and readers have always felt from the moment of Shylock's entrance to his final exit. I wish to argue that these feelings are justified and that such an intuitive response is more natural than the critical sophistries whose purpose is to exonerate Shakespeare from the charge of anti-Semitism. Although few writers on the subject are prepared to concede as much, it is quite possible that Shakespeare didn't give a damn about Jews or about insulting England's minuscule Jewish community, and that, if he did finally humanize his Jew, he did so simply to enrich his drama. It is, of course, interesting to speculate on whether Shakespeare was an anti-Semite, but we cannot rise beyond speculation on this point.

The image of Jewishness which *The Merchant of Venice* presents is contrasted with the image of Christianity to which it is made referable and which ultimately

From *Shakespearean Motives* (London: Macmillan, 1988), pp. 104–18.

encompasses and overwhelms it. Though it is simplistic to say that the play equates Jewishness with evil and Christianity with goodness, it is surely reasonable to see a moral relationship between the insistent equation of the *idea* of Jewishness with acquisitive and material values while the *idea* of Christianity is linked to the values of mercy and love. In this chapter I wish first of all to demonstrate that *The Merchant of Venice* is an anti-Semitic play by examining the image of Jewishness which it presents and by placing that image in the contrasting context of Christianity to which it is automatically made referable. Secondly, I wish to examine the paradox which follows from my assertion of the anti-Semitic nature of the play—that is, the way in which Shylock is humanized in his final scene and made simultaneously both the villain of the drama and its unfortunate victim.

Let us first ask what is meant by anti-Semitism when that term is applied to a work of art. Leo Kirschbaum suggests that it is a 'wholly irrational prejudice against Jews in general, noting it would be difficult to accuse any of the Christian characters in *The Merchant of Venice* of such a vice'.[2] This seems to be John Russell Brown's view as well; he perceives the play's only anti-Semitic remarks to be Launcelot's statement 'my master's a very Jew' (II, ii, 100) and Antonio's comment about Shylock's 'Jewish heart' (IV, i, 80).[3] While generally acceptable, Kirschbaum's definition seems to me to err in its use of the term irrational. Prejudice is almost always rationalized, and it is rationalized by reference to history and mythology. Jews have been hated for a number of reasons, the most potent among them that they were the killers of Jesus Christ.

I would define an anti-Semitic work of art as one that portrays Jews in a way that makes them objects of antipathy to readers and spectators—objects of scorn, hatred, laughter, or contempt. A careful balance is needed to advance this definition, since it might seem to preclude the possibility of an artist's presenting any Jewish character in negative terms without incurring the charge of anti-Semitism. Obviously, Jews must be allowed to have their faults in art as they do in life. In my view, a work of art becomes anti-Semitic not by virtue of its portrayal of an individual Jew in uncomplimentary terms but solely by its association of negative racial characteristics with the term Jewish or with Jewish characters generally. What we must do, then, is look at the way the word *Jew* is used and how Jews are portrayed in *The Merchant of Venice* as a whole.

The word *Jew* is used 58 times in *The Merchant of Venice*. Variants of the word like *Jewess, Jews, Jew's*, and *Jewish* are used 14 times; *Hebrew* is used twice. There are, then, 74 direct uses of *Jew* and unambiguously related words in the play. Since it will readily be acknowledged that Shakespeare understood the dramatic and rhetorical power of iteration, it must follow that there is a deliberate reason for the frequency of the word in the play. And as in all of Shakespeare's plays, the reason is to surround and inform the repeated term with associations which come more and more easily to mind as it is used. A word apparently used neutrally in the early moments of a play gains significance as it is used over and over; it becomes a term with connotations that infuse it with additional meaning.

The word *Jew* has no neutral connotations in drama. Unlike, say, the word *blood* in *Richard II* or *Macbeth*—where the connotations deepen in proportion not merely to the frequency with which the word is uttered but to the poetic significance of the passages in which it is employed—*Jew* has strongly negative implications in *The Merchant of Venice*. It is surely significant that Shylock is addressed as 'Shylock' only seventeen times in the play. On all other occasions he is called 'Jew' and is referred to as 'the Jew'. Even when he and Antonio are presumed to be on an equal footing, Shylock is referred to as the Jew while Antonio is referred to by name. For example, in the putatively disinterested letter written by the learned doctor Bellario to commend Balthazar/Portia, there is the phrase '*I acquainted him with the cause in controversy between the Jew and Antonio...*' (IV, i, 153–4). Similarly, in the court scene Portia calls Shylock by his name only twice; for the rest of the scene she calls him Jew to his face. The reason for this discrimination is, of course, to set Shylock apart from the other characters. This it successfully does. Calling the play's villain by a name which generalizes him while at the same time ostensibly defining his essence is, in a sense, to depersonalize him. As in our own daily life, where terms like *bourgeois, communist* and *fascist* conveniently efface the humanness and individuality of those to whom they are applied, the constant reference to Shylock's 'thingness' succeeds in depriving him of his humanity while it simultaneously justifies the hostility of his enemies. The word *Jew* has for centuries conjured up associations of foreignness in the minds of non-Jews. When it is repeatedly used with reference to the bloodthirsty villain of the play, its intention is unmistakable. And the more often it is used, the more difficult it becomes for the audience to see it as a neutral word. Even if John Russell Brown is right, then, in pointing out that there are only two overtly anti-Semitic uses of the word in the play, it will surely be seen that overt anti-Semitism very early becomes unnecessary. Each time that *Jew* is used by any of Shylock's enemies, there is a deeply anti-Jewish implication already and automatically assumed.

In Act I, scene iii, after the bond has been struck, Antonio turns to the departing Shylock and murmurs, 'Hie thee gentle Jew./The Hebrew will turn Christian, he grows kind' (173–4). The lines themselves seem inoffensive, but let us examine the words and the gestures they imply. Shylock has left the stage and Antonio is commenting on the bond that has just been sealed. It is impossible to ignore the mocking tone of Antonio's words and the fact that the scorn they express is directed toward Shylock's Jewishness as much as toward Shylock himself. Surely, too, the elevation of one religion over another is accomplished only at the expense of the religion deemed inferior. To imply that Shylock is so improved (however ironically this is meant) that he verges on becoming Christian is an expression of amused superiority to Jews. The relatively mild anti-Semitism implicit in this passage is significant, both because it is so common in the play and because it leads with the inexorable logic of historical truth to the more fierce and destructive kind of anti-Semitism, borne of fear, that surfaces when the object of it gains ascendancy. While Shylock the Jew is still regarded as a nasty but harmless smudge on the landscape, he is grudgingly accorded some human potential by the Christians; once he becomes a threat to their happiness, however, the quality in him which is initially disdained—his Jewishness—becomes the very cynosure of fear and loathing.

In its early stages, for example, the play makes only light-hearted connections between the Jew and the Devil: as the connections are more and more validated by Shylock's behavior, however, they become charged with meaning. When Launcelot, that dismal clown, is caught in the contortions of indecision as he debates with himself the pros and cons of leaving Shylock's service, he gives the association of Jew and Devil clear expression:

> Certainly, my conscience will serve me to run from this Jew my master . . . to be rul'd by my conscience, I should stay with the Jew my master, who (God bless the mark) is a kind of devil; and to run away from the Jew, I should be rul'd by the fiend, who (saving your reverence) is the devil himself. Certainly the Jew is the very devil incarnation, and in my conscience, my conscience is but a kind of hard conscience, to offer to counsel me to stay with the Jew.
> (II, ii, 1–28)

Significant here is the almost obsessive repetition of 'the Jew'. In the immediate context the phrase has a neat dramatic ambiguity; it refers explicitly to Shylock, but by avoiding the use of his name it also refers more generally to the concept of the Jew. The ambiguity of the phrase makes the demonic association applicable to Jews generally.

That Launcelot's description is anti-Jewish more than simply anti-Shylock is to be seen in the fact that the view of the Jew it presents is in accord with the anti-Semitic portrayal of Jews from the Middle Ages on. Launcelot's image of the Jew as the Devil incarnate conforms to a common medieval notion. It is expressed in Chaucer and much early English drama, and it is given powerful theological support by Luther, who warns the Christian world that 'next to the devil thou hast no enemy more cruel, more venemous and violent than a true Jew'.[4] That a fool like Launcelot should take the assertion a step further and see the Jew as the Devil himself is only to be expected. And that the play should show, as its final discovery, that Shylock is only a devil *manqué* is merely to lend further support to Luther's influential asseveration.

A less mythological but more colourful and dramatically effective anti-Jewish association is forged by the frequent and almost casually employed metaphor of Jew as dog. The play is replete with dialogue describing Shylock in these terms. In the mouth of Solanio, for example, the connection is explicit: 'I never heard a passion so confus'd, / So strange, outrageous, and so variable / As the dog Jew did utter in the streets' (II, viii, 12–14). I do not believe that it is going too far to suggest that in this passage the word *strange* carries a host of anti-Semitic reverberations. It recalls to the traditional anti-Semitic memory the foreign and, to the ignorant, frightening Jewish rituals of mourning—rituals which in anti-Semitic literature have been redolent with implications of the slaughter of Christian children and the drinking of their blood. With this report of Shylock's rage and grief comes a massive turning point in the play. The once verminous Jew is implicitly transformed into a fearful force.

To this argument I must relate a point about a passage hardly noticed in the critical literature on the play. Having bemoaned his losses and decided to take his revenge, Shylock turns to Tubal and tells him to get an officer to arrest Antonio. 'I will have the heart of him if he forfeit, for were he out of Venice I can make what merchandise I will. Go, Tubal,' he says, 'and meet me at our synagogue,—go good Tubal,—at our synagogue, Tubal' (III, i, 119–20). This collusive and sinister request to meet at the synagogue has always seemed to me to be the most deeply anti-Semitic remark in the play. It is ugly and pernicious precisely because it is indirect. What is the word synagogue supposed to mean in the context? Shylock has just determined to cut the heart out of the finest man in Venice; worse yet, the knowledge that he is legally entitled to do so brings him solace in his grief. Now what might an Elizabethan have thought the synagogue really was? Is it possible that he thought it merely a place where Jews prayed? Is it not more likely that he thought it a mysterious place where strange and terrible rituals were enacted? Whatever Shakespeare himself might have thought, the lines convey the notion that Shylock is repairing to his place of worship immediately after learning that he can now legally murder the good Antonio. Bloodletting and religious worship are brought into a very ugly and insidious conjunction.

Slightly earlier Tubal is observed approaching. Solanio remarks, 'Here comes another of the tribe,—a third cannot be match'd, unless the devil himself turn Jew' (III, i, 70–1). Incredible as it may seem, this line has been used to demonstrate that the play is not anti-Semitic, because Shylock and Tubal alone among the Jews are so bad as to be like devils. What the lines more probably mean is that these two villains are the worst Jews around, and that as the worst of a very bad lot they must be pretty bad.

In her study of the origins of modern German anti-Semitism Lucy Dawidowicz discerns two irreconcilable images of Jews in anti-Semitic literature,

> ... both inherited from the recent and medieval treasury of anti-Semitism. One was the image of the Jew as vermin, to be rubbed out by the heel of the boot, to be exterminated. The other was the image of the Jew as the mythic omnipotent super-adversary, against whom war on the greatest scale had to be conducted. The Jew was, on the one hand, a germ, a bacillus, to be killed without conscience. On the other hand, he was, in the phrase Hitler repeatedly used ... the 'mortal enemy' (*Todfiend*) to be killed in self-defense.[5]

The Christians in *The Merchant of Venice* initially see Shylock in terms of the first image. He is a dog to be spurned and spat upon. His Jewish gaberdine and his Jewish habits of usury mark him as a cur to be kicked and abused. (Is it likely that Antonio would enjoy the same license to kick a rich Christian moneylender with impunity?)

As Shylock gains in power, however, the image of him as a cur changes to an image of him as a potent diabolical force. In Antonio's eyes Shylock's lust for blood takes on the motive energy of Satanic evil, impervious to reason or humanity.

> I pray you think you question with the Jew,—
> You may as well go stand upon the beach
> And bid the main flood bate his usual height,
> You may as well use question with the wolf,
> Why he hath made the ewe bleat for the lamb:
> You may as well forbid the mountain pines
> To wag their high tops, and to make no noise
> When they are fretten with the gusts of heaven:
> You may as well do anything most hard
> As seek to soften that—than which what's harder?—
> His Jewish heart! (IV, i, 70–80)

In this speech Shylock, is utterly 'the Jew'—the embodiment of his species. And the Jew's Jewish heart is wholly obdurate. He is a force of evil as strong as nature itself. No longer a dog to be controlled by beating and kicking, he has become an untamable wolf, an inferno of evil and hatred. The logical conclusion of sentiments like these, surely, is that the Jew must be kept down. Once he is up, his instinct is to kill and ravage. Indeed, Shylock has said as much himself: 'Thou call'dst me dog before thou hadst a cause,/But since I am a dog, beware my fangs' (III, iii, 7–8). If the play defines Christianity as synonymous with tolerance and kindness and forgiveness, it defines Jewishness in opposite terms. The symbol of evil in *The Merchant of Venice* is Jewishness, and Jewishness is represented by the Jew.

The counterargument to the charge that Shakespeare is guilty of anti-Semitism has always depended upon the demonstration that the portrait of Shylock is, ultimately, a deeply humane one—that Shylock's arguments against the Christians are unassailable and that his position in the Christian world has resulted from that world's treatment of him. This view, romantic in inception, still persists in the minds of a large number of critics and directors. From such authors as John Palmer and Harold Goddard one gets the image of a Shylock who carries with him the Jewish heritage of suffering and persecution, Shylock as bearer of the pain of the ages. This Shylock is religious and dignified, wronged by the world he inhabits, a man of whom the Jewish people can justly be proud and in whose vengeful intentions they may recognize a poetic righting of the wrongs of Jewish history.[6] That Jews have themselves recognized such a Shylock in Shakespeare's play is borne out in the self-conscious effusions of Heinrich Heine, for whom the Jewish moneylender possessed 'a breast that held in it all the martyrdom ... [of] a whole tortured people'.[7]

The usual alternative to this view is that of the critics who see Shylock as no more than a stereotyped villain. For these critics, what his sympathizers regard as Shakespeare's plea for Shylock's essential humanity (the 'Hath not a Jew eyes' speech [III, i, 52ff.]) is nothing more than a justification for revenge. These critics circumvent the charge that Shakespeare is anti-Semitic by arguing that Shylock is not so much a Jew as a carryover from the old morality plays. Albert Wertheim, for example, asserts that 'Shylock is a stylized and conventional comic villain and no more meant to be a realistic portrayal of a Jew than Shakespeare's Aaron is meant to be a realistic Moor.[8] John P. Sisk confidently declares that 'Kittredge was mainly right in his contention that the play is not an anti-Semitic document.'[9] These views are determinedly anti-sentimental and usefully balance the oversensitive opposing position. Their mainstay is dramatic precedent, from which can be deduced the similarities between Shylock and the stereotypical comic villain of earlier dramatic modes. Toby Lelyveld notes striking resemblances between Shylock and the Pantalone figure of commedia dell' arte, for example: 'In physical appearance, mannerisms and the situations in which he is placed, Shylock is so like his Italian prototype that his characterization, at least superficially, presents no new aspects save that of its Jewishness.'[10]

What the two critical opinions have in common is their determination to defend Shakespeare from the charge of anti-Semitism—but from opposite sides of the fence. Shylock is either a better man than we might be disposed to believe or he is not really human.[11] The latter reading seems to me to be closer to what the play presents. It is undoubtedly true that Shylock's 'humanity' has frequently been given full—even excessive—play in the theatre. But it is always useful to bear in mind that he is the play's villain. All his words, even the most convincingly aggrieved among them, are the words of a cold, heartless killer and should therefore be regarded skeptically. Shylock is untouched by the plight of those around him, and he plots the ruthless murder of Antonio. Pity for him therefore strikes me as grossly misplaced, and the view of him as the embodiment of wickedness seems dramatically correct. His argument that he is like other men and that he is vengeful only because he has been wronged by them is a violent corruption of the true state of things. Shylock is cruel and monstrous and utterly unlike other men in their capacity for love, fellowship, and sympathy. Consider his remark that he would not have exchanged the ring his daughter stole for a wilderness of monkeys. Rather than redeeming him, as Kirschbaum points out, it only makes him the worse; by demonstrating that he is capable of sentiment and aware of love, it 'blackens by contrast his inhumanity all the more'.[12] As a sincerely expressed emotion the line is out of character. It is the only reference to his wife in the play, and, if we are to take his treatment of Jessica as an indication of his treatment of those he professes to hold dear, we may reasonably conclude that it is a heartfelt expression not of love but of sentimental self-pity. Shylock is, in short, a complete and unredeemed villain whose wickedness is a primary trait. It is a trait, moreover, that is reinforced by the fact of his Jewishness, which, to make the wickedness so much the worse, is presented as synonymous with it.

And yet, although Shylock is the villain of the play, the critics who have been made uneasy by the characterization of his evil have sensed a dimension of pathos, a quality of humanity, that is part of the play. Audiences and readers have usually

found themselves pitying Shylock in the end, even though the play's other characters, having demolished him, hardly give the wicked Jew a second thought. The
Christians fail to see the humanity of Shylock, not because they are less sensitive
than readers and spectators, but because that humanity emerges only in the end,
during the court scene when they are understandably caught up in the atmosphere
of happiness that surrounds Antonio's release from death. Audiences and readers,
whose attention is likely to be equally shared by Antonio and Shylock, are more
aware of what is happening to Shylock. They are therefore aware of the change
that is forced upon him. To them he is more than simply an undone villain. He is
a suffering human being.

Shylock becomes a pitiable character only during his last appearance in the
court of Venice. It is here that he is humanized—during a scene in which he is
usually silent. Ironically, it is not in his pleadings or self-justifications that Shylock
becomes a sympathetic figure, but in his still and silent transformation from a
crowing blood-hungry monster into a quiescent victim whose fate lies in the hands
of those he had attempted to destroy. How this transmogrification is accomplished
is, perhaps, best explained by Gordon Craig's exquisitely simple observation about
the chief character of The Bells. Craig remarked that 'no matter who the human
being may be, and what his crime, the sorrow which he suffers must appeal to our
hearts . . .'[13] This observation helps explain why the scene of the reversal which
turns aside the impending catastrophe of The Merchant of Venice does not leave
the audience with feelings of unmixed delight in the way that the reversals of the
more conventional comedies do. The reversal of The Merchant of Venice defies a
basic premise of the normal moral logic of drama. Instead of merely enjoying the
overthrow of an unmitigated villain, we find ourselves pitying him. The conclusion
of the play is thus a triumph of ambiguity: Shakespeare has sustained the moral
argument which dictates Shylock's undoing while simultaneously compelling us to
react on an emotional level more compassionate than intellectual.

If it is true that Jewishness in the play is equated with wickedness, it is surely
unlikely that Shylock's elaborate rationalizations of his behaviour are intended to
render him as sympathetic. Embedded in the lengthy speeches of self-justification
are statements of fact that ring truer to Shylock's motives than the passages in which
he identifies himself as wrongly and malevolently persecuted. In his first encounter
with Antonio, for example, Shylock explains in a deeply felt aside why he hates the
Christian merchant: 'I hate him for he is a Christian:/But more, for that in low
simplicity/He lends out money gratis, and brings down/The rate of usance here with
us in Venice' (I, iii, 37–40). It is only as an afterthought that he ponders the larger
question of Antonio's hatred of the Jews. The chief reason Shylock gives for hating
Antonio—and he announces it as the chief reason—is directly related to his avarice
in money matters

Almost all of Shylock's speeches can convincingly be interpreted in this light.
When he speaks, Shylock is a sarcastic character both in the literal sense of flesh-
rending and in the modern sense of sneering. For example, when he describes the
bloody agreement as a 'merry bond', the word merry becomes charged with a

sinister ambiguity. Until the scene of his undoing, Shylock's character is dominated by the traits usual to Elizabethan comic villains. He is a hellish creature, a discontented soul whose vilifying of others marks him as the embodiment of malevolence and misanthropy. After Jessica's escape Shylock is seen vituperating his daughter, not mourning her, bemoaning the loss of his money as much as the loss of his child. His affirmations of his common humanity with the Christians, particularly in the 'Hath not a Jew eyes' speech, are above all meant to justify his thirst for revenge. His allegations that Antonio has disgraced him, laughed at him, and scorned his nation only because he is a Jew are lopsided. He is abused chiefly because he is a devil. The fact of his Jewishness only offers his abusers an explanation for his diabolical nature; it does not offer them the pretext to torment an innocent man. His speech of wheedling self-exculpation is surely intended to be regarded in the way that beleaguered tenants today might regard the whine of their wealthy landlord: 'Hath not a landlord eyes? Hath not a landlord organs, dimensions, senses, affections, passions?' Instead of eliciting sympathy for an underdog, Shakespeare intended the speech to elicit detestation for one in a privileged and powerful position who knowingly and deliberately abases himself in a plea for unmerited sympathy.

Furthermore, in answer to the tradition which defends Shylock on the grounds that Shakespeare gave him a sympathetic, self-protecting speech, we need to be reminded that the assertions it contains are dependent upon a demonstrable falsehood. The climax of Shylock's speech, its cutting edge, is his confident cry that his revenge is justified by Christian precedent: 'If a Jew wrong a Christian, what is his humility? Revenge! If a Christian wrong a Jew, what should his sufferance be by Christian example?—why revenge!' (III, i, 62–4). In fact what happens is that in return for the crime which Shylock commits against Antonio, he is offered not revenge but mercy—harshly given perhaps, but mercy nonetheless—and this in circumstances where revenge would be morally and legally sanctioned. The director who causes this speech to be uttered as a genuine defense of its speaker is thus ignoring one of the play's most tangible morals.

Until the court scene, Shylock remains a readily understood and easily identified villain. His dominant characteristics are the negative qualities normally associated with vice figures. Sympathy for him before the reversal therefore does violence to the dramatic purpose of the play. Completely in the ascendancy, he has power and the law itself on his side. When sympathy finally becomes right and proper, it transcends the narrow bounds of religion and stereotype. When finally we are made to pity Shylock, we do not pity a wrongfully persecuted member of an oppressed minority. Instead we pity a justly condemned and justly punished villain. A potential murderer has been caught, is brought to justice, and is duly and appropriately sentenced. The pity we are moved to feel is as natural and inevitable as the great loathing we were made to feel formerly. It results simply from the sympathy that we are likely to admit at any sight of human suffering, no matter how well deserved it may be.

In the court scene the presence of Portia stands as a direct assurance that

Antonio will not die. While we remain conscious of Shylock's evil intentions, then, our judgement of him is tempered by our privileged awareness of his ultimate impotence. In other words, although we might despise Shylock, we do not fear him. This distinction is critical to an understanding of his character and of Shakespeare's intentions, and it helps explain the readiness with which we are able to extend sympathy to the villain.

The chief explanation, however, goes somewhat deeper. It is simultaneously psychological and dramatic. It is psychological to the extent that we are willy-nilly affected by the sight of Shylock in pain. It is dramatic to the extent that the scene is so arranged as to dramatize in the subtlest possible way the manifestation of that pain. Shylock remains onstage while his erstwhile victims are restored to prosperity by Portia. The publication of Antonio's rescue and of Shylock's punishment takes ninety-six lines, from Portia's 'Tarry a little, there is something else . . .' (IV, i, 301) to Gratiano's gleeful 'Had I been judge, thou shouldst have had ten more,/To bring thee to the gallows, not to the font' (II, 395–6). During this period—about five minutes—Shylock is transformed from a villain into a victim.

In part the inversion is achieved by use of the established fool, Gratiano, who, by trumpeting the victory of the Christians, assumes Shylock's earlier role as one who enjoys another's pain. Gratiano is a character who talks too much, who suspects silence, who prefers to play the fool. His joy in Shylock's downfall becomes sadistic and self-serving. Interestingly, it is not shared in quite so voluble a fashion by the other Christian characters. Portia has done all the work, and yet it is Gratiano— whose real contribution to the scene is to announce Portia's success and to exco- riate the Jew—who cries at Shylock 'Now, infidel, I have you on the hip' (l. 334). Until this point in the play Shylock has been vicious and sadistic, nastily rubbing his hands in anticipation of a bloody revenge, thriving on the smell of the blood he is about to taste. Now that role is taken from him by Gratiano, on whom it sits unattractively. The failure of his friends to partipate in this orgy of revenge suggests that their feelings are more those of relief at Antonio's release than of lust for Shylock's blood.

As the tables are turned upon him, Shylock gradually and unexpectedly re- veals a news dimension of himself, and the farcical pleasure we have been led to expect is subverted by his surprising response to defeat. He reveals a capacity for pain and suffering. As a would-be murderer, Shylock gets at least what he deserves. As a human being asking for mercy, he receives, and possibly merits, sympathy. Shylock recognizes instantly that he has been undone. Once Portia reminds him that the bond does not allow him to shed one drop of blood, his orgy is over and he says little during the scene of dénouement. 'Is that the law?' he lamely asks. Five lines later, he is ready to take his money and leave the court with whatever remaining dignity is permitted him. But an easy egress is not to be his. He is made to face the consequences of his evil. Portia's addresses to Shylock during the confrontation are disguised exhortations to him to suffer for the wrong he has done. She forces him to acknowledge her triumph and his defeat: 'Tarry a little' (l.

301); 'Soft . . . soft, no haste!' (II. 316–7); 'Why doth the Jew pause?' (I. 331); 'Therefore prepare thee to cut' (I. 320); 'Tarry Jew' (I. 343); 'Art thou contented Jew?
What dost thou say?' (I. 388). Shylock is made to stand silently, receiving and
accepting mercy and some restitution from Antonio; he is compelled to bear, not
the stings of revenge upon himself, but the sharper stings of a forgiveness that he
is incapable of giving. His humiliation lies in his inability to refuse the gift of life from
one whose life he maliciously sought. When he requests leave to go from the court,
the change that has come over him is total. He is no longer a figure of vice, and he
has not become a figure of fun (except, perhaps, to Gratiano). He is a lonely,
deprived, and defeated creature feeling pain. The fact that he has caused his own
downfall does not diminish the sympathy felt for him now, in part because of the
protraction of his undoing, and in part because of the dramatic effect of the change
in him. The suddenness of the alteration of his character forces a comparison
between what he once was and what he has become. And where dramatic energy
is its own virtue, the visible eradication of that energy is a source of pathos.

In this scene the word *Jew* has been used like a blunt instrument by Portia and
Gratiano. Now, being used against one who has become a victim, the former
associations of the word are thrown into question. Portia's persistence in doing to
the Jew as he would have done to Antonio has a strangely bitter effect. She hunts
him when he is down; she throws the law in his teeth with a righteousness that
seems repulsive to us primarily because we have long been aware that Antonio was
ultimately invulnerable. Having removed Shylock's sting, she is determined to break
his wings in the bargain. In this determination, she is unlike her somewhat dull but
more humane husband, who is prepared to pay Shylock the money owed him and
to allow him to leave. Portia's stance is beyond legal questioning, of course. What
gives us pause is the doggedness with which she exacts justice. Shylock is ruined by
adversity and leaves the stage without even the strength to curse his foes: 'I pray
you give me leave to go from hence,/I am not well' (II. 391–2). He communicates
his pain by his powerlessness, and the recognition of this pain stirs the audience.

In a brief space, in which his silence replaces his usual verbosity, Shylock is
transformed. A villain is shown to be more than merely villainous. Shylock is shown
to be more than merely the Jew. He is shown to possess a normal, unheroic desire
to live at any cost. The scene of undoing is an ironic realization of Shylock's
previously histrionic pleas for understanding. We now see something that formerly
there was no reason to believe: that if you prick him, Shylock bleeds.

By endowing Shylock with humanity in the end Shakespeare would seem to
have contradicted the dominating impression of the play, in which the fierce diabolism of the Jew is affirmed in so many ways. And indeed, the contradiction is there.
Having described a character who is defined by an almost otherwordly evil, whose
life is one unremitting quest for an unjust vengeance, it seems inconsistent to allow
that he is capable of normal human feelings. The Jew has been used to instruct the
audience and the play's Christians about the potential and essential evil of his race;
he has been used to show that a Jew with power is a terrible thing to behold, is

capable of the vilest sort of destruction. And the play has demonstrated in the person of his daughter that the only good Jew is a Christian. The contradiction emerges almost in spite of Shakespeare's anti-Semitic design. He has shown on the one hand, by the creation of a powerful and dominant dramatic image, that the Jew is inhuman. But he seems to have been compelled on the other hand to acknowledge that the Jew is also a human being.

The most troubling aspect of the contradictory element of *The Merchant of Venice* is this: if Shakespeare knew that Jews were human beings like other people—and the conclusion of the play suggests that he did—and if he knew that they were not *merely* carriers of evil but human creatures with human strengths and weaknesses, then the play as a whole is a betrayal of the truth. To have used it as a means for eliciting feelings of loathing for Jews, while simultaneously recognizing that its portrayal of the race it vilifies is inaccurate or, possibly, not the whole truth, is profoundly troubling. It is as though *The Merchant of Venice* is an anti-Semitic play written by an author who is not an anti-Semite—but an author who has been willing to use the cruel stereotypes of that ideology for mercenary and artistic purposes.

NOTES

[1] Introduction, *The Merchant of Venice*, The Arden Edition (London: Methuen, 1964) p. xxxix.
[2] Leo Kirschbaum, *Character and Characterization in Shakespeare* (Detroit: Wayne State University Press, 1962) p. 19.
[3] Bernard Grebanier, interestingly enough, agrees that the play is not anti-Semitic, but contains instances of anti-Semitism. He remarks that Gratiano 'is the only character in the entire play who can be accused of anti-Semitism' (*The Truth about Shylock* (New York: Random House, 1962), p. 300).
[4] Lucy S. Dawidowicz, *The War against the Jews 1933–1945* (New York: Holt, Rinehart & Winston, 1975) p. 29.
[5] Dawidowicz, p.222.
[6] John Palmer, *Political and Comic Characters of Shakespeare* (London: Macmillan, 1962) pp. 401–39; Harold C. Goddard, *The Meaning of Shakespeare* (University of Chicago Press, 1960) pp. 81–116.
[7] Quoted by Lawrence Danson, *The Harmonies of* The Merchant of Venice (New Haven and London: Yale University Press, 1978) p. 130.
[8] Albert Wertheim, 'The Treatment of Shylock and Thematic Integrity in *The Merchant of Venice*', *Shakespeare Studies*, 6 (1970)75.
[9] John P. Sisk, 'Bondage and Release in *The Merchant of Venice*', *Shakespeare Quarterly*, 20 (1969) 217.
[10] Toby Lelyveld, *Shylock on the Stage* (Cleveland: Press of Western Reserve University, 1960) p. 8.
[11] A fuller analysis of these two critical readings is provided in Danson, pp. 126–39.
[12] Kirschbaum, p. 26.
[13] Gordon Craig, 'Irving's Masterpiece—"The Bells",' *Laurel British Drama: The Nineteenth Century*, ed. Robert Corrigan (New York: Dell, 1967) p. 119.

CONTRIBUTORS

HAROLD BLOOM is Sterling Professor of the Humanities at Yale University and Henry W. and Albert A. Berg Professor of English at the New York University Graduate School. He is a 1985 MacArthur Foundation Award recipient, served as the Charles Eliot Norton Professor of Poetry at Harvard University (1987–88), and is the author of nineteen books, the most recent being *The Book of J* (1990). Currently he is editing the Chelsea House series Modern Critical Views and The Critical Cosmos, and other Chelsea House series in literary criticism.

ELMER EDGAR STOLL was an historical critic of Shakespeare. Among his works are *Art and Artifice in Shakespeare: A Study in Dramatic Contrast and Illusion* (1934) and *From Shakespeare to Joyce* (1944).

JOHN MIDDLETON MURRY was the author of numerous works on social theory and literature. Among them are *Keats and Shakespeare: A Study of Keats' Poetic Life from 1816–1820* (1926) and *Jonathan Swift: A Critical Biography* (1954). He wrote works on D. H. Lawrence and Dostoyevsky, and edited the works of his wife Katherine Mansfield.

JOHN PALMER, English diplomat, critic, editor, author of *George Bernard Shaw: Harlequin or Patriot?* (1915) and *Molière: His Life and Works* (1930), also wrote dozens of popular spy and crime novels under the pseudonyms Francis Beeding and David Pilgrim (co-authored with Hilary Aidan St. George Saunders).

HAROLD C. GODDARD was head of the English department at Swarthmore College from 1909 to 1946. In addition to *The Meaning of Shakespeare* (1951), he published *Studies in New England Transcendentalism* (1908) and edited a 1926 edition of the essays of Ralph Waldo Emerson.

GRAHAM MIDGLEY is Fellow Emeritus of St. Edmund Hall, Oxford. He has edited the works of John Bunyan and has published *The Life of Orator Henley* (1973).

JOHN RUSSELL BROWN is Professor of Theatre at the University of Michigan–Ann Arbor. Among his works are *Shakespeare's Plays in Performance* (1967) and *Effective Theatre: A Study with Documentation* (1969). He is the editor of *Focus on* Macbeth *(1982)*.

BERNARD GREBANIER was Professor of English at Brooklyn College. His works include *The Heart of* Hamlet: *The Play Shakespeare Wrote* (1960) and *Then Came Each Actor: Shakespearean Actors, Great and Otherwise* (1975).

BARBARA K. LEWALSKI is William Kenan Jr. Professor of History and Literature and of English Literature at Harvard University. She is the author of Paradise Lost *and the Rhetoric of Literary Forms* (1985) and the editor of *Renaissance Genres: Essays on Theory, History, and Interpretation* (1986).

ALAN C. DESSEN is Professor of English at the University of North Carolina at Chapel Hill. Among his works are *Elizabethan Drama and the Viewer's Eye* (1977) and *Shakespeare and the Late Moral Plays* (1986). He is also the editor of a new edition of *Titus Andronicus* (1989).

LAWRENCE N. DANSON is Professor of English at Princeton University. He is the editor of a collection of essays on *King Lear* (1981) and is the author of *Tragic Alphabet: Shakespeare's Drama of Language* (1974) and *Max Beerbohm and the Act of Writing* (1989).

RENÉ GIRARD is Professor of French and Italian at Stanford University. He is the author of many studies of literature and the history and psychology of religion, most recently *The Scapegoat* (1986) and *Things Hidden since the Foundation of the World* (1987).

DEREK COHEN, Associate Professor of English at York University in Toronto, is co-editor with Deborah Heller of *Jewish Presences in English Literature* (1990), and frequently writes on seventeenth-century dramatists.

BIBLIOGRAPHY

Anderson, Linda. "Romantic Comedies." In *A Kind of Wild Justice: Revenge in Shakespeare's Comedies.* Newark: University of Delaware Press, 1987, pp. 57–125.

Berry, Ralph. "Discomfort in *The Merchant of Venice.*" In *Shakespeare and the Awareness of the Audience.* London: Macmillan, 1985, pp. 46–62.

––––––. "The Middle Comedies: *The Merchant of Venice.*" In *Shakespeare and Social Class.* Atlantic Highlands, NJ: Humanities Press, 1988, pp. 43–74.

Bloom, Harold, ed. *William Shakespeare's* The Merchant of Venice. New York: Chelsea House, 1986.

Boyer, Clarence Valentine. "*The Merchant of Venice* (1596)." In *The Villain as Hero in Elizabethan Tragedy.* London: Routledge; New York: Dutton, 1914, pp. 226–33.

Bradshaw, Graham. "Appraisal: Venice's Jew and Belmont's Moor." In *Shakespeare's Scepticism.* New York: St. Martin's Press, 1987, pp. 22–32.

Brown, John Russell. "Introduction." In *The Merchant of Venice* (The Arden Edition). 7th ed. Cambridge, MA: Harvard University Press, 1955, pp. x–lviii.

Bullough, Geoffrey. "The Jessica-Shylock-Lorenzo Theme." In *Narrative and Dramatic Sources of Shakespeare, Volume 1: Early Comedies, Poems,* Romeo and Juliet, edited by Geoffrey Bullough. London: Routledge & Kegan Paul; New York: Columbia University Press, 1961, pp. 454–57.

Burkhardt, Sigurd. *Shakespearean Meanings.* Princeton: Princeton University Press, 1968, pp. 206–10.

Burton, Philip. "Shylock." In *The Sole Voice: Character Portraits from Shakespeare.* New York: Dial Press, 1970, pp. 159–74.

Cartelli, Thomas. "Shakespeare's *Merchant,* Marlowe's *Jew:* The Problem of Cultural Difference." *Shakespeare Studies* 20 (1988): 255–59.

Charlton, H. B. "Shakespeare's Jew." In *Shakespearian Comedy.* London: Methuen, 1938, pp. 123–60.

Cohen, Walter. "Angelo and Shylock." In *Demi-Devils: The Character of Shakespeare's Villains.* New York: Bookman Associates, 1963, pp. 66–87.

––––––. "*The Merchant of Venice* and the Possibilities of Historical Criticism." *ELH* 49 (1982): 765–89.

Conolly, L. W. "*The Merchant of Venice* and the Jew Bill of 1753." *Shakespeare Quarterly* 25 (1974): 125–27.

Cox, John D. "Power and Archaic Dramaturgy in *All's Well That Ends Well.*" In *Shakespeare and the Dramaturgy of Power.* Princeton: Princeton University Press, 1989, pp. 128–50.

Dawson, Anthony B. "*The Merchant of Venice.*" In *Indirections: Shakespeare and the Art of Illusion.* Toronto: University of Toronto Press, 1978, pp. 3–19.

Donow, Herbert S. "Shakespeare's Caskets: Unity in *The Merchant of Venice.*" *Shakespeare Studies* 4 (1968): 86–93.

Draper, John W. "Usury in *The Merchant of Venice.*" *Modern Philology* 3 (1935): 37–47.

Dreher, Diane Elizabeth. "Defiant Daughters." In *Domination and Defiance: Fathers and Daughters in Shakespeare.* Lexington: University Press of Kentucky, 1986, pp. 96–114.

Eagleton, Terry. "Law: *The Merchant of Venice, Measure for Measure,* and *Troilus and Cressida.*" In *William Shakespeare.* Oxford: Basil Blackwell, 1986, pp. 35–63.

Echeruo, Michael J. C. "Shylock and the Conditioned Imagination." In *The Conditioned Imagination from Shakespeare to Conrad.* New York: Holmes & Meier, 1978, pp. 24–43.

Frye, Northrop. "The Reversal of Action." In *The Myth of Deliverance: Reflections on Shakespeare's Problem Comedies.* Toronto: University of Toronto Press, 1983, pp. 3–33.

Fujimura, Thomas H. "Mode and Structure in *The Merchant of Venice.*" *PMLA* 81 (1966): 499–511.

Grawe, Paul H. "*The Merchant of Venice.*" In *Comedy in Space, Time, and the Imagination.* Chicago: Nelson-Hall, 1983, pp. 183–203.

Greenblatt, Stephen. "Marlowe, Marx, and Anti-Semitism." *Critical Inquiry* 5 (1978): 291– 308.

Hennedy, John F. "Launcelot Gobbo and Shylock's Forced Conversion." *Texas Studies in Literature and Language* 15 (1973): 405–10.

Hibbard, G. R. "Interplay of Verse and Prose: *A Midsummer Night's Dream* and *The Merchant of Venice.*" In *The Making of Shakespeare's Dramatic Poetry.* Toronto: University of Toronto Press, pp. 144–61.

Hill, R. F. "*The Merchant of Venice* and the Pattern of Romantic Comedy." *Shakespeare Survey* 28 (1975): 75–88.

Hinely, Jan Lawson. "Bond Priorities in *The Merchant of Venice.*" *Studies in English Literature* 20 (1980): 217–39.

Holland, Norman N. "*The Merchant of Venice.*" In *The Shakespearean Imagination.* New York: Macmillan, 1964, pp. 91–108.

Holmer, Joan Ozark. "The Education of the Merchant of Venice." *Studies in English Literature* 25 (1985): 309–35.

Hunter, G. K. "Elizabethans and Foreigners." In *Dramatic Identities and Cultural Tradition: Studies in Shakespeare and His Contemporaries.* Liverpool: Liverpool University Press, 1978, pp. 3–30.

Kirschbaum, Leo. "Shylock in the City of God." In *Character and Characterization in Shakespeare.* Detroit: Wayne State University Press, 1962, pp. 7–31.

Kleinberg, Seymour. "*The Merchant of Venice:* The Homosexual as Anti-Semite in Nascent Capitalism." In *Essays on Gay Literature,* edited by Stuart Kellogg. New York: Haworth Press, 1983, pp. 113–26.

Knapp, Robert S. "Shakespearean Authority." In *Shakespeare—The Theater and the Book.* Princeton: Princeton University Press, 1989, pp. 182–246.

Knight, G. Wilson. "Shakespeare and the English Language." In *Shakespeare and Religion: Essays of Forty Years.* New York: Barnes & Noble, 1967, pp. 241–51.

Krieger, Elliot. "*The Merchant of Venice.*" In *A Marxist Study of Shakespeare's Comedies.* New York: Barnes & Noble, 1979, pp. 8–36.

Leggatt, Alexander. "History and Comedy." In *English Drama: Shakespeare to the Restoration 1590–1660.* New York: Longman, 1988, pp. 34–55.

———. "*The Merchant of Venice.*" In *Shakespeare's Comedy of Love.* London: Methuen, 1974, pp. 117–50.

Levin, Harry. "A Garden in Belmont: *The Merchant of Venice,* 5.1" In *Shakespeare and Dramatic Tradition: Essays in Honor of S. F. Johnson,* edited by W. R. Elton and William B. Long. Newark: University of Delaware Press, 1989, pp. 13–31.

Levin, Richard A. "Odd Man Out in Venice." In *Love and Society in Shakespearean Comedy: A Study of Dramatic Form and Content.* Newark: University of Delaware Press, 1985, pp. 30–52.

Lyon, John. *The Merchant of Venice.* Boston: Twayne, 1988.

Mahood, M. M. "Introduction." In *The Merchant of Venice.* Cambridge: Cambridge University Press, 1987, pp. 1–53.

Mullaney, Steven. "Brothers and Others, or the Art of Alienation." In *Cannibals, Witches, and Divorce: Estranging the Renaissance,* edited by Marjorie Garber. Baltimore: Johns Hopkins University Press, 1985, pp. 72–89.

Nash, Ralph. "Shylock's Wolvish Spirit." *Shakespeare Quarterly* 10 (1959): 125–28.

Novy, Marianne L. "Giving and Taking in *The Merchant of Venice.*" In *Love's Argument: Gender Relations in Shakespeare.* Chapel Hill: University of North Carolina Press, 1984, pp. 63–82.

Overton, Bill. "The Problem of Shylock." In The Merchant of Venice: *Text and Performance.* Atlantic Highlands, NJ: Humanities Press, 1987, pp. 24–34.

Palmer, D. J. "*The Merchant of Venice,* or the Importance of Being Earnest," In *Shakespearian Comedy.* (Stratford-upon-Avon Studies 14.) London: Edward Arnold, 1972, pp. 97–120.

Panitz, Esther L. "Venice and Belmont." In *The Alien in Their Midst.* Rutherford, NJ: Fairleigh Dickinson University Press, 1981, pp. 42–63.

Paster, Gail Kern. "The Nature of Our People: Shakespeare's City Comedies." In *The Idea of the City in the Age of Shakespeare.* Athens: University of Georgia Press, 1985, pp. 178–219.

Perret, Marion D. "Shakespeare's Jew: Preconception and Performance." *Shakespeare Studies* 20 (1988): 261–68.

Potter, Nick. "*The Merchant of Venice.*" In *Shakespeare: The Play of History* by Graham Holderness, Nick Potter, and John Turner. Iowa City: University of Iowa Press, 1987, pp. 160–79.

Pye, Henry James. "*The Merchant of Venice.*" In *Comments on the Commentators on Shakespear.* London: Tipper & Richards, 1807, pp. 68–77.

Quiller-Couch, A. "Introduction." In *The Merchant of Venice.* Cambridge: Cambridge University Press, 1926, pp. vii–xxxii.

Rabkin, Norman. "Meaning and *The Merchant of Venice.*" In *Shakespeare and the Problem of Meaning.* Chicago: University of Chicago Press, 1981, pp. 1–32.

Richmond, Hugh M. "Triangles in the *Sonnets* and *The Merchant of Venice.*" In *Shakespeare's Sexual Comedy: A Mirror for Lovers.* Indianapolis: Bobbs-Merrill, 1971, pp. 123–37.

Roth, Cecil. "The Background of Shylock." *Review of English Studies* 9 (1933): 148–56.

Salingar, Leo. "Is *The Merchant of Venice* a Problem Play?" In *Dramatic Form in Shakespeare and the Jacobeans.* Cambridge: Cambridge University Press, 1986, pp. 19–31.

Schonfeld, S. J. "A Hebrew Source for *The Merchant of Venice.*" *Shakespeare Survey* 32 (1979): 115–28.

Shell, Marc. "The Wether and the Ewe: Verbal Usury in *The Merchant of Venice.*" In *Money, Language, and Thought: Literary and Philosophical Economics from the Medieval to the Modern Era.* Berkeley: University of California Press, 1982, pp. 47–83.

Shirley, Frances A. "Oaths as Structure." In *Swearing and Perjury in Shakespeare's Plays.* London: George Allen & Unwin, 1979, pp. 24–43.

Siegel, Paul N. "Shylock the Puritan." *Columbia University Forum* 5, No. 4 (Fall 1962): 14–19.
————. "Shylock, the Elizabethan Puritan and Our Own World." In *Shakespeare in His Time and Ours*. Notre Dame, IN: University of Notre Dame Press, 1968, pp. 237–54.
Siemon, James Edward. "The Canker Within: Some Observations on the Role of the Villain in Three Shakespearen Comedies." *Shakespeare Quarterly* 23 (1972): 436–43.
Sinsheimer, Hermann. *Shylock: The History of a Character*. New York: Citadel Press, 1964.
Smith, John Hazel. "Shylock: 'Devil Incarnation' or 'Poor Man . . . Wronged'?" *Journal of English and Germanic Philology* 60 (1961): 1–21.
Smith, Warren D. "Shakespeare's Shylock." *Shakespeare Quarterly* 15 (1964): 193–99.
Sundelson, David. "Fathers and Daughters in *The Merchant of Venice*." In *Shakespeare's Restorations of the Father*. New Brunswick, NJ: Rutgers University Press, 1983, pp. 71–88.
Thorndike, Ashley H. "Shakespeare: The Earlier Comedies." In *English Comedy*. New York: Macmillan, 1929, pp. 95–139.
Tretiak, Andrew. "*The Merchant of Venice* and the 'Alien' Question." *Review of English Studies* 5 (1929): 402–9.
Tucker, E. F. J. "The Letter of the Law in *The Merchant of Venice*." *Shakespeare Survey* 29 (1976): 93–101.
Van Laan, Thomas F. "Role-playing and Dramatic Structure." In *Role-Playing in Shakespeare*. Toronto: University of Toronto Press, 1978, pp. 43–72.
Weiss, Theodore. "In Money and in Love: *The Merchant of Venice*." In *The Breath of Clowns and Kings: Shakespeare's Early Comedies and Histories*. London: Chatto & Windus, 1971, pp. 11–57.
Wertheim, Albert. "The Treatment of Shylock and Thematic Integrity in *The Merchant of Venice*." *Shakespeare Studies* 6 (1970): 75–86.
Westlund, Joseph. "*The Merchant of Venice*: Merging with a Perfect World." In *Shakespeare's Reparative Comedies: A Psychological View of the Middle Plays*. Chicago: University of Chicago Press, 1984, pp. 1–35.
Wheeler, Richard P. "' . . . And My Loud Crying Still': The *Sonnets, The Merchant of Venice* and *Othello*." In *Shakespeare's "Rough Magic": Renaissance Essays in Honor of C. L. Barber*, edited by Peter Erickson and Coppélia Kahn. Newark: University of Delaware Press, 1985, pp. 193–209.
————. "Toward Tragedy: The Comedies." In *Shakespeare's Development and the Problem Comedies: Turn and Counter-Turn*. Berkeley: University of California Press, 1981, pp. 167–79.
Whigham, Frank. "Ideology and Class Conduct in *The Merchant of Venice*." In *Renaissance Drama: New Series X*, edited by Leonard Barkan. Evanston: Northwestern University Press, 1980, pp. 93–115.

ACKNOWLEDGMENTS

Character Problems in Shakespeare's Plays by Levin L. Schücking, © 1922 by Harrap Publishing Group Ltd. Reprinted by permission.

"Shylock" by Harley Granville-Barker from *Prefaces to Shakespeare: Second Series* by Harley Granville-Barker, © 1930 by Sidgwick & Jackson. Reprinted by permission.

"Shylock's Pound of Flesh and Laban's Sheep" by Leah Woods Wilkins from *Modern Language Notes* 62, No. 1 (January 1947), © 1947 by Johns Hopkins University Press. Reprinted by permission.

"The Merchant and the Jew of Venice: Wealth's Communion and an Intruder" by C. L. Barber from *Shakespeare's Festive Comedy: A Study of Dramatic Form and Its Relation to Social Custom* by C. L. Barber, © 1959 by Princeton University Press. Reprinted by permission.

"Brothers & Others" by W. H. Auden from *The Dyer's Hand and Other Essays* by W. H. Auden, © 1962 by Random House, Inc. Reprinted by permission.

A Natural Perspective: The Development of Shakespearean Comedy and Romance by Northrop Frye, © 1965 by Columbia University Press. Reprinted by permission.

"Shylock" by E. M. W. Tillyard from *Shakespeare's Early Comedies* by E. M. W. Tillyard, © 1965 by Stephen Tillyard. Reprinted by permission of the Estate of E. M. W. Tillyard.

"The Jew as Stranger; or, 'These Be the Christian Husbands'" by Leslie A. Fiedler from *The Stranger in Shakespeare* by Leslie A. Fiedler, © 1972 by Leslie A. Fiedler. Reprinted by permission of the author.

"Shylock's Frustrated Communion" by R. Chris Hassel, Jr., from *Faith and Folly in Shakespeare's Romantic Comedies* by R. Chris Hassel, Jr., © 1980 by the University of Georgia Press. Reprinted by permission.

"The Lords of Duty" by Mark Taylor from *Shakespeare's Darker Purpose: A Question of Incest* by Mark Taylor, © 1982 by AMS Press, Inc. Reprinted by permission.

"Re-reading *The Merchant of Venice*" by Kiernan Ryan from *Shakespeare* by Kiernan Ryan, © 1989 by Kiernan Ryan. Reprinted by permission of Humanities Press International, Inc., Harvester Wheatsheaf, a division of Simon & Schuster International Group, and the author.

"Shakespeare's Method: *The Merchant of Venice*" by John Middleton Murry from *Shakespeare* by John Middleton Murry, © 1936 by Harcourt, Brace & Co., Inc. Reprinted by permission.

"Shylock" by John Palmer from *Comic Characters of Shakespeare* by John Palmer, © 1946 by Macmillan & Co. Reprinted by permission of Macmillan & Co., London & Basingstoke, and Macmillan Publishing Co., Inc.

"The Merchant of Venice" by Harold C. Goddard from *The Meaning of Shakespeare* by Harold C. Goddard, © 1951 by The University of Chicago. Reprinted by permission of The University of Chicago Press.

"The Merchant of Venice: A Reconsideration" by Graham Midgley from *Essays in Criticism* 10, No. 2 (April 1960), © 1960 by *Essays in Criticism.* Reprinted by permission of the Editors of *Essays in Criticism.*

"The Realization of Shylock: A Theatrical Criticism" by John Russell Brown from *Early Shakespeare* (Stratford-upon-Avon Studies 3), edited by John Russell Brown and Bernard Harris, © 1961 by Edward Arnold (Publishers) Ltd. Reprinted by permission.

"Shylock Himself" by Bernard Grebanier from *The Truth about Shylock* by Bernard Grebanier, © 1962 by Random House, Inc. Reprinted by permission.

"Biblical Allusion and Allegory in *The Merchant of Venice"* by Barbara K. Lewalski from *Shakespeare Quarterly* 13, No. 3 (Summer 1962), © 1962 by Shakespeare Association of America, Inc. Reprinted by permission of *Shakespeare Quarterly.*

"The Elizabethan Stage Jew and Christian Example" (originally titled "The Elizabethean Stage Jew and Christian Example: Gerontus, Barabas, and Shylock") by Alan C. Dessen from *Modern Language Quarterly* 35, No. 3 (September 1974), © 1974 by The University of Washington. Reprinted by permission of *Modern Language Quarterly.*

"The Problem of Shylock" (originally titled " 'The Jew Shall Have All Justice': The Problem of Shylock") by Lawrence Danson from *The Harmonies of* The Merchant of Venice, © 1978 by Yale University. Reprinted by permission of Yale University Press.

" 'To Entrap the Wisest' " (originally titled " 'To Entrap the Wisest': A Reading of *The Merchant of Venice"*) by René Girard from *Literature and Society: Selected Papers from the English Institute,* edited by Edward W. Said, © 1980 by the English Institute. Reprinted by permission of Johns Hopkins University Press.

"Shylock and the Idea of the Jew" by Derek Cohen from *Shakespearean Motives* by Derek Cohen, © 1988 by Derek Cohen. Reprinted by permission of Macmillan & Co., London & Basingstoke, and St. Martin's Press, Inc.

INDEX

JUL 16 1991